W9-DGV-170

THE MYTH *of*
AMERICAN RELIGIOUS
FREEDOM

THE MYTH *of* AMERICAN RELIGIOUS FREEDOM

DAVID SEHAT

OXFORD
UNIVERSITY PRESS
2011

OXFORD
UNIVERSITY PRESS

Oxford University Press, Inc., publishes works that further
Oxford University's objective of excellence
in research, scholarship, and education.

Oxford New York
Auckland   Cape Town   Dar es Salaam   Hong Kong   Karachi
Kuala Lumpur   Madrid   Melbourne   Mexico City   Nairobi
New Delhi   Shanghai   Taipei   Toronto

With offices in
Argentina   Austria   Brazil   Chile   Czech Republic   France   Greece
Guatemala   Hungary   Italy   Japan   Poland   Portugal   Singapore
South Korea   Switzerland   Thailand   Turkey   Ukraine   Vietnam

Published by Oxford University Press, Inc.
198 Madison Avenue, New York, New York 10016

www.oup.com

Oxford is a registered trademark of Oxford University Press

Library of Congress Cataloging-in-Publication Data
Sehat, David.
The myth of American religious freedom / David Sehat.
   p.   cm.
ISBN 978-0-19-538876-3
1. Freedom of religion—United States—History.
2. Christian ethics—United States—History.
3. United States—Church history. I. Title.
BR516.S43 2011
261.7′20973—dc22   2010014076

9   8   7   6   5   4   3   2   1

Printed in the United States of America
on acid-free paper

CONTENTS

PREFACE

I used to be an evangelical. My coming of age included a conversion to Christianity in a mainline Presbyterian church and what might be considered a second conversion to evangelicalism about a year later. In the evangelical world, I discovered that to be a patriot and to be a Christian were often considered the same thing. This conflation of American and Christian identities relied on a story about the past. Claiming that freedom had long been dependent upon evangelical Christianity, evangelicals saw their religion as the source of both America's democracy and its ascendant fortune. Once I left evangelical life, this belief seemed to me a peculiar quirk of the culture that I had gladly left behind. But a few years later I was surprised when I read Alexis de Tocqueville, who wrote in 1835, "Americans so completely confuse Christianity and freedom in their minds that it is almost impossible to have them conceive of the one without the other." Tocqueville's comment suggested an old genealogy to the notion of a Christian America, an ideal that continues to thrive in evangelical circles but seems either unintelligible or offensive to outsiders.[1]

After I left the fold I realized that I still understood this point of view in a way that many outsiders did not, though communication with my remaining evangelical friends had become more difficult. When they explained that they were trying to "win the culture," I thought that they wanted to control other people. When they explained that organizational effectiveness and church-planting initiatives were among the most effective ways to "spread the gospel," I pointed out how often ecclesiastical institutions had become co-opted by partisan politics. When they explained that they had a divine imperative to "take their place at the table" because politics and law drew upon norms that were religious in nature, I asked what the rules for the newly reconstituted table would be, who was going to make them, and whether everyone would be allowed a seat.

At the same time, I talked to my non-evangelical friends and followed the confused murmur of national discourse. I was struck by how flippantly some critics of evangelicalism dismissed the idea of morals or values in politics. Although no longer an evangelical myself, I lacked animus against religious institutions. I was (and am) sympathetic to the metaphysically minded. The certainty of atheism offended me as much as the certainty of religious fundamentalism, and the polar positions of the debate seemed to have more in common than they thought.

I began graduate school as the debate intensified through the 2000 election and before it reached fever pitch with the victory of the values voter in 2004. After evangelical political activists triumphed, many around me were asking, "Who are these people?" Since I had been steeped in the political discourse of the Religious Right, I knew who they were and did my best to explain.

But where had the Religious Right come from?

This was the essential question that shouted from the margin of the debate. When pundits and politicians tried to address the question, their answers usually fell along tendentious political lines. Yet even in their polarized responses, people across the political spectrum seemed to share a common set of assumptions about U.S. politics and U.S. history that I found more and more implausible. As I began focusing my attention on the political debate itself, it occurred to me that this shared belief was a political orthodoxy so foundational that it was almost unthinkable to question it. The American orthodoxy was simple: the history of the United States, whatever its failings might be, was a history of religious freedom.

But what if U.S. religious history was not a history of progressive and unfolding freedom? What if, instead, it was a history of religious conflict? And what if that conflict involved extended periods of religious coercion and the continual attempt to maintain religious power and control? Such questions became the core of this book.[2]

THE MYTH *of* AMERICAN RELIGIOUS FREEDOM

INTRODUCTION

THE MYTH OF AMERICAN
RELIGIOUS FREEDOM

1.

In 1886 a grand jury in New Jersey indicted a man named Charles B. Reynolds on two counts of blasphemy. Reynolds was a former Methodist minister turned agnostic. He had begun holding what were then known as freethought meetings in a tent in order to convince his fellow citizens of the error of their religious beliefs. On the first day of a meeting in Boonton, a mob entered the tent while Reynolds was speaking, pelting him with rotten produce before cutting the guy-ropes and slashing the canvas. Reynolds fled from Boonton to Morristown with the intention of distributing freethought pamphlets there. When the mob followed him, demanding that he be arrested, local authorities responded swiftly. His prosecution was legal and orderly. The authorities tried him before a jury of his peers. Reynolds was convicted on both counts and released with a hefty fine. Shortly afterward, the *New York Times* opined on the decision. "It is well that there should be some means of suppressing a noisy and offensive blackguard like REYNOLDS," declared the paper, "and whether he be suppressed as a blasphemer or merely as a plain blackguard is a matter of very minor consequence."[1]

On first blush, the Reynolds case is shocking. How could a man be convicted of blasphemy in the United States nearly one hundred years after the ratification of the First Amendment? Had not the First Amendment guaranteed religious liberty? And the deeper you look, the more puzzling it becomes. Reynolds retained the counsel of a lawyer named Robert G. Ingersoll, a man who the papers of the day labeled the Great Agnostic or the Great Infidel, depending on one's point of view. Ingersoll spent most of his time giving lectures around the country that called for the separation of church and state and criticized religious belief of any kind. He had a visceral contempt for

Christianity. During the 1880s Ingersoll was threatened with blasphemy prosecution as well, not just under laws dating to the colonial period but also under, to pick one example, Pennsylvania's 1860 blasphemy statute, which was clear in its protection of Christianity. It proclaimed that any person who would "willfully, premeditatedly, and despitefully blaspheme or speak loosely and profanely of Almighty God, Christ Jesus, the Holy Spirit, or the Scriptures of Truth" would face fines and imprisonment.[2]

The case seems mystifying on so many levels because the history of the United States as a bastion of liberty has long been a staple of our schoolbooks. But blasphemy law seems to have no place in that story, which indicates a problem in the story itself. In what follows I retell the story of U.S. religious history through its dissenters, people who fought the connection between religious ideals and the state, such as Ingersoll, the abolitionist and radical Christian-turned-freethinker William Lloyd Garrison, the women's rights activist Elizabeth Cady Stanton, the five-time Socialist Party presidential candidate Eugene V. Debs, and others. To talk about religious dissenters in U.S. history can sound strange. It runs against the idea of the United States as a land of liberty born from a desire for religious freedom. It also suggests that there was a dominant religion that exerted a controlling influence on public life. That implication is intentional. Protestant Christian influence in U.S. history was long-standing, widespread, and, from the perspective of dissenters, coercive. Religious views pervaded law at all levels. Reformers of all kinds, including abolitionists, women's rights activists, labor organizers, and educational reformers often had to contend with Christian—or, more narrowly, Protestant Christian—moral norms that defined and limited their rights. The omission of these stories from the American historical consciousness is a major flaw in our national narrative.

This is a work of history, but it is not only that. I have written it in the belief that our current discussion about religion in public life trades on a series of fables about the American past. These fables make it difficult, if not impossible, to understand the religious politics of the present. Religious liberty, we are told, is a hallmark of American democracy. Having been freed from entanglements with the state, so the story goes, religion has flourished in the United States. It became central to reform movements such as abolition or women's rights that sought to perfect the American project by expanding democracy. Its ubiquity made it central, as the scholars Robert Wuthnow and John H. Evans have claimed, "in strengthening and preserving civic life in America." The narrative is so ingrained in American consciousness that it has become an orthodoxy of sorts. All proclaim the march of religious liberty, in spite of disagreements over its meaning. All see religious liberty as a cornerstone in the development of American political thought, though they disagree on how religious and political thought are related. All look to the American church–state arrangement to explain the powerful energy of the American religious impulse, even if they disagree on the specifics of the model. A belief in "the vigor and vitality of the American story of religious freedom," in the words of the legal historian John Witte Jr., is common to everyone.[3]

The narrative is so dominant that it frames the angry disputes over religion today. Religious conservatives decry what they regard as the forced exile of religion from the public square, a banishment that they worry threatens to take freedom with it. As Mitt Romney claimed in his "Faith in America" address prior to the 2008 presidential primaries, religious freedom is "fundamental to America's greatness." Romney, a Mormon whose position outside the Religious Right posed a problem for his presidential ambitions, sought to appropriate the language and story of conservative Christians and in the process demonstrated that story's power. "Freedom requires religion," Romney insisted, "just as religion requires freedom. . . . Freedom and religion endure together, or perish alone." Religious liberty in this definition seems to mean the ability of believers to bring their beliefs into the public square, thereby sustaining the nation's moral foundations. According to Romney, so deeply is religion tied to the American past that the United States has an essential "foundation of faith upon which our Constitution rests," which in turn sustains the "common creed of moral convictions." Romney's address mirrored the thoughts of many on the Religious Right.[4]

By contrast, many liberal writers have complained that the introduction of religion into public life violates the separation of church and state set out in the Bill of Rights and endangers the Founders' conception of religious freedom, which has served us so well for more than two centuries. Isaac Kramnick and R. Laurence Moore, two academics engaged in a self-described polemic in their book *The Godless Constitution*, claim that rather than the "foundation of faith" of Romney's conception, the Constitution's framers situated the U.S. government on an "intentionally secular base." The liberal evangelical Randall Balmer agrees, claiming that the Religious Right has "failed to appreciate the genius of the First Amendment," with its protection of religious liberty, and has thus "defaulted on the noble legacy of nineteenth-century evangelical activism."[5]

These are all half-truths. Both sides share the idea that the history of American religion is a history of freedom that now needs protection, but both perspectives wither under scrutiny. Mitt Romney is right that religion was prominent in public life in the past, but religious fervor did not always aid the cause of freedom. As Charles Reynolds could attest, religion's place in the public square often had disastrous consequences for individual liberties. Religion constrained individual rights as often as it promoted them.

But the liberal claims of church–state separation are equally specious. In 1833 Chief Justice John Marshall, an evangelical Episcopalian who supported Bible societies and the full range of evangelical activism, handed down a unanimous opinion proclaiming that the Bill of Rights did not apply to the states. Although the opinion did not explicitly address religious rights, it laid out a vision of federalism with important implications for the limits of religious freedom. According to Marshall's ruling, only a particular state's constitution "provided such limitations and restrictions on the powers of its particular government as its judgment dictated." The federal Bill of Rights protected individuals only in the limited area over which the national government had power. Twelve years later, with Marshall no longer on the bench, the Court reaffirmed his decision in an opinion explicitly addressing the religion clauses of the First Amendment. It rejected the claim that the First Amendment protected freedom of religion from state- and municipal-level infringement. States, in other words, were free to prosecute for blasphemy and otherwise constrain religious belief in any way they saw fit. Because most disputes about religious liberty occurred on the state or local level, and because the federal government had limited power until the New Deal, the First Amendment had almost no effect on the protection of religious belief or non-belief until the 1920s, when the federal courts began expanding the protections of the Bill of Rights to include all levels of government. Even then, the Court did not specifically apply the First Amendment's religion clauses until 1940, which meant that for much of U.S. history church and state were never separate in the way that many liberal writers have claimed.[6]

2.

This poverty of narrative, this inability of both the Left and the Right to account for the kinds of coercion that were routine in the past, is the result of *the threefold myth of American religious freedom*. The first myth is that of *separation*, the standard liberal myth that holds that the United States protected religious liberty through the First Amendment's separation of church and state. This is a core of fact shrouded in a cloud of misunderstanding. The idea of church–state separation was important to some of the Founding Fathers, most notably Thomas Jefferson and James Madison. Jefferson and

Madison were proponents of the moderate Enlightenment and supporters of the liberal vision of John Locke, who held that the state could and should remove its tentacles from religion without fear of anarchy. To withdraw state control of religion would, according to Lockean liberals, lead to social peace, which was a powerful and innovative idea. Madison in particular had a sophisticated understanding of how this separation would work.

But the U.S. Constitution and the First Amendment did not create the separation that Madison and Jefferson advocated. Principles of federalism gave the states an enormous reservoir of power to regulate the health, welfare, and morals of its residents, and religious partisans drew from this source to imprint their moral ideals onto state constitutions and judicial opinions. Prosecution for blasphemy was just one of many religious and moral regulations that formed a *moral establishment* that connected religion and the state. Supporters claimed that a religiously derived morality, enforceable by law, was essential to the health of the state. As one religious partisan explained in 1838, everyone granted that there was no legitimate connection between "[e]*cclesiastical* Christianity" and the state—in other words, no legitimate foundation for an official state religion. But "[e]*thical* Christianity" and "the *moral* aspect of the gospel" were so important to the preservation of the state that they required "the concurrent agency of statesmen and politicians." This connection between Protestant Christianity's moral code and state power was commonplace throughout much of U.S. history.[7]

Some have sought to wave away these elements of the past, arguing that they are the expression of a dominant Christian culture that went into decline in the nineteenth century and is now no longer relevant. But this is the second myth of American religious history, *the myth of religious decline.* It holds that the United States, or what would become the United States, was settled by religious believers who fled the persecution of Europe and, in turn, created the structures of tolerance that grew into full-fledged church–state separation. As the United States grew into a modern nation, so the myth goes, the religious sensibilities that were so prevalent in the early centuries waned. Although remnants of this religious culture may still be found in our constitutions or law, they are no longer really pertinent.

Yet the idea that religious belief and adherence has waned is inaccurate. Historical demographers and sociologists have shown that in 1776 only 17 percent of the national population belonged to a church. It appears that an official religion governed an indifferent population for much of the colonial period. Then, in the nineteenth century, under the influence of evangelical expansion, church membership began to increase sharply. By 1850, 35 percent of Americans were church members. By 1906 the number was 51 percent. Sixty-two percent of the American populace belonged to religious institutions in 2000, though not specifically Christian churches. Evangelicals led the expansion. Because evangelical theology demands the intervention of believers into public life in an attempt to shape the world according to the dictates of their conscience, religion has, over the last two hundred years, become more important to the public life of the United States rather than less.[8]

Although the long history of the moral establishment does undermine the liberal claim of separation and the narrative of religious decline, it does not necessarily favor religious conservatives. That leads to the third and final myth of American religious freedom, *the myth of exceptional liberty*, which holds that religious liberty in the United States forms the cornerstone of American liberty more generally and makes the United States into a beacon of freedom to the world. But proponents of the moral establishment claimed that God's will should determine the parameters of American freedom, which opened the door to serious encroachment on American liberty. The history of the moral establishment bears this out, with critics constantly seeking to overthrow the establishment in order to expand freedoms that were honored in principle but curtailed in practice.[9]

Foreign observers of the United States saw this dynamic with particular clarity and were keen to point out that religiously derived, moral coercion seemed endemic to American society and government, in spite of Americans' claims to the contrary. In the early nineteenth century, John Stuart Mill, the British philosopher and liberal theorist, claimed of the United States that "in no country does there exist less independence of thought." This seeming contradiction within the United States puzzled Mill. He took "the rejection of authority, and the assertion of the right of private judgment" to be central aspects of the U.S. national character. But according to Mill, personal autonomy and intellectual independence did not extend to "the fundamental doctrines of Christianity and Christian ethics." Likewise, Tocqueville claimed that "the moral empire" in the United States operated with an "irresistible force" upon individuals through the mechanisms of the state. In Tocqueville's analysis, religion was an essential part of the moral empire, a regime that grew more powerful with the antebellum religious expansion that he claimed to observe firsthand. American religion remained outside the formal domain of American politics, Tocqueville admitted, at least in the sense that there were no religious parties. But he insisted that American religious partisans still sought to direct morals, which eventually worked "to regulate the state" even without formal religious partisanship.[10]

Tocqueville's account of the United States has been subjected to scrutiny in the last fifteen years, as political theorists and historians have questioned many of his assumptions. My point is not to defend all of Tocqueville's analysis, but only to explore his keen insight that it was through the regulation of morals that religious partisans maintained power. This was the rationale for blasphemy law. Blasphemy, its proponents argued, undercut the foundation of morality and needed to be outlawed. Because the morality enforced in law often came from Protestant Christian ideals and was presented as such, behind the claim of exceptional liberty stood the reality of religious control, which worked through much of U.S. history to coerce rather than to persuade citizens to behave according to religious norms.[11]

3.

These myths serve a purpose. They are *civic myths* that politicians, legal theorists, and cultural critics draw upon to advance their aims. They are stories used to explain how the United States as a political community came into being and what its values are. They identify the people who hold those values and, implicitly, who are eligible for membership in the body politic. They are in many respects false, resting as they do upon the slimmest of historical evidence. Yet irrespective of their factual inadequacies, they provide the foundation of the civic identity of the American people. At their best they are inclusive, offering a means by which the many kinds of people who live in the United States can be understood to be part of the American polity. At their worst they are tools to justify exclusion and oppression.[12]

With the polarization of religious and political views in the last fifty years, the preservation of these myths has assumed increased importance. All sides rely on them to buttress their political position in the present. Conservatives argue that Christianity has always, by common consent, had a place in the public life of the nation. The public role for Christianity has been undermined, they claim, by a minority of secularists on the U.S. Supreme Court. This argument ignores past coercion and spurs conservatives to action. It attempts to restore religion to government while disguising conservatives' coercive aspirations in the present. Oddly, liberals tend to agree with certain parts of this story. They see the past as a harmonious arrangement of freedom that sprang from the minds of Jefferson and Madison, received protection in the provisions of the Constitution, and is endangered by religious partisans today. This argument also prompts leftist partisans to political action, while, strangely, denying the coercive arrangement of the past that prompted the U.S. Supreme Court to intervene in the first place.

Because both narratives are detached from a true historical foundation, they have yielded a remarkably unproductive discussion of the role of religion in contemporary public life. The cant that passes for a national debate on religion—demagoguery more than anything else—breaks down once one gains an even passing familiarity with the past. Given this situation, my claim is a simple one. We will never understand the source, the development, or the stakes of the debate about religion in public life until we acknowledge that for much of its history the United States was controlled by Protestant Christians who sponsored a moral regime that was both coercive and exclusionary. Proponents of the moral establishment claimed that religion was necessary to reinforce the moral fabric of the people, which was, in turn, necessary for the health and preservation of the state. But their understanding of religion was decidedly narrow. The New Hampshire Constitution's specification of "evangelical principles" as the correct grounding for "morality and piety" was the norm. Religion usually meant Protestant Christianity. Catholics, Jews, Mormons, and freethinkers, along with a host of others who purportedly failed to demonstrate proper morality, faced active legal and social discrimination that continued in various forms until the U.S. Supreme Court began dismantling the moral establishment, after the 1920s. This book reconstructs that establishment's beginning shortly after the passage of the First Amendment, its historical development and intellectual rationale over the long nineteenth century, and its ultimate dismantling. When the moral establishment went into decline, the Religious Right mobilized to restore it, leaving us where we are today.[13]

My purpose is not to contribute to the shrill partisanship that has dominated the current debate about religion in public life. There are problems on all sides, so to weigh in on one side of the same partisan argument would merely promote an already unhelpful conversation. My purpose is instead to dispense with the historical myths by which each side supports their position and in so doing make way for a new and more meaningful conversation on the public role of religion in the present. When religious conservatives criticize secularists by claiming that the United States was a Christian nation in the past, they are not wrong. In many ways, it was a Christian nation in that Christians had significant control over law and governance and used it to enforce morality. But if it was a Christian nation, it was not so by consent. While church and state may not have been completely separate in the past (however desirable it might be in the present), the presence of numerous dissenters undermines conservatives' claims that they are merely trying to recapture a role for religion that most people desire. If religion supported morals by common consent, there would be no need for the coercion of law.

In this book, to put a fine point on the coercive arrangements of the past, I focus on the experience of dissenters. Because dissenters were in the vanguard of the expansion of rights, they saw the coercion inherent in the moral establishment. Their stories show that the establishment impinged on Americans' freedom. But the dissenters did not interpret the situation perfectly. In their rhetoric they depicted the moral establishment as a singular and dominant entity, an agent of faceless oppression. This is how it seemed to them, though the establishment was never as singular as they suggested. It always suffered the intellectual awkwardness of not acknowledging its own existence. Sometimes the effects of its power outran their justifications. Its enforcement was occasional and, in certain cases, erratic. Sometimes the establishment was clumsy. It often relied upon symbolic stands to obscure the subtler mechanisms by which it maintained control. And most importantly, it changed, remaining fluid and porous—with different people simultaneously speaking for it—so that writers have missed its existence. Yet it was real. Given the public commitment to religious liberty, the shadowy character of the moral establishment was its power.

To get at something so misty and yet persistent requires a flexible approach. In order to bring it into focus I move back and forth from the formal domains of law and politics to the more informal struggles over religion and morals that often occurred simultaneously. My selection of subjects is determined by what I think best illuminates the moral establishment's nature. But in order to demonstrate my claim, in this text I continually return to the law. Partisans constantly asserted that legal norms had moral foundations. The law provided the overarching framework in which other debates unfolded. All sides sought to develop new moral arguments that supported, challenged, or transformed the establishment. The debates were various, but ultimately all the conversations returned to a core issue: the role of religion in determining morals and the relationship of those morals to the coercive power of law.

What follows, then, is not just a work of history in the ordinary sense but what the late historian Richard Hofstadter called a "critical inquiry" into the historical origins of our contemporary situation. This book, like any work, is necessarily selective. I am highlighting one aspect of the national history that, were I writing a general history of the United States, might be reduced in scope. It should also be clear that the cultural, political, and legal history of the United States cannot be reduced to a running argument between those who perceived a religious foundation for U.S. society and those who did not. Nor is it my intention to make such a claim. There are always many who occupy a middle space, or who remain aloof from any divide, having altogether different concerns and different conceptions. But the divide was real, long-standing, and persistent. Ignorance of this divide has warped our historical consciousness and distorted our political debate. This book seeks to alter that consciousness.[14]

PART I

MORAL LAW

1

CONTESTED LIBERTIES

1.

B enjamin Franklin believed in God. He explained this in 1790 to Ezra Stiles, the Congregational minister and president of Yale College. Stiles had written Franklin, the great patron, inventor, diplomat, and constitutional framer, to inquire about Franklin's "opinion . . . concerning Jesus of Nazareth." He reminded Franklin, "I am a christian." His religious belief made him wish for Franklin, then eighty-five years old and sick, "that happy immortality, which I believe Jesus alone has purchased for the virtuous and truly good of every religious denomination in Christendom."[1]

Franklin's response was cordial. He explained that he was not offended by Stiles's curiosity, though he added that he had never before in his life been asked about his religious belief. But because Stiles was a friend, Franklin decided to answer the question. "Here is my Creed," he began. "I believe in one God, Creator of the Universe. That He governs it by his Providence. That he ought to be worshipped. That the most acceptable Service we can render to him is doing Good to his other Children. That the Soul of Man is immortal, and will be treated with Justice in another Life respecting its Conduct in this." He considered these "the fundamental Principles of all sound Religion." Except for a belief in the immortality of the soul, Franklin's credo was almost entirely a religion of this world: the best way to honor God was to treat other people well.[2]

Even if he had left it at that, Franklin would have been saying a lot. He was positively disposed to religious belief when it rendered positive conduct in the world. He was skeptical when it did not. Yet he had not really answered Stiles's question, so he went on. Praising Jesus' "System of Morals and his Religion," Franklin judged the teaching of Jesus as "the best the World ever saw." But he did not think that Christians were the uncontested heirs to Jesus' religion, which had "received various corrupting Changes." Although it was not a subject upon which he had dogmatic opinions, Franklin noted that some dissenters in England even doubted the divinity of Jesus. His comfortable agnosticism on the subject did not mean that Franklin opposed others' belief in Jesus as divine. Believing in the divinity of Jesus would likely mean that his teachings would command greater respect, Franklin thought, thereby prompting people to act better in the world. But he still disliked the entreaties of what he called the "zealous Religionist," whose chief characteristic Franklin identified as impertinence, or the violation of etiquette in the name of religion. Franklin's religion was, after all, a get-along sort of affair. Not wishing to invite controversy, he requested that Stiles not publish any part of his letter. Since Franklin had always supported others in their religious belief even when "unsupportable and even absurd," he wanted "to go out of the World in Peace with them all." Franklin died five weeks later.[3]

The exchange between Franklin and Stiles is revealing on a number of levels. Then, as now, many people looked to the Founding Fathers to provide guidance for the public role of religion in the United States. Yet to describe the Founders' religious beliefs, or even to identify an individual who qualifies as a Founder, is to wander into a thicket without end. Franklin was certainly a Founder, but it seems impossible to reason from his credo into the debates of the present.

It is difficult enough to discern the Founders' views on the debates of their own time. Thomas Jefferson, for example, was certainly a Founder. He had clear ideas about the proper role of religion in society and its relationship to the state. He had clear and, like Franklin, guarded religious beliefs. But because he was the ambassador to France, he was not at the Constitutional Convention and had no hand in its conceptualization or drafting. He even objected to the document when he first read it. Nor did Jefferson have a hand in drafting the Bill of Rights, because he was serving as the secretary of state. Though he supported it, Jefferson was even disappointed with the finished Bill of Rights. Similarly, John Adams was a Founder. His views in support of religion in public life come up repeatedly in our contemporary debate. But Adams was also not present at the Constitutional Convention, because he was the ambassador to England. At the time of the convention, many considered his political thought anachronistic, and by the time he died, it was widely regarded as irrelevant. Even Franklin, who was actually at the Constitutional Convention, did not offer a straightforward way to approach the issue. At the convention's close, he explained in a speech, "I do not entirely approve this Constitution at present; but Sir, I am not sure I shall never approve it." He did not elaborate on his reservations. In spite of them he announced his support, saying, "I expect no better." Aware of the many rifts among the delegates over the Constitution, Franklin counseled unanimity in public, once they left the convention, in order to increase the Constitution's chance of success. This unanimity, which largely held through the subsequent ratification debates, has led some writers to act as though the opinion of the Founders on any given subject can be determined. It usually cannot. Even where the Founders had a direct hand in drafting the Constitution, as Franklin did, they too often disagreed among themselves.[4]

These collected problems mean that although the Founders exercised an important influence on the formation of the U.S. government and its underlying political theory, we cannot simply appeal to them to solve the problems of the present. Rather, we must take a broader perspective, one that seeks to understand the relationship between religion, law, and politics that the Constitution made possible. In order to do that, we have to look at a larger set of debates, ones in which the Founders were important participants, but not the only ones.

2.

American political thought was born of the Revolution. Like any thought that emerges in a fast-changing context, it shared not so much a stable set of ideas as a cluster of intellectual inclinations that needed to be worked out in practice. Following the Continental Congress's 1776 Declaration of Independence, statesmen gathered in statehouses across the colonies to work out this political thought in the new constitutions for each state. The peculiarly American faith in the effectiveness of constitutions was one of the most remarkable developments of the late eighteenth century. It meant, in theory, that law was an expression of the will of the people. But it also entailed a conscious dispute, an extended conversation about the shape, contours, and ultimate source of law. The debate remained an elite affair but no less fractious for being so. Disagreements abounded. Political visions proliferated. Scurrilous attacks occurred alongside high-minded debate. Because political theory and practical necessity combined in unpredictable ways, the constitutions that emerged bore the marks of disagreement, debate, and compromise. They were sometimes self-contradictory.[5]

The place and meaning of religious liberty often produced tension during these debates. Nearly every state concluded that religious belief and civil rights should be connected in some way, so the question was not whether to leave religion alone, at least initially. Because nearly everyone presumed that religious belief supported political stability, the question was how to harness it.

Pennsylvania, with Benjamin Franklin at its head, led the way. It was able to do so because the state adopted a radically democratic constitution in 1776. Pennsylvania's constitution dispensed with the idea of an aristocratic house in the legislature, adopting instead a single-chamber assembly in which the people would directly govern themselves. But this arrangement created complications for received ideas of religious liberty. The problem was democracy. Far from being a universal goal in 1776, democracy was a troubling concept to many revolutionary political thinkers, in spite of their frequent verbal gestures supporting rule by the people. Many thought that the masses could not be trusted, and that they had a tendency toward licentiousness—an inclination to moral lasciviousness. Because the so-called better classes provided a model for the licentious masses, the genteel class had traditionally governed, creating and enforcing the laws that placed restraints on social decay. But Pennsylvania's constitution threatened to remove this privilege of governance. The people could vote for whomever they wished. Given the presumed tendency toward immorality, the result might be social ruin.[6]

In the absence of elite authority, the masses required some other kind of restraint. The answer, many felt, was religion. According to the conventional thinking, religion produced and supported morality. It was a means of social control that acted as a check on the worst excesses of democracy. Even the most radical religious thinkers of the time often supported religious belief among the lower classes. Franklin, for example, privately questioned sin, free will, personal immortality, and God's providence in his youth before retreating into respectable moderation. But he still spoke for many of the educated classes when he warned, "[T]alking against religion is unchaining a tiger; the beast let loose may worry his liberator." In a political system based on popular sovereignty, religion would ensure social tranquility and good governance.[7]

Just how religion could or should be harnessed by the state was a tricky question. Three major groups formed around the issue. The first was made up of the old-line proponents of state monetary support for churches. Episcopalians, Congregationalists, and some Lutherans and old-line Presbyterians fell into this category. In Pennsylvania, the group was led by Henry Muhlenberg, the head of the German Lutherans. Outside of Pennsylvania, many were in favor of the state paying churches. Supporters included John Adams; Timothy Dwight, the past president of Yale; Elbridge Gerry, a future Massachusetts congressman; and Lyman Beecher, one of the leaders of nineteenth-century evangelicalism. Many were members or ministers in churches that were currently receiving state support. Because these churches had more members than any of the other religious groups in 1776, their voice projected forcefully into the public debate.

The second group included proponents of the moderate Enlightenment who looked to religion primarily to provide moral standards. They thought religion had a social function, but they tended to oppose the state paying churches. This group also saw the general affirmation of religion as a social good. They supported the proliferation of religious institutions, which they thought would promote social stability. But they feared religious zealotry. Franklin and other Founding Fathers, such as George Washington and John Jay, fell into this group.

Many moderate Enlightenment proponents would prove amenable to the actions of the old-line Protestants in defense of their traditional institutional prerogatives. Yet the moderates' distaste of zealotry, and their Enlightenment sensibilities, also made them amenable to joining the third group, those who wanted protections against religious control of the state. This protection generally took the form of a complete separation of church from state. Thomas Jefferson, who originated the metaphor of a wall of separation, and James Madison, who was the architect of the U.S. Constitution, were the two principal proponents of this position. The idea of strict separation was radically new. It required a revolution in political theory that involved treating a wide range of behavior and belief as off-limits to the government. But, at least at first, this argument did not persuade many people.

In Pennsylvania the first two positions were the twin poles of the early constitutional debates. Pennsylvania had a large group of moderate Enlightenment thinkers such as Franklin. It also had a large number of Protestant ministers who were concerned about the public place of Christianity and who sought to maintain Protestant prerogatives, though they did not necessarily want the state to pay churches. These different positions produced shifting alliances, resulting in tensions within the new Pennsylvania Constitution. Ultimately, it supported a state-sanctioned Christianity. The constitution declared that "all men have a natural and unalienable right to worship Almighty God according to the dictates of their own consciences and understanding." It proclaimed that the government was created for common protection, "not for the particular emolument or advantage of any single man, family, or sett [sic] of men." But it promised civil rights only to "any man . . . who acknowledges the being of a God." It also excluded Jews and others from government by requiring that all officeholders give an oath: "I do believe in one God, the creator and governor of the universe, the rewarder of the good and punisher of the wicked. And I do acknowledge the Scriptures of the Old and New Testament to be given by Divine inspiration." The oath, many believed, forestalled the possibility that the people would install an immoral unbeliever into office.[8]

The provisions turned out to be enormously controversial. Some were unnerved by the constitution's tether to Christianity. Benjamin Rush, a moderate Presbyterian with Unitarian leanings, complained that the Pennsylvania Constitution, and especially the oath of office, was "contrary" to its own bill of rights, which declared that anyone who believed in God would retain their civil rights. The Unitarian Joseph Priestley, who like Rush was unhappy with the exclusionary oath, wrote Franklin to inquire about the rationale. Franklin replied that he, too, opposed the oath but had been unable to stop it. He thought he had limited the damage by adding the stipulation "that *no further or more extended Profession of Faith should ever be exacted.*"[9]

Others complained that the constitution's provisions were too loose. Old-line Protestants became especially concerned. The rhetoric of rights that floated around in the political discourse of the new nation suggested to them an anarchic tendency. In September 1776, while the constitution was still being debated, a group of ministers led by Henry Muhlenberg met to discuss the situation. The group was concerned, in Muhlenberg's explanation, that with all the rhetoric of liberty "no care at all had been taken to acquire even the outer ramparts" that might protect the state from the rampaging godless. Drawing upon a staple of Christian belief, Muhlenberg regarded the forces of wickedness as always ready to mount an assault upon godly moral norms. This belief created what may seem in retrospect a paranoid search for dark conspiracies. But it was a genuine fear that was widespread in old-line Christian political thought.[10]

The initial group around Muhlenberg was small, consisting of himself, as the German Lutheran representative; a Presbyterian; an Episcopalian; and the provost of the College of Philadelphia (now the University of Pennsylvania). Muhlenberg explained to the group that under the new constitution, it seemed "as if a Christian people were ruled by Jews, Turks, Spinozists, Deists, [and] perverted naturalists [atheistic materialists]." Francis Allison, the Presbyterian member of the group and the vice-provost of the College of Philadelphia, disagreed, arguing that the oath requiring officeholders to believe in God would be sufficient to protect the government. But by the end of the meeting all had agreed to widen the circle and to meet again the following day. By then the group of concerned ministers had grown. It consisted of both the provost and vice-provost of the College of Philadelphia, two Episcopalians, a Swedish Lutheran, an English Presbyterian, and Muhlenberg. At the end of that meeting, they were in agreement that something must be done.[11]

The group dispatched a representative to Franklin. Religious organizations were the near-universal creators of charitable foundations in 1776, the representative pointed out. Likewise, educational institutions were almost solely maintained by religious societies. To disrupt religion and remove its legal protections, the representative argued, would be to remove the public commitment to virtue that many state constitutional framers considered necessary for the maintenance of a republican society. The group suggested that a clause protecting Christian institutional prerogatives should be added to the constitution. Franklin agreed to submit their concern to the convention if they would draft a provision.[12]

When they did so, the convention approved the measure. The resulting provision in Section 45 of the Plan of Government explicitly connected religious associations with public virtue. "Laws for the encouragement of virtue, and prevention of vice and immorality, shall be made and constantly kept in force, and provision shall be made for their due execution," the constitution explained. "And all religious societies or bodies of men heretofore united or incorporated for the advancement of religion or learning, or for other pious and charitable purposes, shall be encouraged and protected in the enjoyment of the privileges, immunities and estates which they are accustomed to enjoy, or could of right have enjoyed, under the laws and former constitution of this state." The provision joined "religious societies and bodies of men," "the advancement of religion or learning," and "pious and charitable purposes," because they were, if not interchangeable, then interrelated. All tended by implication to promote "the encouragement of virtue."[13]

Muhlenberg was careful. When his group petitioned the assembly, they wanted to be clear that they supported "the common cause of civil and religious Liberty" and desired only "to preserve and keep fast the sacred religious Privileges and Immunities heretofore possessed and enjoyed." But to Muhlenberg and his allies, religious liberty meant a full protection of Protestant Christian church prerogatives—everything short of paying churches. Others had different notions.[14]

When the constitution was submitted to the people for a vote, debate on the religion clauses exploded. Among the sharpest critics of the constitution were old-line Protestants who saw it as a revocation of their governing prerogative. Someone writing under the name "A Follower of Christ" noted in the *Evening Post* that William Penn's original Declaration *of Rights* had prohibited

"Deists, Jews, Mahomedans [*sic*], and other enemies of Christ" from holding office. This was true. But, misreading the constitution, the writer thought that those bars had been removed by the promise of civil rights to all. Henry Muhlenberg also turned against the constitution. He complained sarcastically that the framers were asking Protestant congregations to "give up life and all else to retain the priceless freedom of conscience." Because the state constitution had declined to endorse an official religion—even though it excluded Jews and freethinkers from public office—he warned, "you need believe in no Redeemer, no Spirit, no Word of God," adding, "If you only acknowledge a Superior Being with the mouth, you may assist in the government. . . . [I]f such incarnate spirits of elevated taste should succeed, there would very soon arise such grand, politic, free republics as flourished before the Flood, in Sodom, and before the destruction of Jerusalem."[15]

Others responded with equal vociferousness in support of the constitution. One proponent wrote to the *Pennsylvania Journal* both to acknowledge the effectiveness of Muhlenberg's campaign and to criticize it for demagoguery. He claimed that opponents relied on "irritating religious spleen" to convince the masses "that the *church*, and indeed our land was *in danger*, because the Athanasian Creed, Heidelberg Catecism [*sic*], Westminster Confession of Faith, or some other much esteemed *form of sound words* was not literally *transcribed* into our Constitution, and every man obliged to make solemn oath that he believed that formula before he could enjoy the rights of a citizen." Although ultimately the supporters of the constitution carried the day, no one was entirely happy. The debate's bitterness and the substantive controversies it evoked foreshadowed a dispute over religious liberty that was just beginning.[16]

3.

Disputed though it was, Pennsylvania's constitution created a model that subsequent states were free to modify, build upon, or reject altogether. Several facets of the debate over religion in Pennsylvania would frame the conversation as it moved forward elsewhere.

The first issue was whether to fund churches. Although Pennsylvania declined state funding, after 1776 five states—Maryland, Massachusetts, New Hampshire, South Carolina, and Vermont—had constitutional provisions to use public money to pay churches, thereby maintaining institutional religious establishments by law. Connecticut, which did not pass a constitution for forty-two years, had a provision by statute to do the same.[17]

The other states refused institutional establishments, but that did not mean that they left religion alone. Their constitutions were often just as skewed in support of Christianity as those that included state funding for religious groups—and the debates over their adoption were just as riddled with intellectual tension as Pennsylvania's. The North Carolina Constitution of 1776, for example, forbade an "establishment of any one religious church or denomination in this State, in preference to any other." That clause forbade state funding for churches. Yet preceding the constitution's disestablishment clause, the convention delegates inserted a provision that "no person, who shall deny the being of God or the truth of the Protestant religion, or the divine authority either of the Old or New Testaments, or who shall hold religious principles incompatible with the freedom and safety of the State, shall be capable of holding any office or place of trust or profit in the civil department within this State." Likewise, the New Jersey Constitution of 1776 offered a series of provisions guaranteeing religious liberty that created real liabilities for non-Protestants. It offered freedom of conscience as a guarantee that "no person shall ever, within this Colony, be deprived of the inestimable privilege of worshipping Almighty God." But its promise was that only "no Protestant inhabitant" would be denied the enjoyment of civil rights and stipulated that only Protestants could hold public office.[18]

Many writers have sought to understand these constitutional provisions as expressions of concern for public morality that stemmed from civic republicanism, the ancient political belief, inherited from the Romans, that republics were sustained by the virtuous public-mindedness of their citizenry. Civic republicanism provided many revolutionary political theorists with the intellectual justification for the American Revolution. The British parliament's policy of denying American representation while levying taxes—and the failure of King George to extend to the colonists the protection of British citizenship—convinced the revolutionaries that the British Empire was suffering a decline of virtue and slow corruption that, according to the categories of civic republicanism, would lead inexorably to tyranny. The maintenance of virtue was crucial to protecting the citizenry from political domination.[19]

But like so much related to the subject of religious freedom, the general agreement about the necessity of virtue rested on a fundamental question of meaning: what was the source and specific moral content of virtue? Civic republicanism affirmed an abstract notion of virtue, defined primarily by the ability of citizens to divorce themselves from their self-interest in order to pursue the common good. Yet what might be called Christian republicanism, put forth by Henry Muhlenberg and other old-line Protestants, defined virtue more narrowly: the ability or willingness of individual citizens to submit to the moral law of God as revealed in the Old and New Testaments. This was the idea behind the general connection of virtue with Christianity in Pennsylvania and its explicit link to Protestantism in New Jersey and North Carolina. The clearly sectarian thrust of the specific moral ideas advanced by Christian republicans, many of whom were also old-line proponents of state financial support, drew more from John Winthrop, the Puritan divine who saw New England as a Christian city upon a hill, than from the civic republicanism of Rome.[20]

For a time, civic and Christian republicans were able to work together. In Pennsylvania, Franklin was not opposed to the idea that the maintenance of morals was a necessary prerequisite for social stability. Nor was he overly troubled by the sectarian character of Christian republican claims. He assumed, true to his intellectual orientation toward the moderate Enlightenment, that the empire of reason was sufficiently broad that most people could agree on general moral obligations, whether the specific content of those obligations came from revelation or from reasoned moral thought. Muhlenberg, by contrast, was a Christian republican. When he complained that the new constitution endangered Christian institutional prerogatives, his concern grew out of a Christian republican notion of religious liberty. Still, Franklin and Muhlenberg's shared language of virtue allowed them to compromise.[21]

As the controversy deepened in other important states, the differences between the Christian and civic republicans' views became more apparent, and the critical ambiguity about the meaning of religious liberty became harder to finesse. One year after Pennsylvania, New York opened its constitutional debate not in a special convention but during the legislative session of its provincial congress. John Jay, a moderate who had sought reconciliation with Britain until the Declaration of Independence, became the most important voice in the New York debate. He would later become, on George Washington's nomination, the first chief justice of the U.S. Supreme Court. He also cowrote the *Federalist Papers* with Alexander Hamilton and James Madison. Jay was a dedicated Anglican, an adherent of an old-line branch of Christianity. He did not seem inclined toward state financial support for any particular group, but he also was not in favor of a radical break between church and state. New York's legislators were of mixed opinion on the issue of religion, so Jay was free to set the parameters of the debate.[22]

The resulting church–state provision in New York's 1777 constitution seemed, at first blush, straightforward. "[T]he benevolent principles of rational liberty," the constitution explained, required the framers "to guard against that spiritual oppression and intolerance wherewith the bigotry and ambition of weak and wicked priests and princes have scourged mankind." To that end they guaranteed "the free exercise and enjoyment of religious profession and worship, without discrimination or preference." But the guarantee was qualified. The framers wanted it understood that "the liberty of conscience, hereby granted, shall not be so construed as to excuse acts of licentiousness, or justify practices inconsistent with the peace or safety of this State."[23]

Behind this language lay a determined battle over the extent of religious liberty. On the first reading of the constitution after it emerged from the drafting committee, John Jay proposed that freedom of religion be limited, offering this proviso: "nothing in this clause shall be construed to extend the toleration of any sect or denomination of Christians, or others, by whatever name distinguished, who inculcate and hold for true doctrines, principles inconsistent with the safety of civil society." Jay's target was vague. After a long deliberation with the other legislators, Jay withdrew his motion in favor of a more specific limitation that revealed his true target. Free religious exercise is the right of all, Jay proposed:

> Except the professors of the religion of the church of Rome, who ought not to hold lands in, or be admitted to a participation of the civil rights enjoyed by the members of this State, until such time as the said professors shall appear in the supreme court of this State, and there most solemnly swear, that they verily believe in their consciences, that no pope, priest or foreign authority on earth, hath power to absolve the subjects of this State from their allegiance to the same. And further, that they renounce and believe to be false and wicked, the dangerous and damnable doctrine, that the pope, or any other earthly authority, have power to absolve men from sins, described in, and prohibited by the Holy Gospel of Jesus Christ; and particularly, that no pope, priest or foreign authority on earth, hath power to absolve them from the obligation of this oath.[24]

Jay's problem with Roman Catholicism was similar to the views held by many Protestants. He was not opposed to the connection of religious ideals to the state in the abstract. As he would later explain, the civil law ought to comport with what he called "the whole moral law." The moral law was "ordained by a legislator of *infinite* wisdom and rectitude," in other words, by God. Because God was unchanging and the moral law stemmed from his will, the moral law had to be "exactly the same" as it had been "before the flood." Jay's problem with Roman Catholicism was that it blurred the structures of spiritual and civil authority in a way that he found unacceptable. In Jay's conception, the spiritual and the temporal were connected only through the moral law, not through the pope or through an ecclesiastic structure, as in Roman Catholicism. The moral law kept the structures of authority separate but acknowledged the foundation of civil law in divine law. With that distinction in mind, Jay claimed, "[I]t is the duty as well as the privilege and interest of our Christian nation to select and prefer Christians for their rulers."[25]

His fellow legislators were not convinced that overt discrimination against Catholics was desirable, but the specifics of the debate were not recorded. After another lengthy battle, Jay's motion was defeated nineteen votes to ten. Finally, Jay proposed language that the convention passed and later modified to its final form, with minimal controversy. The final form promised free exercise without preference, but included the limitation that freedom of conscience did not "excuse acts of licentiousness, or justify practices inconsistent with the peace or safety of this State." In a telling objection, Gouverneur Morris, who would later serve on the Committee of Five that drafted the specific wording of the U.S. Constitution, protested this final amendment. It was "the same in substance" as the one Jay had previously withdrawn, Morris complained. But the delegates overruled Morris's objection, evidently preferring the vague limitation of religious liberty that the amendment seemed to offer. Jay's proviso worked in tandem with the thinly veiled anti-Catholicism in the first part of the paragraph, which claimed that religious liberty was important to protect against the "spiritual oppression and intolerance wherewith the bigotry and ambition of weak and wicked priests and princes . . . scourged mankind." Together the two clauses suffused New York's guarantee of religious liberty with Protestant sectarianism, in spite of its apparent separation of church and state. That would become important for judicial interpretation of the constitution in the future.[26]

The problem in each of these disputes was that the framers were groping for a shared meaning of religious liberty. As they did so, they did not move closer together. Instead, their divergent positions became clearer. As the debate moved from New York to Virginia two years later, the positions reached full articulation. Virginia had ratified its constitution in 1776. Thomas Jefferson, James Madison, and George Mason were among the many important delegates at the Virginia convention, but, again, the delegates did not share a singular conception of the relationship of religion to the state. The resulting provision in Section 16 of Virginia's Declaration of Rights included the same kind of tension as in Pennsylvania and New York. It declared that because religion "can be directed only by reason and conviction, not by force or violence . . . all men are equally entitled to the free exercise of religion, according to the dictates of conscience." This suggested that religious liberty was an individual right. Yet the provision countered this idea by connecting the free exercise of religion with "the duty which we owe to our Creator," and explained that all citizens still had "the mutual duty . . . to practise Christian forbearance, love, and charity towards each other."[27]

Behind this juxtaposition of individual freedom and Christian duty resided the fundamental issue of the meaning of religious liberty. In one definition, religious liberty was a product of Christianity and in service to Christian religious expression; the guarantee of religious liberty was a guarantee of institutional religious rights. In the second definition, religious liberty was the right of the individual to believe as he wished without interference from the government. This definition had a corollary: religious groups had to be prevented from using the government to violate the rights of others. In other words, it required complete separation of church and state.

The tension between these two positions came to a head in 1779 when Jefferson tried to pass what he called a Bill for Establishing Religious Freedom. Jefferson sought to force the issue by separating religious belief from civil rights. He controlled the early drafting of the legislation while it was in committee—but before it could reach the assembly, he was elected governor. Because governors did not take part in legislative wrangling, Jefferson—with all his persuasive powers—was removed from the debate, which limited the ultimate prospects for his bill. When it came before the full assembly on June 12, 1779, the bill's central provision was both succinct and sweeping. "[Because] our civil rights have no dependence on our religious opinions," it read, "all men shall be free to profess, and by argument to maintain, their opinions in matters of religion, and . . . the same shall in no wise diminish, enlarge, or affect their civil capacities." But in attempting to separate civil rights and religious opinions, Jefferson's bill revealed the differing ideals of religious liberty that had produced such contradictory constitutional provisions in other states. Accordingly, it met with controversy. Before proponents could muster the necessary support, the legislative session had expired, so the assembly postponed the bill's consideration until after the summer recess. In the interim the battle of the broadsides intensified. When the legislators returned they found numerous petitions on religious freedom; all but two opposed Jefferson's bill. Emboldened by the popular response, other legislators supported a measure to modify the Declaration of Rights in order to erode freedom of conscience by limiting the civil rights of non-Christians. If implemented, it would have created a broad Christian establishment in Virginia. Unable to come to a decision on either bill by the end of the session, the assembly did nothing.[28]

With the two definitions of religious liberty now articulated, only Massachusetts, with its long and important history, had yet to weigh in. But given the general trend in Pennsylvania, Virginia, and the other states, when the Massachusetts delegates met the following year the outcome was predictable. John Adams, an aloof lawyer whose conservative disposition grew out of a principled elitism, led Massachusetts. He had been raised a Congregationalist but eventually turned to Unitarianism, which provided the kind of rational faith to which he was inclined. Adams believed that religion served a necessary social function, and the Massachusetts Constitution reflected this idea. Massachusetts allowed that no person should "be hurt, molested, or restrained, in his person, liberty, or estate, for worshipping God in the manner and season most agreeable to the dictates of his own conscience, or for his religious profession or sentiments." It limited the equal protection of law to "every denomination of Christians, demeaning themselves peaceably." It required officeholders to declare their belief in the Christian religion. It nominally made room for Catholic officeholders, providing that they affirmed that "no foreign prince, person, prelate, state, or potentate hath, or ought to have, any jurisdiction, superiority, preëminence, authority, dispensing or other power, in any matter, civil, ecclesiastical, or spiritual, within this commonwealth." But because denying the authority of the pope would have been abhorrent to any Catholic who wished to remain Catholic, in practice they were excluded. In the end, the constitution defined religious liberty as the perpetuation and support of Protestant Christianity.[29]

Adams was effusive in his praise of the church–state arrangement in Massachusetts. As he would later explain, the government was "founded on the natural authority of the people alone, without a pretence [sic] of miracle or mystery." The success of American constitutionalism, of which Massachusetts was the crowning flower, stemmed from the ability of the framers "to disabuse themselves of artifice, imposture, hypocrisy, and superstition." The result was the perfection of Christian civilization, a post-Reformation and post-Revolution reconfiguration of the relationship of religion to the state. "The experiment is made, and has completely succeeded," he exulted. The constitution ensured that the "authority in magistrates and obedience of citizens" found support through "reason, morality, and the Christian religion, without the monkery of priests or the knavery of politicians."[30]

Others were less sympathetic, and their criticism laid bare the essential dilemma in the meaning of religious liberty. Isaac Backus, for example, was a

Reformed Baptist opponent of the Massachusetts institutional establishment. He nevertheless approvingly noted of the Massachusetts Constitution, "No man can take a seat in our legislature till he solemnly declares, 'I believe the Christian religion and have a firm persuasion of its truth.'" The constitution needed to go further, in Backus's estimation, in order to provide "equal Christian liberty." Yet his telling phrase outlined the outer limits of the concept: religious liberty was applicable only to Christians. By contrast, John Leland, the radical and iconoclastic Baptist leader from Massachusetts and Virginia, complained that the Massachusetts Constitution was "as good a performance as could be expected in a state where religious bigotry and enthusiasm" had so predominated. The protection of religion in the Massachusetts Declaration of Rights "would read much better in a catechism than in a state constitution," Leland claimed, "and sound more concordant in a pulpit than in a statehouse." Leland wanted the complete separation of church from state so that "a Jew, a Turk, a Pagan, or a Christian of any denomination" whose good standing "as a civilian" would provide sufficient "confidence of the public" to permit him to hold office. But Leland's largely secular ideal was not to be found in any state prior to the 1787 U.S. Constitution. Even then, it would become the subject of dispute.[31]

4.

These early constitutional debates were complex and often not fully developed. Rather than articulating a stable body of political theory, they were instead a cluster of intellectual tensions. As the comments of Adams, Backus, and Leland showed, everyone purported to uphold the ideal of religious liberty. But the appeal to religious liberty did not grow out of any fixed connection to the revolutionaries' ideas of political freedom. It was instead a key component of political symbolism that hid deeper theoretical disagreements. Because all sides were eager to claim the symbolic high ground in the debate over religious liberty, it became a rallying cry for those who wanted to create a Christian commonwealth, and for those who wanted to establish a secular state.

But the invocation of religious liberty should not be confused with the actual distribution of power and the formation of political institutions. In the early disagreements about religious liberty, the protection of Christian institutional prerogatives tended to emerge triumphant. Jefferson's argument that civil rights had no connection to religious opinion did not persuade many people. Many state constitutional framers implicitly believed that such a separation threatened the state's foundation in morality. At the same time, moderate Enlightenment proponents such as Franklin remained open to the arguments of Muhlenberg and other old-line Protestants that the perpetuation of traditional institutional religious privileges was necessary to protect the state from man's inherent vice.[32]

Taken as a whole, the cooperation between Christian and civic republicans produced a hazy agreement after the first round of constitution-making. Most states promoted the perpetuation of religious freedom as a means of supporting congregations. They did so in order to buttress the state. "[T]he happiness of a people and the good order and preservation of civil government," the Massachusetts Constitution claimed, "essentially depend upon piety, religion, and morality."[33]

The agreement was unstable, though. Like godlessness, false religion could undermine established morality and be disruptive to the social order. When people succumbed to enthusiasms that sometimes swept through the masses and that were instigated by what the educated classes considered religious demagogues, then the state needed protection from religious zealotry. Maryland's 1776 Declaration of Rights, for example, modified its freedom of conscience clause to exclude those cases in which "under colour of religion, any man shall disturb the good order, peace or safety of the State, or shall infringe the laws of morality." Delaware (1776), North Carolina (1776), Georgia (1777), New York (1777), and New Hampshire (1784) each enacted similar provisos. The constitutions maintained that morality and virtue connected to the proliferation of religious institutions were necessary for the maintenance of the nation, but some moralities based on some religious claims fell outside the protection of law.[34]

That distinction provided an important opening for religious partisans and raised several questions that would become important in the creation of the moral establishment. Who was to decide when religion was properly supporting morality and when it turned disruptive? What standards were to be used? How would those standards be enforced and who would enforce them? As the tensions over state constitutional formation demonstrated, framers were uneasy with looking to religion *in general* to support morality. Not all religions were equal. Religion supported morality up to a point, but ultimately the government determined which religions supported morality, which did not, and where the limits were. If religious partisans could gain control of the state political or judicial apparatus, they could set those moral standards, thereby setting up a religious establishment under another name.

To that end, most constitutions ratified before the 1787 U.S. Constitution also included limits on the kind of people who could be elected to office. Eleven of the fourteen constitutions prohibited Jews and agnostics from holding office. Seven of fourteen prohibited Catholic officeholders. Nine of the fourteen limited civil rights to Protestants (five), Christians (three), or theists (one). Many states declined to enfranchise Jews, Unitarians, and agnostics. A person's demurral from swearing or affirming his belief in God could limit his ability to testify in court. Religious organizations ran the schools, in which religious practice was a frequent part of instruction. Non-theists could not hold or convey property in trust and could not establish philanthropic organizations to propound their religious beliefs. Whatever religious liberty meant at the time of the Revolution, its limits were clear.[35]

2

A GODLESS GOVERNMENT?

1.

In 1776 the majority of church members were Congregationalists, Episcopalians, or Presbyterians. But the most vital and dynamic force in American religion was evangelicalism. To be an evangelical in 1776 was to be a part of a mildly disreputable group. Evangelicals stressed individual conversion as a response to God, the importance of religious feeling as the hallmark of piety, and strict attention to a tightened moral code that prohibited dancing, drinking, and gaming. In an age of deference to those of the higher classes, condescension toward those of the lower classes, and careful awareness of one's place in the social hierarchy, the evangelical creed seemed to profess that every person was equal before God. That belief ran up against the hierarchical society of the South, where Anglicanism had received financial support from the state. In the North, evangelical groups' lax educational standards for their ministers butted against the highly educated Congregational and Unitarian parishes of New England and the Presbyterian and Lutheran congregations of the mid-Atlantic states. Finally, the ascetic theology of many evangelical preachers rejected dominant parts of the popular culture in all of the colonies.[1]

Although evangelicals played a limited role in the deliberations over the early state constitutions, their aggressiveness in winning new converts made them into a growing force by the late eighteenth and early nineteenth centuries. With their growth, evangelicals had the potential to destabilize the argument of Christian republicans. This was particularly true in Virginia, which became the main front in the debate over religious liberty. By the 1780s Virginia had a thriving evangelical population. It also had the chief proponent of separating religion and the state, Thomas Jefferson.[2]

The relationship between evangelicals and Jefferson was complicated. With his Bill for Establishing Religious Freedom in 1779, Jefferson had become the spokesman for the minority idea that there ought to be no civil punishment for any religious belief, unless it disturbed the peace. In Jefferson's estimation, religious liberty was not the right of groups. Rather, it protected individuals from groups. Jefferson also did not reject the idea that religion supported morality, only the idea that paying churches supported morality. According to Jefferson, paying churches encouraged institutional indolence. "[I]t tends," Jefferson explained, "to corrupt the principles of that very religion it is meant to encourage by bribing . . . those who will externally profess and conform to it." Paying churches kept religious institutions alive, whether or not anyone believed their precepts. State churches also required official adherence to a specific creed, which often, Jefferson claimed, created exterior conformity but private nonconformity, thereby encouraging a hypocrisy that undermined morality. This argument was attractive to evangelicals, because it mirrored many of their own arguments against their state-supported religious competitors.[3]

Yet Jefferson and the evangelicals did not agree on everything. Evangelicals rejected Jefferson's notion of complete separation, in part because old-line proponents of paying churches often accused evangelicals of trying to divorce religion from government, a charge the evangelicals did not wish to bear. Removing state financial support was not, to evangelicals' minds, the same as separating religion from the state. Isaac Backus, for example, was one of the most prominent evangelicals in the eighteenth century. Staunchly opposed to paying churches, Backus still condemned the radical idea of individual rights and the separation of religion and state. As he explained in a 1773 tract, there were many who at that time spoke "great *swelling words* about *liberty*, while they *despise government*." Evangelicals were not among them. "The true liberty of man," Backus explained, was "to know, obey, and enjoy his Creator, and to do all the good unto, and enjoy all the happiness with and in, his fellow creatures that he is capable of." Religious liberty was an extension of this broader Christian liberty. It was a liberty to do what was right. It was granted by God and designed not as a means of separating religion from the state and certainly not as an expression of an unqualified individual right. Religious liberty was intended to support those who wanted to know, obey, and enjoy their Creator, while allowing a measure of diverse belief within Protestant Christendom. Those who were unable to recognize the undeniable connection of religious obligations and liberties were, Backus emphatically explained, "*servants of corruption.*" In attempting to separate morality from its foundation in religion, proponents of church–state separation introduced an amoral impulse that would, Backus contended, inevitably bring down the republic.[4]

Backus's understanding of liberty and his rejection of individual rights clarified the debate between the old-line proponents of state monetary support for churches and evangelicals such as Backus. It was a debate about means, not about ends. Both wanted a nation in which religion was connected to state governance. Such an arrangement was necessary, they agreed, because the individual must always consider, or be made to consider, the social whole. Because the good of the whole required upholding the system of morals that religion provided, the separation of church from state should not mean a removal of religious ideals from government. The scope and limits of that connection were at issue, but not whether there should be a connection at all. This consensus, though widely shared, was submerged beneath the disagreement over whether to pay churches through the state.[5]

Modern historical narratives have ignored this basic agreement and its implications for the meaning of religious liberty. In the usual historical narratives, Jefferson and Madison together passed religious-liberty legislation in Virginia before moving on to the U.S. Constitution and the First Amendment. This movement then supposedly established religious liberty in the United States. But the alliance between Jefferson (and later Madison) and the evangelicals was a classic case of strange bedfellows. All that they agreed on was that the state should not pay churches. They disagreed on whether religious liberty was designed to protect the group or the individual. They disagreed on whether religious liberty only protected religion from the state or whether it also protected the state from religion. They even disagreed on the role of religion in promoting a morality that was shared by all. As this coalition made a concerted push to stop states from paying churches, the ambiguities of their vision, first in Virginia, then at the Constitutional Convention, and finally in the debates over the First Amendment, threatened to unravel their alliance. The result was an uncertainty of meaning that would suffuse the First Amendment, an uncertainty that allowed for the creation of the moral establishment. But at the same time, Madison, the architect of the U.S. Constitution, would introduce a notion of religious liberty and of rights that those disagreeing with the moral establishment could draw upon repeatedly over the next two centuries.

2.

It began in Virginia, with high stakes. Virginia was the most populous state in the young nation. Its prominence was obvious in the number and quality of Revolutionary leaders that it produced, including George Washington, Thomas Jefferson, James Madison, and Patrick Henry. If Christian republicans could succeed in their desire to pay Virginia churches, the outcome would tilt the national debate over religious liberty toward the old-line Christians. The debate had long been deadlocked. Each year since 1776 the assembly had suspended payments for the established clergy, but they had been unable to eliminate the idea of an institutional establishment. With the continued lack of state monetary support, Christian republicans in Virginia worried that the cause of Christianity was suffering, and with it the cause of morality. In 1783 they found new momentum. That fall, when the legislative session opened, the House received three petitions supporting payment for churches. As one explained, "Vice and Immorality, Lewdness & Prophanity [sic]" had replaced the proper observance of Christianity following the American Revolution. The petition went on to call for a general tax to pay for churches, which would be established "[o]n the Broad Basis of Gospel Liberty & Christian Charity—Divested of Past Prejudices and Bigotry." It was the first time that the legislature had received any petitions calling for an institutional establishment since Jefferson's bill had been defeated four years prior.[6]

Patrick Henry, who emerged from the Revolution as the most popular leader of the assembly, championed the petitioners' cause. Henry needed another year to make a serious legislative push, but finally in 1784 he brought a bill before the legislative body. Explaining that "the general diffusion of Christian knowledge hath a natural tendency to correct the morals of men, restrain their vices, and preserve the peace of society," the bill proposed to pay Christian ministers from public funds. The money would be disbursed to a "society of Christians," or a church, which would then use the money to support the leaders of their ministry. Henry's support of the legislation gave it immediate credibility. As George Washington would later explain of Henry's place in the Virginia legislature, "He has only to say let this be Law—and it is Law."[7]

Henry's power in 1784 was even greater than it had been when he successfully opposed Jefferson's bill on religious liberty in 1779. Jefferson himself was out of the country serving as the ambassador to France. Many of his one-time supporters had moved on or changed sides. Stepping into the leadership void was James Madison, a young political theorist and wily parliamentary tactician, but in some ways an unlikely figure to succeed Jefferson in the battle. Madison was among the most singular thinkers in the new nation. But he lacked the personal charisma of Jefferson, the gravitas of George Washington, or the rhetorical power of Henry. In 1784 he was just thirty-four, nineteen years younger than Washington and eight years younger than Jefferson. He also possessed a much less imposing physical presence. Washington and Jefferson both stood an imperious six feet plus. Madison was slight and stood at no more than five-foot-four. By build, temperament, and cultivation, his skills lay not in leading, nor in charming, but in thinking. In spite of all appearances to the contrary, Jefferson could not have picked a more skilled protégé.[8]

Given the pronounced advantages Henry enjoyed, the first thing Madison did was push the final vote on the bill into the winter recess, which allowed him to gather his supporters in order to launch a counterattack. But after that legislative success, he decided to go further. In seeking to expose the bill's dangerous tendency, Madison took intellectual stock of the subject of religious liberty as a whole. In doing so, he would clarify the dispute as never before. Setting to work, Madison produced an anonymous petition to be delivered to the assembly at the next legislative session, the famous Memorial and Remonstrance against Religious Assessments. The memorial has been heralded as one of the two signal statements of religious liberty in the United States (the other being Jefferson's Bill for Establishing Religious Freedom). Its central contention was radical. Madison explained that freedom of religion was "an unalienable right" taking precedence over the power of government. Henry's bill had overstepped the legislature's province by looking to religion as "an engine of Civil policy," which Madison characterized as "an unhallowed perversion of the means of salvation." The risk in such a perversion was that it attempted to buttress religious belief in order to shore up a dilapidated civil authority. It was an act of governance born of desperation. In place of Henry's notion of religious liberty, Madison suggested a reconfigured relationship between religion and the state, in which the state opted out of the business of religion entirely. Explaining that a "just Government" whose goal was to perpetuate "public liberty" would "be best supported by protecting every Citizen in the enjoyment of his Religion," Madison suggested that the only thing for Virginia to do was to leave religion alone.[9]

But the significance of Madison's Memorial and Remonstrance went beyond the disestablishment battle in Virginia. It signaled a watershed in political thought. In much of the eighteenth century, when political theorists talked about the protection of rights, the rights they talked about belonged to the people, not the individual. This was the vision that informed Pennsylvania's radical 1776 constitution. The goal of a properly constructed politics was to protect the people from the abuse of government. In practice, that meant that the people as a whole had to have access to the machinery of governance. This would ensure that the government acted at the behest of the people. In arguing against establishment, though, Madison reconfigured both the relationship of church and state and the more fundamental relationship of rights to government, making explicit what had been implicit in Jefferson's earlier arguments. Madison recognized that majorities could use their access to government to suppress and tyrannize minorities. Therefore, the rights of the minority had to be protected from the will of the majority. That formulation made no sense when rights belonged to the people at large, as they had in much of eighteenth-century political thought. To make sense of this puzzle, Madison suggested that individuals had rights that the government, even when supported by the majority, could not trample. Religious belief in particular was the most fundamental individual right, according to Madison, and in order to protect it the government needed to stay out of religion altogether.[10]

The brilliance of this intellectual leap can obscure that the memorial was also—even primarily—a political document, written as a petition and circulated through several Virginian counties during the legislative break in order to muster opposition to paying the churches. It was only one among the hundred or so petitions to the Virginia legislature that arrived when the new legislative session opened. Only eleven supported Henry's bill. But, unfortunately for Madison's ultimate goal, the majority of petitions that rejected payments for churches did not share Madison's notion of strict separation. The General Committee of the Baptists, for example, explained their rejection of state financial support by declaring that the clergy were "Voluntary Servants of the Church," which prohibited state support. Yet the Baptist delegates went on to explain that their rejection of state monetary support did not mean that they wanted the government to do nothing. The General Assembly could contribute to Christianity by "supporting those Laws of Morality, which are necessary for Private and Public Happiness." In that way the assembly would do its duty as the "Guardian" of the people.[11]

A distinction was emerging. As the Virginia debate made clear, at the end of the eighteenth century many saw the American religious establishment as consisting of three components: institutional, ceremonial, and moral. The institutional establishment consisted of state monetary support for churches. The ceremonial establishment provided ways to recognize God in state ritual, including the oaths of office, which ended with "So help me God"; the practice of state governors to call for days of prayer and fasting; and the custom (if not obligation) of taking the oath of office on the Bible. The moral establishment upheld the moral ideals of Christianity in the name of the public good. Henry promoted all three. Evangelicals rejected institutional establishment, claiming that it unfairly involved the state in the life of institutional churches, which put evangelicals at a disadvantage with the more established denominations. But that did not mean that they gave up on using religion as a means of maintaining a moral populace or as a ceremonial aspect of government. In fact, they argued that the legislature should pass more-stringent moral laws, whose content, they claimed, came directly from the Bible. What they were advocating was the disestablishment of institutional religion, but the continued establishment and the strengthened legal enforcement of Christianity's moral ideals. That is, they wanted to do away with the institutional establishment but to strengthen the moral one.[12]

Madison wanted the complete eradication of the establishment, putting him at odds with the evangelicals over the long haul. But, in the short term, they forged an effective political alliance. When the Virginia Assembly reconvened, Madison used the widespread opposition to Henry's bill to beat back what had originally seemed a strong legislative push in its favor. Then, in an attempt to capitalize on the momentum, Madison reintroduced Jefferson's long-neglected Bill for Establishing Religious Freedom. Because the proponents of paying the churches seemed shell-shocked by the popular response, he had little trouble getting it through the assembly. He did have to compromise slightly on the preamble's original claim that "the opinions and belief of men depend not on their own will, but follow involuntarily the evidence proposed to their minds," which might have sounded both too rationalistic and too individualistic. Opponents of Madison's and Jefferson's notion of rights made several attempts to change the preamble to include Section 16 of the Virginia Declaration of Rights, with its assertion that citizens have "the mutual duty . . . to practise Christian forbearance, love, and charity towards each other," which would have mitigated Madison's individual-rights claims. After much back and forth, the assembly compromised by deleting the objectionable sentences of the preamble and dropping their demand to include Section 16. The assembly also deleted Jefferson's declaration "that the opinions of men are not the object of civil government, nor under its jurisdiction," a deletion that not only repudiated complete separation but also kept open the possibility of state regulation of certain kinds of individual belief. But in spite of the legislative wrangling, the bill's central contention remained in place. Because "our civil rights have no dependence on our religious opinions," the bill explained, "all men shall be free to profess, and by argument to maintain, their opinions in matters of religion, and . . . the same shall in no wise diminish, enlarge, or affect their civil capacities." It was a major milestone in the history of church–state law. Although the practical application of this rule would require more deliberation about its limits and implications, the bill declared that individual rights were, for the first time in American history, at least in some sense independent of religious opinions.[13]

3.

I t would be nice if we could use Madison's triumph in Virginia as a succinct summary of the meaning of American religious liberty as a whole, and that is how many historians and jurists have used it. But such a claim is too simple. The Virginia bill was not a constitutional provision, even in the State of Virginia. It could be overturned at any time by any Virginia legislature, a fact recognized in the bill itself. Although it was important in a symbolic sense, it did not provide any permanent or national foundation for religious liberty in the United States. Only insofar as Jefferson's bill informed the debate over the Constitution and its First Amendment did it provide any kind of authoritative text on religious liberty.

As Madison moved into the national arena, he began to see the limited authority of the bill as one of the deficiencies inherent in the Articles of Confederation. The confederation allowed each state a maximal autonomy, seeking only to coordinate states in the few ways in which the United States acted as a nation. The patchwork of regulations under the articles, in which states passed a whole host of laws applicable only in their state, undermined any discernible sense of national life or consistent protection of rights on a national level. It was, as George Washington wrote to Madison, "[t]hirteen sovereignties pulling against each other, and all tugging at the foederal [*sic*] head." This disagreement threatened, in Washington's fears, to "bring ruin on the whole." Madison agreed. Taking the lessons he learned in the Virginia legislature, Madison began developing a new political theory that he hoped to apply to the entire nation.[14]

But as Madison began to develop his thinking, the implicit divide between him and the evangelicals became more apparent. While Madison caucused with the Virginia delegates in anticipation of the Constitutional Convention, he began preparing what he euphemistically called "some materials" on behalf of the delegation. In April he laid out his thoughts in a memorandum entitled "Vices of the Political System of the United States," which drew upon his experience in the recent Virginia debates. The biggest problem in a republican government, according to Madison, was that majorities would use their power to oppress the minority. "Place three individuals in a situation wherein the interest of each depends on the voice of the others, and give to two of them an interest opposed to the rights of the third," Madison suggested. "Will the latter be secure?" Madison listed the usual means of restraining majorities. Civic republicans claimed that the ability of citizens to divorce themselves from their self-interest for the good of the whole would prevent it.

Others thought deference to public opinion would serve the same purpose. Christian republicans looked, of course, to religion. The first two restraints Madison dismissed out of hand as inadequate safeguards in the protection of rights. Madison reasoned that if anything could be counted upon, it was that individuals would pursue their self-interest in all its various forms, irrespective of the pretension to self-control. Public opinion failed as a safeguard because what was public opinion but the expression of a majority? As for religion, Madison argued that it was too often "a motive to oppression," rather than a restraint from it.[15]

In dismissing the prevailing ideas about the protection of rights, Madison's refined notion of rights and their relationship to government gave his political thought a transformative edge. He did not simply assert rights. What was the point? Any assertion of rights could be trumped by a majority who would do as it pleased. Madison's ingenious solution was to enlarge the government. That is, government should be national, because only on a national scale would society be "broken into a greater variety of interests, of pursuits, of passions, which check each other, whilst those who may feel a common sentiment have less opportunity of communication and concert." Only a national arrangement, with a large diversity of groups, would protect government from the united force of a particular religious vision, thereby preserving the rights of the individual. As he later explained to Jefferson, "Divide et impera [divide and conquer], the reprobated axiom of tyranny, is[,] under certain qualifications, the only policy, by which a republic can be administered on just principles." In addition to enlarging the sphere of government, Madison wanted to divide the offices of governance into branches that would act as a check and a balance upon one another. In this way, Madison hoped to make government "sufficiently neutral between different parts of the Society" so that no group could use government to control another.[16]

Though he did not say so explicitly, it became apparent in the way Madison talked about rights that his goal was a godless government, sufficiently protected from the encroachments of the religious to ensure individual liberty. But this was not the goal of evangelicals, who were alarmed at what emerged from the Constitutional Convention under Madison's direction. Madison had arrived in Philadelphia for the convention in early May 1787, even though a quorum was not achieved for another two and a half weeks, in order to take steps to ensure that his philosophy drove the agenda. In his caucus with the other delegates, he turned his abstract political theory into three practical policy goals. First, he wanted a national government in which individuals chose national representatives, rather than the federal system in which individuals interacted with the national government only through their states. Second, he wanted proportional representation in the national legislature, rather than the equal representation of states, in which each state got one vote regardless of population, as under the articles. Third, and most controversially, Madison wanted the federal government to be able to veto the laws of individual states, because individual states would be more likely to be controlled by a single group, such as a particular denomination.[17]

These practical policy formulations became known as the Virginia Plan. The plan gained the support of Massachusetts and Pennsylvania early in the convention, which was then oriented around Madison's ideas. With this strategic victory, the battle was largely won. Rather than looking to religious ideals, the system of institutional safeguards that eventually characterized the U.S. Constitution grew out of Madison's ideas about proper governance and the preservation of rights. The separation of governmental branches, the balance of their powers, and the checks that they exercised upon one another presumed that the guarding of institutional self-interests, rather than the ability to divorce oneself from self-interest, would limit the power of any one governmental branch. This view rejected civic republicanism. Agreeing with Madison that the citizenry and their political leaders could not be counted upon to act in virtuous good faith, the convention decided that the mutual vigilance that each branch would exercise on every other should keep each branch in check, thereby protecting individual rights by restraining the government's power. Rights would be secured by institutional and structural design rather than by their mere assertion.[18]

But at what seemed the moment of triumph, victory began to slip from Madison's grasp. The convention had gone against him in one crucial arena, rejecting his vision of national supremacy and declining to grant Congress the ability to veto the laws of the states. Toward the end of the convention Madison wrote to Jefferson in France to express his dismay. Utilizing a code to prevent circulation of the letter—the code is deciphered in italics—Madison glumly predicted to his mentor, "[T]he *plan* [of the Constitution] *should* it *be adopted* will neither effectually *answer* its *national object* nor prevent the local *mischiefs* which every where *ex[c]ite disgusts* ag[ain]st the *state governments*." It was a gloomy prediction from someone so closely associated with the Constitution. But Jefferson did not share his melancholy. Unbeknownst to Madison, a crack between Madison and Jefferson had developed while the latter was across the Atlantic. Madison's political theory had moved beyond Jefferson, who only wanted a modification of the articles and continued to uphold civic republicanism as adequate protection against tyranny. Unlike Madison, he opposed a strong central state, seeing it as a means of oppression rather than as a guarantor of rights. Jefferson wrote to say that he was pleased that Madison did not get what he wanted. Regarding national veto power, as he had earlier explained to Madison, "Primâ facie I do not like it." Madison's vision went too far in the direction of a national government. It addressed what Jefferson saw as a series of small problems under the articles with too radical a remedy.[19]

At the same time, evangelicals rejected the framers' reliance on institutional checks and balances rather than a religiously buttressed morality among the people. The Constitution prohibited, in contrast to many state governments, any religious test for office on the federal level. With the exception of the phrase "the Year of our Lord," in Article 7, it omitted the concept of God. Revealing the wide divergence between Madison and his allies, after news of the godless Constitution spread, religious partisans began to mobilize against what they feared was the institution of a secular government that would infringe upon their religious rights. As they did so, Jefferson's opposition became a problem. Although he had been in France for a long time (and was still there), he remained an important figure whose approval of the Constitution would be important to its passage. Jefferson was also a staunch ally in Madison's fight for the rights of conscience. A split between the two would weaken their effective front, made even worse by evangelical skepticism of the Constitution and Christian republican hostility toward it. Madison sought to shore up his fragile coalition with his mentor by again explaining his vision of rights. National control over the states was key "to secure individuals ag[ain]st encroachments on their rights," he claimed. In fact, it was "[t]he mutability of the laws of the States" that undermined individual rights and had made it possible, though he did not say so explicitly, that at some future point someone might overturn the Bill for Establishing Religious Freedom in Virginia. The new government was supposed to address this. Yet because the Constitution did not, in Madison's opinion, "make provision for private rights" since it did not grant the national government veto powers over state laws, it was "materially defective" and needed to be strengthened, not weakened as Jefferson claimed. But they could not come to any real agreement. Jefferson replied that it was not national veto power but a bill of rights that would protect rights. This would become Jefferson's crucial mistake. Far from making rights secure, as Jefferson had hoped it would, what would become the First Amendment instead limited the expansive protection of liberty that Madison had envisioned.[20]

4.

As the debate over ratification moved forward, disagreements over the meaning of religious liberty, its purpose, and its limits broke apart the coalition of Madison, Jefferson, and the evangelicals. The result was an amendment of such utter ambiguity that religious partisans could assert their control. Jefferson's ideas were similar to the views of those who opposed the Constitution, not just evangelicals but the other Anti-Federalists who feared a strong central power and wanted a bill of rights to limit federal encroachment. To many religious leaders who lined up against the Constitution, the omission of God suggested a depraved sensibility that betokened the downfall of the Christian nation and implied a threat to Christian practice and belief. Jefferson's criticism of the Constitution, though he disagreed with Christian republicans on their view of religion and the state, still strengthened their call to modify or even reject it.[21]

This desire to modify the Constitution rose in volume even as states began to ratify it. In the nine months following the federal convention's conclusion in September, eight states (Delaware, Pennsylvania, New Jersey, Georgia, Connecticut, Massachusetts, Maryland, and South Carolina, in that order) quickly ratified the Constitution. Rhode Island rejected the constitution 2,711 to 239 in a statewide referendum. New Hampshire appeared deadlocked after a first session in February 1788. Because the Constitution required only nine states' support for it to take effect, by May 1788 the debate had come down to Virginia. If Virginia ratified the Constitution, it would go into effect, but if it failed, it had the potential to tip the balance against the Constitution in the remaining states in which there was large anti-federal sentiment. Even after New Hampshire guaranteed ratification while the Virginia debate dragged on, Virginia's potential failure to ratify it might call into question the document's legitimacy, given Virginia's size and importance.[22]

Now Jefferson's position became a problem. As Madison was gearing up for the Virginia ratification convention in June, word came from Daniel Carroll of Maryland that a letter, purportedly from Jefferson, was circulating in Maryland (and soon elsewhere) that seemed to reinforce the Anti-Federalist cause. The letter was, in fact, a version of Jefferson's letter to Madison in which Jefferson explained that he disliked the Constitution because, in Daniel Carroll's words, it was "without a Bill of rights."[23]

Four days after Madison received Carroll's warning, the Virginia ratification convention began. Jefferson's letter was ammunition for the opponents of the Constitution, most prominently Patrick Henry, who charged that the

Constitution introduced "a consolidated Government" that threatened liberty. The lack of a bill of rights was his biggest complaint. Ever the demagogue, Henry sought to inflame Christian fears against Madison's understanding of religious liberty. "There is many a religious man who knows nothing of argumentative reasoning," Henry thundered. "That sacred and lovely thing Religion, ought not to rest on the ingenuity of logical deduction." In a sly maneuver, Henry even drew upon Jefferson's letter to make his point. Misconstruing Jefferson's argument, he explained to the convention that Jefferson advised them "to reject this Government, till it be amended." He added, "His sentiments coincide entirely with ours."[24]

Madison was unimpressed but found himself in a tough position. He rose to object to Henry's invocation of Jefferson, who Madison sought to portray as sympathetic to the Constitution. But since he was not comfortable pursuing this argument for long, given the uncertainty about Jefferson's opinion, Madison tried to change the subject. "Is it come to this then," he asked rhetorically, "that we are not to follow our own reason?" Having parried Henry's criticism, Madison turned more explicitly to the subject of religion but struggled to respond because any attempt to explain the logic of the Constitution and its protection of rights would be subject to Henry's charge of syllogistic reasoning. He plunged ahead anyhow, in part relying on his reputation as a proponent of religious freedom to defend against Henry's attacks. As the convention proceeded, Henry kept reiterating the same points, with more elaboration and flourishes each time. Madison answered with calmness and reason. As he did so, Henry's criticism appeared increasingly paranoid and belligerent, eroding his credibility. The convention ratified the Constitution by a vote of 89 to 79.[25]

Yet Henry was still not finished. Although Madison had triumphed, what Jefferson and the Anti-Federalists had done was to make a bill of rights important to assuaging fears of a godless government. Since the question of a bill of rights would be worked out during the first session of Congress, Madison knew that he needed to be there to continue his work. Henry sought to keep him out, first using his influence in the state legislature to block Madison's election into the U.S. Senate (a feat made possible because at the time state assemblies, not the voters, elected U.S. senators). Madison did not want a senate seat anyway, and he immediately announced he would stand for election to the U.S. House of Representatives. Henry again attempted to stand in Madison's way by drawing the legislative district for Madison's seat to include several counties that were dominated by Anti-Federalist sentiment. Henry and his allies then began circulating rumors in the Anti-Federalist counties that

Madison was opposed to changes to the Constitution in any form, further inflaming Anti-Federalist hostility. Madison was not even present to aid his own cause. After the Virginia ratification he went back to New York to finish the final session of the Congress under the Articles of Confederation. Friends kept him abreast of the developments, pleading with him to return home to campaign for the House.[26]

While Madison pondered what to do, he and Jefferson continued their correspondence, with Madison trying to get his rogue ally back on board. Jefferson sent his congratulations on the acceptance of the Constitution, which he called "a good canvas, on which some strokes only want retouching." What he had in mind, of course, was "the general voice from North to South, which calls for a bill of rights." In response, Madison reiterated his pragmatic objections to a bill of rights. Madison regarded declarations of rights as "parchment barriers" whose efficacy had failed in states where the majority disregarded rights to do as it pleased. He was also wary of the motivations of others who were calling for a bill of rights, especially when it came to religious liberty. They seemed to want not the protection of rights but a guarantee of religious control. "I am sure that the rights of Conscience in particular, if submitted to public definition[,] would be narrowed much more than they are likely ever to be by an assumed power," Madison wrote. "One of the objections in New England" to the Constitution, and one of the reasons for their desire for a bill of rights, he explained, was that the Constitution's lack of religious tests for office had "opened a door for Jews Turks & infidels." This confirmed for Madison the risk in opening a debate on religious liberty. He preferred to leave the idea of religious liberty implied, rather than risk the narrowing of its scope. To further explain his political thinking to Jefferson, Madison sent along a copy of *The Federalist*. Although Jefferson replied a month later, once he had read *The Federalist*, to commend Madison's political theory, he still had reservations, explaining, "As to the bill of rights[,] however[,] I still think it should be added."[27]

Faced with criticism from both sides, Madison seems to have had a partial change of heart. Concluding that the activities of Henry and his allies were "most injurious" to his prospects of being elected to the House, he began writing letters to several prominent people in the counties that made up his district. Madison explained that he had opposed amendments in order to get the Constitution ratified. But now that it was ratified, as he clarified to the Baptist minister George Eve, it was his "sincere opinion that the Constitution ought to be revised, and that the first Congress meeting under it . . . ought to prepare and recommend to the States for ratification . . . the most satisfactory provisions for all essential rights." Madison explained that he wanted to protect "particularly the rights of Conscience in the fullest latitude."[28]

Madison was ever wily. He had written earlier to Jefferson that he had "always been in favor of a bill of rights." But to his would-be constituents he promised only amendments. As it turned out, he wanted to amend the text of the Constitution itself, possibly as a way of reinstating his push to create a national veto power on any state action that violated essential rights. Though in the long run the Bill of Rights has altered and expanded national power, its design in the late eighteenth century was to limit federal power, a power that Madison still wanted to expand. By promising only amendments to the Constitution, he seemed to be hoping that most voters would assume he was talking about a bill of rights and not perceive that he still wanted to install national supremacy. This was probably not what his constituents had in mind, but his careful promises seemed to be enough to satisfy them. When the counties voted on February 2, 1789, he made it into the House with 1,308 votes to his opponent's 972.[29]

It was not a wide margin of victory for someone so central to the political development of the new nation, a fact that he did not need to be reminded of when he arrived in Philadelphia for the start of the first Congress. Needing to keep his promises if he wanted a second term, within a couple of months of the beginning of the first session Madison had drawn up a list of revisions to the Constitution. When he put forward his proposals on June 8, 1789, his proposed list of amendments was long, but two revisions in particular addressed the issue of religious freedom. His first amendment would have been inserted between the third and fourth clauses of Article 1, Section 9 of the federal Constitution. Sweeping in its defense of individual religious rights, it read: "The civil rights of none shall be abridged on account of religious belief or worship, nor shall any national religion be established, nor shall the full and equal rights of conscience be in any manner, or on any pretext, infringed." His second was, in some ways, more radical. It would have been inserted between the first and second clauses of Article 1, Section 10. It read: "No state shall violate the equal rights of conscience, or the freedom of the press, or the trial by jury in criminal cases." This was a comprehensive plan to limit both the power of Congress and the power of the states to protect freedom of conscience and individual religious exercise (or non-exercise). Had they passed together, they would have given the national government the power to protect individual rights against encroachment by the states.[30]

But Madison's fears that, as he had explained to Jefferson, the rights of conscience would be "narrowed" when "submitted to public definition" came to pass. The House was not interested in drafting Madison's amendments. It decided, instead, to refer the issue of amendments to a select committee. When the First Amendment emerged on August 15, 1789, it had been trimmed, simply stating, "[N]o religion shall be established by law, nor shall the equal rights of conscience be infringed."[31]

This was not a major alteration, but it hinted at the modifications to come as Madison's vision suffered the death of small changes. Even the more modest version provoked complaint when the House debated the committee's recommendations. Peter Sylvester, a representative from New York, fretted that some might misunderstand the point of the amendment, reading it as an attempt "to abolish religion altogether." Elbridge Gerry, the representative from Massachusetts who had declined to sign the U.S. Constitution in part because it did not contain a bill of rights, wanted the amendment to read: "[N]o religious doctrine shall be established by law." He seemed worried that the amendment as it stood could prohibit the right of states to maintain a state religion (as Massachusetts did until 1833). Madison explained that he understood the words to prohibit Congress from establishing "a national religion." But that did not resolve the issue. Benjamin Huntington of Connecticut, which also had a religious establishment, complained that he thought "the words might be taken in such latitude as to be extremely hurtful to the cause of religion." He wanted the language changed so that it would "secure the rights of conscience, and a free exercise of the rights of religion," while not protecting "those who professed no religion at all."[32]

Huntington's objection most clearly expressed the view of both the old-line religious groups who supported state-level institutional establishments and the newer dissenting groups, such as Baptists and Methodists, who wanted the amendment to guarantee their religious freedom. Both agreed that the amendment should support religious expression but not add protection for the irreligious, which would undermine social stability and the good order of government by removing the foundation for morality. To appease the objections of the various parties, the House changed the wording to "Congress shall make no law establishing religion, or to prevent the free exercise thereof, or to infringe the rights of conscience," before sending the proposal to the Senate.[33]

Madison's other amendment, which limited the power of the states to infringe upon "the equal rights of conscience," also met some resistance, but not as much as one might have expected, given Madison's intention. Thomas Tucker of South Carolina, which had an institutional establishment that Madison's amendment might have prohibited, complained that instead of limiting federal power the amendment actually seemed to offer only an "alteration of the constitutions of particular States." Tucker preferred that the Constitution "leave the State Governments to themselves." In response Madison invoked the idea of inalienable rights, objecting that this was "the most valuable amendment in the whole list." "If there was any reason to restrain the Government of the United States from infringing upon these essential rights," he explained, "it was equally necessary that they should be secured against the State Governments." Because state governments were more likely to abuse the rights of conscience, in Madison's opinion, this amendment was crucial to the protection of rights. On this occasion Madison's defense was successful. The amendment went to the Senate almost as he proposed it.[34]

As the House debated the amendments, Madison grew sick of the entire process, which was unfolding as he had expected. Writing to Richard Peters, a Pennsylvania assemblyman, Madison complained of "the nauseous project of amendments," which had "not yet been either dismissed or despatched [sic]." He was particularly bothered by the House's decision to turn his package of amendments into a bill of rights, which came up when they first began the debate but was not resolved until the day before the amendments were sent to the Senate. Roger Sherman of Connecticut proposed the change, complaining that if they "interweave our propositions into the work itself" the revisions would have the tendency of being "destructive of the whole fabric." Madison, of course, wanted to strengthen the fabric by incorporating national supremacy. He responded to Sherman that the "form is of some consequence." Modifying the Constitution itself had the benefit of simplicity and clarity. But if a list of amendments were appended to the end, Madison noted, the Constitution's meaning could "only be ascertained by a comparison of the two instruments," a process that might create "a very considerable embarrassment." He added that it would be "difficult to ascertain to what parts of the instrument the amendments particularly refer," threatening an ambiguity that would compromise the protection of rights. John Vining of Delaware agreed. If the amendments were added as a bill of rights, "the system would be distorted, and, like a careless[ly] written letter, have more attached to it in a postscript than was contained in the original composition." Michael Jenifer Stone of Maryland got to the heart of the issue. "Now if we incorporate these amendments [into the body of the text], we must undoubtedly go further," he explained, "and say that the constitution so formed was defective, and had need of alteration; we therefore propose to repeal the old and substitute a new one in its place." Madison did in fact believe that the Constitution was defective. His goal was to protect rights in such a way as to guarantee national supremacy, which had not occurred in the convention. But two-thirds of the House agreed with Sherman. "It is already apparent," Madison complained to one of his correspondents, "that some ambiguities will be produced by this change [to a bill of rights], as the question will often arise and sometimes be not easily solved, how far the original text is or is not necessarily superseded, by the supplemental act."[35]

This change to a bill of rights created a particular problem for Madison, in his desire to protect the rights of conscience. Yet if the amendments had stayed in the linguistic formulation that Madison originally desired, there might not have been as much ambiguity as he predicted. But Madison's concerns about limiting religious liberty would prove especially prescient in the Senate debates, which were not at all friendly to Madison's formulations. Because the Senate met behind closed doors with no record of debate until 1794, it is difficult to say exactly what objections the senators had. When what would become the First Amendment emerged from the Senate, it had been changed to "Congress shall make no laws establishing articles of faith, or a mode of worship, or prohibiting the free exercise of religion." That was close to Elbridge Gerry's proposal. The Senate's version prohibited Congress from prescribing doctrine or worship, but it would still allow Congress to pass legislation to support religion or even to create a broad establishment of religion as the Christian republicans had attempted in Virginia. Even more importantly, the Senate deleted Madison's amendment to prohibit states from violating the rights of conscience, which killed Madison's attempt to establish national supremacy in the protection of rights.[36]

Madison was, of course, unhappy with the changes, though he was not necessarily surprised. When the Senate sent back their version, he wrote to Edmund Pendleton, explaining, "[S]ome alterations . . . strike in my opinion at the most salutary articles." His plan was falling apart. The difficulty was a familiar one. No one agreed on exactly what they were trying to do in their attempts to protect religious liberty. Madison had wanted to create a protection for "the full and equal rights of conscience" on both the state and national level. His Christian republican opponents wanted to prohibit any attempt to restrain religious expression, by which they primarily meant Protestant Christian expression. "The difficulty of uniting the minds of men accustomed to think and act differently," Madison explained wearily to Pendleton, "can only be conceived by those who have witnessed it."[37]

The two sides met in conference to hammer out the final version of the First Amendment's religion clauses, which ultimately read: "Congress shall make no law respecting an establishment of religion, or prohibiting the free exercise thereof." The final version included the kind of narrowing of protection that Madison had feared, though he had gotten as much out of the negotiation as he could. In agreeing to the final change, he had to abandon both his hope for national supremacy and his desire for an explicit affirmation of "the full and equal rights of conscience." The final version also added ambiguity—as Madison had predicted—by obscuring the nature of the protection afforded by the amendment. Did it create a government supportive of religion and tolerant of unbelief, or did it support the secular government of the godless Constitution while tolerating religious belief? It was totally unclear.[38]

In the short term Madison had failed; the First Amendment resolved nothing. It fell short of clarifying the proper relationship of religion to the state, and it could plausibly be read as an expression of all positions at once. At the same time, the amendment's limited application to only the federal government made the passage of the First Amendment a symbolic moment of little import. When Congress sent the Bill of Rights to the states in 1789, six states still paid churches and were able to continue to do so under the provisions of the First Amendment. The ambiguity and limited applicability of the First Amendment meant that the issues were, if anything, only more confused.

Initially, even Jefferson was disappointed. When Madison sent him a copy of the Bill of Rights as Congress neared the end of the drafting process, Jefferson responded, "I like it as far as it goes." But he thought the bill should have gone further in protecting essential liberties, which tempered his enthusiasm. It is difficult to understand why Jefferson was surprised. Madison had warned him that a bill of rights would not accomplish what Jefferson had hoped and that the rights of conscience in particular would be narrowed by legislative debate. The process proceeded exactly as Madison had predicted. Because the final version of the First Amendment was the result of a deep ideological divide, it was garbled at best and meaningless at worst, which might have been the best Madison could do. The lack of definition in its essential terms reflected a deep conflict among the legislators. The result was confusion about the amendment's basic purpose. What was the point of protecting religious liberty, however understood? Was it that it formed an individual and essential right, as Madison would have it? Or was it that such protection was a means of encouraging religious expression to shore up social morality and thereby strengthen the state, as others suggested?[39]

The debate over the First Amendment—along with the earlier debate in the Virginia Assembly—had established the symbolic import of religious liberty. But passage of the First Amendment muddied the clear waters of what had been a godless Constitution. Rather than providing a clear institutional-ized form of religious liberty, the First Amendment created an ambiguous legal framework in which religious partisans could use the levers of law and politics to create a moral establishment while claiming religious freedom. It was exactly the result that Madison had feared.

3

THE MORAL ESTABLISHMENT

Madison's failure would become evident with the expansion of evangelicalism. The numbers are startling. Scholars place colonial church adherence or attendance across the thirteen colonies at between 10 percent and
20 percent in 1776. Those who advocated state support of churches were acting
on the not unreasonable fear that if the state got out of the religion business
churches might fold. But, beginning in the 1790s, urban church construction
exploded, signaling the beginning of a religious expansion that intensified
throughout the first half of the nineteenth century. Historians now call this
expansion the Second Great Awakening. It was led by evangelicals. In 1776,
Congregationalists, Episcopalians, and Presbyterians accounted for 55 percent
of all religious members. The evangelical Methodists and Baptists accounted
for 19 percent. By 1850 their positions would be exactly reversed.[1]

Evangelical expansion was rapid and broad, with intense social effects.
Church membership doubled from 17 percent in 1776 (or 668,000 church
members) to 34 percent in 1850 (7.8 million church members). Even more
startling, between 1775 and 1845 the number of ministers grew at three times
the rate of the population (which was itself nearly six times larger in 1850 than
it had been in 1790). Put simply, in 1850 there were many more churches,
many of which were evangelical, with many more church members, many of
whom were evangelical, and many more ministers, many of whom were evangelical. Each category made up a much larger percentage of a much larger
population in 1850 than in 1790.[2]

These statistics do need some explaining. Prior to the Civil War, more
people came within the orbit of a church than belonged as members. These
unconverted "hearers" occasionally came to services and might even adhere to

some general tenets of a faith without ever joining it. But even if membership growth over the course of the nineteenth century came merely from capturing these adherents on the church rolls, it still had a powerful effect on the legal and political environment.[3]

Viewed from one angle, the revival impulse at the heart of the Second Great Awakening was schismatic, since it created numerous religious organizations that disagreed with one another on arcane points of doctrine. But beneath the dizzying array of theological controversy remained a core of agreement that united these groups under the banner of evangelicalism. This evangelical synthesis was so complete among Protestant religious groups that even people who could not be described as evangelical in the eighteenth century had succumbed to the tide of evangelicalism by the nineteenth. Except for a few old-line holdouts, even the Presbyterians, formerly part of the old-guard establishment, joined evangelicals. The Episcopalians, Lutherans, and Congregationalists also had prominent evangelical branches.[4]

The growing prominence of evangelicals transformed the debate over religious liberty. Evangelicals had been important in Virginia, but they had not yet attained sufficient national standing to move the argument in the federal Congress. But as their numbers grew, they began to reshape the political landscape and clear the way for the moral establishment.

They were able to do this because evangelicals were driven by a clear purpose. Many writers have claimed that evangelical religion was individualist and apolitical—concerned primarily with saving souls. But there was actually widespread agreement among evangelicals that God had given them a mandate for societal transformation. Evangelicals saw the Bible as central to life and worship—it provided the standard to which all must be made to conform. They regarded missionary expansion, both at home and abroad, as a core duty. And, most importantly, they believed in the public relevance of evangelical moral ideals. Their widespread agreement created a powerful cultural force that worked against Madison's prediction that diverse sects would counterbalance one another.[5]

The fixed moral ideals of evangelicalism had connections to a second, more profound social change: the intensification of American capitalism and the beginning of the Industrial Revolution. Although the United States, even as a colony, had a commercial orientation, after ratification ever-larger segments of society became involved in the market at the exact same time that political participation was expanding rapidly. The decline of barter systems, characteristic of a rural peasantry, and the development of large commercial centers that utilized wage labor reordered American society and upended traditional hierarchies.

Yet the rise of capitalism caused unease among religious leaders. Capitalism required the embrace of self-interest. That might be fine in general, but when combined with the political ideals of the Revolution it seemed threatening.[6]

This combination of problems was one that other industrializing nations had not faced. Tocqueville is again helpful here. The social structure of Great Britain during the Industrial Revolution was aristocratic. The chief benefit of aristocracy, according to Tocqueville, was that each individual understood himself in relation to a whole. Those of higher social status were required, at least in theory, to assume some responsibility for those below, which had the effect of holding the society together. "Noblesse oblige," the practice was called.[7]

Democratic capitalism, by contrast, obliterated the notion of noble self-sacrifice that formed the core of noblesse oblige. "[D]emocracy breaks the chain" that held an aristocratic society together, according to Tocqueville, because, at least in theory, everyone is of equal social status in a democracy. With everyone pursuing his own self-interest and no upper class looking out for the rest, society threatened to unravel.[8]

Democracy, then, required something to hold society together. By the 1830s Tocqueville thought that Americans had come to a unique solution to this problem. "The doctrine of self-interest well understood," which included long-range planning ability, the embrace of deferred gratification, and a sense of balance between consumption and savings (money management), tempered the absolute pursuit of self-interest by requiring individuals to internalize a code of restraint. Religion was a key part of this principle, since many evangelical moral ideals fit into the requirements of the market. "If the doctrine of self-interest well understood had only this world in view, it would be far from sufficient," Tocqueville explained, "for there are a great number of sacrifices that can find their recompense only in the other world." The Christian belief in the future state of rewards and punishments would compel believers to behave according to these principles, mitigating the anarchic tendencies of democratic capitalism.[9]

But what if not everyone could agree on what "self-interest well understood" meant? Or what if they refused to go along with the doctrine? Then, Tocqueville implied, they must be made to conform.[10]

2.

The rapid changes in American society in the years following ratification intensified the debate about the relationship of religion to the state. But it was the evangelical response to these changes that broke the impasse over the meaning of religious liberty. Evangelicals agreed with Christian republicans that the self-interest of the masses, if unchecked, would result in anarchy and corruption. But evangelicals were uniform in their rejection of payments for churches. As evangelicalism expanded, they began to make up a much larger proportion of religious groups than ones that received state funding. Although old-line churches resisted the efforts of evangelicals to do away with institutional establishment, it was, at the end of the day, a numbers game. And the evangelicals won. As they eclipsed the old-line in numbers, institutional establishment came to an end in state after state, though the process took forty years.

But the end of institutional establishment was hardly the end of entanglements between religion and government. Evangelicals, too, believed that unrestrained individualism was dangerous. So, while states dropped government funding of churches, they still allowed for significant connections between church and state. They shifted from an institutional establishment to a moral establishment, one that placed significant limits on religious freedom.

The shift began during the debate over the First Amendment and continued in its immediate aftermath. Between 1789 and 1792, four states altered their constitutional clauses on religious liberty. Georgia (1789) and South Carolina (1790) removed all limits to civil and political participation based on religious belief, though South Carolina added that the freedom of conscience did not "excuse acts of licentiousness, or justify practices inconsistent with the peace or safety of this State." Pennsylvania's 1790 constitution dropped its Christian oath of office and extended equal protection to nonbelievers. But it still maintained that officeholders must acknowledge "the being of a God and a future state of rewards and punishments." Delaware (1792) also dropped its oath of office requiring belief in the Trinity, but it added a section to its freedom of exercise and freedom of conscience clause, asserting that although citizens could not be coerced, it was still "the duty of all men frequently to assemble together for the public worship of the Author of the universe," because worship promoted the "piety and morality, on which the prosperity of communities depends."[11]

As evangelicals spread into the Northeast, even those states most committed to institutional establishment had to give way. Yet their new laws still placed important limits on religious liberty, limits that evangelicals supported. Vermont dropped both its institutional establishment and all civil sanctions against non-Protestants with its new constitution in 1793, but it maintained its requirement of good moral character for holding public office. It did not explain what good moral character was or who was to decide whether an officeholder had it. Maryland did away with its institutional establishment by amendment in 1810 but left in place its prohibition against Jews and atheists holding office. In 1818 Connecticut drafted its first constitution in part to remove its institutional establishment. The new constitution forbade the state from acting preferentially toward "any Christian sect or mode of worship," which still allowed discrimination against non-Christians of all kinds. It also promised "equal powers, rights, and privileges" only to "every society or denomination of Christians." With this clause, Connecticut explicitly defined religious liberty as a right of Christian organizations rather than individuals. New Hampshire's institutional disestablishment in 1819 preserved its declaration that "morality and piety, rightly grounded on evangelical principles" were essential to the security of government. The legislative act also left unaltered the constitution's prohibition against non-Protestant officeholders, which remained, in spite of repeated efforts to change it, until 1877. Massachusetts accomplished its institutional disestablishment by amendment in two steps, first in 1820 by removing the Christian oath of office, and then in 1833 by removing any state mechanism for collecting money from the populace and distributing it to churches. But the amendment left in place the constitution's original claim that "the public worship of God" and "piety, religion, and morality" were essential to good government. Even North Carolina, which had done away with its institutional establishment in 1776, amended its constitution in 1835 to admit Catholics to office. But it still prohibited Jews and atheists.[12]

The changes were not uniform, but their goal was. Each sought to minimize the anarchic tendencies of individuals under democratic capitalism. Some limited religious liberty to Christian or Protestant organizations. Some continued to prohibit non-Christians or non-Protestants from holding office. Most relied on the regulation of morality, often defined in religious terms. The emphasis on morality was in keeping with evangelicalism. Although evangelicals detested the idea of paying churches, most had never claimed that religion should have no relationship to the state. Even the Baptists, the most democratic, separatist, nonhierarchical, and anti-statist of the new religious groups, upheld the notion that the state should enforce a morality defined by religion. In a petition to the General Assembly in 1786, the Baptist General Committee of Virginia had argued that the legislature should contribute to Christianity by "supporting those Laws of Morality, which are necessary for Private and Public Happiness." In that way the Assembly would do its duty as the "Guardian" of the people. Evangelicals hoped to project their moral values onto society, a goal that required the use of the state and prompted the cultural, political, and legal campaigns that would become a hallmark of American life for the next century.[13]

One of the chief figures in the development of this evangelical activism was Lyman Beecher. Beecher would become an archetype of the new religious leader in the nineteenth century. He was from a new generation who had neither served during the Revolution nor drafted the U.S. Constitution. He focused on cultural reformation as much as the propagation of religion. His descendants, including Harriet Beecher Stowe, the author of *Uncle Tom's Cabin*; Catharine Beecher, a conservative domestic reformer and women's right advocate; and Henry Ward Beecher, the most famous preacher of the late nineteenth century, followed his pattern of political and cultural reform. Many historians have portrayed a divide between Jacksonian evangelicals, who were suspicious of the state, and the more traditional, old-line Whigs of the nineteenth century, who looked to the state for religious support and economic development, but this divide has been overstated. Beecher was a Whig and among the most reformist of Christian Whigs. Yet his activism and his vision of the moral establishment crossed party lines and would become a dominant part of American culture within his lifetime.[14]

Beecher had been part of the old-line establishment in Connecticut. As a Congregational minister, he was at the forefront of the fight to keep paying churches after evangelicals began to move into the state. According to Beecher, this issue caused a rupture in what should have been a natural alliance between the two groups of well-meaning Christians. Evangelical desire to cease church payments had caused an unnatural alliance with atheists, who were interested only in resisting "[t]he efforts we [Christians] made to execute the laws and secure a reformation of morals." The alliance meant that "the democracy, as it rose, included nearly all the minor sects, besides the Sabbath-breakers, rum-selling tippling folk, infidels, and ruff-scuff generally." It was this alliance, Beecher surmised, that brought institutional establishment to an end in Connecticut in 1818.[15]

After the state stopped paying churches, the coalition of evangelicals and secularists broke down, which made Beecher more favorably disposed toward institutional disestablishment. "The consequence unexpectedly was, first, that the occasion of animosity between us and the minor sects was removed," he recounted, "and infidels could no more make capital with them against us." At the same time, the evangelicals "began themselves to feel the dangers of infidelity, and to react against it, and this laid the basis of co-operation and union of spirit." The realignment made perfect sense. Evangelicals had never wholly shared Madison and Jefferson's view of religious liberty as an inalienable individual right. They agreed with Christian republicans that religion needed a connection to state governance. Once the issue of state support was out of the way, their more natural alliance with Christian republicans such as Beecher would reemerge, not just in Connecticut but also across the new nation.[16]

As this realignment was occurring, Beecher became one of the chief spokesmen for the moral establishment. He found support across the religious spectrum for his condemnation of what he variously called "political atheism" or "moral atheism." Both terms were shorthand for Madison and Jefferson's view of religious liberty. Their liberal notion of individual rights presumed that humans came together to form society as a means of mutual cooperation. It presumed an orderly and innate goodness that allowed individuals to cooperate for higher purposes. Beecher, by contrast, viewed humans as "desperately wicked." Individual humans did not come together to form a society of their own accord in order to accomplish larger purposes. There was no social contract. Societies existed from the beginning. They trained individuals. They were not the result of the voluntary congregation of individuals.[17]

The dispute, at heart, was over which was most basic: societies or individuals. Madison presupposed the primacy of the individual, whose inalienable rights needed protection. Beecher, along with many evangelicals, believed in the primacy of society over the individual. Humans, in Beecher's explanation, could not "be qualified for good membership in society without the influence of moral restraint." Society acted on individuals to make them fit to live together. Because societies were primary, the kind of individual rights that Madison espoused was a dangerous fiction. Government was not the result of the natural human tendency to cooperate for higher ends, with each individual retaining their inalienable rights. Government was a necessary instrument "of self-defence against the violent evil propensities of man." Civil government joined a constellation of governing authorities that included the family, the church, and religious education. These mediating institutions ensured cooperation among ministers and magistrates in their effort to build a morally sound society.[18]

Here we can appreciate the acuteness of Tocqueville's observation that American religion sought first to regulate morals, which ultimately worked to harness the state. There was little separation between Beecher's religious thought and his moral thought, or between the religious and moral thought of many evangelicals. The family, the church, and religious education used informal pressure to influence behavior. Civil government used the coercion of law. The two were connected. Both sought to mitigate the anarchic tendencies of individuals. In Beecher's view, if society charged government alone with restraining the individual, despotism could be the only result. But without the power of governmental coercion behind them, other institutions would be unable to restrain recalcitrant individuals. Anarchy would thus result. The most effective plan required that "moral suasion and coercion . . . be united." Either individuals would freely internalize the moral restraint they were taught or the policing power of civil government would compel them to obey moral laws. For those searching for a model, Beecher held up New England, where "pastors, churches, and magistrates coöperated. And what moral constraint could not accomplish was secured by parental authority and the coercion of the law."[19]

To create a moral nation, evangelicals such as Beecher started national organizations that sought to impose their moral norms on law. Groups such as the American Bible Society, the American Sunday School Union, and the American Board of Foreign Missions connected large groups of people across denominational lines. By 1837 evangelicals had begun at least 159 moral-reform associations, many of them operating across a broad geographic area, with the express purpose of curtailing the immorality of the masses. The prohibition of alcohol, the creation of vice and obscenity squads, the perpetuation of Sabbath enforcement, and the accomplishment of other evangelical Christian goals all grew out of these reform federations.[20]

Many historians have suggested that moral-reform societies were an expression of democratic politics, but it might be more accurate to say that, though they were a response to democratic politics, they were not themselves entirely in favor of democracy. That was how Beecher saw them. Moral associations guarded against an unfettered democracy. These organizations provided, in Beecher's explanation, an influence "distinct from that of the government, independent of popular suffrage, superior in potency to individual efforts, and competent to enlist and preserve the public opinion on the side of law and order." They needed to be distinct from government to act as a watchdog. They needed to be independent of popular suffrage, because the mass of people could not be counted upon to maintain high moral standards. They needed to pressure politicians, because politicians were often unwilling to risk professional injury by enacting moral laws that would result in popular discontent. Voluntary associations, Beecher predicted, would act as "a sort of disciplined moral militia" that would "repel every encroachment upon the liberties and morals of the State" and strengthen "the hands of the magistrate." Religion set the morals to be enforced by the state, and religiously directed voluntary associations ensured that the state did its work. As a result, Beecher predicted that a biblical ethos would pervade all aspects of society, though the formal institutions of church and state remained separate.[21]

Beecher's agenda did encounter setbacks. After 1810, when the U.S. Congress began requiring post offices to stay open on Sundays, evangelicals led a movement that sought to strengthen the enforcement of the Christian Sabbath. Beecher joined the movement in 1814, eventually taking the lead. He did not seem to regard ending Sunday postal delivery as an end in itself, but as a first step in requiring Americans to observe this crucial institution for the protection of morality. In 1829 he launched a petition drive to plead with Congress to repeal the 1810 law and to halt mail delivery on Sunday. After five months Congress had received 467 petitions, which would swell to more than 900 by May 1831. Yet Beecher would come up short. Legislators dismissed his concern as part of an organized evangelical cabal that threatened to overturn what Richard M. Johnson of Kentucky, the leader of the anti-Sabbatarian group in the Senate, considered the wise judgment of the framers in making Congress a "civil institution, wholly destitute of religious authority." Some anti-statist and more-populist evangelicals such as Alexander Campbell, the founder of the Disciples of Christ, backed away from Beecher's reform efforts. But Beecher had broad support among all the major Protestant denominations. The controversy eventually fed the polarization of political parties, as the anti-moralist concerns of the anti-Sabbatarians fit well into the thrust of the Democratic Party, while many evangelical reformers fled to the Whigs.[22]

Yet this episode, which operated according to a party logic rather than anything else, did not demonstrate the secular character of the American government or the speciousness of the ideal of the Christian nation. It proved, instead, the correctness of Madison's belief that national supremacy would make it more difficult for factional interests to put together a coalition to trample rights. As evangelical power grew through the nineteenth century— and evangelical opinion became more homogeneous as a result of the rise of the religious press and voluntary associations—it would eventually claim a more majoritarian defense for evangelical Christian morality. In the short term, though, evangelicals' loss in the Sabbath controversy confirmed their suspicion of democracy as a form of government that relied upon the masses and their too-beholden representatives. It also reinforced for them the need to work at the state level, where effective coalitions could be more easily created. Beecher and others therefore turned to state constitutional regulation, careful lobbying of state politicians, and, above all, state courts. Rather than demonstrating the futility of efforts to create a Christian nation, the setback in the Sunday mail controversy suggested a path to its eventual triumph.[23]

3.

The combined front of old-line Protestants and evangelicals proved powerful. Evangelical moral associations pressured legislatures and sought changes in state-level law that, because of the evangelicals' persistence and numbers, proved hard to resist. The results would be seen in the last decades before the Civil War. At the same time, Christian activists were at work in the courts. The judicial structure provided a most potent institution to check the excesses of democracy because it was not beholden to the masses and did not require the complicated political trade-offs that legislation often did. Since judges could rule as they wished, with only limited fear of popular reprisal— even after judicial elections were implemented in the decades prior to the Civil War—courts were at the vanguard of setting up a moral establishment. State courts, in particular, tended to read state constitutions conservatively. In the process, they sided with Protestants on all the church–state issues that came before them: blasphemy trials, challenges to Sabbath laws, and the role of Christianity in public education.

The fact that state courts decided many of the cases did not limit their effect. At a time when the Supreme Court offered only minimal state-level guidance in American jurisprudence, state court judges had a powerful influence on U.S. law, with the opinions of the most important judges in the most important cases enjoying a wide readership. One of the best-known state court judges, second only to John Marshall in the development of antebellum jurisprudence, was the chief justice of the New York Supreme Court, James Kent. Kent's *Commentaries on American Law*, published between 1826 and 1830, established him as the first of the great law-treatise writers of the nineteenth century.[24]

It was Kent who provided the founding principle of the moral establishment in the 1811 New York Supreme Court case *People v. Ruggles*. The case raised many issues that would reappear later. A man named Ruggles, probably under the influence of alcohol, had shouted in a public venue, "Jesus Christ was a bastard and his mother must be a whore." The authorities arrested him and charged him with blasphemy. He was convicted, and appealed to Kent's court. New York did not have a blasphemy statute, so Ruggles argued that he could not be charged with having broken any law. And even if there had been such a statute, he claimed, the charge of blasphemy impaired his right to free religious exercise, violating New York's constitutional declaration that the state should not display a preference when it came to religion.[25]

Kent wrote for a court composed of three Democrats and two Federalists. He was himself a Federalist. If there was a partisan divide over the enforcement of the moral establishment, it should have shown up here. Instead, ruling for a unanimous court, he rejected all of Ruggles's arguments and upheld the conviction. Kent decided that irrespective of the guarantee of religious freedom in the New York Constitution and the lack of a blasphemy law in the civil statutes, Christianity was still a part of the common law of the state. Common law was an evolving body of law derived from England and based on custom and prior decisions of legal courts and treatise writers. Because Christianity was a part of Anglo-American common law, Kent concluded, blasphemy was punishable in New York.[26]

Kent's opinion foreshadowed the logic of the moral establishment as it would unfold in the courts. Christianity provided "moral discipline" and "those principles of virtue, which help to bind society together," he explained, especially in the face of the centrifugal forces of democratic capitalism. These were necessary restraints that could not be compromised by the defendant's claim of his free exercise of rights. "The free, equal, and undisturbed enjoyment of religious opinion," Kent completely granted, but he held that the abuse of that right, as in the case of blasphemy, had a tendency "to corrupt the morals of the people, and to destroy good order," adding, "Such offenses have always been considered independent of any religious establishment or the rights of the Church. They are treated as affecting the essential interests of civil society." The defendant's free-exercise argument, Kent thought, was touched by the anarchic licentiousness that the moral establishment was designed to constrain. Free exercise had limits precisely to prevent such license. Although Kent conceded that the New York Constitution had established a regime of toleration, he was insistent that the toleration "never meant to withdraw religion in general, and with it the best sanctions of moral and social obligation from all consideration and notice of the law." The courts could never just ignore religion, Kent summarized, because Americans were "a christian people."[27]

By linking Christianity to the common law, Kent's decision set a precedent on which other courts freely elaborated. To be sure, common law would eventually be codified by legislative statute, but statutes could never do away with case law, the body of precedent established by a court system. Because the state constitutions and the court systems were so new and because the common law had not yet been codified by the state legislatures, many of the early religious-liberty cases were the first such cases to be heard in U.S. courts, so there was no body of precedent. *Ruggles* offered one.

It was a precedent that other courts received with eagerness in their own efforts to constrain what they saw as the pernicious side of individualism. In an indecency case four years after *Ruggles*, the Pennsylvania Supreme Court began laying the basis for the moral establishment in that state. Pointing out the courts' crucial role as "guardians of public morals," the opinion argued that the preservation of morality was essential to state security. To protect the cohesiveness of society, in the words of the concurring opinion, any offense that could be "destructive of morality in general" was "punishable at common law," even if it was an offense committed in private.[28]

Lest anyone think this rationale was part of a generic moral consensus, the same court two years later elaborated its rationale in a Sabbath law case. A Jewish businessman convicted of violating the Sabbath by conducting business on Sunday claimed that the Sabbath law was a violation of religious freedom, an argument that the court rejected. Citing the legislature's prohibition of work on "the Lord's day, commonly called Sunday," the court pointed out that the Sabbath law was part of a larger section of laws created for "the prevention of vice and immorality," which could not be overturned on what it characterized as "technical niceties" affecting free religious exercise. Because the act construed the "breach of the sabbath as a crime injurious to society," the court found the defendant's appeal to the state constitution's clauses providing for free religious exercise and freedom of conscience irrelevant to his conviction. The point of the ruling was not to defend Christian prerogatives, the court claimed, but rather to preserve morals. "Laws cannot be administered in any civilized government unless the people are taught to revere the sanctity of an oath, and look to a future state of rewards and punishments for the deeds of this life," the court ruled. It therefore upheld the required observance of the Christian Sabbath so that people would "be reminded of their religious duties at stated periods."[29]

Seven years later, in a blasphemy case, the court completed the circle by acknowledging that their definition of morality came from Christianity, citing Kent's *Ruggles* opinion, among others. The defendant had claimed that the Christian Scriptures were "a mere fable." The court characterized his statement as an "invective so vulgarly shocking and insulting" that no one in a Christian land should have to hear it. Christianity had always been part of the common law of Pennsylvania, but it was not Christianity, the court was quick to assert, "founded on any particular religious tenets; not Christianity with an established church." Rather, it was nonsectarian Christianity that upheld public morals. The reason for prosecuting blasphemy against the Christian God was that it was "the highest offence *contra bonos mores* [against good morals]."[30]

In each of these cases, Christianity received protection in order to enforce morality, lest society collapse. In doing so, Kent and the Pennsylvania jurists invoked what has been called the *bad tendency* test, originally advanced by the famous English jurist William Blackstone to explain the conditions under which a court could curtail free speech. Blackstone originally argued that speech could be punished if it tended to produce behavior prohibited by a statute or to undermine general morals and the preservation of good order. But in the hands of Kent, it had a wider application, and early American courts took it even further. They maintained that blasphemy, indecency, and Sabbath-breaking, by offending or criticizing the religious mechanisms of moral obedience, threatened to destroy good order and corrupt morals. Because the protection of Christianity for its own sake would make Christianity an established religion, they suggested that they were not protecting Christianity as an end in itself. It was the supposed bad tendency of blasphemy, Sabbath-breaking, and indecency that permitted their suppression by the courts.[31]

This was not a persuasive distinction to those who objected to the moral establishment. At the 1821 New York Constitutional Convention, called to update the 1777 state constitution, this distinction came under scrutiny from both sides, with Kent emerging triumphant. During the first reading of the new constitution, General Erastus Root, a freethinker who viewed Kent's *Ruggles* decision as an outrage against the 1777 constitution's free-exercise provisions, proposed additional language to outlaw the protection or promotion of religion by the state. Professing a desire for true "freedom of conscience," he suggested adding another clause that would read: "The judiciary shall not declare any particular religion, to be the law of the land; nor exclude any witness on account of his religious faith." Kent rose to criticize Root's characterization of his *Ruggles* opinion. He had not declared religion to be the law of the land, Kent explained, relying on a fine-grained, and, from the perspective of dissenters, disingenuous, distinction that he had upheld the conviction "not because christianity was established by law, but because christianity was . . . the basis of the public morals." Ruggles's criticism of Christianity threatened morals and had to be suppressed accordingly.[32]

Root was not convinced. To better address the issues, he split the provisions. His new amendment, which relied on the passive voice to avoid offending the jurists at the convention, proclaimed, "It shall not be declared or adjudged that any particular religion is the law of the land." That amendment passed on a 62 to 26 vote. Strangely, Kent voted in favor of the new amendment, and rose to explain the apparent inconsistency. His conviction of Ruggles, even under the proposed provision, would still have been in accordance with New York law, he claimed, because it did not make Christianity the law of the land. Instead, his opinion only noted that Christianity simply was the religion of the nation and so determined its morals. The convention went on to reject Root's second amendment that "no witness shall be questioned as to his religious faith" in a vote of 94 to 8. The same defense of morals came into consideration here, with Kent weighing in again. In New York, as in most states, a witness had to swear belief in a supreme being and in a future state of rewards and punishments to testify. Kent regarded that provision as the only appropriate means of measuring the veracity of testimony. He wondered what the evidence provided by an unbeliever could be worth and agreed with the statement of another delegate that "the testimony of the atheist and infidel" was rightly excluded.[33]

Root was ultimately unsuccessful in making his case to the convention, because even his successful amendment came up for discussion again two days later. When Kent had adjudicated *Ruggles,* he was chief justice of the New York Supreme Court. But in 1814 Kent became chancellor of the State Court of Chancery. The new chief justice was Ambrose Spencer, a Christian republican even more devoted than Kent to the protection and promotion of Christianity in law. During the final reading of the constitution, Spencer rose to reopen the debate on Root's successful provision. Spencer, like Root, seemed to regard Kent as insincere. The protection of Christianity for its own sake was the real rationale behind prosecution for blasphemy, according to Spencer, and rightly so. But in response, Kent reiterated his position that Christianity could not be declared the legal religion of the state, "because that would be considering Christianity as the established religion, and make it a civil or political institution." As he sought to avoid the obvious religious control through law that he continued to support, Kent's distinctions became ever finer. Although he maintained that "the duties and injunctions of the Christian religion" were "interwoven with the law of the land," and "part and parcel of the common law," he insisted that Christianity was not thereby established by law. Although Kent and Spencer appeared to be at an impasse, they shared a common enemy in Root. When Root's amendment came up for another vote, both agreed that an amendment against making any particular religion the law of the land was undesirable. Kent's moderate position, when combined with Spencer's more explicitly partisan position, swayed the convention. It then reversed its prior decision, rejecting Root's amendment 74 to 41. The moral establishment had triumphed.[34]

4.

Three years later Thomas Jefferson got involved. Jefferson had always been unrealistic about the power of the First Amendment, but the actions of the courts seemed to shake him out of his complacency. In a long letter that he subsequently published, Jefferson objected to "the judiciary usurpation of legislative powers" that had occurred through "their repeated decisions, that Christianity is a part of the common law." Because the common law began while the English were pagans, before they had "heard the name of Christ pronounced," Jefferson claimed that the common law could not possibly include Christianity. He also decried the attempt by state courts to enforce Christianity as contrary to the spirit of the revolutionary ideal of religious liberty. "What a conspiracy this, between Church and State!" Jefferson exclaimed.[35]

But his claim was more a political posture than an argument. There was no singular revolutionary ideal of religious liberty. The emergence of a more outspoken opposition that included Jefferson himself did not slow the expansion of the moral establishment, because most jurists did not accept Jefferson's view. In Jefferson's own party, Joseph Story, who was a devout Unitarian, an associate justice of the U.S. Supreme Court, and soon to be the Dane Professor of Law at Harvard, and who was, along with Kent, one of the architects of antebellum jurisprudence, rejected Jefferson's claims. If the partisan divide over the moral establishment was as strong as some have claimed, it would be hard to explain how a Democrat such as Story would be so forcefully in support. Explaining his reasoning in a letter, Story claimed that it was "inconceivable" that anyone would agree with Jefferson that Christianity was not part of English common law. If Christianity was not a part of the common law of England, Story asked in a subsequent article that addressed the issue, "[w]hat becomes of her whole ecclesiastical establishment, and the legal rights growing out of it on any other supposition?" Of course, the United States was not supposed to have an established religion, so the entire debate begged the question of how England's common law could be relevant to the United States.[36]

As the legal opinions kept coming, the slippage between the proclamation of disestablishment and its continuation in another form became ever clearer. In 1837 in Delaware, a man appropriately named Thomas Jefferson Chandler was convicted of blasphemy for claiming, in words echoing Ruggles, that "the virgin Mary was a whore and Jesus Christ was a bastard." In Chandler's case the conviction was based not on common law but on Delaware's general criminal statutes of 1826, which provided penalties for blasphemy, murder, rape, perjury, sodomy, and treason. Chandler claimed that the law showed a preference for Christianity in violation of the Delaware Constitution. He also tried to anticipate the objection that Christianity was part of the common law by quoting Jefferson's letter on the subject. In rejecting Chandler's claim, Chief Justice John M. Clayton, writing for a unanimous court, offered a twofold argument. First, he declared that it had "been long perfectly settled by the common law" that blasphemy was an indictable and punishable offense. To make his case he criticized Jefferson's letter and cited *People v. Ruggles,* among others. Second, he quoted the Delaware Constitution, especially its provision that worship remained a general duty of all men because it promoted "piety and morality, on which the prosperity of communities depends." Reasoning from the wording of the constitution, Justice Clayton claimed it was obvious that "the religion of the people of Delaware *is christian,*" although that did not mean that Christianity was the state religion. Instead, rewarming Kent's formula, Clayton claimed, "The distinction is a sound one between a religion preferred by law, and a religion preferred by the people, without the coercion of law." So long as this distinction was honored, the people themselves could "claim the protection of law guarantied to them by the constitution itself" in order to punish blasphemers against their beliefs. This was unpersuasive and circuitous reasoning, but it was still legally binding. It resulted in a fine of ten dollars for each act of blasphemy, ten days of solitary confinement, and four hundred dollars in sureties to ensure that Chandler did not blaspheme again.[37]

In another famous blasphemy case in Massachusetts in 1838 (five years after Massachusetts's official disestablishment), the Massachusetts Supreme Court continued the evasion by convicting the prominent antebellum free-thinker Abner Kneeland of blasphemy under a 1782 law. Kneeland claimed that the blasphemy conviction was contrary to the Massachusetts Constitution. The majority of the court seemed offended that Kneeland would call into question the validity of the blasphemy law, noting that it seemed "somewhat late to call in question the constitutionality of a law, which has been enacted more than half a century, which has been repeatedly enforced." The court's opinion recounted the constitutional provisions of New Hampshire, Vermont, Maine, and New York, pointing out the similar limitations on free speech and religious expression when they offended "good morals and manners of society" or consisted of "acts of licentiousness." Blasphemy, according to the court, was "not intended to prevent or restrain the formation of any opinions or the profession of any religious sentiments whatever, but to restrain and punish acts which have a tendency to disturb the public peace." For that reason, blasphemy laws were perfectly in accord with the constitution's guarantee of free religious exercise. The Massachusetts Constitution had coupled its provision that "no subject shall be hurt, molested, or restrained, in his person, liberty, or estate . . . for his religious profession or sentiments," the court noted, with a proviso similar to those of other states, that under the cover of religion one could not "disturb the public peace or obstruct others in their religious worship." That was all blasphemy laws were attempting to accomplish. The court upheld the conviction, though this time with one Jacksonian justice in dissent. Kneeland served sixty days in prison.[38]

The reasoning of the various state courts showed how limited disestablishment was. Both sides in the dispute agreed that blasphemy prosecution was indicative of the place of Christianity in the legal system that its proponents lauded and its opponents decried. Jefferson complained of the "repeated decisions" that Christianity was part of the common law. Delaware Chief Justice Clayton declared that the legitimacy of blasphemy prosecutions had "been long perfectly settled by the common law." All of this demonstrated the limits of any institutional church–state separation.[39]

The issue soon reached the U.S. Supreme Court, where it came into the hands of Jefferson's critic and fellow Democrat, Joseph Story. In 1844 the High Court affirmed the opinions of the state courts, ruling in *Vidal v. Philadelphia* that Christianity was part of the common law of the State of Pennsylvania (and, by implication, every other state that had not specifically rejected it by legislative statute). Christianity's "divine origin and truth are admitted," the Court ruled, "and therefore it is not to be maliciously and openly reviled and blasphemed against, to the annoyance of believers or the injury of the public." The case was complicated, involving a dispute over the terms of a will created by Stephen Girard, who founded a school for orphans to be administered by the city. Girard required that no cleric, missionary, or minister could hold any position at the school or even step on its grounds. His justification for their exclusion was that it would shield the young minds from theological disputes while teaching them the principles of morality. The provision was widely, and probably correctly, seen as an anticlerical and therefore antiChristian position.[40]

The U.S. Supreme Court, rather than the Pennsylvania Supreme Court, heard the case, because one of the parties was a French national. The appellants, several potential heirs who wanted the trust dissolved so that they could get the money, claimed that the will was unchristian and therefore against Pennsylvania's law. The defendants, the City of Philadelphia and some of Girard's nieces, were represented by Daniel Webster, the famous future senator. Webster claimed that the concept and motivation of charity came solely from Christianity, not being present in Judaism or among the pagans. Any attempt to divorce charity from Christianity was incoherent on its face. As for Girard's desire for pure morality, Webster suggested that the purest principles of morality could be found only in the Bible, which was in perfect accord with Pennsylvania law. Writing for a unanimous court, Joseph Story agreed with Webster, acknowledging that had Girard established a school "for the propagation of Judaism, or Deism, or any other form of infidelity," his will might have been against Pennsylvania law. But Story noted that Christianity could still be taught to students at the school. Story's opinion showed just how easily the declaration of moral instruction bled into the defense of the Christian religion. Girard's command that pure morality be taught at his school suggested to Story that Christianity, qualified in nonsectarian terms, could be taught by laymen in the interests of cultivating morality. After all, he asked,

> Where can the purest principles of morality be learned so clearly or so perfectly as from the New Testament? Where are benevolence, the love of truth, sobriety, and industry, so powerfully and irresistibly inculcated as in the sacred volume? The testator has not said how these great principles are to be taught, or by whom, except it be by laymen, nor what books are to be used to explain or enforce them.[41]

One year later the U.S. Supreme Court unanimously rejected any attempt to appeal to the Bill of Rights for the protection of religious liberty against state law. In explaining its ruling, the Court claimed that the U.S. Constitution did not protect the rights of citizens within states, where state constitutional and statutory provisions prevailed; rather, it limited the federal government in the circumscribed portion of society over which it had power. The implications of Madison's failure were now clear. In many states the inability to swear belief in the existence of God and an afterlife prohibited freethinkers from acting as witnesses in court. Religious societies were so closely connected to charitable foundations and educational organizations that the law often treated them as one and the same. As the *Vidal* case showed, there was some question as to whether a charitable organization could be created independently of the Christian religion under Pennsylvania law (which resembled the law of many other states). And blasphemy laws constrained free speech and even freedom of the press.[42]

Mostly, as Chief Justice Spencer explained at the 1821 New York Constitutional Convention, non-Christians were "tolerated" so long as they did not criticize Christianity, violate moral norms, or expect to be treated equally. Toleration is considerably more liberal than outright persecution, but it does not entirely comport with the usual laudatory narrative of American religious liberty. Rufus King, a longtime New York senator, elaborated on Spencer's point to make clear the kind of toleration that was on offer in New York, the state with the most liberal provisions on church and state. "While all mankind are by our constitution tolerated, and free to enjoy religious profession and worship within this state," King explained, "yet the religious professions of the Pagan, the Mahomedan [sic], and the Christian, are not, in the eye of the law, of equal truth and excellence. . . . While the constitution tolerates the religious professions and worship of all men, it does more in behalf of the religion of the gospel."[43]

Ultimately, the end of institutional establishment did not much change the role of religion in public life. It turned out to be just one leg of a long-standing political theology, a religious understanding of public life that looked to Christianity to provide the foundations of civil government. After institutional establishment fell, the moral establishment became more important. It provided the essential rationale for the post-1776 connection of religion to the state. Protestant Christian moral norms needed the force of law because, proponents claimed, in the absence of Christian moral enforcement the nation would devolve into anarchy, licentiousness, and ultimate ruin.

Yet even as the moral establishment expanded, the extent and meaning of religious freedom remained controversial. The debate exposed deep disagreements about the nature of the American experiment, the political and moral basis of the union, and what many took to be the genius and genesis of American ascendancy. Religious partisans won more battles than they lost, at least in the short term. In that space between the establishment of Christianity by law and the adherence of a growing number of people to Christianity—who in turn provided the moral standards to be enforced by law—religious partisans found ample room for legal and political maneuvering. Religiously derived moral standards assumed a legal standing that was applicable to believers and unbelievers alike. Moral law became the mechanism of religious control.

PART II

CHALLENGERS

4

THE MORAL PURPOSE OF SLAVERY
AND ABOLITION

1.

The moral establishment was the creation of an active religious minority who believed that God had established moral norms and that it was incumbent upon them to enforce those norms through law. Yet the fairly obvious contradictions in Kent's claim that "the duties and injunctions of the Christian religion" were "interwoven with the law of the land," but that it was not an official religion, brought the moral establishment into constant dispute. Problems set in almost immediately, centered on the most contentious moral issue of the first half of the nineteenth century: slavery.[1]

Originally, there had been no disagreement. In the colonial period, supporters of slavery justified the institution by noting that African slaves were not Christian. As a colonial court ruled in 1694, "[Negroes] are heathens, and therefore a man may have property in them, and . . . the court, without averment made, will take notice that they are heathens." Virginia, the first sustained North American British colony, followed this law, but there the equation of race with slavery was not immediate, though the equation of slavery with spiritual unfaithfulness was. As early as 1618 a blue law required each person to go to church on Sunday and on holy days. Any transgressor would have to "be a Slave the week following." The next year a Dutch ship brought, in John Rolfe's words, "twenty Negars" to the colony. Over the next fifty years, slavery became a racialized institution, justified by the non-Christian status of Africans. The legislature and the courts juxtaposed Christianity and whiteness with heathenism and blackness to muster support for slavery.[2]

Yet as some African slaves converted to Christianity, race became the primary legal justification for slavery, though many continued to believe that Africans' legacy of heathenish barbarism justified their enslavement. This trend continued on both sides of the Atlantic until the latter half of the eighteenth century, when Britain and the American colonies diverged and the colonies began to disagree among themselves about the moral propriety of slavery, which would eventually create problems for the moral establishment.

Antislavery activism had begun in midcentury, when a group of Quaker activists started to question the legitimacy of slavery, though their efforts would not gain notice until the Revolution. Relying on their connections with believers in other port cities, Quakers were among the most prosperous traders in the new market economy. Networks of faith made them wealthy. Their commercial success allowed them to see how they were implicated in the slave trade, whether or not they themselves owned slaves. Just as someone today might be confronted with the uncomfortable realization that to buy sneakers is to be implicated in sweatshops in Asia, Quakers were able to see that every time they bought cotton, tobacco, indigo, or anything else connected to slave labor, they were embroiling themselves in the entire system. The slave catcher, the slave buyer, and the consumer of slave-produced goods were, in the words of the early Quaker abolitionist John Woolman, "concerned in the same work" of mistreating the slave and so had "a necessary connection with and dependence on each other."[3]

For some Quakers this became intolerable, in part because of their religious belief. Quakers, who called themselves Friends, held that God communicated with each person by means of an Inner Light that every person possessed. Because the Inner Light was present in every human being, Quakers posited a fundamental equality among all; thus, they rejected formal clerical leadership. Unlike evangelicalism in the North and South, with its concern for structures of authority to curb man's inherent wickedness, there was a radical individualist streak in Quaker thought. Unlike most other religious groups, Quakers allowed slaves and free persons of color to participate fully in their meetings, in which congregants sat facing one another waiting until one of them had a word of God to share with the group. If a slave or free Negro had a word from God, in principle he or she was equally free to share it.[4]

In the mid-eighteenth century, some Quakers began reconsidering how the system of slavery fit with their theological commitments. The idea that a slave could be a bearer of God's word, speaking with God's Inner Voice, and then walk out of a meeting to become subject to the will of his master became an unbearable contradiction to some. They began to persuade their fellow slaveholding Friends to renounce slavery and to emancipate their slaves. After persuasion reached its limits, they moved to ban slavery among those who wanted to remain in fellowship. By 1776, having decided to outlaw slavery among themselves, they also turned to eradicating slavery in the nation as a whole, which was in keeping with the realization that even if no Friends held slaves, they were still implicated in slavery through the mechanism of the market. It was a remarkable campaign, surely one of the most successful and most profound reorientations of moral sensibility in the history of activism. But unlike other forms of religious activism, it was not sectarian. The Quaker campaign grew out of religious commitment but invoked the rights of man as often as the Golden Rule, and it drew on the rhetoric of universal rights that was a constant theme in the American Revolution. In state actions throughout the North, Quakers petitioned legislatures and cajoled the public into accepting the fundamental rights of man. The Northern states responded. Vermont outlawed slavery in its constitution of 1777. In 1783 Massachusetts's state Supreme Court declared an end to slavery. New Hampshire followed suit shortly thereafter. By the end of the American Revolution in 1783, the Pennsylvania, Rhode Island, and Connecticut legislatures had either enacted laws to gradually abolish slavery or were moving toward their passage. That left only New York and New Jersey among the Northern states that still allowed slaveholding post-Revolution. But they would soon abolish it as well, with New York introducing the gradual abolition of slavery in 1799 and New Jersey becoming the final Northern state to outlaw slavery, in 1804, though the institution would continue to be a feature of daily life almost until the Civil War, given the extremely gradual nature of the emancipation.[5]

The abolition of slavery in the North at times appeared so painless that we might excuse eighteenth-century activists for believing that slavery would be swept away in the South in a couple of decades. But the purity of religious vision and the intensity of pursuit that had such a remarkable success in the Revolutionary era foundered on the shoals of a rising sectionalism between North and South over slavery. The obstacle was not entirely obvious. Resistance to slavery had become a national movement by the end of the eighteenth century, with regional or state organizations consolidating. At the first national meeting of antislavery societies in 1794, Quakers dominated the proceedings. Although Quakers were a small denomination whose already marginal numerical strength would further diminish as evangelical expansion began in the early nineteenth century, the future nevertheless looked bright. Many of the early evangelicals seemed to have an inclination toward abolitionism. The Methodists, in particular—along with the Baptists the fastest-growing evangelical group—were outright supporters of abolition. At the 1796 Methodist General Conference, the denomination declared itself "more than ever convinced of the great evil of the African slavery which still exists in these

United States." It established a series of regulations that checked the degree to which a slaveholder could become involved in a church or denominational body. It even requested that the ministers "and other members of our [Methodist] society" consider the subject of slavery until the next general conference, so that they could enact practical steps to eradicate the "enormous evil" of slavery from the church as a whole.[6]

But just four years later, at the next Methodist General Conference, the delegates rejected a motion to exclude slaveholders from membership in Methodist churches while still affirming "the necessity of doing away with the evil" and requiring preachers to emancipate their slaves. The resistance to slavery was weakening, with Southern ministers acquiescing to the fierce opposition of their church members. At the next conference, in 1804, the tide turned as delegates further retreated from making the abrogation of slavery a doctrinal issue in the *Discipline*, which governed Methodist religious life and practice. The conference instead allowed each regional conference to do as it saw fit when it came to slavery, which enabled Southern Methodist churches to proclaim slavery an institution of Christianity and enabled Northern churches to adopt a variety of positions, from outright abolition, to colonization schemes, to indifference.[7]

2.

The Methodist divide over slavery was replicated in most of the new denominations of the nineteenth century, with the abolition movement floundering in the early republic even as it triumphed in Great Britain. After Methodists accepted the place of slavery in the nation, the moral establishment drifted in opposing directions. Northern establishmentarians began to question slavery, and Southern establishmentarians began to see it as a linchpin to a moral society. The difference centered upon the place of slavery in the panoply of institutions that were supposed to tame the individual. Moral establishmentarians in both the North and the South agreed that God had created various authority structures designed to check the licentious tendencies of the individual. But Northern establishment supporters began to see slavery as an expression of individual licentiousness rather than as a legitimate structure of authority. This disagreement became impossible to overlook. Because slavery exerted such an extraordinarily powerful influence on the political, social, and economic organization of the nation, if slavery was immoral, then U.S. society required a near-total transformation.

It took some time before Northern moral establishmentarians came to that conclusion. Northern evangelicals focused their attention in the early part of the nineteenth century not on abolition but on the various campaigns to Christianize American society by eliminating drunkenness, Sabbath-breaking, and the like. To the extent that many evangelicals did participate in the call for abolition, it was through the American Colonization Society, a national organization that joined conservative antislavery advocates, Southern liberals, and evangelical reformers. The group believed that slavery was wrong, but, in accord with the sentiments of the Southern moral establishment, it saw domestic emancipation as a threat to the body politic. As the society explained to Congress in 1820, the free black population was growing rapidly, and it was universally agreed that they could not be "either useful or happy among us [Americans]." Believing that there was a fundamental incompatibility between the two races, the Society considered it "beyond dispute" that the presence of free people of color required "a separation." To that end, the colonization society suggested that slaves should gradually be shipped to Liberia, the society's colony in West Africa, and released upon their arrival. Lyman Beecher was fervent in his support of colonization and gradual emancipation, but, like many Northern evangelicals in the early nineteenth century, his larger focus was on the advancement of temperance and the defense of the Sabbath.[8]

The colonization movement was an imperfect reform vehicle for evangelicals. Its plea for gradualism was out of sync with the fervent moralism of evangelicalism, which was usually uncompromising in its denunciation of sin. Beecher himself faced this problem. He had no hesitation impugning those who questioned the notion of the immediate prohibition of alcohol but somehow made room for gradualism in abolition. The reason, not often articulated by Northern evangelicals, was that they believed Africans had a defective moral compass.[9]

In this, Southern establishmentarians agreed, but unlike Northern evangelicals they used the belief in black moral degradation to support slavery. While Northern evangelicals pursued other forms of moral regulation, the South became more rigid in affirming that slavery was central to the Southern moral order. Beginning with the Great Revival in Kentucky in 1801, itinerant preachers and religious enthusiasts began moving throughout the Southeast, seeking the chance to preach the evangelical gospel to Southern slaves and their masters. Because they needed the permission of masters to get access to their slaves, slave evangelization required an elaborate set of calculations in the contested relationship between master and slave. Masters initially resisted slave evangelization, worrying that it might prompt insurrection or claims of equality. In time, they would come to realize the utility of slave conversion to ensure quiescence and resignation.[10]

Yet black Christianization did not quite live up to planters' hopes, as slaves combined Anglo and African religious forms to create an alternative black Christianity that defied the expectations of their masters. By the 1830s, faced with the realization that the plan had not quite worked, white Southern evangelicalism began to harden. White Southern preachers looked upon the Africanisms that existed in slave Christianity as evidence of only a thin veneer of Christian civilization cloaking a core of barbarism. Charles Colcock Jones, a Presbyterian missionary to the slaves in Georgia, provided a representative white response to slave religion in his widely read book *The Religious Instruction of the Negroes in the United States*. Slaves were inclined to understand religion, he explained, as a "profession, in forms and ordinances, and in excited states of feeling." They also relied on "dreams, visions, trances, [and] voices" to denote true conversion. Their entire body of religious practice, he thought, bore "a perfect or striking resemblance to some form or type which has been handed down for generations, or which has been originated in the wild fancy of some religious teacher among them." The continuation of long-standing religious practices stemming from Africa, according to Jones, called into question the Christian status of slaves. Many shared his assessment. The Kentucky Union for the Moral and Religious Improvement of the Colored Race, for example, concluded, "After making all reasonable allowances, our colored population can be considered, at the most, but semi-heathen."[11]

The heathenism under a veil of Christianity accounted for what Southern moral establishmentarians regarded as the moral incapacity of slaves. The list of putative moral failings among slaves was long, but widely agreed upon by Southern slaveholders. Charles Cotesworth Pinckney, the son of a prominent Revolutionary family and the namesake of his uncle, a delegate to the Constitutional Convention and a two-time presidential candidate from South Carolina, provided another representative view. The younger Pinckney complained, in a famous 1829 address in Charleston, that the morals among slaves on plantations proved "the doctrine of human depravity." Parents and elders among the slaves demonstrated a "mischievous tendency" that was passed onto "the little negro," who then perfected the practice of iniquity with age. Christian slaveholders were particularly upset by the code of silence by which slaves protected one another and excluded masters from their religious lives. Charles Colcock Jones complained, "[M]embers of the same church are sacredly bound by their religion not to reveal each others' sins, for that would be backbiting and injuring the brotherhood." Slaves' protection of one another suggested to him, somewhat contradictorily, their inability to transcend the desires of individual appetite in order to enforce a proper communal system of values. "They take little interest in the moral improvement of their own color," he noted. "They live not together as communities having common ties and interests which would prompt them to promote the public piety and virtue, but very much as independent individuals and families." Their supposed inability to internalize moral norms meant that individual conduct remained "so much [at] variance with the Gospel" that too often God's grace was "turned into lasciviousness." The result, according to another prominent critic, Frederick Dalcho, an Episcopal bishop in South Carolina, was moral dissipation. Slaves were "[i]gnorant and indolent by nature, improvident and depraved by habit, and destitute of moral principle," he explained. That moral failing meant that generations or even ages might come "before they could be made virtuous, honest, and useful members of the body politic."[12]

Precisely because slaves could not be trusted to become members of the body politic, given their alleged moral depravity, Southern moral establishmentarians claimed that Christian slavery was a system of governance that was appropriate for slaves. Care for the religious lives of their slaves, in the explanation of many masters, was part of their obligation to God. Slaves needed the Christian oversight of masters in order to prosper. But this glossed over the problem at the heart of chattel slavery: slaves were supposed to be both things and people at the same time. By putting forth an alternative understanding of slavery that detached it from the marketplace in which slaves were bought and sold, slaveholders elided this contradiction. Just as children were people who lacked certain rights because they were incapable of moral self-determination, so, too, in the understanding of Southern moral establishmentarians, slaves lacked rights because of their damaged moral capacity and were therefore placed under the protective care of a master. Southern Christians claimed biblical justification for this paternalism, but it was, in the end, only a rhetorical justification for a form of property management. It involved "a specific metaphor of legitimate domination," according to the historian Elizabeth Fox-Genovese. By invoking the rule and protection that a father provided to his family, paternalism legitimated the master's rule over his slaves, which purported to follow the model of the Father in heaven.[13]

The claim of paternalism found widespread support in the Christian churches of the South. Some historians have claimed that Southern religion was apolitical and individual in orientation. The Southern evangelical impulse was primarily to save souls, so the argument goes, and they upheld what some called the spirituality of the church doctrine, or the idea that the church was concerned primarily with religious rather than political affairs. Yet the white Southern church was integral to shoring up slavery as a legal institution and to distributing power to elite planters. Many of the loudest proponents for the spirituality of the church, usually Southern Presbyterian theologians, were at the forefront in defending slavery as a Christian institution. These preacher–theologians of the South had their nuanced theological, temperamental, and personal differences. But they all forcefully affirmed slavery as a divinely con-stituted hierarchy and a vital part of the Southern social order. This was nei-ther apolitical nor individualistic. It was a comprehensive social vision that engaged law and politics to lend religious sanction to the Southern racial regime.[14]

No one stated the case more forcefully than Robert L. Dabney, a Presby-terian pastor–theologian who served as chief of staff to Thomas "Stonewall" Jackson in the Confederate army. He was exceptional not so much for his views, which found wide adherence among many architects of the Southern moral establishment, but for the clarity with which he presented them, laying out the moral vision of the master class and its attendant political vision with acute precision. For Dabney, slavery was a divinely ordained, hierarchical relationship. It provided a paradigm of political governance that he thought characterized the Southern moral order as a whole. Given the slave's moral degradation, which resulted from his religious corruption—his African heritage of barbarism—the Southern moral order placed the slave under the subordination of his master for his own protection and betterment. In this way Southern paternalism constituted a form of God-mandated racial discipleship—though not one from which slaves would ever emerge. It was, Dabney explained, "the genius of slavery, to make the family the slave's com-monwealth." The family served as the slave's "State," with the master as "mag-istrate and legislator." The master functioned as the slave's chief representative, under whom the slave remained "a life-long minor" in moral "tutelage."[15]

Dabney's invocation of moral depravity as the central justification for the slave system involved an elaborate anti-liberal political philosophy that was similar in many ways to Lyman Beecher's. He noted that the "[d]omestic ser-vitude" in which the master governed the slave was "but civil government in one of its forms." Because all government was a form of restraint to bind indi-viduals in order to make them fit for civil society, in Dabney's estimation slav-ery merely extended that principle of governance. Slaves' ostensible moral condition simply required a more severe form of restraint than other forms of governance offered. "As long as man is a sinner," Dabney explained, "restraint is righteous. We are sick of that arrogant and profane cant, which asserts man's 'capacity for self-government' as a universal proposition." Those who argued that all were fit to govern themselves were simply not in touch with reality as God had created it. God was the originator of moral distinctions and gave each person (and race) their place. So, Dabney concluded, "If there are certain things which he [the slave] is restrained by authority from doing, which the superior grades may do, these things are not rights to him. His inferior character, ignorance, and moral irresponsibility, have extinguished his right to do them."[16]

The Southern courts agreed with Dabney in asserting that the moral failings of slaves forfeited any claim to rights. In the absence of specific rights, masters possessed near-total power, acting as ruler and judge over slaves, which courts justified by referencing masters' Christian paternal obligation. Large tracts of society were excluded from the purview of the law. As the Virginia Supreme Court explained, because "the common law could not operate on" the system of slavery—since the common law would give slaves some rights as servants—the rules governing slavery had to come from "the positive enactments of the lawmaking power, or . . . be deduced from the Codes of other countries, where that condition of man was tolerated." The court's willingness to reason from the code of other countries included the biblical code of "the Theocratic Jews." It noted that among the Jews slavery originated from "the paternal curse of Noah upon the descendants of his grandson Canaan," thereby invoking the biblical curse of Ham that many Southerners used to justify American slavery's racial component. The court went on to explain that in each of the ancient codes, and in Virginia, a master could do as he wished, short of killing a slave. In the case before the court, a man named John Turner had been convicted of cruelly beating his slave and appealed to the Virginia Supreme Court. The court lamented that "an offence so odious and revolting as this" could exist but declared that the supreme court had no jurisdiction and no "power of correction." The integrity of the household and the independence of the master as the slave's ruler were absolute, short of murder. John Turner evaded punishment.[17]

The Virginia Supreme Court's argument was a common one, particularly after 1830, when the courts began warming to the notion that slavery was an absolute property relationship. As the North Carolina Supreme Court noted in another case, there was a difference between the relationship of the master and slave and the relationship of the pupil and governor. The difference went to the heart of the reason for slavery. The governor used physical punishment only as an addition to "moral and intellectual instruction." Coercion and physical punishment made the governor more "effectual" in training the pupil toward maturity. But the slave could never reach maturity. The slave was "doomed in his own person, and his posterity, to live without knowledge." He had to submit his will to another. The slave's inability to control his own will meant that the master had to rely on violence as a means of controlling the wayward tendencies of his slaves. "The power of the master must be absolute," the court explained, "to render the submission of the slave perfect." The court acknowledged that such a proposition was harsh, but it was inherent in "the curse of slavery," a likely reference to the curse of Ham. In the case before the court, a master had beaten his slave. When the slave tried to run away in the middle of the beating, he shot her in the back, wounding but not killing her. The court set the master free, again declaring its lack of jurisdiction. A slave must always understand, the court explained, "that there is no appeal from his [or her] master; that his [the master's] power is in no instance, usurped; but is conferred by the laws of man at least, if not by the law of God."[18]

In another case, the Georgia Supreme Court went even further, ruling that even killing a slave was not a felony. This was harsh even for most Southern courts. After a man named William Neal killed a slave, whose name was not recorded, the slave's owner brought suit in civil court. Neal lost and appealed to the Georgia Supreme Court, citing the rule that a civil suit could not go forward in cases of a felony until the criminal trial had yielded a conviction or acquittal. The court rejected Neal's argument, ruling that because it was not a felony to kill a slave, he was required to pay the restitution ordered by the civil court. In explaining how he could kill a slave without facing a felonious indictment, the court noted, "The curse of the Patriarch rests still upon the descendants of Ham." Because Negroes had been cursed of old, the court explained, the slave and master were "but fulfilling a divine appointment." The court added, "Christ came not to remove the curse; but recognizing the relation of master and servant, he prescribed the rules which govern, and the obligations which grow out of it, and thus ordained it an *institution of christianity*." The laws of the State of Georgia honored this institution of Christianity. The court went on, invoking Christian paternalism as the heart of the slave institution:

> It is the crowning glory of this age and of this land, that our legislation has responded to the requirements of the New Testament in great part, and if left alone, the time is not distant when we, the slave-holders, will come fully up to the measure of our obligations as such, under the christian dispensation. The laws of Georgia, at this moment, recognize the negro as

a man, whilst they hold him as property—whilst they enforce obedience in the slave, they require justice and moderation in the master. They protect his life from homicide, his limbs from mutilation, and his body from cruel and unnecessary scourging. They yield to him the right to food and raiment, to kind attentions when sick, and to maintenance in old age; and public sentiment, in conformity with indispensable legal restraints, extends to the slave the benefits and blessings of our Holy Religion.

The court declined to address the contradiction in its claim that the laws of Georgia protected slaves from homicide when, in fact, the slave in question had been subject to a homicide. The key point was that slaveholders needed to be "left alone," to fulfill the "divine appointment" bestowed upon them "under the christian dispensation."[19]

Given the belief that African Americans required the guiding hand of slavery, the presence of free persons of color was distressing to the Southern jurists. Because many were also of mixed blood, the courts struggled to define the rules that governed them. The rationale of the moral establishment helped. In South Carolina in 1835, an appeals court noted that the state legislature had nowhere defined the terms *mulatto* or *persons of color* in the various legal regulations that it had put forth. The court suggested, "[I]t may be . . . proper, that a man of worth . . . should have the rank of a white man, while a vagabond of the same degree of blood should be confined to the inferior caste. . . . It is hardly necessary to say that a slave cannot be a white man." In drawing such a rule, the court declared that the moral character of a person would determine his racial category. Yet free persons of color did not have the same rights as white men; as the Georgia Supreme Court explained, "They have always been considered in a state of pupilage, and been regarded as our wards." Society itself also had to act as the guardian of the free person of color, the court concluded. If a free black man or woman did violate norms, there were remedies. It was not uncommon to sell a free black man into slavery when he was convicted of a felony. His conviction proved his putative need for the guidance of slavery and the presence of a more extreme form of restraint. The white community was also permitted a certain amount of extrajudicial violence. In a North Carolina case, the supreme court ruled that a white man could beat a free black man who demonstrated "insolence." "It is unfortunate, that *this third class* exists in our society," the court complained. "If a slave is insolent, he may be whipped by his master, or by order of a justice of the peace; but a free negro has no master to correct him, a justice of the peace cannot have him punished for insolence, it is not an indictable offence, and unless a white man, to whom insolence is given, has a right to put a stop to it, in an extra judicial way, there is no remedy for it. This would be insufferable."[20]

The jurisdictional integrity of the household, the reliance upon the master to act as a restraint on the licentiousness of the slave, the status of a free black man as a ward of society without civil rights, and the danger of commingling to a racial hierarchy ordained by God all came together in the infamous 1857 U.S. Supreme Court case *Dred Scott v. Sandford*. The Court ruled that no descendants of slaves, whether emancipated or not, could be U.S. citizens. The opinion was the crowning expression of the antebellum Southern view of American society. Pervading Justice Roger B. Taney's *Dred Scott* opinion was the notion that moral competency, and by implication religious belief, constituted an immovable barrier to African Americans' fitness for the rights of citizenship. He invoked the putative moral depravity of slaves in a manner similar to Robert Dabney. For at least a century, the Court maintained, Africans had "been regarded as beings of an inferior order, and altogether unfit to associate with the white race, either in social or political relations; and so far inferior, that they had no rights which the white man was bound to respect." Because of African degradation, American laws had held "that the negro might justly and lawfully be reduced to slavery for his benefit." American law also regulated the relations between the races. Citing the many prohibitions against miscegenation in both Great Britain and the United States, the Court concluded the twin heritage of barbarism and heathenism was so great that, perhaps in reference to the curse of Ham, a "stigma, of the deepest degradation, was fixed upon the whole race." That stigma meant that miscegenation was both "unnatural and immoral." Because Africans were "so far below them [whites] in the scale of created beings," black moral degradation required "a perpetual and impassable barrier . . . between the white race and the one which they had reduced to slavery." This supposed moral degradation, the Court maintained, created political incompatibility, which both justified slavery and required the exclusion of slaves and free Negroes from citizenship in the body politic.[21]

3.

The concerns of moral establishmentarians were, of course, not unique to the South. Northern evangelicals also fretted about democracy and feared the loosening of social restraints. As Beecher had argued, God placed the individual under society and its institutions of family, church, and school. These institutions mediated between the person and the state, shaping him so that he was fit for society. Beecher's understanding did not differ much from that of Dabney or others of the Southern moral establishment. Dabney, like Beecher, looked to the mechanisms of society, with the coercive power of law behind them, to restrain the individual. Moral establishmentarians, both Northern and Southern, agreed on the relation of religion, law, and morals in principle, only disagreeing on the legitimacy of slavery in practice.

This tacit agreement was eclipsed by the increasingly clamorous debates over the future of slavery. In 1820 the nation averted crisis with the Missouri Compromise, which established the boundary between future slave and free states. It was, like most compromises regarding slavery, an imperfect agreement that bothered both sides. But as Christians North and South puzzled over what to do, a revolution was beginning. While many Christians continued to look to the permanent removal of African Americans as the solution to the slavery issue—and as a catalyst in the missionary conversion of the continent of Africa—other Christians began to radicalize. In the 1820s a group of Quakers following Elias Hicks refined their theology to claim that Jesus was revealed not solely through the Bible but through the Inner Light, the Christ Within. All Quakers had earlier agreed that God spoke to each individual, but the revelation of Jesus through the Bible had some level of preeminence over any word that a person might receive through the Inner Light. The Bible acted as boundary-defining revelation, helping individuals distinguish a true word from a false one. With the teaching that the revelation of the Inner Light was on par with the revelation of Jesus from the Bible, Hicksite Quakers removed those boundaries and transformed Quaker religious praxis, distancing it from Bible reading and prayer, and recognizing an ongoing personal reformation through experience in the world. An individual acting in the world could experience Jesus in the same way as someone kneeling in prayer or reading the Bible. Such an understanding tended to minimize the importance of Bible-reading and prayer and sacralized Quaker social activism.[22]

The shift was important because it changed arguments against slavery, ultimately causing a split in abolitionism and revealing the intellectual connections between evangelical abolitionists and the proponents of the Southern moral establishment. The dilemma that Hicksite Quakers raised was that of the exact connection between religion and morals. Early Quakers and Methodists had suggested that slavery was immoral because it ran against their theological beliefs. Abolitionist evangelicals would continue to argue in this vein, claiming that because slavery was a sin it must be rejected. With the advent of Hicksite Quakerism, theological belief became detached from any scriptures, focusing instead on moral argumentation. Hicksite abolitionists came to increasingly rely on an Enlightenment mode of reasoning: the secular rationale for abolition that drew upon the rights of man. These two modes of argument entailed two divergent understandings of abolition. Northern evangelicals could argue for abolition as part of their attempt to effect a reformation of morals that would make the nation Christian. To Northern evangelicals, abolition was one prong of a multilateral effort to confront sin and establish a moral rule. By contrast, Hicksite Quakers and those who found them attractive (especially those in the emerging freethought movement, who resisted the influence of religion in public life) grounded antislavery in the perfection of individual and secular rights. This second group often rejected the religious notion of rights that evangelicals supported.[23]

The two factions were able to live together for a time because they seemed to be united in agreeing that slavery was wrong. Their agreement also found joint leadership in a new player in the abolitionist cause: William Lloyd Garrison. He could bring together both the evangelicals and the Quakers and freethinkers because he had a foot in each world. Occasionally attending Lyman Beecher's church in Boston in the 1820s, Garrison imbibed Beecher's belief that stirring controversy was the most efficacious way to effect reform. At the same time, he was friends with many Hicksite Quakers, forging relationships that would blossom in the 1830s.[24]

The question was how long Garrison could hold such divergent factions together. He had attracted the attention of evangelicals as early as 1829, when he accused a Newburyport merchant of "domestic piracy" for moving slaves from the upper South to the Deep South. The merchant sued and then pressed criminal charges for libel, with disastrous consequences for Garrison. The paper in which Garrison published the charge went out of business. Garrison was convicted and fined, and because he could not pay the fine he went to jail. But Garrison's plight aroused attention from Arthur Tappan, an evangelical merchant who had withdrawn from the colonization society the year before because of its connection to the rum trade. Perhaps Tappan saw in Garrison one who might create a sufficient reform vehicle for evangelical beliefs. In any case, Tappan paid Garrison's fine and had him released.[25]

Garrison emerged from jail even more determined. His first step, in January 1831, was to found the *Liberator,* a paper calling for the immediate abolition of slavery. Under Garrison's leadership, the paper rejected colonization and gradual abolition schemes of all kinds. Almost all of the early subscribers to the *Liberator* were free African Americans. Garrison sought to expand this base by making overtures to prominent white evangelicals who might be looking for a different vehicle for the evangelical antislavery reform than the American Colonization Society.[26]

The cooperation between Garrison and the evangelicals would grow in the short term. Two years after founding the *Liberator*, Garrison collaborated with Arthur Tappan; Lewis Tappan, Arthur's brother and a staunch temperance advocate; and Theodore Weld, an evangelical who was converted by the evangelist and abolition supporter Charles G. Finney. Together they formed the American Anti-Slavery Society (AASS) in 1833. It was the first national society in the United States devoted to the immediate and unconditional abolition of slavery. At the first meeting of the society, the delegates drafted a constitution and a document called the Declaration of Sentiments. Garrison was its principal author. The document was remarkable for its shifting mode of argumentation, moving in and out of language that invoked God's will as the foundation of civil law, which moral establishmentarians favored, and more secular language. Declaring the right of slavery "an audacious usurpation of the Divine prerogative, a daring infringement of the law of nature, a base overthrow of the very foundations of the social compact, a complete extinction of all the relations, endearments and obligations of mankind, and a presumptuous transgression of all the holy commandments," the American Anti-Slavery Society rejected all laws protecting "the right of slavery" as "before God utterly null and void."[27]

These shifting justifications betrayed uncertainty in the movement and the still-nascent quarrels among its leaders. Although all parties wanted the abolition of slavery, abolition occupied different places in their larger reform programs. The Tappan brothers were typical of evangelical abolitionists. Abolition was part of their attempt to bring civil law in line with divine law. Because God's law had established the unchanging moral obligations of human beings, it formed the foundation of civil law, even though church and state were institutionally separated. The connection of divine and civil law required that the goal of reform be the sanctification of the state in order to compel people to do what was right. The whole point of the civil government, as Beecher had argued, was to restrain the wicked tendencies of human beings in order to make them fit to live in society. Slavery was a state-sanctioned concession to evil and was, as such, a failure of civil government. The goal of abolitionist evangelicals was to erase this failure, harnessing the coercive mechanisms of the state to abolish not just slavery but a whole host of practices that evangelicals saw as evil: Sabbath-breaking, consuming alcohol, dueling, and other forms of social vice.[28]

Garrison, by contrast, viewed the state with a skepticism that grew with experience. In some ways Garrison was an evangelical, though he would become less so as time went on. He believed in the pervasiveness of sin, in personal reformation through faith, and in the resulting obligation to transform society. But Garrison saw the state as a temporary institution, introduced as a result of human sin and therefore implicated in human sin. The state would be rendered unnecessary with the perfection of society and its submission to God. To rely on the state as part of a reform program or to use the coercive power of the state to compel people to do what was right would be, in Garrison's view, to use an instrument of evil in pursuit of good. Garrison's philosophy entailed a substantial critique of both the Southern moral establishment and of moral establishmentarians from the North who called for the eradication of slavery as a step in the perfection of American moral government.[29]

Trouble between the two factions soon surfaced. Two years after founding the AASS with the Tappans, Garrison went public with his thoughts. He was drawn into criticism of their position tangentially, nibbling at the edges until he found himself gnawing at the center.

In 1835 the Massachusetts Supreme Court upheld the conviction of a man named George Cheever for libel. Having served time for libel, Garrison might have been expected to object to the broad application of libel law. But, in what would become his first salvo against the idea of a moral establishment, Garrison published an editorial in the *Liberator* that went much further, rejecting penal laws altogether. "All penal laws of men are just so many conventional expedients to gratify human selfishness, retaliation and power," he claimed.[30]

To his many supporters, this was a puzzling, even alarming, statement. It seemed like a call for anarchy. Garrison did not stop there but moved on to attacking reform movements and evangelical leaders who seemed indifferent to abolition yet sought to impose their vision of Christianity on the nation. His old minister, Lyman Beecher, became a principal target. Beecher had moved to Cincinnati in 1832 to become the president of Lane Theological Seminary, a new Presbyterian institution not far from the Western frontier. Two years later, he stood by as the seminary's trustees suppressed a group of evangelical Christians who began holding campus antislavery meetings. After the trustees imposed a gag order on those discussing the issue of slavery, Beecher defended the gag order in public while seeking in private to roll back the worst abuses against the students. As criticism intensified and as defenders of the so-called Lane Rebels began heaping scorn on Beecher, his position hardened against immediate abolition. This made his public position on the students' dissent only more untenable, since he was rejecting the kind of agitation on the slave question that he otherwise supported in his crusade against drinking, gambling, dueling, and Sabbath-breaking. Beecher's prominence made him a tantalizing target for Garrison. But in criticizing Beecher, Garrison risked extending his critique to a whole host of ideas supported by evangelical abolitionists such as the Tappans, who looked to the Christian-nation ideal and the religious foundation of morality as their major impetus for the eradication of slavery.[31]

It was a risk Garrison was prepared to take. After Beecher gave a speech calling for the centrality of moral reform in the American experiment, Garrison objected to the Christian millennialism that underpinned Beecher's reform activities. Claiming that Beecher "oracularly asserts in the style of our Fourth-of-July orators" that the United States was undertaking an experiment in liberty upon which the freedom of the world depended, Garrison could not contain his incredulity. "As if God had suspended the fate of all nations, and hazarded the fulfillment of his glorious promises, upon the result of a wild and cruel 'experiment' by a land-stealing, blood-thirsty, man-slaying, slave-trading people in one corner of the globe!" he exclaimed. Garrison's stridency led many evangelical commentators to claim that he was an anarchist. He had affirmed the integrity and autonomy of the individual to such an extent that he threatened to repudiate the entire rationale of the moral establishment. In the ensuing storm of criticism, Garrison wrote a rebuttal to the *New England Spectator*, honing his position. "I am not against government, whether civil or religious," he explained, "but it must be the government of God in the hearts of men, all-directing, all-controlling, all-abiding—not one based upon physical strength, and maintained by powder and ball, and accompanied by stripes, and fines, and jails, and dungeons, and gibbets, and lawyers, and constables, and sheriffs."[32]

His explanation did not satisfy many evangelicals, because, as they pointed out, all government relied on coercion: that was its point—to ensure that wicked people were fit to live together. Garrison's blithe dismissal of this rationale, along with his trust in the individual to follow what was right, seemed crazed to his evangelical critics. It recalled the atheistic and anarchist experiments of the French Revolution and the resultant Terror. As Beecher himself complained, "One of the most alarming indications of our day is, that men are too proud to be free under the law, and are beginning to turn the same glance upon the law, that they turn in Europe upon the despot." Garrison was unconvinced. "It is popular to speak of the Goddess of Reason, of Robespierre and his vindictive associates, of the guillotine, and of the reign of atheism," he responded. "But who dwells upon the fact, that a despotic government, a false religion and a wicked priesthood, had conspired to crush, ruin and enslave the people, so that human endurance could bear no more, and all that was associated with the name of christianity became hateful?" An idol-worshipping moral estab-lishment had sown the seeds of the Terror, Garrison claimed, and Beecher was its heir. "How does it happen," Garrison wondered, "that Dr. Beecher's sym-pathies and fears side only with the rich and the powerful?" By claiming that the Christian association with the structures of power resulted in despotism, Garrison attacked one of the fundamental rationales of the moral establish-ment and threatened both to erode his popular support and to chill the fervor of the AASS.[33]

As tension grew between the Tappans and Garrison, the place of women in the abolitionist movement emerged as yet another flashpoint. Controversy erupted in 1837, just as Garrison's opponents began to criticize his nonresis-tant and Christian anarchist views, when Sarah and Angelina Grimké went on a speaking tour for the abolitionist cause. The appearance of women on a public platform with men in the audience caused a sensation. It defied expec-tations of respectability. The scandal was only heightened because the Grimkés came from a genteel Charleston slaveholding family, which led many to expect more decorum from the brash women. But led by Sarah, who was thirteen years older than her sister, they rejected slavery, abandoned the Presbyterian-ism of their family and the South altogether, and came under the influence of a group of Hicksite Quakers in Philadelphia. Guided by the Inner Light, they defied social prescription, throwing themselves into the abolitionist move-ment and becoming two of the most effective speakers for the cause.[34]

This was a problem for many evangelical abolitionists. In their reading of the Bible and especially of the apostle Paul, God had placed women under men. Paul even commanded that women must remain silent in churches, a mark of their deference to men's spiritual authority and their own subordinate status. In July 1837, shortly after the Grimkés began their tour, the Congregational General Association of Massachusetts sounded an alarm. The association feared that the Grimkés' activities portended social anarchy and moral degra-dation. The Grimkés, speaking tour violated "the appropriate duties and influ-ence of woman," whose primary duty, in the minds of the Association, was to wield moral influence that remained "unobtrusive and private, but the source of mighty power." Men, meanwhile, would lead in public, as God had man-dated. By supposedly abandoning the arena of the family for which God had made them, the Grimkés posed a threat to the moral character of the nation.[35]

The evangelical attacks on the Grimkés began in tandem with the attacks on Garrison, but Garrison, at least, was pleased with the sisters' efforts. "The Grimkés are doing a mighty work here," he wrote to one correspondent, "in the presence of assembled thousands." As women became more active, and as the debate over their participation became more acute, the Garrison faction began to craft arguments for women's inherent right to speak and act in the movement—and in society as a whole. This trend suggested to Lewis Tappan just how far the radical wing of the movement had gone. As he complained in his journal in June 1839, Garrison and his followers had so "loaded the cause with their no-government-woman's-rights-non-resistance &c. notions" that the cause of abolition and the moral purpose of reform were being upended.[36]

By including women in the cause, the Garrison–Grimké faction threatened to reorganize American society around the individual, a goal not shared by the evangelical abolitionists. Objecting to what they considered an extraneous (and dangerous) foray into issues unrelated to slavery, the national leadership grew especially concerned that the AASS, in Garrison's hands, would become something other than a vehicle to perfect the moral establishment. Accordingly, Lewis Tappan began to use his position in the national office to cut Garrison out. In August 1837 Tappan wrote from New York to Amos A. Phelps, another prominent evangelical abolitionist, to assure Phelps that the executive committee was seeking to disassociate itself from the Garrison faction. He thought that Phelps, who was in Boston with Garrison, might begin to do the same up there. He also began working with James G. Birney, an evangelical with connections to Lyman Beecher and a corresponding secretary for the AASS, to set in motion a plan to gain control of the organization.[37]

While Tappan moved against Garrison in private, many ministers signed public petitions against him, attacking him in print and proposing a new abolitionist organization that had an evangelical test for membership. As one petition claimed, Garrison was so outside the mainstream that "the promotion and speedy triumph of the cause of emancipation, and the prosperity of *evangelical religion*" required an organization from which Garrison was excluded. Garrison sought to defuse the issue by forming an alternate organization himself through which he could express his political views not directly related to abolition. In September 1838 he established a society for nonresistance, which was the name he gave to his political philosophy. Yet at the Peace Convention called to form the Non-Resistance Society, Garrison and his allies continued their withering critique of the moral establishment's Christian Nation ideal. Sounding like a revolutionary, Garrison led the convention into a Declaration of Sentiments that was highly critical of all religious attempts to make the U.S. government Christian. "The dogma, that all governments of the world are approvingly ordained of God, and that THE POWERS THAT BE in the United States, in Russia, in Turkey, are in accordance with his will," the convention declared, "is . . . absurd." He believed that all human governments maintained themselves by "the point of the bayonet," seeking "to compel men to do right, on pain of imprisonment or death." Because a nation could never act according to the will of God while resorting to coercion, the overthrow of all governments (including that of the United States) "by a spiritual regeneration" of their citizens, was "inevitable." To make such blanket statements courted the outrage even of his allies, who wondered what kind of political authority or social philosophy Garrison could support.[38]

Garrison's efforts did not quell the controversy, which reached a head in 1839. Tappan decided to raise the issue during a meeting in mid-May. He hoped finally to align abolition with evangelical efforts to perfect the moral establishment. Though he might have prevailed had he handled it correctly, his side's parliamentary fumbling allowed the Garrison faction to stave off any attempt to expel the religiously unorthodox from the organization. Still smarting a week later, Tappan wrote to Gerrit Smith, who would in the 1840s and 1850s run for president multiple times under the abolitionist banner, with a confession that they had likely "erred in associating with ungodly men in the Anti S. enterprise." Still, he worked to expel them. By the end of June, Tappan sought to use the official organ of the AASS, the *Emancipator*, to rally evangelical abolitionists to his cause. He turned to his trusty evangelical colleague James G. Birney to make the case. Writing in the *Emancipator*, Birney sought to persuade the AASS to officially repudiate Garrison's radical positions.[39]

Birney, who would run for president under the Liberty Party banner in 1840 and 1844, laid out the arguments of evangelical abolitionists while at the same time revealing the essential agreement between Southern and Northern moral establishmentarians on the broader issues of religion, morals, and law. What was striking was the degree to which Birney's understanding overlapped that of both Lyman Beecher, who supported colonization, and Robert Dabney, who supported slavery. All three evangelicals shared the view that government acted as a restraint upon human wickedness, that it raised some above others, and that the evangelical goal was to bring civil law in line with divine law. Garrison was a threat to this goal. In Birney's understanding, the principles of nonresistance tended "to strike at the root of the social structure . . . to throw society into entire confusion, and to renew, under the sanction of religion, scenes of anarchy and license" that had, to that point, "generally . . . been the offspring of the rankest infidelity and irreligion." Birney acknowledged that Garrison had sought to separate abolition from nonresistance in a concession to those who opposed his political philosophy, but he wondered how the two issues could really be kept separate. "Is the difference between those who seek to abolish any and every government of human institution, and those who prefer *any* government to a state of things in which every one may do what seemeth good in his own eyes—is the difference between them, I say, so small, that they can act harmoniously under the same organization?" Birney asked. He argued that such a wide disagreement meant that the two sides actually disagreed on the cause of abolition itself, because both sides saw it as a step to a different end. "One party is for sustaining and purifying governments, and bringing them to a perfect conformity with the principles of the Divine government," Birney explained, while "the other [is] for destroying *all* government." Because he was of the party seeking "to purify, invigorate and immortalize" civil government, and because he read the constitution of the American Anti-Slavery Society as supporting that goal, Birney argued that nonresistants needed to leave the society.[40]

Birney's attack precisely delineated their disagreement. Was abolition a step in the purification of government and the moral establishment, or was it a step in their dismantling? The controversy finally ended at the annual meeting of the AASS in 1839. Birney and Tappan were determined to use the society for evangelical political action. When the meeting opened, Birney moved to condemn the doctrines of No Government and Non-Resistance as contrary to the constitution of the society. Lewis Tappan was in favor of Birney's resolution. He had written in his journal a month earlier that he thought Garrison had corrupted the purpose of abolition, having "grown lukewarm on the anti-slavery subject." Garrison, who was in attendance, did not participate in the debate "as a matter of principle," he later explained, saying, "[F]or, as I have never intruded my views of peace and government upon any anti-slavery meeting, so I will not stand up in their defence at any such meeting."[41]

Yet, in spite of Tappan and Birney's co-opting of the *Emancipator*, and the executive committee's tacit endorsement of Birney's proposal, they could not muster the votes to pass the resolutions. A few months after their defeat, Lewis Tappan noted, with a touch of sadness, "The abolitionists now seem to be divided into several parties." He placed the blame on Garrison. Unwilling to remain in the same organization with people they regarded as infidels, in 1840 Tappan and his allies finally left to form the American and Foreign Anti-Slavery Society (AFASS).[42]

4.

The decision to leave was a good one for the advancement of the evangelical cause, though it did not seem so at the time. The war within the AASS exposed a latent tension that had festered for several years. Yet it also showed a fundamental agreement that was not necessarily obvious at first glance. The similarities among the political philosophies of Dabney, Beecher, and Birney showed that evangelicals agreed on the necessary connection of religion, morals, and law and the perpetuation of institutions to shape the individual for society. What they disagreed upon was slavery, and among evangelicals in the North, they disagreed on the best method to eradicate it. That disagreement meant that as soon as the new society was formed Northern evangelicals splintered into competing factions. Some abolitionists, such as Gerrit Smith and Elizur Wright, left the old AASS but did not join the new society, deciding instead to concentrate their efforts on the newly formed Liberty Party, which was based on the single premise of entering formal politics in the cause of abolition. The Tappans, for their part, declined to join the Liberty Party and instead retreated into church reform. What little the new society did accomplish, Lewis Tappan pushed through by himself, because many people who left the old society appeared simply to drift away. Their philosophical (and theological) agreement on the moral establishment awaited the creation of an organization through which they could work toward their common goal.[43]

Yet just when it seemed that Garrison's challenge to the moral establishment had triumphed among abolitionists, an extraordinary event occurred that would provide Tappan the platform to pursue his moral-establishment aims. In August 1839 the slave ship *Amistad* arrived on Long Island. The previous June a group of slaves from the Mendi tribe had mutinied aboard the ship but spared the life of the two Spanish slavers who had bought them so that they could direct the Africans home. The Spaniards deceived the mutineers, sailing the ship northward until a navy cutter seized it, freed the Spaniards, and jailed the Africans. Tappan took immediate interest in the case, first meeting with the Africans on September 6, in jail, where he preached a sermon to them on the providence of God. They knew no English, so the gesture was symbolic. Tappan then arranged for their instruction in English (through Bible-reading and other forms of religious indoctrination), which provided copy for the religious press and served to accentuate the plight of the slave and the piousness of the antislavery cause. Meanwhile, he found legal representation for the captives and won a favorable court ruling that threw out the charges of piracy and murder on jurisdictional grounds. Then Tappan requested the arrest of the two Spanish slavers for imprisonment and cruelty, even accompanying the New York sheriff to their hotel to take them into custody. Tappan handled the case masterfully, using the plight of the Mendi Africans as a symbol of the plight of slaves in general. While winning the case in the court of public opinion, he also made sure to win the legal case. When the case reached the U.S. Supreme Court, he enlisted John Quincy Adams to argue it. The high court upheld the lower court's decision in March 1841. The captives were freed.[44]

It was a stellar performance, which served for a time to focus attention on the plight of slaves. But its most lasting legacy had little to do with the Africans or even with slave law. Tappan had been hoping to use the American and Foreign Anti-Slavery Society to unite evangelicals against slavery and in favor of the subsequent perfection of the moral establishment. As the *Amistad* case drew to a close, it was apparent that the AFASS was not up to the task. Tappan began considering another way to move forward. In August 1841, a few months prior to the return of the Africans to Africa, a black minister from Connecticut named J. W. C. Pennington founded an organization that he called the Union Missionary Society. It sought to use the Mendi repatriation as a springboard for Christian evangelical propagation at home and abroad. Most of its original leaders were black ministers. Taking notice of the new organization, in May 1842 Tappan convinced the leadership of the Union Missionary Society to merge with his *Amistad* Committee, which had directed the *Amistad* case. Shortly after the two organizations merged, Tappan and his white brethren assumed control, replacing several of the black leaders with their own but leaving Pennington as president for the short term. Tappan wrote to Amos A. Phelps to explain that even though the two organizations had merged, he intended to allow "the intelligent & excellent men of color" to participate in what he characterized as "our cause." But soon the white leadership had marginalized the black leaders to minor or meaningless posts.[45]

Tappan's racist paternalism was a sign of things to come. Having found another organization for perfecting the moral establishment, he began to push his agenda. A few years later, in 1846, the society incorporated several smaller associations and reconstituted itself as the American Missionary Association (AMA), an organization dedicated to the abolition of slavery and the Christianization of the United States. The original call to form the new organization explained, "Christianity wages an uncompromising warfare against all forms of sin, public as well as private; social, political, and organic, as well as individual; sins sustained, authorized, enacted, and even required and enjoined by civil rulers, as well as sins forbidden and punished by them." The organization allowed anyone "of evangelical sentiments, who professes faith in the Lord Jesus Christ, who is not a slaveholder, or in the practice of other immoralities" to become a member.[46]

Unlike the American and Foreign Anti-Slavery Society, by then nearly moribund, the AMA became a major vehicle for evangelical antislavery agitation as one part of the promotion of the moral establishment. Part of its success stemmed from its ability to compete with the American Board of Commissioners for Foreign Missions and also the American Bible Society, both of which were conservative on the issue of slavery and which had appointed board members who were either proslavery or held slaves. By exploiting evangelical dissatisfaction with the two dominant missionary societies, the AMA was able to peel off evangelicals who might not have participated in outright antislavery agitation but who did not want to support proslavery missions. As the AMA grew, it could push forward the Northern version of the moral establishment while the nation neared war. Finally, Tappan had found an organization to pursue his vision. The power of the AMA would not fully crest until after the Civil War, but the organizational architecture was fully in place by the mid-1840s.[47]

MORAL REPRODUCTION
AND THE FAMILY

1.

The slavery question raised a host of others. The ultimate goal of the moral establishment was to tame the individual. But the radical branch of abolition, which claimed that slaves had absolute rights, raised the individual above the whole and rejected the entire logic of the moral establishment. This idea quickly spread to other groups that were excluded from the body politic, especially those women who were among the most prominent proponents of the abolition movement and some of the fiercest defenders of its Garrisonian branch.

Women's prominence increased after the split between the evangelicals and the radicals, which allowed Garrison to pursue his vision unobstructed. The place of women in the radical branch served to further highlight the differences between the two sides when they met one final time at the world conference of antislavery societies that convened in London a few months after the organizational break. The conference was cantankerous, not least because the American Anti-Slavery Society (AASS) and the American and Foreign Anti-Slavery Society (AFASS) each sent their own slate of representatives, with the AASS including among their delegates the many women who had a prominent role in the cause. Before the conference had even begun, controversy swirled among evangelicals on both sides of the Atlantic about seating the female delegates. Uncertain of what to do, the male delegates began the convention by debating women's rights for the entire first day. Wendell Phillips, who would assume leadership of the AASS after the Civil War, led the way in pressing the female delegates' cause. "[W]e do not think it just or equitable," he explained, "that, after the trouble, the sacrifice, the self-devotion of a part of those who leave their families and kindred and occupations in their own land, to come three thousand miles to attend this World's Convention, they should be refused a place in its deliberations." But Henry Grew, a minister from Philadelphia, immediately rejected the radical argument with sublime confidence. Seating the women would run against "the ordinance of Almighty God," he complained. The debate continued in that vein, touching on the capacity of women, the customs of England, the prescriptions of theology, and the competing views of individual rights, but it did not end well for the AASS representatives. After a long and weary back-and-forth, the delegates voted to deny the female AASS delegates their seats, which meant that the women had to watch the entire proceedings from the gallery. Garrison, who had not been present at the debate due to a delay at sea, was appalled at the outcome and refused his own seat in silent protest, sitting instead in the women's gallery for the entire ten days of the convention.[1]

Among the others sitting in the women's gallery was Elizabeth Cady Stanton, who would become one of the most powerful advocates for women's rights and one of the fiercest opponents of the moral establishment. Stanton was the daughter of Daniel Cady, a lawyer who served in the U.S. Congress and as a justice of the New York Supreme Court. Cady had doted on his daughter and introduced her to the practice of law. It was by reading his law library that Elizabeth discovered the severe legal liabilities women faced, which she attributed to the untoward influence of Christianity in law. In the third chapter of Genesis, God tells Eve, upon learning that she had eaten of the tree, "I will greatly multiply your pain in childbearing; in pain you shall bring forth children, yet your desire shall be for your husband, and he shall rule over you." In Anglo-American law, this was codified in the doctrine of coverture. When a woman married, she assumed the name of her husband and legally ceased to exist. "[T]he very being or legal existence of the woman is suspended during the marriage," the great English jurist William Blackstone explained, which meant that the few legal acts she was allowed to perform could only be done in her husband's name. Lacking a legal identity and individuality, the married woman, or *femme couverte* (covered woman), became a virtual nonentity. She could not make contracts, except in her husband's name and with his consent. All her property became his upon marriage, unless it had been placed in a trust, in which case she still lost control over it. She could not accrue any property within marriage. Any will she created prior to marriage was dissolved because once she married the property ceased to be hers.[2]

The law of coverture presumed the subordination of women as described in scripture. Wives' responsibility for childrearing and family care went hand-in-hand with the idea that husbands governed the family and represented it before the state. The decision to exclude women as delegates from the London convention and the earlier outrage over the Grimkés' activities grew out of these conservative Christian ideas.[3]

Elizabeth Cady Stanton had already become skeptical of such ideas before her experience in London, but, at the time, her future radicalism was not totally apparent. She was the young bride of Henry Stanton, a supporter of the conservative wing of the abolition movement and a friend of James G. Birney and the Tappans. Given her husband's proclivities, she might have been expected to support the evangelical faction. She had even converted to evangelicalism earlier in life, though her fervor had waned. The controversy over seating the female delegates offered an object lesson in the liabilities and lack of power that came from the religious, political, and legal subjugation of women, while the conference offered her the opportunity to meet Garrison, who she later claimed helped cut her free from the chains of "spiritual bondage." She also met Lucretia Mott, a Quaker matriarch and Garrison ally who would join Stanton as one of the principal leaders of the emerging women's movement. Excluded from the conference, Stanton and Mott concluded that women needed a convention of their own to argue for women's rights.[4]

Although it would take eight years to materialize, the resulting Seneca Falls Convention of 1848 was a pivotal point in the history of individual rights in the United States. Organized by Mott and Stanton, the convention advanced the radical view of rights and the rejection of the moral establishment previously supported by Garrisonian abolitionists. To explain the purpose and goal of their new movement, the attendees produced a document, modeled on the Declaration of Independence and following the example of the American Anti-Slavery Society, that they called the Declaration of Sentiments. Listing the injustices against women just as Jefferson had listed the injustices of the British king against the colonists, the declaration maintained that women were "aggrieved, oppressed, and fraudulently deprived of their most sacred rights" and demanded "immediate admission to all the rights and privileges . . . as citizens of these United States." That demand rejected the idea that women's civic obligations were to their husbands alone, and called for the rejection of coverture so that the government acknowledged women as citizens and individuals, apart from their status as wives or mothers.[5]

Yet there was some ambiguity. Although the delegates' advocacy of women's rights was unequivocal, the rationale for those rights remained obscure. The major impetus for the convention had come from supporters of Garrisonian reform, but the emergent women's movement had philosophical fractures as deep as the abolition movement. Not all women would agree with a radical women's rights vision that rejected the moral establishment. Others embraced the moral role of women, which God had mandated, as justification for their enlarged public presence. Perhaps most important among these more conservative women was Catharine Beecher, Lyman Beecher's eldest daughter. Catharine Beecher partially moved away from her father's theology after her unconverted fiancé died in a shipwreck. According to Lyman's evangelicalism, Catharine's fiancé was doomed to eternal perdition as a result of his failure to believe. Catharine realized after his sudden death that she could not accept the stark conversionary requirement for salvation that played a central role in Lyman's theology.[6]

Her inability to accept this core tenet of evangelical belief eventually led her to question other aspects of her father's religious views, including those that limited women's role in society. But she was still enough of an evangelical that she did not believe in women's unqualified right to political and social equality based on their status as individual moral beings and did not abandon the moral establishment. Instead, Catharine Beecher argued that because women were morally superior, they should have a greater public role. That would inject the principle of religious virtue and motherly love into the broader world outside the home. In other words, she used the argument of the moral establishment that women had a divine obligation to stay in the home in order to argue for women's enlarged public role. It was a paradoxical projection of domestic responsibility onto the larger world.[7]

These separate justifications for women's rights entailed divergent appeals to religious authority and ultimately divergent political goals, but for a time, as with abolition, all were able to work together. Although Seneca Falls was dominated by women like Stanton and Mott, more moderate supporters of both the moral establishment and of women's rights were also present at the meeting, which is reflected in the convention documents. The convention's resolutions seemed to move in two directions, sometimes in support of the radical wing for women's rights and sometimes in line with the Catharine Beecher branch. The convention, for example, condemned "the circumscribed limits which corrupt customs and a perverted application of the Scriptures" had created for women, at least implicitly rejecting the moral establishment. At the same time, the convention gestured toward the maintenance of moral norms, claiming that it was "demonstrably the right and duty of woman, equally with man, to promote every righteous cause . . . especially in regard to the great subjects of morals and religion."[8]

2.

This divide, papered over at Seneca Falls, continually threatened to break into the open and split the movement. Four years later, during the 1852 Woman's Rights Convention in Syracuse, New York, it erupted. By that time the movement had grown to include a host of newcomers, including Antoinette Blackwell Brown, the first female ordained minister in the United States (a Congregationalist); Ernestine L. Rose, a Russian-born freethinker who upset some of the religious members of the movement; and Susan B. Anthony, a Quaker who developed such close ties to Stanton that together they would lead the movement for the next fifty years. The controversy began with a speech by Brown, who introduced a resolution claiming that the cause of women's rights was biblical because the Bible recognized the equality of women and men. Such a resolution accepted the connection of religion and law while altering its content.[9]

By citing the Bible as a support for her cause, Brown raised the issue that had torn apart the abolition movement. The resulting debate lasted for two days, an indication of the tensions that were to come. Some factions claimed that the resolution was central to the success of women's rights, while others claimed that it conceded the most potent means by which the movement could object to the current system. Ernestine L. Rose, the radical freethinker, was adamant about rejecting any appeal to the Bible, claiming "no need to appeal to any written authority, particularly when it is so obscure and indefinite as to admit of different interpretations." Her comments enraged the conservative Christian proponents of women's rights. The debate ended only after Lucretia Mott surrendered her moderator's chair to argue that biblical discussions were generally a waste of time. "[S]elf-evident truths" had no need of "argument or outward authority," she claimed. Her own authority persuaded the convention to drop the subject, but the issue came up again just two years later in almost identical form after Rose was elected the 1854 convention president. That year, William Lloyd Garrison was in attendance. Having completely rejected his early evangelicalism, he joined Mott in shrugging off the Bible controversy and claiming, "We *know* that man and woman are equal in the sight of God." At the same time, he acknowledged the crux of the problem. Women's rights were self-evident to the members of the convention. But "with the American people the case is different," he continued. "The masses believe the Bible is directly from God; that it decrees the inequality of the sexes; and that settles the question." Only if the "incubus" of Protestant churches could be removed, he explained, would the masses join their cause. The Bible resolution failed again.[10]

Stanton joined the radicals but often had to do so from afar. Her young children prevented her from regular attendance at the early conventions, so she weighed in with letters to the delegates that pushed for dismantling the moral establishment. At the 1852 meeting, Stanton asked Susan B. Anthony to read a letter to the convention that further contributed to the controversy. Arguing that women suffered from the tyranny of men in law, Stanton called for mass civil disobedience and the rejection of men's authority in both law and religion. "Priestcraft did not end with the beginning of the reign of Protestantism," she explained. Women had long remained "the greatest dupe" in bowing to religious authority, with ministers existing "like so many leeches" on women's efforts while they still demanded the subjugation of women in all aspects of society. She had nothing good to say about the role of religion in politics, culture, and law that prevailed at the time. Religion had only set back the cause of women, Stanton concluded, making "her bondage but more certain and lasting, her degradation more helpless and complete."[11]

Stanton's letter put her finger on the main issue with more clarity and more force than perhaps many others were prepared to acknowledge. Rather than using religion to claim a larger role for women, Stanton, like Garrison, wanted a complete social transformation that entailed the rejection of any connection between religion and law. This went beyond declining to invoke the Bible for women's rights. It connected the advocacy for women's rights with the movement to destroy the moral establishment as a whole. As Stanton's thinking developed, she thought she saw the linchpin to the system of religious, legal, and political subordination of women, the removal of which would bring down the moral establishment; this linchpin was marriage. In Stanton's view, marriage took the Christian ideals of female subordination and made them legally binding. Only a complete reform of marriage law would liberate women, loosen the improper connection of religion and law, and dissolve the moral establishment.

It looked at first as though she might be swimming with the current. Beginning in 1835 several state legislatures reformed the law of coverture, allowing women to keep estates that they brought with them into marriage. The changes came not from an explicit rejection of Christianity in law but from practical necessity. The coverture arrangement worked fine in a society in which only the rich had land and they sold it infrequently. But in a society with ubiquitous land ownership and a strong real estate market, it proved to be a problem. Although a woman could not own property, she had certain claims upon land while she lived. This placed land in legal limbo and hindered a properly functioning market. At the same time, as the market economy grew and the business cycle intensified, many who might have otherwise rejected women's property rights used a paternalistic rationale to support modification of the law, fretting that in the increasingly unstable business climate the bad bets of husbands too often led their wives into penury.[12]

But allowing women to hold property destabilized the legal system. If wives could keep property, then the law might potentially treat them as individuals separate from their husbands. Yet reforms in property laws always stopped short of abolishing coverture or forthrightly acknowledging women's independence from men. Stanton thought they should go further. At the 1854 convention, with Garrison in attendance and Rose as president, Stanton gave an instantly famous (or infamous) speech on marriage that the convention resolved to reprint and send to the New York State legislature. The speech sought to throw the women's movement's support behind this further modification of laws, with the goal of completely severing religion from law to bring about women's emancipation.[13]

In advancing her claims, Stanton provided a trenchant critique of the moral establishment as a whole. Her motivation in pursuing legal reform, she explained, was the unfortunate tendency of the law to view marriage as a "half-human, half-divine institution." She noted that men such as Chancellor James Kent and Justice Joseph Story, the two dominant treatise writers of the antebellum period, had been careful to uphold the Protestant idea that marriage was a civil contract rather than a religious sacrament, but they hedged the language of the contract to ensure that it stayed within Christian bounds. Unlike other contracts, Kent claimed, marriage had "its foundation in nature" and so was essential to "moral improvement." As "one of the chief foundations of the social order," it could not be dissolved by the agreement of the parties, as most contracts could. Marital rights and duties were to be the subject of law, which was binding upon all for the perpetuation of moral norms and the maintenance of society.[14]

This tendency to mix and match religious and secular reasoning in marriage law sometimes became an explicit affirmation of the role of Christianity in maintaining social norms, an idea that Kent and Story left implicit. One such person to make this connection explicit was Edward Mansfield, whose 1845 treatise, *The Legal Rights, Liabilities, and Duties of Women*, circulated widely. Men and women each had, Mansfield explained, different parts in "the development of that grand Moral Drama, whose Acts fill up all the course of time." Mansfield directly connected marriage to Christian patriarchy. Marriage was nothing less than "an institution of God . . . begun in the garden of Eden" and "perpetuated by the laws of nature, of religion and of civil society." Although he acknowledged that marriage was a civil contract, he insisted, "In

Christian countries, and with Christian people, the revealed law of God, so far as it applies to the relations of society, is the only true foundation of human laws." To demonstrate his claim, Mansfield recited "the leading principles of Scripture" in order to show how much American civil law conformed to divine law. Among the operative principles, scripture regarded the husband and wife "as one person" and taught that "men must govern their families, and women submit to their lawful requisitions." Mansfield's treatise was quite popular.[15]

Such reasoning enraged Stanton. "Would to God you could know the burning indignation that fills woman's soul when she turns over the pages of your statute books and sees there how like feudal barons you freemen hold your women," Stanton vented in her 1854 speech. The law supported men's tendency to mix and match religious and political ideas in a way that always empowered men rather than women. Because marriage was an institution half-human and half-divine, it embodied the worst aspects of both. If marriage was purely a religious institution, Stanton claimed, then the law could not bind it. If marriage was a civil contract, then it must be dissolvable at the will of the parties. Failure to see marriage as anything other than the union of two individuals, she explained, led to "the grossest absurdities and contradictions."[16]

Stanton had a point. Any attempt to construct a coherent rationale for women's subordination to men and exclusion from public life founders on its own contradictions. Women were excluded from public life because they were subjected to men as a result of their sin in the Garden of Eden. It was their lack of moral fortitude, according to proponents of the moral establishment, that resulted in their subordination. But women were at the same time conferred the duty of perpetuating public morals through the rearing of children. So great was women's moral task, Kent explained, that a husband's adultery did not necessarily abrogate the marital contract as would the wife's. Some jurists even regarded the adultery of the husband as beneath the notice of the court since, Kent noted, "it is not evidence of such entire depravity, not equally injurious in its effects upon the morals, and good order, and happiness of domestic life" as the unfaithfulness of a wife. Women were seen as agents of moral reproduction, yet somehow they were not considered morally competent to emerge from the shadow of their husbands.[17]

3.

Over the next decade Stanton pushed the women's movement to take on the moral establishment. She was joined by Susan B. Anthony and Ernestine Rose. Their position was a bold and not entirely popular one that wore on even the radical members of the coalition. In April 1854, the same year that Stanton gave her address on marriage laws, Anthony recorded in her diary a conversation that she had had with Ernestine Rose. Rose, like Stanton, was constantly pushing the movement forward, trying to reform all of society, not just women's place in it. As Anthony and Rose discussed the many failures of those who were supposed to be their allies, Rose began to weep. Given her foreign birth and her radical religious sensibilities, her estrangement from American culture seemed complete. "I expect never to be understood while I live," Rose explained, and Anthony began to cry with her in recognition of their shared isolation.[18]

Yet they could not give up their commitment to the radical cause, trapped as they were by the legal strictures that limited their independence. Reading the writings of these women is at times a melancholy endeavor. As Lucy Stone, another young freethinker who had recently joined the women's rights cause, explained to her soon to be sister-in-law Antoinette Blackwell Brown, she could not accept the limits placed upon women. Stone pledged never to marry in order to preserve her independence. "My heart aches to love somebody," she confessed to Brown, but she could not accept "what a *mere thing*, the law, makes a married woman." After reading Edward Mansfield's legal treatise, Stone became committed to the complete separation of church and state and joined the free-religion movement, which sought to remake religion through an uncompromising dedication to the freedom of individual conscience.[19]

As the decade progressed, Stanton and others sought to keep the movement afloat despite their many responsibilities. Writing to Anthony in 1856 to report the birth of her sixth child, Stanton expressed her dismay at not hearing from Anthony enough: "Where are you Susan & what are you doing. Your silence is truly appalling. Are you dead or married?" Stanton was restless at home and chafing under the responsibilities of motherhood, which might explain her equating marriage with death. Anthony wrote back a few months later, after a visit with Stanton in Seneca Falls, asking her to draft a speech that Anthony could give to the New York Teachers' Association. Anthony understood the burden of her request, having just seen the chaos of Stanton's household, but she was convinced that Stanton had a gift for speechcraft and polemic that she herself lacked. Stanton responded with a touch of acid that she would write the speech only if Anthony would come to Seneca Falls to "hold the baby and make the puddings." "I pace up and down these two chambers of mine like a caged lioness," she sighed, "longing to bring nursing and housekeeping cares to a close."[20]

Seeing the burdens placed upon Stanton, Anthony wrote to Lucy Stone while planning the next year's convention. "Lucy, I want this Convention to strike *deeper* than any of its predecessors. It seems to me we have played on the *surface* of things quite long enough. Getting the right to hold property, to vote, to wear what dress we please, &c &c, are all good," she admitted, "but Social Freedom, after all, lies at the bottom of all—& until woman gets that, she must continue the slave of man in all other things." What the radicals in the movement wanted was public recognition of their individuality and freedom, upheld by fair law and sustained by changes in social and religious practices. Yet social freedom was exactly what the moral establishment was designed to prevent. It sought to constrain the individual by imposing religiously based moral norms. Looked at another way, Stanton was doing precisely what the proponents of the moral establishment required. She remained in the home to care for her young and to see after their moral development.[21]

This dissatisfaction with family life, and the desire to rework society and law to free women from its burdens, finally came into full expression at the Tenth Annual Woman's Rights Convention in New York City. Any observer should have seen what Stanton was planning: she had offered a peek at her maturing vision at that year's American Anti-Slavery Society meeting, also held in New York City just three days before the women's rights convention. Addressing the AASS at Garrison's invitation, Stanton explained that she saw abolition as an expression of what she called the "one idea" of individual equality that had guided all the humanitarian movements to that time. To achieve that one idea would involve a reorganization of society that was total, and she listed the many things that would have to change: "religion, philanthropy, political economy, commerce, education, and social life, on which depends the very existence of this republic, of the state, of the family, the sacredness of the lives and property of Northern freemen, the holiness of the marriage relation, and the perpetuity of the Christian religion." First and last in that list was religion, which in her view affirmed the status quo by rejecting the rights of the individual. Distinguishing between the religion that subjugated certain people to others and a purer form of individual religion, Stanton praised Garrison "as the great missionary of the gospel of Jesus" because Garrison, like Jesus, rejected corrupt religious institutions in favor of individual rights.[22]

Stanton's speech served notice on the moral establishment. Three days later, she followed up with a full-blown assault on the Christian church. Stanton used her address at the Woman's Rights Convention to expand her claim that the logical end of the women's movement should be social transformation and individual freedom. From time immemorial, Stanton suggested, the institutions of civil, political, religious, and social life all taught that the individual must be "sacrificed to the highest good of society." This was the central argument of the moral establishment. But Stanton claimed that it rested on a fundamental error. A society could not suppress the individual and still uphold the highest social good. Only when individuals possessed full freedom could the possibilities of a society be realized. In her mind the most urgent step toward that ideal was the abolition of "the man marriage." Because men had the sole prerogative of regulation over marriage, the man marriage exalted male power and authority while constraining female independence. To reject the man marriage, Stanton explained, required society to repudiate the moral responsibility of women for the family, the subordination of women to men, and the moral establishment's claim that the family was instrumental in the taming of the individual. Stanton, in short, sought to win legal freedom for women by decoupling Christian patriarchy from law and excluding family life from the control of the state.[23]

Stanton's speech provoked immediate and vigorous dissent. She had rejected the connections between religion and the state that many delegates believed in, and mounted a full assault on those religious women who sought to use the moral role of women to expand their rights. But Stanton had the allies to uphold her resolutions, which had the effect of positioning the women's movement in full opposition to the proponents of the moral establishment. As Anthony explained in the debate following Stanton's speech, "By law, public sentiment, and religion, from the time of Moses down to the present day, woman has never been thought of other than as a piece of property. . . . Therefore, in my opinion, this discussion of the marriage question is perfectly in order on this Woman's Rights platform." Stanton's opponents outside the movement greeted her resolutions as proof that women's rights claims were dangerous to the moral order. Horace Greeley, the editor of the *New York Tribune*, future presidential candidate, and an ally of the Tappan brothers, sarcastically wondered if the women's rights "platform should not be altogether replanked, so as to cover all human relations." His sarcasm was misplaced— that was exactly Stanton's goal. "Anything that is outward, all forms and ceremonies, faiths and symbols, policies and institutions, may be washed away," she explained immediately after the convention. For her dream to be realized, the world would have to be born anew.[24]

But with the ordeal of the Civil War, Stanton's dream would be delayed. Within the year, the nation would be awash in blood, and the consuming fire of war burned away more than the faiths, symbols, and institutions that Stanton had rejected. Shortly after the start of hostilities, Stanton decided to cancel the 1861 Woman's Rights Convention and to postpone any further ones. As Anthony explained in a letter to Wendell Phillips, a leader in both abolition and women's rights, "Mrs. Stanton . . . says it is impossible for her to think or speak on anything but the War." Yet they were both still optimistic about their eventual triumph. "What a glorious revolution we are in," Anthony concluded.[25]

But was it really glorious? Did the revolution portend the emancipation of women and the separation of church and state? In a word, no. As Lyman Beecher had earlier claimed, when a woman fulfilled her subordinate role she came to embody "whatsoever things are pure and lovely." Yet should she stray from this God-mandated duty, she would cause destruction on such a scale that she would be regarded as "a paragon of deformity, a demon in human form." Because Stanton's assertion of individual autonomy rejected the idea of the family as the fundamental governing unit in society, proponents of the moral establishment foresaw catastrophe. Although Stanton and others who rejected the moral establishment seemed to be at the center of the reform movement—they remained in control of the abolition movement and provided the driving force in the women's rights debates—they still came against a powerful religious machine. The Civil War promised the abolition of slavery, in Anthony's understanding, but it also threatened to remove the artificial divide between Northern and Southern proponents of the moral establishment. When that reunion occurred, moral establishmentarians could advance their common vision of confining wives to the home. Would the revolution that both Anthony and Stanton saw in the Civil War allow a woman to be an individual without marking her as a demon bent on moral destruction? Could women, in fact, be individuals? Those were the questions that were not yet answered but whose outlook seemed doubtful as the women's movement went into hibernation and the nation took up arms.[26]

PART III

RETRENCHMENT

6

MORALS, CITIZENSHIP, AND SEGREGATION

1.

The Civil War did prove to be a revolution, but not quite in the way Anthony had hoped. The physical destructiveness of the war, and its appalling level of human carnage, defied any reasoned debate or principled stand. Although the Union's win resolved the question of slavery in the abolitionists' favor, the underlying questions that slavery had provoked—about the nature of moral authority, its religious sources, and its connection to law and government—grew only more urgent. In his second inaugural address, Abraham Lincoln addressed the issue, claiming that North and South "read the same Bible, and pray to the same God; and each invokes His aid against the other." The magnitude of death and destruction suffered by both sides was enough to disprove any claim that God had favored one over the other, so Lincoln counseled a careful agnosticism. "The Almighty has His own purposes," he suggested. But Lincoln's advice to avoid theological triumphalism went unheeded.[1]

In a sense, the debate largely picked up where it had left off before the war. Northern moral establishmentarians still remained divided from Southern moral establishmentarians (though they agreed on much), and dissenters to the moral establishment criticized both. The debate did not immediately dissolve because, as the Protestant church historian Philip Schaff explained, "The negro question lies far deeper than the slave question." What he meant was that even among those who agreed that slavery was immoral, not many agreed on what to do with the freed slaves. The question that had divided the Garrisonians from the evangelicals remained unanswered: what was the place of the individual in a democracy? For Garrison, of course, as well as for Stanton, the individual was the litmus test of all legitimacy and authority. As he explained,

"Man is superior to all political compacts, all governmental arrangements, all religious institutions. As a means to an end, these may sometimes be useful, though never indispensable; but that end must always be the freedom and happiness of man, INDIVIDUAL MAN." So committed was he to the individual that he thought the antislavery stance required a position of "total separation from Church and State, and warfare upon both as the existing bulwarks of the slave system."[2]

Yet the Tappans, Birney, Beecher, and Southern evangelical theologians such as Robert Dabney disagreed. For them, authority resided in the institutions that made individuals fit for society. Slavery had been one such institution. "The hands of Providence," Philip Schaff explained, had used slavery to bring "the genial influence of Christianity" to the African. Schaff was not a Southerner but still thought slavery had served a purpose for a time. American slavery provided "a wholesome training school for the negro from the lowest state of heathenism and barbarism to some degree of Christian civilization." With the passing of slavery, the Southern moral order needed a complete restructuring, but not, according to evangelicals, along Garrisonian lines.[3]

Northern establishmentarians thought instead that the South required a reworked establishment, one that did not include slavery but also did not install Garrisonian individualism as the cornerstone of American democracy. When slaves were set free, they entered into a new relationship with the body politic. But Northern establishmentarians worried that perhaps black Christianity, born within a slave structure that relied on exterior compulsion, would not provide the internal moral guidance to enable freed people's success. They wondered if former slaves could be counted upon not to become rogues and thought that former slaves required help to ensure industrious and sober behavior. This is where the American Missionary Association (AMA), the organization begun by Lewis Tappan, stepped in. In keeping with the long-standing belief in the role of Christian institutions in taming the individual, the AMA joined other freedmen's aid societies sponsored by Christian churches to work in close cooperation with the U.S. government to bring about a new moral establishment in the South. Their core belief, common among moral establishmentarians everywhere, was that these groups provided individuals with the necessary moral temperament through educational retraining to make them good and productive citizens.

Yet Northern establishmentarians had a more particular understanding of slaves' needs that was in keeping with what had become, by the time of the Civil War, the dominant Northern ideology. Many writers have observed that the industrial transformation in the North produced a bourgeois class whose dominance supposedly proved the superiority of their system of values. With the expansion of the market, which accelerated throughout the Civil War, the merchant sector, inhabited by people such as the Tappans, became the dominant class in the North. These were people who believed that Protestant Christianity was integral to the American way of life, because Christianity produced the virtues of discipline, moral sobriety, self-control, and seriousness of purpose necessary for economic success. Those who prospered had reaped the just reward for their inner virtue. The poor were poor because of their own shiftlessness, laziness, and self-indulgence. This Christian American civilization, according to proponents, was the highest stage of societal development.[4]

But black Christianity was something else entirely. Slave religion was, to many in the North, the quintessential expression of former slaves' stunted racial development, making them unfit for work in a free-labor system. The benevolent agencies of the North had already devised strategies to prepare freed slaves for the new economic system of the South and to make them compatible with Christian civilization. Central to the plan was that black Christianity needed to give way to the bourgeois Christianity of the North. This was the freed slaves' first step toward acquiring the virtues necessary for economic success.[5]

The key, according to Northern establishment proponents, would be to remake the South to accord to God's law. It was the "Providence of God" that had made the war a success, as Samuel P. Chase, the radical Republican and chief justice of the U.S. Supreme Court, explained to George Whipple, who was soon to head the American Missionary Association. The goal was to pursue "the work of restoration and renovation" in the South in accordance with moral virtue. "Let it be prosecuted with wise patriotism, sincere good will, and impartial justice," Chase suggested, "and who will dare doubt that God will crown this work also with success?" Others went further. "The law of God must pervade the law of the land," explained Aaron Cragin, a Republican representative from New Hampshire. "The foundations of our Republic are to be laid anew."[6]

2.

Southern establishmentarians agreed with their Northern brethren on the need for guidance and control of their former slaves but thought that they were the ones who should be doing the guiding. Freed slaves, of course, sought control of their own lives, which had both Northern and Southern establishmentarians scrambling in response. Immediately following the war, freed slaves left their white-controlled churches en masse, rejecting the spiritual and political oversight of their former masters. They did so because the churches still intended to treat them like slaves. The Alabama Baptist Convention of 1865, for example, confidently proclaimed, "[T]he changed political status of our late slaves does not necessitate any change in their relation to our churches." In churches throughout the South, freedmen were expected to sit, as before, in a segregated area in the back. White church leaders expected the freed slaves to abide by the discipline of white clergy and their former white masters. They allowed black ministers to serve only under strict rules, in some cases requiring them to send white representatives to denominational gatherings in their place. Lucius H. Holsey, an early bishop in the Colored Methodist Episcopal (CME) Church, which broke away from the Southern Methodist denomination in 1866, elaborated on the problem. Although "the war had changed the ancient relation of master and servant," he explained, masters still carried "all the notions, feelings, and elements" of social authority that they had held in the past. In response to white attempts to maintain control, black ministers throughout the South created their own denominations or, more frequently, led their people into autonomous Baptist congregations where the minister and leaders had maximum control over church life. Black churches became the center of black community life, performing civic, cultural, and intellectual, in addition to religious, functions.[7]

This autonomy frightened both Northern and Southern establishmentarians, but they had different responses to the situation. Like Northern moral establishmentarians, Southern church leaders looked to institutions, churches chief among them, to mediate between the individual and the state. But they believed blacks required the continued oversight of their former masters, who knew them and had worked with them under slavery. Because African American Christianity had combined African and Anglo forms of worship—featuring call and response, syncopated musical rhythms, and distinctive ritual practices—many Southerners continued to view black Christianity as but a thin veneer of civilization overlaying a core of barbarism. Proper moral instruction would require vigilance to ensure that former slaves did not backslide. As Thomas R. R. Cobb, a draftsman of the Confederate Constitution and an officer in the Confederate army, had warned, "[R]emove the restraining and controlling power of the master, and the negro becomes, at once, the slave of his lust, and the victim of his indolence, relapsing, with wonderful rapidity, into his pristine barbarism." Absent the restraint of slavery, so the thinking went, blacks would lapse into the heathen savagery that supposedly marked their race.[8]

Partially to avert this impending disaster—and partially to retain economic dominance—Southern states passed the infamous black codes at the war's end. The codes sought to replace slavery with another system of external restraint. Mississippi's black code, which was among the harshest in the South, included punishment for "all rogues and vagabonds, idle and dissipated persons, beggars, jugglers, or persons practicing unlawful games or plays, runaways, common drunkards, common night-walkers, pilferers, lewd, wanton, or lascivious persons, in speech or behavior, common railers and brawlers, persons who neglect their calling or employment, misspend what they earn, or do not provide for the support of themselves or their families, or dependents, and all other idle and disorderly persons, including all who neglect all lawful business, habitually misspend their time by frequenting houses of ill-fame, gaming-houses, or tippling shops." These were qualities and activities that many white Christians associated with freed slaves. To protect the community and to maintain moral standards, such persons would "be deemed and considered vagrants under the provisions of this act," and so would "be fined not exceeding one hundred dollars, with all accruing costs, and be imprisoned at the discretion of the court, not exceeding ten days."[9]

The U.S. Congress did not look favorably on the black codes of the South and invalidated them with the Civil Rights Act of 1866. It followed quickly with the Fourteenth Amendment, subsequently ratified by the states, which shifted power from the states to the federal government. The amendment's key section stated: "No State shall make or enforce any law which shall abridge the privileges or immunities of citizens of the United States; nor shall any State deprive any person of life, liberty, or property, without due process of law; nor deny to any person within its jurisdiction the equal protection of the laws." These three clauses—the privileges or immunities clause (clause 1), the due process clause (clause 2), and the equal protection clause (clause 3)—were not self-explanatory. It would take time for the courts to work out their meanings and implications. But the immediate effect of these two acts of Congress was to thwart Southern whites' attempt to reinstitute slavery under another name.[10]

While Northerners were remaking Southern institutions and holding back Southern white power, they also moved to reconstruct the Southern moral establishment by remaking individual freed slaves. To be sure, Northern establishment proponents were attempting to meet practical needs. Emancipated slaves confronted a hostile world and lived precariously. They lacked money, land, and, in many cases, the goodwill of their former white masters. Mere survival required ingenuity. To meet their needs, a philanthropic battalion of agents from the benevolent societies of the North poured into the South with the advancing army. Their goal was to provide material aid to the freed slaves and to contribute to a Christian reconstruction of the South. At the head of the group was the American Missionary Association, now headed by George Whipple after Tappan's resignation in 1866. By directing post–Civil War Northern philanthropy, the AMA wielded unparalleled influence. In the twenty-five years after the Civil War, the AMA began several institutions of higher education and numerous schools to train teachers throughout the South. Of the estimated fifteen thousand black teachers in the South by 1888, nearly half had been trained in AMA schools. The AMA's commanding position stemmed from its wealth. Although it drew from all parts of Northern Protestantism, as time went on its funding came increasingly from wealthy Congregationalists and Unitarians. Between 1861 and 1889, the AMA's operating budget totaled almost $7 million. That amount was nearly as large as that of all other benevolent societies combined and constituted nearly one-third of all Northern funding for Southern relief over the period. This commanding financial position made the AMA a dominant policy player before Jim Crow.[11]

But the benevolence of the AMA and other missionary societies came with strings. The AMA was committed to inculcating civilization in what it considered the backward races of the South. In its 1875 publication, *The Nation Still in Danger, or, Ten Years after the War*, AMA representatives warned, "[T]he education and morality of the Negro is the only safety for the South and the Nation." The AMA's secretary, the Reverend Michael E. Strieby, elaborated the logic: "The blacks are religious," he acknowledged, but because there was "such ignorance among priests and people . . . with the diabolical training of slavery almost compelling theft, falsehood, and unchastity," he thought that much slave piety was "emotional and immoral." Black religion, as Strieby saw it, could not offer the guidance necessary to preserve moral order in the postwar South. So, the AMA would remake it.[12]

The AMA's mission relied upon a tight connection with the U.S. government. In July 1864 a convention of benevolent associations that included the AMA had met in Indianapolis to discuss how best to cooperate on the religious reconstruction of the South. It declared that the Civil War promised a grand opportunity for Christian benevolence, and expressed disappointment that no bureau had yet been created for oversight of the freed slaves. To that end, the convention spent two days crafting a petition to President Lincoln. Several such petitions finally yielded a bill creating a Bureau of Refugees, Freedmen and Abandoned Lands, popularly known as the Freedmen's Bureau. The bureau assumed "control of all subjects relating to refugees and freedmen from rebel states." The purpose, the bill explained, was to offer "supervision and care" to all loyal freedmen in order to "enable them as speedily as practicable to become self-supporting citizens of the United States." Most significantly, the bill required that the commissioner of the bureau "at all times coöperate with private benevolent associations of citizens in aid of freedmen, and with agents and teachers duly accredited and appointed by them." Because the AMA dominated the field in providing educational services to the freed slaves, the Freedmen's Bureau worked with it as something like an equal partner.[13]

The eventual choice of Oliver Otis Howard to lead the Freedmen's Bureau further reinforced the general affinity between the two organizations. A Union general and devout evangelical who had found Christianity at an 1857 church meeting in Florida, Howard was called the "Christian General" as a term of endearment. Though he denied that he favored the AMA, Howard used his position to coordinate the two organizations. In part, cooperation was natural because both organizations had similar views on the supposed black degradation and moral laxity. Immediately after his appointment, Howard issued his first policy instructions to bureau agents. Presuming the laziness and immorality of former slaves, he wanted it made clear that freedmen should not expect the government to support them "in idleness." Four days later, Howard extended his instruction. He warned that in addition to removing the purported reluctance of former masters to employ their former slaves, agents needed to correct what he later described as the "false impressions sometimes entertained by the freedmen that they can live without labor." Such an assumption was the result of the "singular false pride" that, in his estimation, allowed freedmen to live off contributions rather than work. He reminded his agents that rather than competing with the benevolent agencies already at work in the South, the goal was "to systematize and facilitate them" in their attention to what he characterized as the freedmen's "educational and moral condition." Howard's outlook shaped the organization, and his views were reproduced on the ground. In 1870, for example, a white superintendent of Louisiana schools reported that many black students were religious but not particularly Christian. In the black community "the most heathenish vagaries and superstitions" existed alongside "the grossest immoralities," he explained. Because "their religion takes on gross forms and is not always followed by the virtue of morality," the superintendent continued, religious retraining should be a fundamental task for schools.[14]

The general ideological affinity between the two organizations soon blossomed into a tight administrative cooperation that began at the top. In 1865 the bureau's superintendent of education, John W. Alvord, introduced Howard to George Whipple, who was about to become the AMA's executive. Whipple was concerned that the AMA would be frozen out of assistance from the Freedmen's Bureau. He need not have worried. Alvord himself was an evangelical abolitionist with long-standing ties to Whipple. The AMA had considered employing Alvord as their corresponding secretary the previous year. Within a few months of their meeting, Howard and Whipple had become good friends. In 1866, after Whipple sent Howard a letter explaining how the bureau could best assist benevolent societies, Howard created policies on transportation, rations, and the rental of land and equipment that almost mirrored Whipple's suggestions. This cooperation extended to personnel as well: each fired subordinates at the other's request. In addition, the AMA commissioned many Freedmen's Bureau agents as AMA missionaries. This created an elaborate system of dual appointments that blurred the boundaries between the two organizations and greatly aided the AMA's attempts to reconstruct African American Christians.[15]

Nowhere was this tight cooperation more important than in the creation of a freedmen's industrial school, Hampton Institute, started by another Christian general, Samuel C. Armstrong. Hampton was typical of the institutions for black educational retraining that the AMA began throughout the South. Its most famous graduate was the black leader Booker T. Washington, who would adopt many of Armstrong's ideas and become the chief black proponent of Armstrong's (and the AMA's) vision of the new Southern moral establishment. Armstrong had grown up in Hawaii with missionary parents. It was there that his educational philosophy first emerged. He returned to the mainland to attend Williams College, where he came under the influence of its president, Mark Hopkins, a Congregationalist who would become a leading member of the Evangelical Alliance, another organization formed in 1847 to advance evangelical political ideas in the United States and abroad. After attending Williams, Armstrong commanded a black regiment from Maryland during the Civil War before moving into the Freedmen's Bureau in 1866 as the assistant supercommissioner for the ninth district of Virginia. Almost as soon as he assumed this new position, he drew upon his experience as a missionary and his training at Williams to begin laying the foundation for what he called an industrial school. His first step was to publish an appeal in early 1866 in the AMA's magazine, *American Missionary*, explaining his philosophy of industrial schools and urging their creation to uplift freed slaves in the South. Later that year, Armstrong met with Northern philanthropists and businessmen to further explain the idea of industrial schooling. Because George Whipple, the head of the AMA, was slow to warm to the idea of industrial schooling, Armstrong enlisted Mark Hopkins, the future president James Garfield (whom he knew from his days at Williams), and Edward P. Smith, the AMA secretary and liaison to the Freedmen's Bureau, in lobbying Whipple. By July 1867 Armstrong had secured $44,000 from various Christian businessmen and benefactors for the plan. With a site chosen, money in hand, and the backing of other leaders, Whipple conceded to the plan already in motion.[16]

Armstrong's industrial education was a near-perfect expression of the racial theories and bourgeois values that dominated U.S. policy through the AMA and the Freedmen's Bureau. The schools also revealed the moral establishmentarian ambitions of both organizations. According to Armstrong, bondage had weakened blacks' character, particularly their desire to work. This only compounded the natural handicap of "weak tropical races," in which, he said, "idleness, like ignorance, breeds vice." To combat this, Armstrong lifted his plan of industrial schooling directly from his father's missionary practices in the Hawaiian Islands, arguing that freed slaves and island natives both possessed "not mere ignorance, but deficiency of character." According to Armstrong, slavery had exacerbated African Americans' racial flaws, bequeathing to them a host of unvirtuous habits that crippled them after slavery. Their main problem was not, he claimed, a lack of skill or money. It was instead "one of morals, industry, [and] self-restraint." Gesturing to the connection among religion, moral competency, and the capacity for self-government, Armstrong explained that African Americans did not possess true morality. "[T]hey do not possess its conditions," Armstrong elaborated, "which require self-control rather than pure devotional life."[17]

To combat these problems Armstrong sought to create a school that taught freed slaves the skills necessary for life in the New South and, perhaps most importantly, inculcated them with the character that he thought had been lost or damaged by their time under slavery—if they had ever had it. The curriculum omitted all study of the classics and focused instead on bookkeeping, agriculture, the mechanical arts, and home economics. He required students to work, paying for half of their room and board in cash and half in labor. The trustees found benefactors to pay for student tuition, $70 per student in 1873–74. Although on occasion Armstrong put forward the provision of work as a practical necessity so that poor black girls and boys could attend (though many were actually adults), its economic function was secondary to its educational purpose. Admitting that "such an education must be in the outset expensive," Armstrong dismissed economic concerns because the goal of industrial schooling was not economic self-sufficiency. Instead, he saw manual labor as central to the educational process itself. "Character is the best outcome of the labor system," he explained. "That makes it worth its cost many times over. It is not cheap, but it pays." It conferred upon the laborer diligence, honesty, and virtue, thereby offering reformers the perfect tool to correct the ostensibly deleterious training blacks had received under the slave system. And such labor was not merely for men. Armstrong was a strong believer in the industrial coeducation of men and women, explaining, "[I]f a race is to be saved it is by creating the unit of Christian civilization, the family." Retraining men and women required teaching them bourgeois norms so that freed slaves could enter Christian civilization.[18]

3.

The issues were complicated, but agreement existed across a wide number of groups. Southern partisans, the Freedmen's Bureau, and the Northern freedmen's aid societies (led by the AMA) were united in their worry about the supposed moral degeneracy of freed slaves. They may have disagreed about its causes, but they all sought to correct it by creating a new moral regime built on religious foundations.

Yet this fundamental agreement was obscured by violence, as the South did not submit without resistance to Northern efforts at reconstruction. Following the invalidation of the black codes, Southern religious partisans turned to vigilante terrorism, committed primarily by the Ku Klux Klan (KKK). White churches, now segregated after the black exodus into autonomous African American congregations, became platforms for KKK organizing. Theology also inflected the Klan's ideology. In South Carolina, to become a Klan member one swore upon "the Holy Evangelists of Almighty God." Southern ministers became the intellectual arm of Klan leadership. Meanwhile, black churches and schools—institutions that represented autonomy—became particular targets.[19]

As the reign of terror progressed, Northern religious leaders began calling for forgiveness of the white South. Among the most surprising of those voices was that of Henry Ward Beecher, the son of Lyman Beecher and, in the last half of the nineteenth century, the most popular preacher in the North. Henry Beecher, in contrast to his father, was a powerful voice for abolition. In 1863, the year of his father's death, he conducted a speaking tour throughout England to rally support for the Union cause. He gained notoriety (and infamy, in the South) for holding reverse slave auctions—in which people could buy freedom for slaves—from the pulpit of his church. Toward the end of the Civil War,

Abraham Lincoln tapped Beecher to deliver the major address when the U.S. flag was raised again over Fort Sumter, where the war had begun. But Beecher had always been a controversial figure who seemed not to fit into an organized movement. He adopted the religiously motivated political and cultural reform that his father had pioneered, although his theology was never as strict as Lyman's. Henry Beecher shared the view of African American moral degradation so prominent in the AMA and the Freedmen's Bureau. In 1866, for example, he warned the New England Freedmen's Aid Society that the "large mass of ignorance" found among the freed slaves represented a threat to free government without an attempt "to elevate the freedmen morally and intellectually." When he published his novel *Norwood* in 1868, its only black character, Pete Sawmill, was clumsy, lazy, and lacking in moral fortitude. The book was a huge success, suggesting that the message resonated in the North. "The author [Beecher] had certain ideas of character and morals to work out," the reviewer for the *New York Times* noted. Beecher elaborated those ideas primarily through the main (white) character, but the reviewer still saw in Sawmill an important characterological function. "Unlike most Negroes, as we find them in New-England novels, he is a genuine 'nigger,' not a saint in charcoal, nor a paragon of virtue," the reviewer explained. "It is really pleasant to meet a darkey in a New-England novel who isn't a living reproach to all white men."[20]

The reviewer was almost certainly contrasting Beecher with his sister, Harriet Beecher Stowe, whose depiction of Uncle Tom in *Uncle Tom's Cabin* was widely credited with mobilizing sentiment against slavery prior to the Civil War. In contrast to Stowe's work, Beecher's novel, in the reviewer's opinion, was an example of "[t]he largeness of Mr. Beecher's mind, and his superiority over sectional prejudice." By 1868, when Beecher's novel was published, his sister Harriet had joined her brother in his call for national harmony. Defending her brother from criticism, she claimed that his "instinct to defend the weaker side"—by which she meant the white South rather than the freed slaves—was essentially Christian because it required a "strong impulse to *forgive*." Stowe and Beecher's posture of forgiveness was mirrored across the major denominations, which had split into Southern and Northern branches preceding the Civil War. Although most denominations were unable to bridge their sectional differences prior to the twentieth century, Northern denominational leaders made great efforts to reconcile with the white South, showing a willingness to condone segregated ecclesiastical structures and a qualified notion of rights for African Americans.[21]

This move toward religious rapprochement also coincided with another phase of rapid Christian expansion, the Third Great Awakening, which would catapult church members to a simple majority in 1906. This growth was made possible by the intersectional cooperation. To that end, a number of new evangelists, including most prominently Dwight L. Moody, began moving throughout the nation to spread the evangelical Christian message, bringing together Northern and Southern whites. To smooth the connection, Moody offered softened and nonpolitical accounts of the Civil War, used Southern white ministers in his Northern crusades, and conducted segregated revival meetings.[22]

Meanwhile, dissenters to the moral establishment grew more active. Led now by Elizabeth Cady Stanton since Garrison had retired after the Civil War, the emancipation of slaves had caused Stanton to consider more seriously the fundamental affinity between freed slaves and women. Pursuing a secular path, Stanton began testing a new argument that linked women's rights and black rights in a joint call for universal suffrage. When the war ended, Stanton and Susan B. Anthony called the Eleventh Woman's Rights Convention to put their new plan into action. The convention declared their cause and the cause of the freed slaves as one, and broadened their appeal from women's rights to human rights. Resolving to "bury the woman in the citizen," the convention dissolved their group into a new organization, the American Equal Rights Association (AERA), dedicated to all human rights. The AERA would work for an expanded notion of citizenship in resistance to both the Southern and Northern moral establishment, bringing every individual into the body politic.[23]

But given the prominence of moral establishmentarians in Reconstruction and the renewed efforts of sectional reconciliation, Stanton's early hope that the Civil War might bring both freed slaves and women into a new relationship with the body politic began to wither. Many in the moral establishment did not support the logic of equal rights because it downplayed differences between men and women and was predicated on the notion that society was nothing more than a collection of individuals. Their aversion to individual rights became a problem for the AERA's central post-emancipation project of universal suffrage. Because enough establishment supporters favored an amendment to enfranchise freed black men, a narrowly crafted amendment had enough support to pass. But a universal-suffrage amendment ran headlong into the moral establishment's suspicion of individual rights, which made its prospects uncertain. Seeing that things were not going in a good direction, in 1867 Stanton made a strategic and unfortunate alliance with the anti-Negro, pro–women's rights Democrat George Francis Train in an attempt to break the partisan gridlock on the amendment. Others within the association, led by Wendell Phillips, Lucy Stone, and Henry Blackwell, decided that it was better to get a partial victory of black male suffrage than to risk not gaining any victory at all, though they remained in support of the equal rights amendment in principle. When the suffrage amendment emerged from Congress, it guaranteed suffrage to citizens over the age of twenty-one but implicitly denied the vote to women. Phillips, Stone, and Blackwell lined up in support even though the amendment fell far short of their goal, and the amendment, passed in 1870, was subsequently ratified by the states and became the Fifteenth Amendment to the U.S. Constitution.[24]

The ensuing fallout fractured dissenters at the moment that moral establishmentarians, North and South, were coming together. Already suspicious of concessions to the moral establishment, Stanton and Anthony became convinced that only women could be trusted to work for their enfranchisement. To effect a properly radical effort, they left the AERA in 1869 to form the National Woman Suffrage Association (NWSA), which initially allowed only women to preside as officers. But Stanton also turned on her erstwhile black allies. Embittered by what she considered their betrayal, she began putting out racist propaganda against the Fifteenth Amendment. Backing away from Stanton's NWSA, that same year Lucy Stone and Henry Blackwell formed a rival, ultimately more conservative group, the American Woman Suffrage Association (AWSA).[25]

The breakup of a coherent dissent, just as establishmentarians gained strength, proved to be momentous. It left dissenters without a unified organization at the moment that the consensus among moral establishmentarians, both North and South, finally began to resurface.

That emergent consensus became most apparent in the U.S. Supreme Court, which aligned with public opinion to eviscerate the expansive notion of equality and of individual rights that the Fourteenth Amendment seemed to promise. At issue were the rights and location of citizenship. Prior to the war, it was the states that granted citizenship, but that function was suddenly and radically nationalized by the Fourteenth Amendment. This constitutional revolution left many questions unanswered. Did national citizenship erase the notion of state citizenship? How would national citizenship alter or reconstitute the system of federalism established by the Constitution? In 1873 the U.S. Supreme Court finally began to sort out the issues. In a group of cases collectively known as the *Slaughterhouse Cases*, a five-person majority began to limit the power of the Fourteenth Amendment. The actual ruling in the case was less relevant than the reasoning it employed. The Court rejected an expansive reading of the privileges or immunities clause, which promised that states could not infringe on the privileges and immunities of U.S. citizens. Citing the police power of the states, upon which "the security of social order" depended, the majority claimed that an individual maintained a dual citizenship in both the state-level and the national-level polity. The Court then defined "the privileges or immunities of citizens of the United States" so narrowly as to be nonexistent, leaving great latitude for the states to use their police power to restrict civil liberties, effectively allowing a new Southern order to take shape that did not permit blacks civil rights.[26]

The decision also had significant implications for the shape of white Christianity within this new Southern establishment. The majority claimed that police power was "and must be from its very nature, incapable of a very exact definition or limitation," which seemed to hold that almost any right could be abrogated for the public good. Even the minority opinion seemed to endorse this expansive view of police power, noting, "That power undoubtedly extends to all regulations affecting the health, good order, morals, peace, and safety of society . . . and in almost numberless ways." Because the majority of the Court declined to specify the limits of police power, moral establishmentarians could continue to use it to justify the enforcement of a religiously derived morality in the maintenance of what they considered a Christian social order that subjugated the supposedly immoral former slaves.[27]

All of this suggested the eventual end. The combined effect of the white South's campaign of violence, the expansion of evangelicalism, the widespread agreement on the supposed moral degeneracy of freed people, the decision of the Court in the *Slaughterhouse Cases*, and the fracturing of dissent all moved toward the rejection of individual rights that Stanton and her allies had sought. Their defeat looked almost total when Reconstruction ended in 1877 and the tentative commitment of Northern moral establishmentarians to African American rights—never secure because of the widespread belief in black moral degeneracy—ended with it.

4.

It was in this context that a new black leader, Booker T. Washington, made his debut. Washington became a symbol of the emerging agreement between moral establishmentarians of North and South. He was born a slave but came of age during the AMA's reign in the South, and he received his education at Hampton, where he internalized the values of the civilizing mission. Samuel Armstrong was so pleased with him that in 1881, after the Alabama legislature created a school, called the Tuskegee Institute, to train African

Americans, he recommended Washington for the new position of principal. But when Washington arrived in Alabama, his school existed only in theory, with no buildings, no books, and no teachers. Because the legislature had already set the state budget before Tuskegee was created, it was a full year before he had funding. He managed to scrape together enough money to buy land, build a school, and hire teachers, but his first decade at Tuskegee was difficult, with more students always arriving, not enough space to put them in, and never enough money. Because soliciting funds to keep the school afloat was an almost overwhelming task, Washington quickly settled into a fundraising role, spending up to six months of the year in the North passing the hat in churches and other venues.[28]

Washington read the signs. He was a singularly shrewd leader who appealed to the moral establishment's suspicions in his fundraising efforts. By far, most of Washington's money came from the abolitionist contingent of New England and friends of the American Missionary Association who had previously supported the Hampton Institute. Seizing on the Northern fear of black degradation, he promised his audiences that he would instruct Southern blacks in the moral, religious, and industrial standards that they—and he— held. Washington put particular emphasis on the issue of black ministers, stressing that because African American clergy were at the center of black religious life (with its ostensibly dubious character), they were among the most important subjects for the civilizing mission. Before a meeting of the National Education Association in 1884, for example, Washington disparaged the "so-called leaders" of African Americans, who he described as being "as a rule ignorant, immoral preachers or selfish politicians." Faced with such poor leadership, Washington decried that the average black man had "no standard by which to shape his character." The poor quality of black leaders, Washington went on, was evident on one of his recent visits to a black church near Tuskegee that had two hundred members and nineteen preachers. Noting that the number of preachers was "legion," he alluded to the biblical story of a man haunted by demons whose collective name was "Legion," at once deferring to his audience's religious sensibilities and impugning those of the African American ministers.[29]

He also elaborated on Armstrong's belief connecting character to work, portraying the movement of so many black men into the ministry as a calculated attempt to get out of manual labor, thereby causing them to miss out on its virtue-inducing properties. At a speech before the Women's New England Club in 1890, after repeating the story of the church with nineteen preachers, he embellished it with a parable of a man who might as well have been a minstrel figure. Washington claimed that the work ethic of most black preachers could be summed up by a man in a cotton field at the end of a hot July day who stopped, looked up into heaven, and cried, in Washington's rendering, "Lord, de work is so hard, de cotton is so grassy, and de Sun am so hot, dat I believe dis darkey am called to preach." His use of the vernacular was likewise calculated—the spelling is from a text that he himself corrected—stressing both his understanding of and separation from the poor black ministers he was trying to civilize.[30]

Washington never limited himself to criticizing ministers but argued that they encouraged and relied upon moral degradation among their parishioners. In doing so, he endorsed the moral-establishment ambitions of the AMA. Reasoning backward, if a person failed to demonstrate proper (bourgeois) character, which required discipline, emotional equilibrium, and conscious, rational control, that person had a defective religion. Washington never tired of pointing out that black Christianity fell very short of the bourgeois standard and frequently derided what he saw as the emotionalism of black Christianity as evidence that many African Americans were not authentically Christian. In his 1890 speech before the Women's New England Club, for example, he conceded that many ministers were religious but argued that their religious sensibility reveled "largely in emotion." "[I]n real practical Christianity," he claimed, they were wanting. What was true of ministers was equally true of members. Washington warned that although the great majority of black people in the South belonged to a church, "a large proportion of these people" were "Christian heathen," who required "as much missionary's effort as the heathen of foreign fields." With that, he quickly turned to a plea for money to educate the black people of the South.[31]

His rhetorical assault on black ministers and their parishioners got the attention of many in the AMA. In 1890 Lyman Abbott, a prominent liberal minister, asked Washington to contribute an article on African American clergy to Abbott's journal, the *Christian Union*. Abbott was a central figure in Northeastern philanthropic circles, and his publication, formerly edited by Henry Ward Beecher, was a leading organ for northeastern abolitionist sentiment. By publishing his attack in the *Christian Union*, Washington could present his arsenal of effective critiques before a national audience because supporters of the AMA mission—who were readers of the *Christian Union*—had spread throughout the South as teachers and administrators in AMA schools. He jumped at the chance, again repeating the story of the church with many ministers and the black man who received the call on a hot day in July. He also expanded his critique, layering statistics with anecdotal observations that resulted in large-scale generalizations, such as his claim that "three-fourths of the Baptist ministers and two-thirds of the Methodists are unfit, either mentally or morally, or both, to preach the Gospel to any one or to attempt to lead any one." He particularly highlighted what he saw as the self-serving nature of many black ministers. Although "[n]ot one in twenty" ministers had any standing as businesspeople in their communities, Washington snidely claimed that much of black religious service seemed "to revolve itself into an effort to get money." While he attacked ministers for their ignorance and moral vice, he repeated his claim that black religious ritual, cultivated and supported by black ministers, was in fact an expression of their parishioners' backwardness and moral degradation. Because the standard for good preaching was the extent to which a preacher was "able to set the people in all parts of the congregation to groaning, uttering wild screams, and jumping, finally going into a trance," he argued, African American religion pandered to the lowest impulses of the congregation and proved that many black parishioners were "as ignorant of true Christianity . . . as any people in Africa or Japan."[32]

Washington's solution was in keeping with the goals of the moral establishment. He looked to educational institutions to reform black religion. In the article, Washington advocated the creation of a theological school that would reform black ministers, who could then lead the effort to retool black churches and, in turn, retrain individual members. After noting that only a small proportion of black ministers had received theological education of any kind, he suggested that a school be established "at some central point in the South, on a thoroughly Christian but *strictly* undenominational basis, with a one or two years' course covering such branches as would fit a student to get a comprehensive idea of the Bible, to teach him how to prepare a sermon, how to read a hymn, how to study, and, most important, how to reach and help the people outside of the pulpit in an unselfish Christian way." The obvious place for a new Bible school was at Tuskegee. He even went so far as to suggest that $1,500 or $2,500 would be enough to pay for teachers and to operate the school, though where the facilities, books, and other teaching materials were to come from, he left to the readers' imagination. Within two years he had the money for both his Bible school and a building to house it. Washington's supreme gift in fundraising was an ability to tell Northern white audiences what they wanted to hear. His appeal before white groups North and South relied upon their shared view of black moral degeneracy and black religious heathenism, which fed his fundraising prowess and raised his profile as a channel of philanthropic largesse to combat black moral degradation.[33]

While Washington consolidated his position with the moral establishment, the courts continued to limit black rights. In 1883 in *Pace v. Alabama*, the U.S. Supreme Court upheld the conviction of a black man named Tony Pace who was arrested for living with a white woman. He had been convicted of living in a state of adultery or fornication and sentenced to two years in the state penitentiary. The couple was prohibited from marrying by Alabama's anti-miscegenation statute but was also prohibited from living together outside of marriage by its statute prohibiting fornication. In his initial appeal, the Alabama Supreme Court upheld the conviction, claiming that the laws were not in violation of the Fourteenth Amendment. The court justified the law, explaining, "The evil tendency of the crime of living in adultery or fornication is greater when it is committed between persons of the two races, than between persons of the same race. Its result may be the amalgamation of the two races, producing a mongrel population and a degraded civilization, the prevention of which is dictated by a sound public policy affecting the highest interests of society and government." The putative moral incapacity of African Americans threatened to pollute the white gene pool and bring down Southern Christian civilization. The U.S. Supreme Court upheld the ruling, finding that the law did not violate the Fourteenth Amendment's equal-protection clause, though the states could not set different penalties for white and black infringement of the law. The Court's ruling endorsed the proliferation of anti-miscegenation legislation that spread throughout the nation but became an especially important part of the new Southern moral establishment.[34]

That same year, the High Court decided a collection of five cases known as the *Civil Rights Cases*, which were brought by African Americans against private organizations or individuals for discriminating against them in public spaces. The plaintiffs invoked the Civil Rights Act of 1875, which outlawed racial discrimination at inns, in transportation services, and in places of public amusement. The eight-person majority ruled that Congress did not have the power, based upon the Fourteenth Amendment, to regulate the actions of private individuals or organizations. Its power was limited to regulating state-governmental action—an understanding that became known as the state-action doctrine. The Court's ruling had the effect of differentiating between political and social equality, so that political equality could be guaranteed while social inequality, arising out of the presumption of different social capacities in the different races, could not. Yet the separation of political and social equality also reduced the meaning of political equality to an empty shell because of the widespread assumption that blacks were inferior and dangerous to the body politic. That decision opened the way for racial segregation throughout the United States, and especially the South.[35]

The general trend was clear. Southern states began erecting what would become the legal apparatus of the Jim Crow South, with courts signing off on each provision along the way. This new moral establishment would rely upon segregation and the denial of black political and social rights. By limiting African Americans' rights, the thinking went, whites could limit the damage done by black immorality. It was a movement that Booker T. Washington seemed to endorse. In 1895 he gave a speech at the Atlanta Cotton States and International Exposition that was widely reported in the press and sealed his stature as the preeminent spokesman for black people in the United States. Later dubbed the "Atlanta Compromise" by his rival, W. E. B. Du Bois, the speech seemed to offer an exchange of black political and social rights for economic advancement. Washington made the speech against the backdrop of the Southern codification of segregation enforced by law and lynching throughout the South. Urging black Southerners, "Cast down your bucket where you are," he warned that the "greatest danger" in the leap out of slavery was that black laborers might forget that blacks would "prosper in proportion" as they learned "to dignify and glorify common labour, and put brains and skills into the common occupations of life." To his Southern white listeners, Washington urged beneficence and tolerance, while assuaging their concern over social mixing. He explained that black Southerners stood ready to braid "industrial, commercial, civil, and religious life" with that of whites in a way that would "make the interests of both races one." This interlacing of civil and religious life was exactly what his Northern moral-establishment supporters had sought in their attempt to reform black religious life. He also seemed to accept segregation and political disfranchisement. "In all things that are purely social we can be as separate as the fingers," he explained, "yet one as the hand in all things essential to mutual progress."[36]

Given this general trend, the full-scale acceptance of Jim Crow was unsurprising, even at the time. In 1896, in the now infamous case of *Plessy v. Ferguson*, the court ruled that state-mandated segregation did not violate the Fourteenth Amendment. Drawing upon its prior distinction between political and social equality, the Court conceded that the purpose of the amendment was to ensure equality before the law. "[B]ut, in the nature of things it could not have been intended to abolish distinctions based upon color, or to enforce social, as distinguished from political equality, or a commingling of the two races upon terms unsatisfactory to either," the Court explained. Laws requiring racial segregation, in the reasoning of the Court, had been "generally, if not universally, recognized as within the competency of the state legislatures in the exercise of their police power." The same was true of anti-miscegenation laws. The case turned on what the opinion called "the question of reasonableness." The Court held that it was completely reasonable that the state was "at liberty to act with reference to the established usages, customs and traditions of the people, and with a view to the promotion of their comfort and the preservation of public peace and good order." Because any state legislature was powerless to abolish "racial instincts," the Court thought the distinction between social and political equality was inevitable, and the segregationist policies of the South were the result of the incapacity of law to remedy the basic lack of affinity between the two races. *Plessy* gave the High Court's blessing to large-scale segregation as a fixture of the Southern moral establishment.[37]

By divorcing social and political rights and by linking what the Court considered the natural capacity of a race and its moral fortitude with political rights, the Court tacitly gave Southern states permission to strip African Americans of political rights as well. Southern states responded in earnest. In 1901, for example, the State of Alabama convened a Constitutional Convention with the stated intention of perpetuating white supremacy and disenfranchising African Americans. Each day began with a prayer that, in a typical example, asked God "to shine into all our hearts the knowledge of the light and glory of God as it shines in the face of Jesus Christ" in order to guide the delegates in their work. On the second day of the convention, its president explained that they had been called to establish white supremacy, which was "justified in law and in morals" because of the Negro's "intellectual and moral condition." "There is in the white man an inherited capacity for government, which is wholly wanting in the negro," he explained. "This principle of inherited moral capacity" was first proposed, he claimed, "by the inspired Apostle . . . Paul." Booker T. Washington, again a symbol of agreement among Southern and Northern moral establishmentarians, seemed to accept the strictures of this new arrangement. In a letter to the convention, he "beg[ged]" the delegates "to keep in mind in dealing with the problems that grow out of our presence" that African Americans had shown moral improvement since coming to America. "We have gotten the habits of industry, the English language, and the Christian religion," Washington elaborated, "and at the same time, we have tried in a humble way to render valuable service to the white men."[38]

The new establishment had wide support in the North as well. Two years after Alabama established white supremacy in law, Booker T. Washington held a fundraiser in New York City, inviting the leading lights of both North and South to attend. The former president Grover Cleveland began the meeting with a speech he took to be sympathetic to Washington's cause. Proclaiming that emancipation did not erase the "racial and slavery-bred imperfections and deficiencies" among Negroes, Cleveland explained that their chief problem was a lack of moral standards, most importantly, "a grievous amount of ignorance, a sad amount of viciousness, and a tremendous amount of laziness and thriftlessness." He claimed full sympathy with the white South and averred that because nine-tenths of the black population lived in the South, white Southerners were "entitled to our [Northerners'] utmost consideration and sympathetic fellowship." It was "their material prosperity, their peace, and even the safety of their civilization interwoven with the negro problem." But precisely because "the solution of the negro problem must . . . bear the heat of the day and stagger under the weight of the white man's burden," he threw himself behind Tuskegee's goal of helping fit the Negro for "his place." He also proclaimed himself a friend of the Negro, while supporting the moral establishment's erosion of black rights. Cleveland was not alone in intertwining praise for Washington with racist and denigrating comments about black people, which sustained the moral establishment. Edgar Gardner Murphy, an Episcopal minister from Montgomery, Alabama, and a member of the several educational boards that replaced the AMA as the dominant educational presence in the South, warned that "the rotting body" of black ignorance and moral decay was "polluting the atmosphere" Southerners breathed. He assured his audience that "amid all the bewildering and rasping nonsense of pro-negro sentimentality," Tuskegee stood apart "with incomparable dignity and sanity." Finally, Lyman Abbott came to the podium. "[T]he negro problem" was not a Southern problem, he explained, but "a National problem." It was the nation that had decided "to bring the negro here [to America]." But, according to Abbott, "because in the North we couldn't use him in our industrial development, we let him go to the South." Yet now that slavery was abolished, it was apparent that Northerners could not "compel by force the elevation of the black man." Unable to internalize moral norms, African Americans had forfeited their political rights, while they awaited the retraining needed for full incorporation into the body politic.[39]

"The negro question" that Philip Schaff had noted after the Civil War had now become, in Abbott's phrase, "the negro problem." Both Northerners and Southerners assumed that African Americans did not possess the moral fortitude to be productive citizens. They also had little faith in black Christianity as a civilizing agent, given its detachment from the moral establishment. Even Booker T. Washington disparaged black preachers and their congregants, appealing to the white assumption that U.S. citizenship required training in self-control to sustain the blessings of liberty. The call to civilizing benevolence that the AMA sounded, that Washington echoed, and that the U.S. government supported embraced a moral establishment guided and directed by white Protestants. When this failed to yield the transformation that Northern whites and Washington had anticipated, many Southern whites argued that segregation was necessary for the good of American society and the maintenance of the Southern moral order. The white Southern vision of the moral establishment emerged dominant at the end of the nineteenth century, in which maintaining moral order, in this case with a decidedly racial cast, overcame the black argument for individual and equal rights.[40]

WOMEN'S RIGHTS, WOMAN'S INDIVIDUALITY, AND THE BIBLE

1.

The basic question posed by the freeing of the slaves would assert itself repeatedly after the Civil War. To moral establishmentarians, the question was, given the emerging strain on the social order created by the expanding market economy and the demographic shifts in national life, what was the best means to restrain the individual? In the case of African Americans, they fell upon the idea of segregation and political disfranchisement. Exclusion was the only means of keeping their supposedly immoral tendencies at bay. A similar question would arise with the women's movement.

The breakup of the movement into radical and conservative branches after the debacle of the Fifteenth Amendment allowed Stanton and Anthony to emerge from the shadow of abolition even more radicalized, though it also allowed them to step back in certain respects from their transformational agenda. Turning away from their earlier commitment to equal rights for all, they instead focused exclusively on women's issues, but they were pulled back into conflict with the moral establishment even so. The National Woman Suffrage Association (NWSA) would provide a vehicle to wage a frontal assault on the moral establishment now unconstrained by the presence of their more conservative allies. From her new perch at *Revolution,* a magazine begun by Stanton in 1868 and bankrolled by George Francis Train, Stanton began criticizing moral-establishment proponents both within the women's movement and outside it as the Northern and Southern establishment began to come together again at the end of Reconstruction. This had the effect of further radicalizing her rejection of the establishment in a way that others in the movement could regard only as politically naïve.

But Stanton had other ideas. After being burned by the American Equal Rights Association (AERA) controversy, Stanton wanted to be sure to attract only those equally committed to destroying the moral establishment in order to emancipate women. She presumed that once a sufficient organization came together, she could use it to mount a political and legal assault, regardless of the political delicacy of the situation. Yet as committed as she was to total resistance, neither Stanton nor Anthony were completely lacking in political savvy. Stanton made sure to save her most extreme comments for private gatherings. In the early 1870s, before a society of reformers, she revealed the full extent of her radicalism by admitting that her ultimate goal was the abolition of all laws governing marriage so that men and women could couple and uncouple as they saw fit. She supported, to use the parlance of the times, free love, a scandalous and dangerous position, given the widespread belief that women's rights would lead to moral degradation and the unleashing of the licentious tendencies of the unrestrained female. There was a remarkable irony here. Stanton agreed with moral-establishment proponents that any move toward women's rights would require a host of other reforms to transform society in ways that would expand what establishmentarians considered immoral. Some in the movement did not see it, though. "[A]ll reforms and innovations stand logically affiliated with each other," she warned, so any who might have qualms about this ultimate outcome of women's rights, which was inevitable in their reform, should "for safety get out" right away, for delays would be "dangerous."[1]

Her statement turned out to be more portentous than even she realized. Although Stanton understood the personal risks of criticizing the place of religion in law and so operated with a modicum of discretion, others attracted to her movement were not always so careful. One of those women, who would play a major role in the coming legal and political confrontation with the moral establishment, was Victoria Woodhull. Woodhull had a wildly extravagant temperament that made her sympathetic to Stanton's agenda. She had grown up in Ohio, married a man who turned out to be an alcoholic, and moved to California where she supported her husband and two children through acting and casual prostitution. By 1866 she had left her husband, traveled back East, and taken up with Colonel James Blood, a freethinker and avowed free lover. She also became a spirit medium, channeling the dead for the benefit of the living. Two years later she arrived in Manhattan with Blood and her sister, Tennessee Claflin, where they called on the industrialist Cornelius Vanderbilt at his residence. Soon her sister tended to Vanderbilt's body as his mistress while Woodhull served as his medium to the dead. Drawing upon her wide contacts among the many New York prostitutes who served elite bankers and businessmen, Woodhull offered financial advice to Vanderbilt while in a trance state. He found her assistance so invaluable that he began giving both Woodhull and her sister a split of the profits, which they used to open a stockbrokerage firm. Together they became the first two female brokers on Wall Street. In 1870 Woodhull publicly endorsed women's suffrage and somehow managed to get a hearing before the Judiciary Committee of the U.S. House of Representatives, where she laid out the dominant women's rights strategy after the collapse of the American Equal Rights Association. Called the New Departure, it sought victory in the courts by arguing that the Fourteenth and Fifteenth amendments had already laid the legal foundation for female suffrage.[2]

Woodhull's entrance on the scene was both sudden and momentous. She offered a proxy through whom Stanton could confront the hypocrisies and inconsistencies of the moral establishment without much risk to herself. Woodhull's rise to prominence came so suddenly that not much was known about her past, either within or outside of the movement, but even a passing knowledge of her personal history raised suggestions of disreputable behavior. As more came to light, the question for the women's movement became whether to embrace Woodhull, and thereby admit that they sought total social transformation, or to break with Woodhull in order to preserve the appearance of propriety. Stanton embraced Woodhull fully. Although the details of Woodhull's past were still vague in the spring of 1871, Isabella Beecher Hooker, another one of Lyman Beecher's daughters who had earlier rebelled against her father and become a leader in the NWSA, confronted Woodhull with a series of letters that purported to detail an illicit personal history. Trying to warn the others in the NWSA, Hooker gave copies of the letters to both Stanton and Martha Coffin Wright, a radical Quaker (and Lucretia Mott's sister). With rumors swirling, Stanton rallied to Woodhull's defense. She even gently rebuked Mott, by now an aged matriarch of the movement, for the "great impertinence" of prying into Woodhull's private affairs. Unconcerned with past moral lapses, Stanton instead sensed a conspiracy. The "sentimental, hypocritical, prating about purity," she complained, was "one of man's most effective engines, for our division, & subjugation."[3]

Meanwhile, a more profound revelation was brewing, one that would set the stage for a morality play with the moral establishment. Henry Ward Beecher was at its center. At the 1866 Woman's Rights Convention, the women's suffrage movement had gained Beecher's personal endorsement. He cited women's equal participation in public affairs as "God's growing and least disclosed idea." In giving his endorsement, Beecher explained to the convention that the central question in women's suffrage was, "Who has a right to construct and administer law?" His question cut to the heart of the justifications that religious partisans used to explain their cultural and legal authority. Beecher was a cagey figure, a large man of flowing hair, fashionable appearance, and amiable ideas who was exquisitely attuned to the sensibilities of his upper-class parishioners. His endorsement of forgiveness to the South after the Civil War and his affirmation of the connection between religion, morals, and law placed him with moral establishmentarians. Even his support of women's suffrage came on the moral establishment's terms. "[T]he questions of politics are to be more and more moral questions," explained Beecher, who looked to "those whom God made to be peculiarly conservators of things moral and spiritual [i.e., women] to come forward and help us in that work."[4]

When Beecher first announced his support for women's suffrage at the convention, one of his parishioners, the newspaper editor Theodore Tilton, introduced him. Yet not long after Beecher endorsed women's suffrage, rumors began circulating that Beecher and Tilton's wife, Elizabeth, had formed a closer friendship than was normally permitted outside of marriage. The story was long and involved. It had been kept quiet by mutual agreement in order to protect everyone's reputation. To ensure accountability, Beecher and the Tiltons had entrusted papers that documented their agreement, including letters back and forth, apologies, admissions of guilt (though without specifics), and pledges of silence, to a disinterested third party, Francis Moulton.[5]

Given Henry Ward Beecher's prominence and his connection to the Beecher clan, he must have struck Stanton as a perfect example of the hypocrisy of the moral establishment. That was what he would become, anyhow, if she had her way. Meanwhile, Woodhull decided to confront her critics, as her situation had only gotten more precarious. While the Beecher affair was unfolding in secret (though not without rumors), news had gotten out that not only had Woodhull's second marriage been a sham but that she also kept a stable of men in her home. Among them were her second informal husband, Colonel James Blood; her ex-husband, Canning Woodhull; and the anarchist and notorious free-love advocate Stephen Pearl Andrews. To those charging the women's movement with moral anarchy, this was unseemly in the extreme. It raised the specter of the rapacious woman, unconstrained by ties of family and home.[6]

But just as public criticism of Woodhull—and by extension, of the women's movement—became more shrill, Woodhull learned of the Beecher–Tilton scandal through multiple sources, including, of course, Elizabeth Cady

Stanton. To Woodhull (as to Stanton), the Beecher affair seemed to offer a powerful lesson in hypocrisy and a perfect way to deflate what she saw as the facile connection made by moral establishmentarians between theological rectitude and moral and sexual probity. Sinking under the weight of public contempt, Woodhull grasped the slender reed that rumors of the Beecher affair offered. Her goal was a confrontation. Cleverly, she owned up to her illicit past, all the while scheming to reveal the commonality between Henry Ward Beecher and herself. In early 1871 Woodhull put in motion a plan, attempting to leverage her knowledge to persuade Beecher to introduce her at that year's Spiritualist Association meeting. She later claimed that she was trying to get him to proclaim his adherence to free love, but she may have merely been trying to forge a connection in the public mind between herself and Beecher.[7]

When Beecher refused, she took an alternate route and had Theodore Tilton introduce her to the meeting. Her address, entitled "The Principles of Social Freedom," achieved instant infamy. It was her public proclamation, in defiance of her critics, of her support for free love. In the face of numerous and repeated hisses from the crowd, Woodhull laid out the connection between women's rights and free love with a clarity never achieved even by Stanton herself. To a considerable extent Woodhull's argument reflected the anarchism of her houseguest, Stephen Pearl Andrews, without rejecting government entirely. Contrary to the claims of the moral establishment, she understood self-government quite literally: all should be entrusted to govern themselves and to act according to their own wishes in the pursuit of individual happiness. Because individual sovereignty was the guiding principle of social freedom, the individual rather than the family became the basic unit of government. In making this argument, Woodhull put forward a radically libertarian position that rejected all authority except that which was acknowledged by the individual. She claimed that aggregates of individuals formed communities (again, not families) that enacted governments in order to guard individual rights. Because the individual was the basic unit of government, society must safeguard individual rights even when its members disliked what the individual was doing.[8]

Woodhull's argument for the sovereignty of the individual promised the complete reevaluation of marriage. Law that was based on individual rights, she asserted, would recognize marriage as a true contract, terminable under the same provisions governing other contracts and not beholden to divine decree or religious foundation. The lack of freedom in marriage became for Woodhull a symbol of society as a whole. All nods to religious and political freedom in theory were, in practice, suffocated by a "*society*-despotism." Only true religious and political freedom would yield social freedom, she explained, and social freedom was, in two words, free love. As the hisses grew, Woodhull waxed prophetic, claiming that the spiritualization of marriage, which involved the free coupling of individuals, was necessary for the transformation of all of society to accommodate the principles of social freedom. The "spiritually constituted" family would herald "the most wonderful transformation of human society," a transformation that was "at the very door." The result would be "a nobler manhood and a more glorified womanhood; as, indeed, the veritable gateway to a paradise regained."[9]

The effect within the women's movement was explosive. Stanton may have been pleased, but the NWSA did not know what to do. Even prior to the convention, some had begun to wonder if Woodhull was doing more harm that good. Isabella Beecher Hooker, Henry Ward Beecher's sister, had confronted Woodhull directly. In response to Hooker's intervention, Woodhull adopted a messianic tone, explaining that she would not have chosen the cause for herself but could not resist her "mission." She possessed secret knowledge—surely a reference to the Beecher affair—but she regretted, "I cannot yet divulge it." Woodhull did offer a glimmer of prophecy, proclaiming "the near approach of the grandest revelation" yet known to the world. She continued, "[F]or the part you shall play in it thousands will rise up and call you blessed." If that did not sound ominous to Hooker, it should have. Because the public outcry against Woodhull seemed to place their movement in jeopardy, some in the NWSA began wondering if they should temper their call for a social revolution. It was a suggestion echoed by Henry Ward Beecher, who was upset that his name had begun appearing in connection with an avowed practitioner of free love. In response to a concerned letter from his sister Isabella, Henry begged her not to make any stand in the coming year "*except upon suffrage.*" His plea effectively truncated her reform message to its most conservative core and rejected the idea of individual rights. He also begged her, gesturing toward the rumors swirling around him, to maintain "*silence* and a silencing influence on all others," adding, "A day may come for converse. It is not now. Living or dead, my dear sister Belle, *love me*, and do not talk about me or suffer others to in your presence." Others, meanwhile, began pulling away from Woodhull to limit the damage that she could do. Susan B. Anthony, writing in her diary a few weeks later, confessed that the day struck her as sad. She explained, "Our movement as such is so demoralized by the letting go the helm of ship to Woodhull—though we rescued it— it was as by a hair breadth escape."[10]

But Anthony had spoken too soon. After Woodhull's speech, Beecher's allies began to mobilize against her to discredit the radical branch of women's rights. Two more Beecher sisters, Catharine Beecher and Harriet Beecher Stowe, launched an attack in the pages of Henry Beecher's journal, the *Christian Union*, accusing Woodhull of licentious behavior that revealed the danger of individual rights. Simultaneously, they worked to undermine her remaining support through their large network of influential friends, which hurt Woodhull's stockbrokerage business. Observing the ruthless assault upon her by proponents of the moral establishment, Woodhull concluded that she was out of options. Her only remaining course was to publicize the connection between herself and Beecher in order to demonstrate the hypocrisy of religiously based moral norms in law. But, first, Woodhull tried to blackmail Beecher. Noting the efforts of his two sisters to smear her reputation and to resist her mission, Woodhull warned him, "You doubtless know that it is in my power to strike back, and in ways more disastrous than anything that can come to me; but I do not desire to do this." Still the attacks did not stop. Woodhull reached a breaking point. Writing again to Beecher, she explained, "The social fight against me . . . is becoming rather hotter than I can well endure. . . . Now, I want your assistance." When Beecher made no reply, Woodhull moved forward with her plan. In September 1872 she was reelected president of the National Association of Spiritualists. In her speech before the convention in Boston she unveiled her knowledge that the Reverend Henry Ward Beecher was a secret believer in the most-advanced doctrines of free love and had had affairs with any number of his parishioners, including Elizabeth Tilton, the wife of his close friend, Theodore. To ensure a wide distribution, Woodhull reprinted the charges in her own newspaper, *Woodhull and Claflin's Weekly*, shortly after her speech. In her preface to the charges, she explained that she wanted the article to "burst like a bomb-shell into the ranks of the moralistic social camp," adding, "I am engaged in officering, and in some sense conducting, a social revolution on the marriage question."[11]

It was a stunning act of self-immolation. To criticize the moral establishment was dangerous. To do so while advocating free love was even more hazardous. To attempt to destroy one of the moral establishment's golden sons was courting disaster. In her own explanation, Woodhull was driven to do it by the rampant hypocrisy of the age. The Beecher affair provided her with an example of what she regarded as a phenomenon inherent in the moral establishment. The use of law to enforce morality drove people to dishonest moral behavior, she claimed; so although she normally honored the privacy of the individual above all things, Woodhull offered Beecher's affair as an indictment not of an individual but of the system. She hoped that exposing a man of Beecher's eminence would send an "inquisition through all the churches and . . . conservative society" by demonstrating the deep folly of the moral establishment. Noting that the age was "pregnant with great events," Woodhull prophesied that once "the pious ejaculations of the sanctimonious" were "expended," everyone would see the hypocrisy of the age and the social revolution would come.[12]

It is difficult to overstate the magnitude of the scandal in the trials that followed. The public demand for Woodhull's accusation seemed insatiable, and print run after print run of her magazine sold out. With the situation careening out of control, religious partisans began to intervene. Anthony Comstock, the vice reformer, stepped in a month after Woodhull published her article and arrested both Woodhull and her sister on the charge of obscenity. Comstock would become the embodiment of Lyman Beecher's vision, a young apostle of righteousness committed to using voluntary associations and the coercion of law to maintain the moral uprightness of the nation. His arrest of Woodhull was his first highly publicized vice reform effort, and he would use it as a platform for more-intrusive moral laws in the coming years. Upon jailing Woodhull, he seized her presses so that no more magazines could be republished to meet the demand for the Beecher issue.[13]

But Woodhull would not go away. After her jail stay in January 1873, she delivered and subsequently published a lecture claiming that she had just emerged from "the American Bastille," to which she had been "consigned by the cowardly servility of the age." With Woodhull further stoking press coverage of the affair, in March 1873 some of Beecher's most prominent parishioners, acting independently of their pastor, decided to drop Tilton from the roll of Beecher's congregation. They assumed that he had spread the rumors about Beecher that had fed the frenzy. To Tilton it seemed that he was being made a scapegoat, and the pact of secrecy began to crumble on all sides. Beecher, who began to worry that his reputation would never recover, declared his innocence and appointed members of his church to conduct an ecclesiastical investigation. Although the outcome of the investigation was largely predetermined, the process only furthered the media scandal. Newspapers around the nation carried daily transcripts of each session. In the latter half of 1874 the *New York Times* alone offered 37 editorials and 105 news articles on the trial.[14]

The controversy destroyed reputations as charges of free love, which were potent because they connected theological and sexual infidelity, flew in all directions. The accusations raised two possibilities: either Beecher was a hypocrite and the moral establishment he supported was a sham, as Woodhull claimed, or the moral establishment was correct and Woodhull and the radical branch of women's rights fabricated the charges to cover their own licentious tendencies. Though public opinion remained divided, all the participants in the scandal sought to claim the mantle of righteousness. Theodore Tilton echoed Woodhull by portraying both Beecher and Elizabeth Tilton as secret proponents of free love. Beecher returned the accusation, claiming that Theodore did not even bother to conceal from the members of his own household his numerous sexual conquests after what Beecher called "a marked change in his [Tilton's] religious and social views." Elizabeth Tilton joined Beecher's side by assuming the pose of a chaste woman devoted to her children's moral and religious upbringing. She rejected Theodore's victim posture as "a lamentable satire upon the household where he himself, years before, laid the corner stone of Free Love."[15]

With religious partisans clamping down on Woodhull, and Beecher's church members defending their pastor's morals, the radical branch of the women's movement was thrown into disarray. Beecher began distancing himself from all parties. His criticism extended beyond Theodore Tilton to "one wing of the Female Suffrage party [that] had got hold of the story in a distorted and exaggerated form." The radical wing of the reform movement, Beecher claimed, sought to discredit by way of slander anyone who became noted as a reformer but resisted their revolutionary goals. As it turned out, he was not above slander himself, furthering the connection between free love, women's rights, and unorthodox theology. The Beecher team procured one of Tilton's former domestic servants to say that several female friends of Mr. Tilton—including Stanton, Anthony, and, of course, Victoria Woodhull— were often at the Tilton house. Woodhull had stayed for several months. As the servant explained, Mr. Tilton "seemed to be very fond of her; he was with her a great deal; he used to caress her and kiss her; he was very much taken with her in every way." When the chair of the committee prompted her about the other women, she responded that Tilton was not much interested in other women, except Stanton and Anthony.

Q. How was it with them?
A. He seemed to think a great deal of Mrs. Stanton and Miss Anthony; I saw her sitting on his lap on one occasion when I was coming into the parlor, and she jumped up pretty quick.
Q. Miss Anthony?
A. Susan B. Anthony.

Q. What was his conduct with Mrs. Stanton?

A. Well, I never saw him caressing her, but he used to be alone with her a great deal in his study; they used to play chess until two or three o'clock in the morning; frequently they were up until after the family had gone to bed—quite late.[16]

Unhelpfully, at least to the NWSA, Woodhull continued her theatrics. Providing coverage and commentary throughout the trial, in 1874 she published a tract entitled "Tried as by Fire; or, The True and the False, Socially." It reiterated her intent to conduct "a campaign against marriage." The entire Beecher incident had revealed to her just how much the United States needed social freedom. As she saw it, after her revelation about Beecher, "the American Pope," his allies rallied to his support to suppress her. "[T]he United States authorities, urged on by the minions of the Church—the Y.M.C. Assassination Association—swooped down upon me and carried me off to jail," she explained, "not for libel on the Pope, but for obscenity." Waiting in jail, she trusted that the public's outrage would secure her release, but it did not come and the ensuing spectacle did not seem to be going as she had hoped. She realized in the aftermath that though her own arrest ought to have produced outrage, "Beecher was bigger than a free press—of more consequence than free speech. His danger cowed the whole country into silence; and the people sneaked after the trail of the popular preacher, in abject submission."[17]

The entire sordid affair only strengthened the moral establishment. After another year of trial and testimony, this time in a New York court, when Theodore Tilton filed a suit against Beecher for criminal conversation with his wife, Beecher's vindication was complete: a hung jury allowed him to go free. The others fared less well. When Elizabeth abruptly changed her story (for a third time), claiming that she had in fact had an affair with Beecher, she was promptly excommunicated from the Plymouth church and ostracized by everyone for the remainder of her life; she died lonely and blind in her daughter's Brooklyn apartment in 1897. Theodore, prevented from finding journalistic work by the numerous influential members of the Plymouth church, emigrated to Paris, where he lived in poverty and wrote poetry until his death in 1907. Woodhull did not last more than two years in the United States after the trial's end. In 1877 when Cornelius Vanderbilt died, some of his squabbling heirs fretted that their father's consultation with spirit mediums and his insatiable sexual appetite might be grounds to challenge his sanity and, therefore, the will. They paid Woodhull to leave the country to ensure their fortune. Because her stockbrokerage firm had been closed during her jail stay—and because her life was increasingly beset with financial strain and social ostracism—she took the money and her daughter to England, where at one of her speeches on free love she met her wealthy future husband—her third. She had discarded her previous two prior to leaving the United States.[18]

2.

Although the Beecher–Tilton affair certainly provided spectacular entertainment, it was more than just spectacle. In the view of conservatives, such as E. L. Godkin, the editor of the then-conservative weekly the *Nation*, the scandal was "a symptomatic phenomenon . . . illustrative of the moral condition of American society generally." Godkin extended blame to that "large body of persons," by which he meant reformers such as Stanton, who with great hubris sought to "tackle all the problems of the day—men's, women's, and children's rights and duties, marriage, education, suffrage, life, death, and immortality—with supreme indifference to what anybody . . . ever thought." Rather than a new age, these reformers heralded "a kind of mental and moral chaos," Godkin claimed.[19]

He was not alone in his sentiments. The presence of a more militant and focused women's rights movement alarmed establishmentarians, especially since that movement seemed to be behind the recent scandal. Proponents of the moral establishment saw the Beecher–Tilton affair as an example of what happened when the constraints of law and moral pressure broke down. And the women's movement led by Stanton wanted those constraints permanently removed! To resist the movement and to protect the nation from moral degradation, moral establishmentarians began to reformulate the legal mechanisms to keep women under control.

Beginning in the early 1870s, judicial writers in particular began to turn their attention to the laws granting property rights to married women. Treatise writers had enormous power to shape the law without having to bother with the legislature. Although legislatures had passed the property rights acts prior to the Civil War, they did not specify how those acts meshed with the idea of women's coverture, which placed wives under the care of their husbands and made them a nonentity before the law. Coverture arose out of common law, or case law, and needed to be reconciled with the statutory laws passed by state legislatures. This is where treatise writers came in. They codified case law in legal treatises, offering authoritative guides that judges could consult and cite when deciding cases. Although they would have never admitted it, this power of codification allowed them the ability to make law, which enabled them to rework the law to protect against the kind of licentiousness that the Beecher–Tilton affair seemed to betoken.

The two most important post–property act treatise writers were James Schouler and Joel Prentiss Bishop. So great was their influence that in wake of the property acts' passage, many jurists, when explaining their decisions, employed the phrase "according to Bishop" or "according to Schouler." Both were uniformly hostile to the property acts. Schouler complained that they had put family law into complete disarray, because the passage of women's property acts had established two separate legal systems, one based on common law and one based on civil law. The common law system began with the assumption of unity in marriage, during which the wife's legal existence was suspended, and therefore comported with the Christian ideal. Though Schouler admitted that she sacrificed her property interests and was placed almost entirely in her husband's keeping, she was also entitled to his protection and support, which was enforceable by law. This, in Schouler's estimation, ensured the general unity of family life. By contrast, civil law paid little attention to the unity of the pair, and instead acknowledged the personal independence and individuality of husband and wife, especially in their property rights. To Schouler, the civil law scheme threatened to bring about the kind cultural and familial atomization of which the Beecher–Tilton affair was an example. He warned that if the legislators continued to reinforce women's separate rights, the legislation would likely "weaken the ties of marriage, by forcing both sexes into an unnatural antagonism; teaching them to be independent of one another." Such a condition was "unnatural" because "God's law points to family and the mutual intercourse of man and woman as among the strongest safeguards of human happiness."[20]

To strengthen the old common law scheme that was so important to the moral establishment, both Schouler and Bishop interpreted the laws in the narrowest possible way. Schouler, for example, acknowledged that women's property rights were necessary because of past instances of abuse but suggested that they did not really modify the common law scheme of coverture, which continued as before. Bishop likewise emphasized "how little of the old law" had really changed, but he took the opportunity to elaborate what he considered "a new branch of the law" that the women's property statutes had created. This allowed him to reformulate the doctrine that marriage was a civil contract, an idea that had always caused discomfort to proponents of the moral establishment because it allowed women's rights activists to argue that it ought to be dissolvable by consent. Bishop argued that it was actually engagement that was a contract, one that ended upon marriage. Rather than a contract, marriage, he claimed, was a "civil status." Because it was a civil status, it could not be dissolved at the whim of the parties, and, following a circular logic, because the individuals could not dissolve it at will, marriage could not be a contract.[21]

Bishop also reformulated the rules governing divorce. Because marriage was essential to the perpetuation of society, Bishop explained, the public was the "third party" in a divorce suit. Therefore, the public's interests needed to be protected as much as, or even more than, those of the husband and wife. And the public's primary interest was the maintenance of moral norms. One way to protect this interest, Bishop noted, was by making it "the duty of the public prosecuting officer to oppose all suits for divorce," a system already in place "[i]n Kentucky, Indiana and perhaps one or two other states." In the states that did not have a public prosecutor, the court itself was to exercise "a constant watchfulness over the public interests in the cause." Whatever the mechanism, before a judge could grant a divorce the court needed to establish that the marriage did more harm than good to the community, rather than to the individuals in the marriage, thereby "satisfying the conscience of the court." Bishop's and Schouler's arguments were quite successful, in part because of their willingness to spell out in exhaustive detail a judicial process whereby judges could maintain the provisions of the common law by fending off or limiting the effectiveness of civil laws that granted women a minimal level of autonomy.[22]

While jurists buttressed the common law provisions of the moral establishment, alarmed legislators stepped back from the implicitly egalitarian impulse that had underwritten the married women's property acts, seeking instead to reinforce the prescribed social roles within the family and to limit the rising divorce rate. Leading the charge was Theodore Woolsey, the former president of Yale, a supporter of the AMA, and a leading member of the Evangelical Alliance, the organization begun in 1847 to further evangelical political action at home and abroad. In 1881 Woolsey added another organization to his affiliations when he began the New England Divorce Reform League, which he reorganized as the National Divorce Reform League in 1885 in order to petition the U.S. Congress for a federal study of marriage and divorce. The status of the signatories—who, in addition to Woolsey, included Noah Porter, the president of Yale; Samuel W. Dike, the nation's leading divorce statistician; Elisha Mulford, a minister and professor at Episcopal Theological School in Cambridge, Massachusetts; Charles Comfort Tiffany, a prominent Baltimore clergyman; and Theodore William Dwight, a professor of law at Columbia and the grandson of Yale's former president Timothy Dwight—caught the attention of Congress. The resulting Bill Providing for the Collection of Statistics Touching Marriage and Divorce led to a comprehensive statistical survey published two years later under the auspices of the U.S. secretary of labor, Carroll Wright. The report detailed what, to moral establishmentarians, seemed a disturbing trend. Wright found that the majority of the states retained the language of "civil contract" in their laws, rather than Bishop's "more modern, and apparently more accurate view" of marriage as a civil status. At the same time, divorces had increased every year, nearly tripling (in absolute numbers) from 1867 to 1886.[23]

The problem facing the National Divorce Reform League was that marriage was not regulated at the federal level, so they began working on a state-by-state basis. They did have some success, but what emerged out of the struggle was a messy arrangement. Earlier in the century both Maine and Indiana had enacted liberalized divorce laws that included judicial discretion in permitting divorce, in addition to the usual grounds of adultery and abandonment. If a judge were so inclined, he could allow a divorce simply because the parties were unhappy, a provision that alarmed moral establishmentarians. Because the U.S. Constitution required states to acknowledge the "public acts, records, and judicial proceedings" of every other state, Indiana and Maine became divorce havens to which people moved to establish residence in order to get divorced, before moving back to their previous state of residence. But pressure from states with strict divorce laws was relentless, and before the century was up both Maine and Indiana had repealed their liberal laws. Yet it was not a total victory. Other states stepped in. First the Dakotas, and then Nevada, became the divorce havens of choice. Couples who really wanted a divorce could get one, but the process was expensive and time consuming, which in the minds of moral-establishment proponents at least limited the potential for abuse.[24]

But this never satisfied proponents of the moral establishment. The National Divorce Reform League began pushing for a constitutional amendment to allow Congress to regulate marriage and establish uniform grounds for divorce. Although they failed to garner the necessary support, even if they had, the amendment was unlikely to have had the desired effect. The disappearance of liberalized divorce laws ran up against the real desire of many couples to get out of their marriages. Whole industries rose up to procure the often fabricated evidence of adultery or cruelty that was required to meet the grounds for divorce in the strictest states. Collusion between the divorcing parties often included the courts, which either could not or would not challenge the obvious fraud that litigants perpetrated to make their case. In many respects the efforts of religious partisans to strengthen the moral establishment verified Woodhull's claim that "an organized hypocrisy" had become the norm in late nineteenth-century American society. The system created, as the legal scholar Lawrence Friedman has pointed out, "a regime of massive lying and deceit," adding, "In almost every state, perjury or something close to it was a way of life in divorce court." Yet Stanton and Woodhull's attempts to liberalize divorce law had stalled. The resulting standoff lasted until the 1970s.[25]

3.

Faced with the hostile reactions of jurists, legislators, and religious lobbyists, the leaders of the women's movement confronted the familiar dilemma of whether it ought to oppose the moral establishment or whether the moral establishment itself provided the fundamental reason for women's enlarged public role. The dilemma was made more acute by the abrupt failure, just as the Beecher affair was coming to its sad conclusion, of the movement's New Departure strategy, which had looked to federal legal challenges to argue for suffrage. It was not a completely surprising development. In 1873 the U.S. Supreme Court had ruled in an 8–1 decision against Myra Bradwell, who was suing the State of Illinois for refusing to allow her to join the bar because she was a woman. Although the majority rejected her suit by claiming that the federal government had no power to regulate the state bar, the concurring opinion, which agreed with the result of the majority opinion but offered different reasoning and legal grounds, provided a larger rationale. Although they claimed to support the work of reform, the signers of the opinion indicated that the organization of the family, which was "founded in the divine ordinance," relegated women to the home as the proper sphere for their work. The opinion also noted, in echo of Schouler, that husband and wife possessed a harmony of interests and that the common law of coverture, which presumed that harmony, remained in force in most states. That harmony of interests required that Bradwell remain under the direction of her husband rather than pursuing an individual career. Harmony meant subordination, as the Court fully acknowledged. The Court explained, "This is the law of the Creator."[26]

In 1875 the U.S. Supreme Court went further by unanimously rejecting the claim that the Fourteenth Amendment granted women suffrage with the simple assertion that the Constitution did not include voting as an essential part of citizenship. With Schouler and Bishop ensuring that women's rights in marriage hewed to common law rules, and with legislators tightening the permissible grounds for divorce, the High Court now declared that the national citizenship promised in the Fourteenth Amendment did not offer women the access to the political process that it gave to men. Given this shrinking sense of possibility, some in the women's movement began to suggest a more strategic approach.[27]

Stanton was not one of them. She emerged from the Beecher–Tilton affair even more committed to the Garrisonian idea that all injustice needed to be confronted. Taking up Woodhull's argument that social freedom required a revolution in the social and legal system—and a rejection of its religious foundations—she sought to incorporate women's rights into the broader world of freethought. In a letter to Francis Abbot, a leader in the free-religion movement and the editor of the freethought publication the *Index*, Stanton claimed that because so many women were "held in bondage" by their religious beliefs, there was not an "Orthodox woman" among the women's rights activists. But she acknowledged that this had caused problems, especially in the controversy over the Beecher–Tilton affair. To get the women's rights movement out of the dire position it was in, Stanton thought they needed to identify with the broader struggle that Abbot and others were making to reject religion in public life as a whole. She also began to draw closer to Robert Ingersoll, the late nineteenth century's most infamous agnostic, who toured the nation giving polemical lectures about the role of religion in national life. While planning for the next women's rights convention in 1877, Stanton wrote to Isabella Beecher Hooker that she wanted to find someone to show "how degraded woman has been under all forms of religion," and suggested Ingersoll be tapped to make the argument. Anthony had also written him earlier that year asking him to attend the convention or, in lieu of that, to provide a letter in support of women's rights that could be read to the delegates. Ingersoll did not make the convention, but he included as part of his rhetorical arsenal a speech entitled "Liberty of Man, Woman, and Child," which linked the subjection of women with the reign of the church, and the improper connection between church and state.[28]

Stanton interpreted the efforts of Schouler, Bishop, Woolsey, and other religious activists to further tighten the moral establishment's provisions governing women as indications of the all-absorbing nature of the fight. The conclusion of the Woodhull affair seemed to confirm that for her. Only by breaking the authority of Christianity in public life, she suggested, could women be freed from their legally prescribed obligation to the family in order to stand as individuals in the eyes of the law and in the political process. She did have some success in positioning women's rights in opposition to the role of religion in public life. The high point came in 1878, three years after the end of the Beecher–Tilton affair, at the movement's thirtieth anniversary celebration in Rochester, New York. Serving on the committee for resolutions that year were an array of Stanton allies: Matilda Gage, Lucy Colman, and Amy Post, all freethinkers who agreed with Stanton's claims that the improper union between church and state had created a regime of laws that ensured women's subordination. Among the resolutions they proposed, three ignited fierce debate because they singled out Christianity as uniquely responsible for the degradation of woman, having perverted woman's religious nature in order to stunt her individual development and keep her in subjection through "priestcraft and superstition."[29]

Amid the many objectors was Susan B. Anthony. If Stanton had broadened her vision after the Woodhull affair, Anthony had the opposite response. She considered the Woodhull affair an unmitigated disaster. Seeing the personal harm it had caused all participants and the public relations nightmare it created for the women's movement, Anthony turned shrewd and pragmatic, apparently concluding that the strength of the moral establishment was too great to resist. The growing power of religious organizations in the last thirty years of the nineteenth century convinced Anthony that the women's movement needed to pursue specific goals rather than social revolution. Her pragmatic inclination frequently put her at odds with Stanton. As she complained to Isabella Beecher Hooker, a go-between during the entire Beecher–Tilton debacle, "Has Mrs. Stanton come to that, that she would *ask nothing* of the tyrants but just what she *expects* them to grant?" The inability to think strategically and to recognize stark political realities, Anthony maintained, was detrimental to the movement as a whole. "But *if* the *Women's Rights women* were only *alive* to the *one work* of *assertion* & *assumption* of the *Citizens right to vote*," Anthony wrote emphatically, "we should soon walk into the kingdom en masse." Anthony's pragmatic turn aligned her, in opposition to Stanton, and to her friend's dismay, with the religious proponents for women's rights who sought the right to vote in order to increase the moral and religious tone of public life.[30]

But in 1878 at the Rochester Convention, Stanton and her allies possessed just enough rhetorical and organizational strength to pass her resolutions against Christianity in American life. Once passed, Stanton used the resolutions in a letter to Francis Abbot, published in the *Index*, that sought to assuage the concerns of some in the freethought movement who worried that because women were often more religious than men, giving women the vote might further increase the role of religion in U.S. public life. She explained, "I think our liberal friends will find those touching the religious element of woman's nature sufficiently broad to assure them that these women, armed with ballots, will not prove the dangerous element so many fear on the side of priestcraft and superstition." Abbot had organized so-called Liberal Leagues around the country as part of his effort to complete the separation of church and state. In response to the convention's resolutions, he called upon Stanton to give speeches jointly sponsored by the Liberal League and NWSA, which she happily accepted. But the cracks within the women's movement were beginning to show. Many Liberal Leagues also offered to organize Anthony's lectures, though she was less enthusiastic, noting that such sponsorship deterred "the religionists."[31]

Anthony's demurral signaled the turning tide. Stanton had won a minor battle in 1878, but she was to lose the war. The Thirtieth Anniversary Resolutions were the last major resolutions that Stanton was able to pass. As Anthony consolidated her organizational control, she began to narrow the vision solely to suffrage. Perhaps sensing the shift, Stanton began withdrawing from NWSA conventions, although Anthony did try to keep her involved. In 1880 Stanton warned Anthony not to let her name come up for consideration in the NWSA officer selection. "I *positively decline*," she wrote. "My work in conventions is at an end; they are distasteful to me." But she did not withdraw completely from the movement. In 1881 Stanton, Anthony, and Matilda Joslyn Gage published the first of what they originally conceived as a three-volume series entitled *The History of Woman Suffrage*. It represented Stanton's attempt to influence the direction of the movement by narrating its past. The text bore the unmistakable mark of Stanton's hand, often drawing lessons from past battles with the church to explain the folly of truncating the reform effort, which, in Stanton's evaluation, was simply to capitulate to forces they had once overcome. She described the early battles that had occurred in the 1840s and 1850s as a contest with the church that the movement had won, although she acknowledged that in the past "[t]he fear of a social revolution thus complicated the discussion." The book began with a portrait of Frances Wright, a radical freethinker from the early nineteenth century, on the frontispiece, visually evoking her critique of religious influence in public life. Perhaps most provocatively, the authors concluded with an essay by Gage, entitled "Woman, Church, and State." It continued Stanton's argument that the Christian religion was historically responsible for female subordination and that the improper connection of church and state in the United States fixed the degradation in law.[32]

Such sentiments were less and less characteristic of the women's movement of the 1880s, as Anthony and her lieutenants stultified Stanton's supporters at the conventions. In 1885 and 1886 Stanton sought to repeat the success of 1878, proffering amendments that renewed the call for a rejection of the moral establishment. Though the resolutions created extended controversies each time, they were voted down by Anthony's fervent opposition. After the 1890 merger between the NWSA and the American Woman Suffrage Association (AWSA) to form the National-American Woman Suffrage Association (NAWSA), Stanton's position became even more tenuous, because the AWSA was filled with evangelical suffragists such as the Woman's Christian Temperance Union president Frances Willard. Willard was part of the rising tide of religiously motivated political activists who emerged with the evangelical expansion at the end of the nineteenth century. By asserting the place of Christianity in U.S. public life, she endorsed the move to exclude black Americans that was becoming characteristic of the Southern moral establishment. Explaining in 1890 that she pitied white Southerners, Willard noted, "The Anglo-Saxon race will never submit to be dominated by the Negro so long as his altitude reaches no higher than the personal liberty of the saloon and the power of appreciating the amount of liquor that a dollar will buy." In Willard's mind, Southern African Americans used liberty to pursue the licentiousness found in the saloon, while "[w]ould-be demagogues," an oblique reference to black preachers and politicians, led their black followers "to destruction." By contrast, "a more thoroughly American population than the Christian people of the South" did not exist, she claimed.[33]

Stanton might not have disagreed, but Willard's embrace of a Christian white supremacy remained dangerous to Stanton because it assumed religious norms in law. After the merger Stanton withdrew even more, focusing her energy on the publication of her *Woman's Bible*, which emerged in two parts in 1895 and 1898. Her intention was to expose the patriarchy that ran throughout the Bible in order to limit its influence and undercut the argument of evangelical suffragists such as Willard. The book was a remarkable document, part critical commentary, part cranky tirade. It was not, in spite of its title, a new version of the Bible, but a selection of passages that touched upon women, with commentary from a selected group of women who made up what she called the Revising Committee. Her strategy was to point out the biblical contradictions affecting women, most fundamentally the two different creation stories in the first two chapters of Genesis. In the first chapter, man and woman were created at the same moment, equally in the image of God, and jointly given dominion over all the earth. In the second, woman was created, in Stanton's words, as "a mere afterthought." She explained, "The world [was] in good running order without her. The only reason for her advent being the solitude of man."[34]

Taken as a whole, the *Woman's Bible* sought to reject the concept of women's responsibility for perpetuating society's moral norms. But it was not internally consistent, since moral establishmentarians were included on the committee in order to help Stanton make her point more forcefully. As Stanton's critical edge became clearer, some members of the Revising Committee grew concerned that her tone did not more reverently acknowledge "the Word of God." Recording the controversy in the pages of the *Woman's Bible* itself, her response was unequivocal. Stanton asked, "Does anyone at this stage of civilization think the Bible was written by the finger of God, that the Old and New Testaments emanated from the highest divine thought in the universe?" She pointed out that the Bible was written over a long period of time by numerous people, edited by forgotten editors, copied by forgotten scribes, translated by committee, published in multiple forms, and subject to multiple commentaries, all of which demonstrated that the Bible was an ongoing conversation, not complete and unalterable truth. Stanton offered her commentary on the Bible as part of that conversation, not because she viewed it authoritatively but because others did. She wanted to divest it of authority in order to release its hold on both the popular mind and the partisans within the women's movement.[35]

The furor that attended its publication went partially according to Stanton's plan. She had both expected and counted upon criticism from religious conservatives. Their criticism resulted in publicity, and publicity generated curiosity, and curiosity generated sales, with the paradoxical result, as she wryly observed, that "bigots promote the sale." Once it was published, everyone understood that the *Woman's Bible* was largely Stanton's product, and, ignoring her protestations that it was the result of a committee, they attacked it as the work of a pernicious mind, a heretical sensibility, and the logical outcome of the women's rights movement. Because it was largely her product, she had to defend it herself, which she did with gusto. When a clergyman claimed that the *Woman's Bible* was "the work of women, and the devil," Stanton retorted, "This is a grave mistake. His Satanic Majesty was not invited to join the Revising Committee, which consists of women alone. Moreover, he has been so busy of late years attending Synods, General Assemblies and Conferences, to prevent the recognition of women delegates, that he has had no time to study the languages and 'higher criticism.'"[36]

What Stanton did not expect was censure from her own organization. The furor over Stanton's work worried the leaders of the National-American Woman Suffrage Association. NAWSA delegates (and NWSA delegates, before that) had tolerated Stanton's pronouncements, robbed of official endorsement, out of respect for her role in the movement's past. But when Stanton's *Bible* was published, religious denunciation and the public mind immediately connected it with the women's movement—to the extreme displeasure of NAWSA leaders. It did not help that Stanton had used the *Woman's Bible* to address her opponents, calling their reluctance to provoke religious opposition "but another word for *cowardice.*" Women's complete emancipation could not occur, Stanton maintained, "without the broadest discussion of all the questions involved in her present degradation." She continued, "For so far-reaching and momentous a reform as her complete independence, an entire revolution in all existing institutions is inevitable."[37]

The National-American Woman Suffrage Association was not looking for a revolution just then, especially not one that rejected the role of Christianity in American life. The following convention would show just how out of step Stanton now was. As the 1896 convention began, someone whispered to Anthony after she had started speaking that the meeting had not been opened with a prayer. Deferential to her young lieutenants, Anthony called upon Anna Howard Shaw, a religious conservative who would become one of the movement's leaders, to offer an invocation. Perhaps missing the omen, Anthony offered another indication of her cluelessness. After the prayer she praised Shaw and Carrie Chapman Catt, who would succeed her as president, and noted her delight in seeing "these girls develop and outdo their elders." With Anthony apparently oblivious, the convention buzzed on the floor with the controversy, which exploded into the open after Rachel Foster Avery read an annual report containing the resolution subsequently known as the Bible Resolution, which disclaimed any "official connection with the so-called 'Woman's Bible.'" It was widely, and correctly, viewed as a stinging rebuke to Stanton. Once Avery had read the resolution, the public jockeying began, with Anthony's own lieutenants aligned in favor of its passage. Anthony herself maintained a conspicuous silence for most of the debate, which took place over several days. Finally, after prompting from Stanton's supporters, Anthony rose from her chair to come to her friend's defense, belatedly invoking the principles that had long been central to the women's movement. "I shall be pained beyond expression if the delegates here are so narrow and illiberal as to adopt this resolution," Anthony remarked, beseeching the convention not to embark on a path that stank of "censorship" and "inquisition." Anthony pled "for religious liberty" as a core principle that they ought to follow, trying to show the full magnitude of their act. Notwithstanding Anthony's impassioned argument, the resolution passed 53 to 41. The National-American Woman Suffrage Association censured its honorary president.[38]

Stanton, of course, was personally wounded, but the censure vote only solidified the contraction of the women's movement only to the acquisition of suffrage while disavowing any radical challenge to religious power in public life. Stanton's rejection of religious authority became politically anathema to pragmatists such as Anthony, who, whatever their personal preferences, looked to the continued hold of the moral establishment as the strongest basis on which to argue for female entrance into public life. That decision is a sign of the establishment's continued strength at the end of the nineteenth century. Pragmatists ultimately joined religious partisans in yoking women's rights to their avowed goal of strengthening moral prescriptions in national life. The host of NAWSA convention resolutions concerning Sabbath-breaking, temperance, and what Frances Willard called "home protection"—the women's suffrage ballot as a way to protect the Christian values of the home—demonstrated the rejection of the individual-rights philosophy that Stanton had advocated, in favor of the communal social ideals of the moral establishment. Women, in their capacity as stewards of the home, were to act as ciphers of a divinely sanctioned morality. Although the projection of that responsibility onto the world at large would require a greater public role, it actually entailed an extension and intensification of the rationale for the moral establishment, not the fundamental challenge that Stanton, Woodhull, and Anthony had earlier offered. In spite of their early provocations, or possibly because of them, proponents of the moral establishment remobilized in the last half of the nineteenth century, further sacrificing woman's individual rights for the good of the whole and punishing those who stepped too far in the direction of social transformation.[39]

8

RELIGION, MORALS, AND LAW

1.

The rationale for the moral establishment was internally inconsistent, claiming to support religious liberty while in fact promoting religious control. At issue was the meaning of religious liberty. When Anthony pled for the National-American Woman Suffrage Association (NAWSA) not to censure Stanton by invoking religious liberty, her speech begged the question of what exactly religious liberty required of the delegates. Moral establishmentarians had long dismissed the assertion that religious liberty entailed freedom *from* religion in public life. They asserted instead that it required the freedom of believers to bring their religion into public life to establish an ordered society. That definition of religious liberty seemed to offer a successful rejoinder to Anthony, Garrison, and Stanton's claim that moral establishmentarians were guilty of religious intolerance. It redefined behavior that dissenters considered intolerant as a necessary expression of an ordered society founded upon a religiously based morality. But given the redefinition of citizenship as both a national and a state-level phenomenon in the Fourteenth Amendment, the dispute over the moral establishment inevitably moved from the state to the national level, which involved groups whose claims to religious liberty were not so easily rejected. As Catholics, Mormons, and freethinkers all became serious players after the Civil War, they too challenged the moral establishment's notion of religious freedom. But unlike women and African Americans, each of these groups was explicitly religious (or anti-religious), which meant that establishmentarians had a harder time disguising their naked claims to religious power.

Catholics took the lead. Although Catholics objected to the entire panoply of preferential connections between Protestantism and the government, the battle played out most explicitly in the schools. To take but one illustrative example, in 1859 an eleven-year-old Catholic boy named Thomas Whall was beaten for refusing to recite the Ten Commandments in school. Protestants used a version of the Ten Commandments that included a prohibition against graven images that the Catholic version excluded. The school was two-thirds Catholic yet used the Protestant version of the Ten Commandments, and the Protestant King James version of the Bible was used in religious exercises. Both Whall's father and his priest objected to the arrangement and encouraged the boy to defy his teachers and the school administration. After a standoff lasting two days, the teacher turned to physical coercion. She called upon an assistant to the principal, McLaurin F. Cooke, who, upon entering the room, announced, "Here's a boy that refuses to repeat the Ten Commandments, and I will whip him till he yields if it takes the whole forenoon." Cooke whipped the boy's hands with a three-foot-long rattan rod, pausing to ask him if he would recite the commandments and resuming when he refused. He twice took the boy to the sink to soak his cut and swollen hands in water before continuing. After thirty minutes, with his hands bleeding, the boy relented. In the subsequent fallout, three hundred students were discharged from the school for also refusing to recite the Protestant Ten Commandments, and Cooke was arrested and charged with assault and battery. The trial was held in the police court of Boston. All charges against him were dismissed.[1]

Whall became the living personification of the dispute between Catholics and Protestant supporters of the moral establishment. Both agreed that one purpose of schooling was the perpetuation of virtue and morality. Neither nineteenth-century Catholics nor Protestants found it odd that public schools featured chapel service, Bible-reading, prayer, public recitation of the Ten Commandments, and other forms of religious exercise. State governments saw no contradiction in promoting Christianity in public schools while simultaneously claiming to uphold religious freedom. But the question was: whose Christianity? The evangelical awakening in the first part of the nineteenth century overlapped with the states' creation of public schools, and evangelicals mustered the political muscle to control school curriculum and administration.[2]

To proponents of the moral establishment, such an arrangement was inevitable. The school, Lyman Beecher had suggested, worked in tandem with the family and the church to strip individuals of their sinful and antisocial tendencies so that they were fit to live in a democratic society. This link between democratic citizenship and Christian morality ran deep. The State of Massachusetts commanded that teachers inculcate in their students "piety, justice, and a sacred regard to truth, love to their country, humanity and universal benevolence, sobriety, industry, and frugality, chastity, moderation, and temperance." It did so after the state had abandoned the idea of paying churches, but, as the architect of Massachusetts's common schools, Horace Mann, asked, "Are not these virtues and graces part and parcel of Christianity?" It was such logic that led to Thomas Whall's thrashing.[3]

Mann was a Unitarian, among the most liberal denominations in the United States, but his belief in the moral function of religion reflected a typical Protestant view. The common-school movement unapologetically embraced what it considered nonsectarian Christianity, which presumed the broad moral consensus that arose out of the Second Great Awakening. It thus excluded Catholicism, Judaism, Mormonism, Chinese Buddhism, and freethought. In practice, nonsectarianism meant reading the Bible without comment as part of a daily devotion. That way, schools avoided theological disputes and the Bible remained the foundation of morals. But this flew in the face of Catholic belief. Catholics did not read the Bible themselves. It was the function of a priest to inform the parishioners what the Bible said as part of the liturgical service and in the care he offered as a shepherd of the congregation. The use of the King James version furthered this implicit connection of nonsectarianism with Protestantism and promoted the Protestant form of worship that relied upon the self-sufficiency of individual Bible-reading without priestly mediation. Because Bible-reading and recitation remained at the center of the American common-school curriculum for much of the nineteenth century, so did the Protestant doctrine of *sola Scriptura,* or scripture alone. There was nothing nonsectarian about it.[4]

Catholics did not sit idly by while Protestants ran the schools, but rather pressed the states to allow separate devotional services, or, better yet, to allow separate Catholic schools funded by taxpayer money. But because the common-school movement was corroded by the desire to make immigrants, many of them Catholic, less of a menace to society, many proponents of the school movement, and by extension of the moral establishment, were unmoved. The judge's opinion in the Whall case serves as an exemplar of the moral establishment's response to Catholic dissenters. The opinion began by quoting the Massachusetts Constitution, which prohibited the use of taxpayer money by "any religious sect, for the maintenance, exclusively, of its own schools." Then, quoting the statutory law that governed public schools, the judge noted that all had been formed to perpetuate morals, including "the principles of piety, justice, and a sacred regard to truth, love to their country, humanity and universal benevolence, sobriety, industry, and frugality, chastity, moderation, and temperance." He dismissed the notion that these values were in any way controversial. Instead, the judge noted that the provisions of religious worship found in schools were at the time upheld by Massachusetts's "constitution and laws, and the almost unanimous voice of the people." By citing an almost unanimous public voice, the judge rendered Catholics mute. He had to. To acknowledge the protest of Roman Catholics would be to acknowledge the coercive rather than consensual basis of the moral establishment.[5]

Unwilling to recognize the forms of Protestant power that the court was sustaining, the judge closed his opinion with a ringing endorsement of the establishment. The major problem in allowing Whall and other Catholic children an exemption to the Protestant recitation, the judge explained, was that such a move would lead to the rejection of the Bible for use in schools at all. If Whall could claim objection to a particular version of the Bible, what would stop someone from objecting to the use of the Bible itself? To recognize a diversity of religious sentiments and practices would suggest a diversity of moral standards, which would in turn undermine a common morality and destroy the American way. All were required to acknowledge the Bible because it was the central means of protecting and inculcating a shared moral framework, which promoted the goals of the common school, the judge concluded, while protecting it from sectarian abuse.[6]

But nonsectarianism only evaded the problem, by suggesting that religious liberty was but a thin disguise for the forms of Protestant control that were the norm. In microcosm, the Whall case demonstrated the entire nexus of dilemmas Catholics raised for the moral establishment, which led to widespread religious conflict that grew as the number of Catholics increased through massive immigration over the course of the nineteenth century. By 1890 Catholicism was the largest denomination in the United States, with 7.3 million adherents. Methodists were next, at 7.1 million, followed by Baptists, at 5.9 million. Their organizational growth gave Catholics power to pressure the moral establishment.[7]

The difference, though, between Catholics and other dissenters was that Catholics sought a more forthright connection between church and state, one that allowed Catholic children to get religious education in their own tradition. Catholics had long rejected any idea of separation of church and state and even scoffed at the notion of religious liberty. As Pope Gregory XVI had explained in his 1832 encyclical, *Mirari Vos,* the separation of church and state had produced gross error in which "all that is sacrilegious, infamous, and blasphemous . . . gathered as bilge water in a ship's hold, a congealed mass of all filth." Because some people's claims of conscience were instances of error and immorality masquerading as religious belief, the pope rejected the notion of universal liberty of conscience as an "absurd and erroneous proposition." "When all restraints are removed by which men are kept on the narrow path of truth," which the Church alone could impose, then people inevitably strayed, following their evil natures from the path of righteousness into ruin. In a proper government, according to the pope, a divinely constituted authority that centered on the papal hierarchy protected individuals from their worst selves. To Catholics this required a connection not just between religion and the state, as evangelicals claimed, but "between temporal authority and the priesthood."[8]

This forthright argument for a state-run Church, directed by the pope and connected to state authority, exposed the hypocrisy of the moral establishment, which maintained a religious establishment but denied it. The friction between these two positions—both of which were authoritarian but only one of which acknowledged it—animated the debate over school control. Given the pope's categorical rejection of a church–state separation, which made any secular compromises difficult, clerical activism against Protestant-controlled schools increased. At the Second Plenary Council of Baltimore, in 1866, one of the three national meetings of American bishops in the nineteenth century, the prelates issued a decree condemning the public schools. Attending a school exposed Catholic children "to great danger to faith and morals," they explained. The risk to the faith was inherent in school readings that promoted "either a false religion or none at all" and that impugned Catholics' "most Sacred Religion and teachings, yea even the Saints themselves." The cumulative effect of such schools, the bishops explained, was to weaken "the force and virtue of true Religion" in the minds of Catholic children, destroying the faith by robbing it of future members.[9]

After bitter disputes in Philadelphia, Boston, and other East Coast cities prior to the Civil War, the epicenter of conflict moved to Cincinnati, Ohio, in the late 1860s. It had been brewing for some time, since Cincinnati was popular with the newer Catholic migrants and yet old enough to have an established Protestant population. Lyman Beecher had moved to Cincinnati in 1832 in order to Christianize the American West, and his death in 1863 did not diminish the desire of his evangelical followers to continue their mission. As was true elsewhere, the school curriculum featured the Bible as a central text in order to shape the moral impulses of students. By the late 1860s the number of Catholics had grown so large and so many of them had moved their children to private sectarian schools that some Protestants feared the shadow Catholic school system might undermine the civic foundations of the city.[10]

Finally, in 1869 a newly elected Catholic member of the school board, F. W. Rauch, introduced a plan to merge Cincinnati's public schools and private Catholic schools. This would, in effect, divide the public school fund in a way that Catholics had long hoped. The board, made up of two Jews, ten Catholics, eighteen Protestants, and ten marginally religious or unaligned members, seemed open to the idea. The public was divided. As debate proceeded, Samuel Miller, a board member who had no public religious affiliation, offered an amendment that seemed a practical necessity for such a merger to move forward. His resolution outlawed "religious instruction, and the reading of religious books, including the Holy Bible . . . in the Common Schools of Cincinnati." He claimed that the resolution sought "to allow the children of the parents of all sects and opinions, in matters of faith and worship, to enjoy alike the benefit of the Common School fund." It also might have had a more devious design. The provision was either a friendly amendment that recognized practical problems in merging schools with different religious agendas or it was a poison pill designed to kill support from both Catholics and Protestants, making the merger untenable.[11]

Whatever the intent, the effect was to end the merger. As the so-called Cincinnati Bible Wars heated up, hysteria infected all sides. After the school board voted to approve the measure by a vote of twenty-two to fifteen, Protestant activists filed a motion with a judge on the Superior Court of Cincinnati, who issued a temporary restraining order. When the court met to consider the case in late November 1869, the arguments went to the heart of the moral-establishment controversy. Ohio's constitution established that because "[r]eligion, morality, and knowledge" were all "essential to good government," the school board was obligated to protect every denomination in the peaceable enjoyment of their public worship "and to encourage schools and the means of instruction." Simultaneously, the constitution prohibited any "religious or other sect or sects" from having "any exclusive right to or control of any part of the school funds of this state." It was a plausible interpretation that schools must teach religion and morality as much as they must teach knowledge. The plaintiffs argued that the constitutional provision meant that Bible-reading was essential in schools. Although this was not spelled out explicitly in the constitution, it had been standard practice in most public schools for most of the century, which gave them the benefit of historical precedent.[12]

The ambiguity of the constitutional phrasing became central to the subsequent opinions and appeals. In a 2–1 decision, the superior court held for the plaintiffs, asserting that Ohio's constitution required the teaching of religion, which subsequently required the use of the Bible. The issue yielded three separate opinions. Justice Bellamy Storer articulated the moral-establishmentarian position clearly. He explained that in the United States and in the State of Ohio, all were allowed "the largest liberty of believing or disbelieving." But Christians, he continued, "advocate the plenary inspiration of that volume which gives us our only safe guide through this world." Christian belief had relevance in deciding the case because the nation had long been directed and sustained by Christianity. Reasoning from historical usage, Storer claimed, "Revealed religion, as it is made known in the Holy Scriptures, is that alone that is recognized by our [Ohio's] Constitution, and has, by a long series of legislative enactments, been sustained by the General Assembly. On no other ground could blasphemy be made criminal, not merely against the Supreme Being, but extended as it is to the Son and the Holy Ghost, names to be found only in the Bible." Storer noted that the argument of the defendants seemed to be that the doctrines of the Bible were sectarian. He was not prepared to "admit the assertion, in whole or in part," explaining, "What we understand by sectarianism is the work of man, not of the Almighty." Teaching the Bible alone could not be sectarian, he asserted, because it simply propagated the revealed will of God. His opinion placed the Protestant position into law without any recognition of its sectarian origins.[13]

Finally, the case made it to the Ohio Supreme Court. The court had already declared that Christianity was not part of the common law of Ohio, in a famous, though singular, 1854 decision that still upheld Ohio's Sabbath law. In keeping with its earlier position, the supreme court ruled in favor of the school board. Quoting the aphorism "Knowledge is the hand-maid of virtue," the court claimed that "[t]he fair interpretation" of the Ohio Constitution required only the belief that knowledge aided religion and morality, not that the schools must teach all three. Given that the legislature had not explicitly required the teaching of the Bible and the school board was ready to drop the practice, there was nothing in the constitution or any statute that would require the court to intervene. But because it was a matter for the legislature to decide, there was also nothing to prevent the legislature or the school board from later decreeing that the Bible must be taught in the schools. The court did not indicate whether such a move would be constitutional.[14]

Yet the court did permit itself a significant amount of comment upon the issues raised by the case, though they were not relevant to the decision. Noting that the situation touched upon "religious convictions and prejudices" that jeopardized "the harmonious working of the state government," the court again addressed the idea that Christianity was part of the law of the state. Reiterating its 1854 claim, the court asserted that Christianity had no part in common law. Claiming that this was for the best, the court explained, "[A]ll history shows us that the more widely and completely they [religion and the state] are separated, the better it is for both." It also went well beyond its earlier ruling by suggesting that there ought to be no connection between church and state whatsoever. Summing up its view, the court called its doctrine "hands off," adding, "Let the state not only keep its own hands off [of religion], but let it also see to it that religious sects keep their hands off each other." This was a secular vision, in which both Protestants and Catholics needed the regulation of a religiously neutral state. Against the claim that Protestants had a preferential role in law and governance because of their superior numbers and long heritage in the United States, the court asserted that the state's primary role in religion was to ensure that the minority received the protection of the state's constitution because "[t]he majority can protect itself." Lest it be accused of promoting novel doctrine, the court invoked James Madison in support.[15]

Given the continued opposition of Catholics and the movement by the Ohio Supreme Court to define the debate, moral-establishment supporters again responded with an attempt to use the fig leaf of nonsectarianism to further their interests without acknowledging the coercive nature of their power, taking it to the national level. In 1875 President Ulysses S. Grant proposed an amendment to the U.S. Constitution banning sectarian religious instruction in schools and prohibiting any public monies to be used in support of sectarian schools. His meaning was a bit vague, probably intentionally. It was unclear at first whether the amendment was designed to maintain Protestant control of schools or to secularize them. Newspapers around the nation reprinted the speech, with both Protestants and freethinkers praising the idea. The Protestant *Christian Advocate* called the notion "full of wisdom in respect to both the past and the future." The *Index*, edited by the freethinker Francis Abbot, also initially supported the idea. In an open letter to President Grant, the paper interpreted Grant's call to be an expression of the freethought principle that "religion should be left entirely to the citizens in their private capacity, and that the Church and the State should be absolutely and forever separate." Momentum built as Grant's fellow Republican James G. Blaine, the former speaker of the House of Representatives, who harbored presidential ambitions, proposed an amendment to the U.S. Constitution in December 1875 that would become known as the Blaine Amendment. It read:

No State shall make any law respecting an establishment of religion, or prohibiting the free exercise thereof; and no money raised by taxation in any State for the support of public schools, or derived from any public fund therefor, nor any public lands devoted thereto, shall ever be under the control of any religious sect; nor shall any money so raised or lands so devoted be divided between religious sects or denominations.[16]

Because it was widely seen as an attempt to curry favor for his presidential campaign the following year, the proposal languished for several months as Republicans and Democrats geared up for their respective nominating conventions. Republicans used the opportunity to insert support for the Blaine Amendment into their platform, but they rejected Blaine the candidate and instead settled upon Rutherford B. Hayes, an evangelical teetotaler who had been elected governor of Ohio on an anti-Catholic platform.[17]

The nomination of Hayes hinted at the amendment's ultimate purpose without fully acknowledging it. Noting the change, the *Index* stepped back from its earlier endorsement. The paper claimed that the Republican platform had been worded ambiguously in order "to catch (if possible) the Evangelical and the Liberal votes at the same time." The paper defined liberals as those who resisted any religious influence in schools. All who wanted religion in the schools were "illiberal and sectarian, since they would give to Evangelical Protestants or to Catholics an unjust superiority in civil affairs over Jews, freethinkers, and all non-Christians, whose equal rights they would thus unhesitatingly trample underfoot."[18]

After the party conventions Congress again resumed consideration of the Blaine Amendment. The chief question, which had been carefully skirted until then, was its purpose. Was it to prohibit the division of public school funds in order to squash Catholic schools? Was it to ban the use of the Bible in the school curriculum? Or was it to end religious exercises altogether? Evangelicals wanted to ban only support for Catholic schools. Freethought liberals wanted to ban all three in an effort to create secular schools. The debate in the House, which was controlled by Democrats, for whom Catholics made up a significant constituency, failed to clarify the matter. House Democrats felt the need to pass the amendment, lest they allow Republicans to represent them as tools of the Catholic hierarchy, but could not pass the bill without turning off the many Democratic Catholics. The House compromised by modifying the amendment with the proviso, "This article shall not vest, enlarge, or diminish legislative power in the Congress," which made it unenforceable. Having gutted the amendment, the House passed it 180–7, with 98 representatives abstaining, and sent it to the Republican-controlled Senate.[19]

It was there that the purpose of the amendment finally became clear. Partisans did not want to create secular schools, but only to prohibit Catholic ones from receiving state funding. The amendment that emerged from the Senate committee explicitly perpetuated Bible-reading with the phrase: "This article shall not be construed to prohibit the reading of the Bible in any school or institution." It left unaddressed whether the continuation of nonsectarian religious exercises was allowed, but since Bible-reading was at the heart of these exercises, the bill extended an implicit approval.[20]

Senator Frederick Frelinghuysen, a prominent evangelical from a long line of evangelical statesmen, became the amendment's primary spokesman. "There is nothing in it [the amendment] that prohibits religion as distinguished from the particular creed or tenets of religious and anti-religious sects and denominations [from] being taught everywhere," he explained. "That pure and undefiled religion which appertains to the relationship and responsibility of man to God and is readily distinguishable from the creeds of sects; that religion which permeates all our laws, which is recognized in every sentence against crime and immorality, which is involved in every oath," he noted, was still allowed, and in fact expected, to continue its place in public life as before. After quoting Joseph Story, Daniel Webster, and George Washington on the state's obligation to foster religion for the perpetuation of the moral order, Frelinghuysen concluded that the Bible's continued presence in the curriculum was necessary because it was "a religious and not a sectarian book." Supporting Frelinghuysen was the appropriately named Senator Isaac P. Christiancy, who noted that he could "see no possible reason, resting upon any true or just principle," that anyone who supported "an entire separation of church and state . . . full religious toleration and freedom of conscience and . . . perfectly equal rights among churches, sects, and societies" would not be able to vote for the amendment.[21]

Yet all were not convinced. Lewis Bogy, a Democratic senator, made explicit the anti-Catholic sentiment that had lurked beneath the surface of the debate. "I think I know the motive and the animus which have prompted all this thing," he complained. "I do not believe it is because of a great devotion to the principles of religious liberty." Bogy claimed that Republicans were in search of a wedge issue to sustain their electoral majority now that the North and South had turned public attention away from the plight of the former slaves, which made the Negro question "for party purposes in a manner dead." Acknowledging "that this thing is played out, and that 'the bloody shirt' can no longer call out the mad bull," the Republicans hoped to unite in opposition to "the old Pope of Rome." Ultimately the partisan animus that the bill created was enough to doom it, but it remained close until the end. The final count was 28 to 16 in favor, with 27 abstaining. The many abstentions in both the House and Senate votes were an indication of how rancorous the debate was and how unclear to many politicians the political fallout might be. Given this uncertain political environment, though there seemed to be strong initial support, the amendment fell just two votes short of the two-thirds majority required to pass.[22]

Faced with such concerted opposition, Catholics were unsure how to respond. Some supported a liberalized approach that sought mutually acceptable solutions short of dividing public school funds into Catholic and Protestant pools. Many accepted that the complete removal of religion from the schools was preferable to using their children as proxies in a sectarian war. In New York and Chicago, school boards rejected Bible-reading and religious instruction. Michigan and other Northern progressive states at least began movements to reject religious exercises as well, though not all came to fruition. Buffalo and Rochester banned Bible-reading and religious exercises in 1875. All had large Catholic populations, a significant number of freethinkers, and enough moderate Protestants that the various factions were able to coalesce around a compromise solution.[23]

But because many other Catholic prelates still required that education be Catholic, and because many Protestant supporters of the moral establishment continued to see Bible-reading in schools as the foundation of morality, the controversy did not die down. While both sides jockeyed for position, Pope Leo XIII weighed in with a series of encyclicals. He did not necessarily focus on the United States, but his encyclicals were binding on the American Catholic hierarchy and helped drive the debate. Leo saw the intellectual contradiction in the Protestant formulations. In 1878 he produced *Inscrutabili Dei Consilio*, an encyclical that noted the proliferation of evil-doing and licentiousness in the modern world and offered "the Church's aid" to restore order and security to governments. The moral disorder of the modern world proved, in the pope's reasoning, the rightness of the Catholic belief that religious authority sustained the state. His claim echoed those of the Protestant supporters of the moral establishment while providing the basis for Catholic critique of the moral establishment's Protestant bias. Three years later Leo elaborated this line of thought. In *Diuturnum*, an encyclical on the origin of civil power, the pope claimed that "the divine power of the Christian religion" had both "given birth to excellent principles of stability and order for the State" and "penetrated into the customs and institutions of States." Civil power emerged through the diffusion of Christian ideals, which the Church promoted and which required a clear institutional connection between church and state. Four years later, in *Immortale Dei*, an encyclical on the Christian constitution of states, the pope further explored the nature of the connection between temporal and religious power. God had established civil society as a separate sphere from the church, he explained, but the authority of its rulers rested on God's natural law and will. Because the church was the interpreter of the divine laws and will that framed civil society, the pope explained, "There must, accordingly, exist between these two powers a certain orderly connection, which may be compared to the union of the soul and body in man." The Protestant Reformation disrupted this connection, leading to the unrestrained license that the pope thought cleared the way "for enmities and contentions between the two powers" and that caused "evil result to both."[24]

Ironically, the pope had laid bare the internal contradictions of America's cherished notion of religious liberty. Protestants wanted a connection between religion and the state that relied on both a common nonsectarian Christianity and an institutional separation between church and state while still protecting absolute religious freedom. This was an impossible position. Given this lack of intellectual clarity, the moral disorders of the modern world made sense, the pope seemed to claim, springing as they did from a muddled desire to have Christian moral authority without any Christian institutions receiving explicit state support. Three years later, in 1888, Leo put the crowning touch on his assault on what he considered a befuddled pattern of thought. His encyclical, *Libertas*, on the nature of human liberty, denied that the Catholic Church was against freedom, rightly understood. Many civil laws existed for the protection of morality. "[W]ithin the sphere of this kind of laws the duty of the civil legislator is, mainly, to keep the community in obedience by the adoption of a common discipline and by putting restraint upon refractory and viciously inclined men, so that, deterred from evil, they may turn to what is good, or at any rate may avoid causing trouble and disturbance to the State," the pope claimed. This sounded almost exactly like Lyman Beecher's argument for the moral establishment. It entailed from one point of view a curtailment of liberty, the pope admitted, but "the true liberty of human society" did not consist in "every man doing what he pleases, for this would simply end in turmoil and confusion, and bring on the overthrow of the State." Instead, true liberty was made possible "through the injunctions of the civil law" so that all citizens might "more easily conform to the prescriptions of the eternal law." Naturalists, rationalists, and supporters of liberalism, according to the pope, all undermined this true liberty by severing morality from its proper authority. This was the ultimate absurdity in the doctrine of church–state separation, he claimed. It tended toward the moral perversion of naturalists, rationalists, and liberals. In making his claims the pope also dismissed freedom of speech, freedom of the press, freedom of conscience, and the idea of toleration itself, all of which ran against the perfect equation of liberty with obedience to God's laws supported by the Holy Church. This was an absolutely consistent position, though it was also fantastically illiberal. In contrast to the Protestant defense of the moral establishment that theoretically affirmed all the above liberties while in practice curtailing them, the pope rejected those liberties and called for a forthright connection between church and state.[25]

The dilemma eventually came to an uneasy detente on two fronts. Subsequent attempts to pass the Blaine Amendment in the U.S. Congress never got as close as its 1876 vote, but religious partisans, still fearful of Catholic control, also began to work on the state level. Because state law governed education and because the use of the Bible was common, religious partisans correctly concluded that a federal amendment was unnecessary. They merely needed to pass state constitutional amendments to protect what was already the prevailing practice. Partisans worked on state constitutions to pass prohibitions of sectarian education in states throughout the nation, often drawing upon the proposed language of the Blaine Amendment. These prohibitions had been rare prior to the 1870s, but faced with an insurgent Catholic population that challenged Protestant control, thirty-seven of the forty-nine constitutions ratified starting in 1874 contained provisions similar in wording and in purpose to the Blaine Amendment, with twenty-one out of twenty-five passed between 1874 and 1900. The great majority of states had these prohibitions by the twentieth century.[26]

Given the continued Protestant hostility to Catholic educational demands and the rejection of any attempt to divide state funds, the Catholic hierarchy recommitted itself to building the Catholic school system. In 1875 Rome had issued a directive that affirmed the position of hard-line bishops against public school education, given its Protestant or, more rarely, liberal tendencies. When the Third Plenary Council of Baltimore met in 1884, although the hierarchy was initially divided, the bishops decided that the pope's specific directive, the political thrust of his encyclicals, and the past Catholic ineffectiveness in eliminating Protestant control short of embracing complete secularism required them to move forward with Catholic parochial schooling. The council commanded that by 1886 parochial schools be built near any church that did not have one. Pastors who neglected to build the schools could be removed from their posts, and Catholic parents were commanded to send their children to parochial schools. Faced with rampant Protestant hostility, ultramontane sentiment, and an inability to make any large-scale compromise, the American hierarchy opted for devotional purity, moving at full speed to create the alternative Catholic parochial school system that would become such an important feature of American Catholic life. By 1920 the parochial school movement constituted a kind of shadow national school system, offering a haven for Catholics without creating the explicit church–state connection that their theology required.[27]

2.

The ability to expose Protestant hypocrisy and the contradictions of the moral establishment was not limited to Catholics. Mormons also pressed for a more honest connection between church and state. Mormonism—later known as the Latter-Day Saints movement—had already become one of the most important religious movements in a nation characterized by a bewildering number of new religious groups. Founded by Joseph Smith, a young man in Upstate New York who started having visions in the 1820s, Mormonism quickly blossomed into an important and indigenous American religion. Mormons, like Catholics, were persecuted from the start, a persecution that stemmed from the Mormon doctrine of the Restoration. According to the *Book of Mormon*, God's revelation had ceased with the death of Jesus' twelve apostles and began again with Joseph Smith. The Latter-Day Saints represented the restoration of the true church, which included a political kingdom ruled by Mormon leaders. With Smith's death, in 1844, the movement fragmented. The largest branch went West under the leadership of Brigham Young to set up God's kingdom amid the salt flats of the Utah territory. But Mormonism's absolute identification of God's law and human law was a problem to many non-Mormons. Evangelical Protestants might agree that human law rested upon the foundation of God's law, but they would never claim an absolute identification of the two with each other.[28]

Mormon political theology had another, more peculiar, tenet that appalled proponents of the moral establishment: plural marriage. Mormon men were directed by God to take on multiple wives. Joseph Smith had more than one wife by 1835, though his church had not yet publicly proclaimed polygamy or plural marriage as official church doctrine. In 1843 he finally put the doctrine into writing but kept it secret from all but a select few among the leadership. The delicacy of the issue demanded this approach. To proponents of the moral establishment, plural marriage would have sounded a lot like free love. In 1852, when Brigham Young finally announced the doctrine of plural marriage to the public, evangelicals and their allies mobilized. The U.S. Constitution, a moral document in evangelical eyes, could not be allowed to shield such barbarism. The Mormon Question, as it became known, was a catalyzing issue in nineteenth-century struggles to define religious liberty. Like Catholics, Mormons wanted a more forthright acknowledgment of the role of religion in public life. By looking for the restoration of God's rule on earth and by advocating plural marriage, Mormons joined Catholics in demonstrating that the proclaimed separation of church and state actually meant the maintenance of Protestant evangelical control.[29]

Though Mormons lived in tension with the moral establishment, their removal to Utah provided a buffer. Full-scale constitutional conflict did not emerge until well after the Civil War. Faced with a large and flourishing Mormon population, the U.S. Congress moved to address the Mormon question at about the same time that it sought to reject Catholic schooling. In 1874 it included anti-bigamy and anti-polygamy provisions in its revised statutes, which could then be used to prosecute Mormons in federal courts. Although anti-polygamy laws had existed before that time, the provisions had been nearly impossible to enforce because the Mormon hierarchy controlled every governmental branch in the Utah territory. But, in a surprise decision, the Mormon hierarchy decided to challenge the law by offering a test case. George Reynolds, a young and quiet man with only two wives, was selected for the cause and accordingly presented himself to federal authorities, who arrested and charged him. After his conviction, Reynolds appealed his case up to the U.S. Supreme Court, claiming that the laws of the United States that were in force in Utah territory deprived him of his religious right to marry multiple women. Because Reynolds resided in federal territory, the federal Bill of Rights applied to him. Since the Court had ruled in 1833 that the Bill of Rights did not apply to the states, this case provided the first opportunity for the Court to clarify the meaning of the religion clauses of the First Amendment, ninety years after the amendment's ratification.[30]

In a unanimous opinion in 1879, the Court ruled that free religious exercise, promised in the First Amendment, could not be an excuse to violate the sacred obligation of monogamous marriage by taking on multiple wives. "Congress was deprived of all legislative power over mere opinion," the Court explained, "but was left free to reach actions which were in violation of social duties or subversive of good order." The Court thus appeared to embrace a secular rationale while actually continuing de facto Protestant control over the definition of "social duties" and "good order." The Court continued: "Polygamy has always been odious among the northern and western nations of Europe, and, until the establishment of the Mormon Church, was almost exclusively a feature of the life of Asiatic and of African people." Upon the foundation of marriage "society may be said to be built, and out of its fruits spring social relations and social obligations and duties, with which government is necessarily required to deal." The Court's distinction between its inability to regulate belief but its ability to regulate practice, even where that practice might have a basis in religious belief, committed moderate Protestants to the enforcement of morals, without explicitly acknowledging that those morals came from Christianity. Because polygamy would be injurious to "good order" and was a "violation of social duties," it could not hide behind the claim of religious exercise.[31]

Some historians have seen *Reynolds* as a largely secular opinion, noting that the Court cited James Madison in its reasoning and seemed to avoid any mention of a Christian foundation for morals. But in spite of these gestures toward secularism, the Court actually upheld the claim of evangelicals who argued that the doctrines of the Restoration and of plural marriage could not receive the protection of religion because they were, in the words of the famous nineteenth-century historian Robert Baird, "irreligion—opinions contrary to the nature of religion, subversive of the reverence, love, and service due to God, of virtue, morality, and good manners." Protecting plural marriage in the name of religion was absurd, because religion, so the thinking went, could be known by its fruit. True religion produced morality. Irreligion, though perhaps constitutionally protected error, produced only licentiousness, which it was the duty of the state to mitigate. It was that duty, in line with the moral establishment, that the Court upheld.[32]

The Court was not finished, either. Associate Justice Stephen J. Field, one of the brightest minds of the Court, led the way. Field had been on the losing end of an 1858 case in California that overturned the enforcement of the Christian Sabbath for the first and only time in the nineteenth century. But he had the last laugh just a few years later when a reorganized California Supreme Court, with Field now sitting as chief justice, reversed itself, which showcased the kind of reasoning that Field would bring to the U.S. Supreme Court. In recognition of Christians' growing numerical superiority, Field moved toward a new legal paradigm that downplayed an explicit connection of Christianity to law. Accepting that legislation could not specifically promote religion, this new vision upheld legislation if it had any conceivable civil end, even if that civil end was rooted in religious concerns and seemed to support preferential religious ideals. This new argument could be seen as early as Field's 1859 dissenting opinion in *Ex Parte Newman,* the California decision that over-turned Sabbath law. Disagreeing with the majority of the court, Field had argued that California's Sabbath law was legitimate because it was part of a legislative requirement to oversee "the preservation of health and the promotion of good morals." Unlike the 1817 Sabbath law case of *Commonwealth v. Wolf* in Pennsylvania, when the state Supreme Court ruled that Sabbath law was necessary so that people would "be reminded of their religious duties at stated periods" and thereby be more likely to fulfill their moral obligations, Field pointed toward a legislative obligation ungrounded in religion as such. If legislation had the support of religious belief, it was better for it. But so long as it worked toward a civil, nonsectarian end—health and morals, in the case of Sabbath law—then that legislation was permissible even if it seemed religiously preferential toward Christianity, as Sabbath law did.[33]

Field was appointed to the U.S. Supreme Court by Abraham Lincoln in 1863. There he would preside over the reorganization of the moral establishment's legal rationale, a necessary shift given the Mormon question. The essential rhetorical move, which seemed to be present in the *Reynolds* opinion, required maintaining the appearance of secularism but shading the opinion so that it maintained the religious status quo in favor of the moral establishment. In 1890, in *Davis v. Beason,* Field continued the trend when he wrote for a unanimous court that a congressional law disenfranchising Mormon practitioners of polygamy in Idaho territory was constitutional. "Bigamy and polygamy are crimes by the laws of all civilized and Christian countries," Field wrote. Rejecting again the petitioners' claim that plural marriage was an expression of religious belief, Field noted that it had never been within the purpose of the First Amendment to allow it to "be invoked as a protection against legislation for the punishment of acts inimical to the peace, good order and morals of society." That was because religion dealt with what one believed in relation to a Creator, whereas the forms and rituals of a religion did not receive the protection of religion in the First Amendment. In particular, practices that "shock the moral judgment of the community," conceived in majoritarian terms, were not permitted. "However free the exercise of religion may be," Field explained, that right remained "subordinate to the criminal laws of the country, passed with reference to actions regarded by general consent." By claiming general consent, Field gestured to the democratic processes that had presumably set up the laws of marriage under which Mormon religious claims now had to be subsumed. Repeating himself later in the opinion, he claimed that it had been "the general consent of the Christian world" that submitted marriage to legal jurisdiction. His opinion left unclear what would happen if the general consent changed, suggesting at times that democratic processes created moral norms and at other times that it was the general consent of the more narrow Christian world that upheld legally enforceable norms. The opinion also furthered the distinction between regulating religious thought and regulating religious practice, especially when that practice was objectionable on moral grounds, but with only minimal acknowledgment that the morals were defined by Protestant norms.[34]

That same year, Joseph P. Bradley, who had earlier argued in *Bradwell v. Illinois* that the law of the Creator relegated women to the home, wrote for the majority in a 6–3 opinion that the United States possessed the power to dissolve the charter of incorporation of the Church of Jesus Christ of Latter-Day Saints and to seize its lands for its failure to disavow plural marriage, which Congress and the courts held as "repugnant to public policy." "The organization of a community for the spread and practice of polygamy is, in a measure, a return to barbarism. It is contrary to the spirit of Christianity and of the civilization which Christianity has produced in the Western world," Bradley explained. Citing *Davis v. Beason,* Bradley noted that the state possessed the right to outlaw polygamy. The charter of incorporation was given under the law of charities, which had been evident "in all civilized countries pervaded by the spirit of Christianity." When the trustees of a charitable corporation failed to provide for the public interest, the ownership of the property reverted to the state, he claimed, which could then appoint new trustees to ensure that the purposes of the corporation were met. Given the danger of polygamy to Christian civilization, Bradley ruled that the corporation was rightly dissolved and that the property correctly passed to the state, awaiting a reconstitution of the church without the doctrine of plural marriage. Writing for the dissent was Chief Justice Fuller, with Field and Lamar in concurrence. The dissent did not disagree that Congress had the power to suppress polygamy but objected only to the lack of any explicit constitutional authority for seizing the property. The chief justice granted that Congress had the power to craft legislation for the territories and that part of the power was an ability to restrain crime even when that crime took on "the form of a religious belief or creed."[35]

Although their victory seemed complete, partisans also worked on the state level to ensure that Mormon polygamists could not hide behind the veil of religion. Taking their cue from an earlier tactic but using it much more extensively and single-mindedly, they sought to connect improper religious ideas with immorality in order to allow the state to regulate Mormon behavior and belief. Partisans added the now-familiar proviso to many state constitutions' freedom of religion clause that prohibited them from being used to endorse acts of licentiousness and practices endangering the peace and safety of the state. Twenty of the forty-nine state constitutions (a little more than a third) that were ratified after 1874 contained these provisos, compared to twenty-two of ninety-one constitutions (a little less than one-fourth) ratified before 1874. Five states explicitly outlawed bigamy and polygamy, sometimes connecting that prohibition in an explicit fashion with the "acts of licentiousness" clause.[36]

3.

Having won their battles against Catholics and Mormons, supporters of the moral establishment went for the trifecta: the quelling of freethought. The freethought movement had been around since the late eighteenth century but gained prominence with the beginning of labor radicalism in the early nineteenth century. It remained small prior to the Civil War, important primarily in its connection to abolition and women's rights. Following the Civil War, though, it emerged as a movement of its own, largely through the effort of a single prominent figure, Robert G. Ingersoll. The son of a revivalist Presbyterian minister and a staunchly abolitionist mother, Ingersoll had been a Free Soil Democrat before bolting the party to join the Republican cause. He saw combat in the Civil War, was taken prisoner at Shiloh, and returned home to great acclaim. His impeccable credentials suggested a bright political and legal future, but this conventional career was not to be. Shortly after the war he gave his first iconoclastic lecture, in which he asserted that the church had enslaved the mind of humanity and retarded the progress of the human race. Because many of his would-be constituents did not share his religious sentiments, two years later he lost the 1868 Illinois gubernatorial nomination to Major General John M. Palmer, the founder of the Republican Party of Illinois, after Ingersoll's support among the convention delegates wilted over concern that his anti-religious beliefs would be a liability for the party.[37]

The experience radicalized Ingersoll, who turned his religious heterodoxy into a political mission. Ingersoll aimed to get the United States to completely remove Christianity from public life. To effect such a change he began delivering a series of lectures with titles such as "The Gods" and "Individuality," which rankled clerical sensibilities and drew large, interested crowds. His central theme was that the changing social order that had produced abolition and the women's movement would bring about progress heretofore unknown in human society, liberating individuals from the oppressive social structures that had held them back. As Ingersoll saw it, the forward movement of the nineteenth century necessarily meant the secularization of the world and the reeducation of individuals to rely on themselves rather than on an "aristocracy of the air." His most basic intellectual inclination was an absolute trust in the capacity of individuals. As he put it, "Every mind should be true to itself— should think, investigate and conclude for itself." As he became more provocative, his reputation grew. He was soon known nationally as an arresting orator and a dangerous infidel.[38]

As Ingersoll gained a following, evangelicals began to move against him. Anthony Comstock led the way. Comstock was the religious firebrand who jailed Victoria Woodhull during the Beecher–Tilton affair. That proved to be a brilliant maneuver that raised his national profile among the many concerned and powerful U.S. congressmen who supported the moral establishment. It served to establish Comstock's authority when he began lobbying for passage of tougher laws against moral indecency the following year. He started small. In 1872 he sent a letter to the Young Men's Christian Association (YMCA) warning of myriad institutions and cultural practices that endangered "the morals of the young." After his letter caught the attention (and won the monetary support) of the industrialist Morris K. Jesup, a strong supporter of New York's YMCA and also of Booker T. Washington, Comstock founded the New York Society for the Suppression of Vice. He transferred his newfound cachet into a remarkably successful lobbying effort. The result, a mere year later, was the passage of the so-called Comstock Law of 1873, one of the most important tools of the late nineteenth-century moral establishment, which called for a $5,000 fine and up to ten years of hard labor for distribution of each item of literature that Comstock deemed obscene, lewd, or lascivious. He even had himself appointed as a special agent for the post office so that he could carry a gun and make arrests for any violation of the Comstock law. He interpreted the law to include freethought literature as well because, he argued, freethought always went hand-in-hand with the degradation of morals, so it had a tendency toward obscenity and licentiousness that made it subject to his oversight.[39]

After the passage of the Comstock Law, Robert Ingersoll gathered fifty thousand signatures on a petition to Congress to repeal the law or narrow its application to exclude freethought, claiming that the law threatened free speech, freedom of the press, and individual religious liberty. When Congress ignored the petition and strengthened the law three years after its initial passage, other freethought groups went ahead with a Court challenge in 1877. Writing for the U.S. Supreme Court in a unanimous opinion was Stephen J. Field, who used his evasive civic justification for the defense of morality in order to reject the freethought arguments. Against the claims of freethought groups that the law infringed upon their freedom of religion and their freedom of the press, Field claimed that it had not been the object of Congress to deny any "rights of the people." Rather, adopting Comstock's view, Field explained that the law's sole object, which was within legitimate legislative authority, was merely to limit "the distribution of matter deemed injurious to the public morals." Now unmoored from religion in any explicit sense and yet all the more likely to be Christian, given American Protestantism's organizational power, the protection of morals became the major means of suppressing anti-religious organizations and their publications.[40]

Faced with this hostile legal regime, freethought opposition to the moral establishment, again led by Ingersoll, intensified through the 1880s. Ingersoll looked upon the evasions of the moral establishment with contempt. Religious partisans claimed to support religious liberty and church–state separation, he claimed, while at the same time so clearly flouting it. The tension of their position was, to Ingersoll, an example of the dishonesty of evangelical leaders. For their part, moral establishmentarians saw in Ingersoll the specter of complete moral dissolution. Quite apart from his secularism, his championing of progress, and his attacks on religious leaders, he served as a symbol of a society that no longer acknowledged the mutual accountability and tacit submission to religious authority that the moral establishment sought to perpetuate. As Anthony Comstock explained, freethought's claim to support liberty was in fact a call to license. "Liberals and infidels," Comstock complained, had mounted "a systematic and organized effort, to defend the dealers in obscene literature, or repeal the laws of Congress prohibiting the transmission through the mails of this infamous matter." Leading the charge, according to Comstock, was Ingersoll, "the great American blasphemer." Ingersoll's efforts threatened to destroy "the fastenings which are the only restraints of vice" by calling into question divine existence and, by extension, divine retribution. To Ingersoll's claim that Comstock was infringing upon their liberty, Comstock responded emphatically: "Liberty is not endangered. Moral purity is. There is a wide difference between the patriot's liberty and the Liberal's so-called liberty—license."[41]

The question was: where did liberty end, and mutual obligation and social solidarity begin? If Ingersoll symbolized the breakdown of a social order sustained by the moral establishment, he also defined the limits of religious liberty by putting a fine point on an issue that religious partisans wanted to keep rather vague. Ingersoll demanded that the moral establishment withdraw its restraints so that people could achieve individual empowerment and self-control. Religious conservatives could not see how to do so without risking the dissolution of society into moral anarchy. That disagreement constituted an unbridgeable gap.

Faced with this mutual incomprehension, moral-establishment proponents moved to coerce Ingersoll into silence. Comstock himself had no luck in catching Ingersoll in violation of the Comstock law, but Ingersoll suffered various legal intimidations, receiving fines for lecturing on Sunday, the last-minute closing of venues where he was schedule to speak in accordance with Sabbath law (though they were open on other Sundays for other purposes), and the like. In 1881, moral establishmentarians in Delaware enlisted the support of Joseph P. Comegys, the chief justice of the Delaware Supreme Court, to shut down one of Ingersoll's planned lectures. Prior to the lecture a grand jury was convened and the chief justice urged it to indict Ingersoll under a 1740 blasphemy law, because his lectures, Comegys wrote, tended to upend the social order by promoting a social philosophy that undermined public morals. The entire proceeding smacked of legal showmanship, especially after the grand jury declined to indict Ingersoll before he had even given his lecture. But it did offer Ingersoll the warning that if he did speak, he would learn that blasphemy was in fact a crime in Delaware. When many liberal papers around the nation criticized the court, Ingersoll cancelled the lecture with the consolation that the press had made his point for him. The threat of prosecution lingered again in 1884 in Philadelphia, this time under an 1860 law promising fines and imprisonment for anyone who would "willfully, premeditatedly, and despitefully blaspheme or speak loosely and profanely of Almighty God, Christ Jesus, the Holy Spirit, or the Scriptures of Truth." Ingersoll had had enough and went ahead with his lecture, labeling attempts to censor speech "in this day and generation" as "exceedingly foolish" and "idiotic." When asked what he would do if they attempted to arrest him, he replied, "Nothing, except to defend myself in court." The prospect of a court battle with Ingersoll, even if the law was on their side, dissuaded clergy, and nothing came of it.[42]

As Ingersoll grew in prominence, establishment hardliners fretted. Given all these challenges that faced the nation, they began to worry that the U.S. Supreme Court's recent reluctance in the Mormon cases to explicitly acknowledge the Christian bases of moral norms relinquished too much ground. Someone such as Ingersoll might, at some point in the future, exploit a legal rationale that had worked against the Mormons. This concern coalesced in a growing organization called the National Reform Association (NRA). It had been founded during the Civil War but took on life in the 1870s and 1880s as Ingersoll's provocations increased and the Court, led by Field, began to rework the moral establishment's rationale by emphasizing an unspecified morality as a way to maintain de facto Christian control without acknowledging its coercive power. To the NRA this suggested instability inherent in the moral establishment. Warning that "[t]he enemies of our national Christianity" were active and that the "Christian institutions of government" were under attack, the NRA called on all patriots to fight on "the field of moral conflict." It rejected what it called "the secular theory of civil government" or the idea that government had "nothing to do with religion but to let it alone." The NRA claimed that it opposed "both secularism and the union of Church and State" but supported "Christianity in the State." In other words, rejecting the desires of both freethinkers and Catholics, the NRA wanted to maintain the specific connection between Protestant Christianity and the enforcement of moral norms, because it regarded anything less as too easily exploited by the many enemies of the moral establishment.[43]

The question then was not whether religion and civil government should be connected but how. In the face of multiple challengers, the NRA decided that the implicit connection of the moral establishment now needed a permanent, visible foundation. Acknowledging their somewhat weak constitutional position, the NRA claimed that the moral establishment was grounded in a delicate balance between what it called the written and the unwritten constitutions. The written Constitution established the essential political and social principles and offered "authoritative sanction to the distinctive fundamental features of the national life" that were drawn, so the reasoning went, from the unwritten or vital constitution of a people. In the U.S. republic, the vital constitution "in reference to morals and religion" was always "unquestionably Christian." According to the NRA, the written Constitution was not responsible for constituting the American people. It was, instead, but the written expression of the nation's vital constitution or character, buttressing it and providing legal sanction for its enforcement. For various reasons that the NRA declined to specify, the constitutional framers had neglected to include an explicit affirmation of Christianity, which resulted in the unstable relationship of "[a] non-Christian written Constitution and an unwritten Christian Constitution." Only a constitutional amendment to acknowledge the vital Christian constitution of the nation would ensure that the minority of secularists did not exploit this instability in order to demolish the Christian character of the U.S. government and laws. To those who misguidedly touted the freedom of the individual, the association responded in unapologetically majoritarian terms, pointing to "the right of society as against the so-called rights of the individual."[44]

Although the National Reform Association never mustered enough support to modify the Constitution, it codified the several strands of evangelical political thought that could then be picked up by jurists. Among its most important judicial proponents was David Josiah Brewer, the son of Congregational missionary parents and the nephew of Stephen Field, whom he joined on the U.S. Supreme Court in 1890. When he arrived on the bench, Brewer assumed the intellectual leadership of a voting bloc of justices that guided the Court after Field's retirement in 1897. He also became an instantaneous celebrity, as bar associations and religious groups courted him for speaking engagements to elaborate his justification for the moral establishment, which clashed at key points with his uncle's. This was because, in line with the NRA, Brewer supported an explicit connection between Christianity and the state rather than a de facto one.[45]

Though he spoke and wrote on a wide variety of themes, the subject that occupied almost all of his utterances was the role of Christianity in the formation of the nation and its subsequent greatness. Rejecting the evasiveness of some religious partisans, including his uncle, Brewer insisted that Christianity was essential to the maintenance of a national moral character, not only because those who had internalized Christian ideals were more likely to maintain individual morality but also because Christianity itself provided the moral standard by which any action was measured. "Christianity has been so wrought into the history of this republic, so identified with its growth and prosperity, has been and is so dear to the hearts of the great body of our citizens, that it ought not to be spoken of contemptuously or treated with ridicule," he explained. Having laid the foundation for blasphemy law, Brewer elaborated the positive duties of U.S. citizens toward Christianity. Respecting Christianity implied respecting "its institutions and ordinances." Regarding the Sabbath, in particular, he was explicit: "The American Christian is entitled to his quiet hour." Most broadly, reiterating the views of Story, Kent, Lyman Beecher, and the NRA, Brewer held that because Christianity had been "a potent and healthful factor in the development of our [U.S.] civilization," it was a positive duty of every citizen "to uphold it and extend its influence." Following his own principle, it was Brewer who wrote in 1892 for a unanimous U.S. Supreme Court that the wide variety of historical sources, common law provisions, and state constitutional claims confirmed the United States was "a Christian nation." Because Christianity provided the foundation of all law, Christian moral norms had preeminence.[46]

4.

By the end of the century, evangelical political thought and its corollary in the courts had moved in a few different directions in justifying the moral establishment. When it came to Catholicism, partisans continued to affirm the role of nonsectarian Christianity in promoting morals but claimed that such a promotion was consistent with, as Senator Christiancy claimed, "an entire separation of church and state . . . full religious toleration and freedom of conscience . . . and of perfectly equal rights among churches, sects, and societies." Meanwhile, faced with the Mormon problem, the courts began to increasingly emphasize the secular power of majorities to set public policy in a way that still maintained the right of society to protect Protestant Christian moral standards. This had the appearance of secularism, thereby shielding courts from the obvious intellectual instability of the anti-Catholic movement, while maintaining the status quo of Protestant religious control. This second argument was also used against freethinkers, though some jurists became concerned that obscuring the place of Christianity as the foundation of morals introduced a further instability into the moral establishment that might backfire. The intellectual move that Field pioneered involved a feint in the direction of secularism, necessary to disavow the specter of coercion that haunted the moral establishment, with a simultaneous and concealed attempt to maintain religious control that narrowed the freedom of the moral establishment's challengers.[47]

The central issues of these debates—over religion and the basis of society, the source of moral restraint, the meaning and possibility of religious and intellectual liberty—were clear, even if the rationale for the moral establishment was not. The most forthright Christian defenders could not see how a nation founded on Christian principles and sustained by its moral imperatives could survive and maintain its greatness should those principles be eroded. The NRA and the Catholic Church agreed on this. Others, like Field, purported to uphold religious liberty while allowing for the enforcement of majoritarian moral norms. These claims often collapsed when subjected to too much scrutiny, because majoritarian moral norms limited the religious liberty of minorities. At the other end of the spectrum were freethinkers led by Ingersoll, who tried to argue with greater theoretical than historical plausibility that the United States had become great precisely because religion was left out of its government. In place of the moral establishment he argued for radical individualism.

Although challengers had revealed the establishment's intellectual instability, the moral establishment remained strong. As with those who had argued for black rights and women's rights, those who argued for minority religious rights were consistently thwarted because the establishment controlled the levers of power. In making all of these arguments, moral-establishment proponents relied upon a variety of rhetorical justifications, but ultimately it did not require a coherent rationale. The establishment was sustained by an elite network of politically powerful men and women. Theodore Woolsey, who mobilized the National Divorce Reform League, associated through the American Missionary Association (AMA) and the Evangelical Alliance with Mark Hopkins, who mentored Stephen J. Field and Samuel Armstrong, Booker T. Washington's teacher. Lyman Abbott, occupying Henry Ward Beecher's old pulpit, brought Booker T. Washington before a national audience by using the same AMA-friendly paper that Harriet Beecher Stowe and Catharine Beecher had used to mobilize the moral establishment against Victoria Woodhull. Morris K. Jesup supported Booker T. Washington and gave money to Anthony Comstock, who jailed Woodhull and used her provocations to justify his lobbying effort before Congress to pass the Comstock law, which he then used to control freethinkers such as Robert Ingersoll. The examples multiply. All these actors were connected through an ad hoc network of organizations—the AMA, the Evangelical Alliance, the YMCA, the Woman's Christian Temperance Union, and various structures of Christian business—that functioned as a "disciplined moral militia," just as Lyman Beecher had predicted they would. The net result, as it had been in the other cases, was the subordination of individual and minority rights to establishmentarian efforts to preserve order, moral stability, and their peculiar sense of American freedom.[48]

PART IV

FRAGMENTATION

9

A CONFLICT OF AUTHORITIES

1.

By the end of the nineteenth century, the moral establishment had emerged triumphant. Its proponents had shored up public support by building upon a familiar foundation: subjugating blacks, corralling the women's rights movement, and denying minority religious rights. But they had built their edifice upon shifting sands. The challenge would come on two fronts, one economic, the other intellectual.

The maturation of the industrial economy in the latter half of the nineteenth century produced new wealth, new social relations, and new anxieties. Prior to the Civil War, capitalism was entrepreneurial, with most companies owned by individual proprietors. After the war, the economy shifted to a more corporate form, in which large firms were owned by many shareholders, often controlled by a smaller group of preferred shareholders, and run by salaried managers. The creation of vast corporate firms, which pooled large amounts of wealth and had tremendous influence on American life, created a series of dilemmas for both moral establishmentarians and dissenters. The moral issues arising from the growth of the industrial market economy—the place of the individual in a system based on the pursuit of self-interest, the fear of mass licentiousness, and the worry that democratic society would come apart with no attention to social obligations, all of which had motivated the creation of the moral establishment in the first place—took on greater intensity in this new context.[1]

The Great Railroad Strike of 1877 signaled the beginnings of the shift, though its full implications would not become clear for several decades. The strike began on the Baltimore and Ohio railroad when John Garrett, who had just built his son a fifty-four-room mansion with a twenty-three-karat gold leaf toilet seat, imposed wage cuts on his workers. The ostentatious display of personal wealth infuriated the workers, who demanded the restoration of their wages. To suppress the strike, the governor of Maryland called out the militia in Baltimore, but not before a more serious strike had broken out in Pittsburgh. There the authorities attempted to call out the local militia, who, out of sympathy for the strikers, refused to deploy. The governor of Pennsylvania then called in troops from Philadelphia, who did not have the same empathy for the locals. The out-of-town troops ended the strike at the cost of twenty-five lives, which in turn prompted violence from incensed citizens and unemployed or aggrieved workers who had gathered in opposition. Before police and concerned citizens could restore order, the mob had exacted between $5 million and $7 million dollars of property damage. And that was just the beginning. The authorities' violent response may have checked the Pittsburgh strike, but it also prompted sympathy strikes throughout the nation, crippling transportation networks and bringing large portions of the economy to a standstill. Desperate to quell the unrest, President Rutherford B. Hayes, the evangelical teetotaler, called out federal troops, who eventually broke the strikers' will. By the end of July the trains were running and the strike was over. It had lasted about two weeks.[2]

The shock of the Great Railroad Strike did not soon fade, and it especially shook up the moral establishment. They saw society as a moral unit whose members were bound together by a shared Protestant morality. It was now clear that a web of economic connections not only linked people to a greater extent but made the immoral activities of one group of people—striking industrial workers, for example—consequential for all. To many moral establishmentarians, the ability of nascent labor unions to bring the nation's economic system to a standstill suggested dark conspiracies of anarchism and licentious disorder—and the potential downfall of Christian America. This reading of events revealed just how implicitly hierarchical and authority-based establishmentarian political thought was. Surveying the industrial carnage from the Great Railroad Strike, Henry Ward Beecher, for example, explained the position of many in Protestant Christian churches. "God has intended the great to be great and the little to be little," he insisted, dismissing labor's demands for fair wages as irreligious. According to Beecher, God was on the side of ownership.[3]

Dissenters, meanwhile, faced a choice. Throughout the nineteenth century, they had largely adopted a posture of libertarian radicalism. They rejected the moral establishment's submission of the individual to the larger collective and instead pled for self-determination. Their argument made a certain amount of sense, given the demands of the market, which relied on self-interest, and, in fact, many businessmen appealed to individual rights to justify their actions. Individuals, according to these corporate boosters, were able to contract for whatever wages they desired (or were forced into by their circumstances), which was a necessary component of liberty. That dissenters shared an argument with corporate boosters revealed the problem with nineteenth-century dissent. Libertarian radicals were so extreme in their libertarianism that their conception of society and of social obligation—to the extent that they acknowledged either—tended so far in the direction of abstraction as to be meaningless. As the market and Industrial Revolution gained steam through the nineteenth century and saw its share of violence, libertarian radicals' exclusive focus on the individual became an even greater problem, since such a focus offered no way to address the emerging power of corporations that would, somewhat unexpectedly, align with proponents of the moral establishment. In an economic world dominated by corporations and Christians, libertarian radicalism seemed quaint, unable to provide any coherent opposition.[4]

That realization would change the nature of dissent. In order to counterbalance the power of corporations, industrial activists were forced to act through larger entities such as labor unions and political parties in order to articulate a more coherent philosophy of social obligation. They began to coalesce around a coherent moral vision that reconfigured the relationship of the individual to society—a moral vision to rival that of the moral establishment.

At the forefront of the new dissent were the social theorists who created a new form of knowledge built on social research and housed in universities. But, initially, they ran up against the traditional structures of the American college, which functioned as a continuation of the primary school in inculcating Christian moral norms into pupils and acted as a bridge between the home and the wider world. Many college presidents were clergy, and a significant percentage of college graduates went into the ministry, though the number had declined over the nineteenth century. A religious ethos pervaded the college and extended to the curriculum, which culminated in a capstone course on moral philosophy taught by the university president. Seeking to transmit a fixed and timeless body of knowledge that emerged from the canons of Western thought and represented the crowning achievement of Christian civilization, the goal of the curriculum was to produce cultured and moral leaders for Christian society. As Noah Porter, the president of Yale and a moral establishmentarian, observed, "The position which we occupy is that [quoting another divine] 'the Christian faith is the perfection of human reason'; that supernatural and historical Christianity is the only Christianity which is worth defending or which is capable of being defended on the grounds of reason or history; and that such a Christianity, when interpreted by enlightened judgment, as to its truths and its precepts, is not only friendly to the highest form of culture, but is an essential condition of the same." Christianity, not some open and empirically measurable truth, was the body of knowledge to be passed along to students. The fact that many college trustees were also clergy limited the ability of professors to stray far from the moral logic of the curriculum or to pursue controversial research. These limits, its proponents claimed, maintained the institution as an inculcator of moral values for the perpetuation of Christian civilization.[5]

Yet this happy marriage between Christian rule and knowledge had grown tempestuous during the nineteenth century. New scientific discoveries in biology and fresh investigations into the origins of the Bible began to erode the intellectual credibility of scripture as a source of biological or historical truth. Darwin's 1859 publication of *On the Origin of Species* disrupted the Christian creation narrative by suggesting the irrelevance of God in human origins. Meanwhile, biblical critics, particularly in Germany, began to formulate the new discipline of Higher Criticism, which saw the Christian scriptures as a literary product of the Ancient Near East rather than as a divine revelation. Many began to consider the Bible not a timeless repository of truth but a literary expression of a particular historical moment. Humanity and the human social order, these new discoveries seemed to suggest, could be understood through history, biology, and culture alone—without any supernatural foundation.[6]

As the seamless Christian curriculum of the university grew more strained, critics began to reject the traditional organization and function of the university, seeking to remake it into a place of free and open-ended inquiry into the whole spectrum of human and natural existence. Distinguishing science, which they saw as open and empirical, from religion, which they regarded as fixed and dogmatic, critics began to call for a reorientation of the university around scientific research. But this would mean a wholesale rejection of the university as an institution for the preservation of Christian civilization. Traditionalists reacted accordingly. John W. Burgess, a legal scholar at Columbia University who became instrumental in the founding of U.S. political science, later reminisced about the hostility of traditionalists to his own research agenda at Amherst in the 1870s. "They regarded the college as a place for discipline, not as a place for research," he explained. "To them the truth had already been found. It was contained in the Bible, and it was the business of the college to give the preliminary training for acquiring and disseminating it. Research implied doubt. It implied that there was, at least, a great deal of truth still to be found, and it implied that the truth thought to have already been found was approximative and in continual need of revision and readjustment." Traditionalists, Burgess claimed, believed that an orientation to research was "more or less heretical."[7]

Their reaction was not overblown. The new threat became most apparent as university reformers successfully pushed for an end to the teaching of moral philosophy as a capstone course in the 1870s. Their rejection of the moral philosophy capstone went hand-in-hand with the reorientation of the curriculum around the new disciplines as the German PhD became fashionable in the United States. American scholars who trained in Germany adapted their own graduate programs from the German model that they observed firsthand. One of their major innovations was the introduction into graduate education of the seminar method, which stressed original research as a contribution to a growing and catalogued body of knowledge. Several new universities, beginning with the Johns Hopkins University in 1876 and the University of Chicago in 1892, organized their faculties according to the new disciplines emerging from Germany and added new research and publishing responsibilities for their faculty members. New scholarly societies brought specialists from universities together to further professionalize knowledge. So great was the transformation that by the end of the nineteenth century the traditional curriculum, in which students as a cohort took classes that culminated in a course on moral philosophy taught by the president, had been largely replaced by an elective system in which a student majored in a specific field of knowledge and received training in that field by choosing from a group of relevant classes. Although amateurs continued to publish works of history and to engage in social analysis, the professionalization of knowledge created an ascendant class of people whose authority as experts promised to provide a more certain basis of knowledge about the world.[8]

2.

Although these changes alarmed many religious conservatives and revealed cracks in the foundation of the moral establishment, conservatives did not fundamentally alter their thought. Instead, they sought to reassert their power by aligning themselves with owners in the ongoing industrial conflict. And they drew intellectual support from allies still in the U.S. college system. As Mark Hopkins, the president of Williams College, a member of the

Evangelical Alliance, and a prominent moral-establishment supporter, emphasized as early as 1862, the rights of property were God-given and therefore
sacred. Ownership was a characteristic of the God in whose image man was
made. "If God had no ownership, he would not be God," Hopkins explained,
"and if man had none, involving dominion, he would not be in his [God's]
image." Applying this principle to the labor situation, Hopkins suggested that
owners used their dominion as an agent of God and that their dominion
extended to the workers' labor. Should the worker consider his wages inadequate compensation for his labor, he could either quit or not accept the job in
the first place, establishmentarians maintained, but he could not strike or otherwise disrupt company operations, because that interfered with an owner's
God-given dominion.[9]

Many historians have argued that Protestants' emphasis on individual salvation and personal transformation made them hostile to collectivist or class-
based justice and guided their support for owners over workers. But this
misrepresents the thought that undergirded the moral establishment. Protestants, led by evangelicals, were happy to support communal moral norms as a
means of stifling the individual tendency to licentious anarchism and taming
the market. But by the end of the nineteenth century, they had shifted to allow
for economic libertarianism under the protective canopy of moral norms.
They coupled their nascent embrace of economic individualism with a forthright and nearly continuous rejection of socialism in all its forms. In this way
moral establishmentarians balanced the economic responsibility of the individual with the social and moral rights of the community.[10]

The concept of authority was the way that they justified this balance.
According to moral establishmentarians, God had laid down certain structures of authority—the family, the church, the primary school, and the
college—that perpetuated morality. The individual submitted to the forms of
authority required by God and enforced by the community. The industrial
economy threatened to destroy these forms of authority as it moved women
out of the home, children out of the school, and working people of all kinds
out of the church and into the factory and the saloon. But because many Protestants had become convinced that God had created the market as part of his
plan for moral governance, they needed some mechanism to reconcile its operations with their wider moral vision. To make sense of these inconsistencies,
moral establishmentarians devised a new system of noblesse oblige that combined authority and property. Owners could compel workers to behave
according to God's wishes because God had given them property. In turn, the
government aligned with owners for the maintenance of moral control.

In other words, by the last quarter of the nineteenth century the corporation had joined the family, the church, and the school as an institution perpetuating Christian moral authority. As the Christian ethicist Daniel Seeley Gregory explained in an 1875 textbook that was widely used in colleges, property was a means of achieving divine ends. A property holder had influence over numerous dependents, increasing his power to do good. And he certainly would do good, because God, the original owner, had arranged the world so that only persons of moral character could acquire property in the first place.[11]

The actual behavior of industrialists revealed a weak point in this scheme. Their rapaciousness and their seemingly casual disregard for Christian decency in their treatment of workers required some kind of justification. To explain what might seem like shortcomings, many moral establishmentarians shifted the blame from the owners to the workers, claiming that industrialists were forced to address the degraded moral condition of the workers who, like slaves, required stricter forms of control. Because Christianity provided the foundation for morals, the Christian owner had a duty to exercise what Gregory called "social control," which he defined as the maintenance of moral and religious constraints for the good of society. Wealth provided the means for the man of property to exert social control by extending "his moral mission" and "his moral work" to permit him to control those who labored under him. The state then ought to support owners over workers, as it did in the Great Railroad Strike, because God had created the state, just as he had created wealth, to enforce his moral norms. "The coercive power of civil authority," Gregory believed, had to be combined with the natural authority of owners in order to achieve "any certain efficacy in regulating the public conduct of men."[12]

Beneath all of this talk lurked a fierce anti-Catholicism. As the Protestant minister Samuel Lane Loomis of Brooklyn explained in his popular work, *Modern Cities and Their Religious Problems,* fully half of the workingmen in the United States were Catholic. Although he gave no source for this claim, it was certainly true that a quite large percentage of workers were Catholic or Jewish. Because to Loomis's mind only the Protestant Christian religion could provide a bond that would unite rich and poor, he emphasized that the presence of non-Protestant workingmen undercut the authority of the moral establishment through "radical differences in faith and doctrine." "Ours is a Protestant land in name, institution, and tradition," he noted. "Among Americans of native stock the proportion of Romanists is insignificant. It may, therefore, be said that the people engaged in the professional and mercantile occupations in cities"—in other words, the ones with money who employed the rest—"are mostly Protestants." Faced with a body of Protestant owners and a larger body of Catholic and Jewish workingmen, the allegiance of the moral establishment seemed clear. Workers needed Protestant owners to guide them. The tendency of Christian writers such as Hopkins and Gregory to bathe industrial mendacity in the cleansing waters of Christian morality combined with the anti-Catholicism of writers such as Loomis to support owners against workers through the formidable machine of the moral establishment. These arguments often required bald-faced fabrications and willful blindness to the real state of labor relations.[13]

Yet faced with the specter of growing poverty and state-supported violence against workers, a small minority of Protestants began backing away from such rhetorical justifications, objecting to the attempt to shield industrial magnates from moral culpability. These progressive Protestants began to advocate a changed conception of the relationship between the individual and the state that rejected the sacralized social Darwinism of their conservative brethren. Leading the way in what would become known as the Social Gospel movement was a liberal Congregationalist minister named Washington Gladden. Gladden had been raised in an evangelical household. He had supported the American Missionary Association's postwar civilizing mission to the South and had stood as an early supporter of Booker T. Washington. But Gladden came to the conclusion that the mere regulation of individual moral behavior, which remained the moral establishment's chief goal, could not address the problems of industrial conflict. Just as the individual needed to be tamed to fit into society, so society and its structures needed to conform to the ethical imperatives of Jesus.

In 1886 he published a landmark book entitled *Applied Christianity: Moral Aspects of Social Questions,* which began to chart a new course. But Gladden's departure from his more conservative brethren was not total. Rather, he extended the idea that religion formed the basis of society by providing the morals to be enforced in law that could tame industrial capitalism, an argument similar to the moral establishment's original vision. And he believed that Christian civilization relied upon private property. The question for Gladden was not the fact of wealth but its distribution. The competition over resources and the hoarding of wealth by industrial magnates led Gladden to declare American industrial capitalism both "anti-social and anti-Christian." He dismissed the fiction that the market always produced moral behavior from property holders through some obscure mechanism that rewarded character with wealth. Instead of offering platitudes, Gladden suggested that when a Christian man made money he had the responsibility to enter into a profit-sharing agreement between labor and capital. Such an arrangement would honor the partnership that actually existed between the two sides, he explained, and would honor the law of love that Jesus had promoted.[14]

Ultimately, the appearance of Gladden's book marked the beginning of a split within Protestantism, but that split was neither immediate nor decisive. Historians have often spoken of the Social Gospel as ascendant in the last quarter of the nineteenth century, but such a claim overstates the degree of its influence and the delicate position in which Gladden found himself. He challenged conservative Protestants to become consistent in their moral vision. He criticized secular reformers for their inattention to religion in reforming the industrial system. And he sought to woo workers into a Christianity that maintained its relevance in the new industrial age. But his results, at least in the nineteenth century, were meager.[15]

By contrast, the ideas of the conservative moral establishment made their way into law. The driving force in aligning the moral establishment with corporate capitalism was none other than Stephen J. Field, who had been so instrumental in clearing the way for Jim Crow and in maintaining the Comstock laws. Field had been trained originally by Mark Hopkins, so he was steeped in the moral establishment's dominant patterns of thought. When he moved on to the bench he brought with him Hopkins's belief that God had anointed property. As early as 1873 Field had claimed that, with the passage of the Fourteenth Amendment, the Declaration of Independence's promise of life, liberty, and the pursuit of happiness, the last of which he understood as property, had been incorporated into constitutional doctrine through that amendment's privileges and immunities clause. But he had come out on the losing end of the *Slaughterhouse Cases* in 1873, when the Court stripped the privileges and immunities clause of any meaning. In Field's argument, the Fourteenth Amendment limited the powers of state action but left individuals to work out social decisions among themselves. There was no worry, according to Field, that it might strengthen black civil rights since the majority-white population in the South could always control their former slaves through informal social mechanisms. After the majority rejected his view, Field shifted his attention to the due process clause of the Fourteenth Amendment, which asserted that the state could not "deprive any person of life, liberty, or property, without due process of law." In many ways this clause offered a better peg on which Field could hang his constitutional doctrine because the due process clause, which limited the actions of state governments, mirrored the language of the Fifth Amendment, which prohibited the national government from depriving anyone of "life, liberty, or property, without due process of law." Together, the two amendments offered a way to forbid both national- and state-level governments from interfering with the property rights of owners, thereby privileging the rights of corporations over those of unionized workers.[16]

The Court swung to Field's interpretation three years later in the case of *United States v. Cruikshank.* The case actually had nothing to do with property rights, so it showcased how the acceptance of a racial hierarchy often marched hand-in-hand with other forms of control. In 1873 an armed militia of white men in Louisiana attacked black Republican supporters in what has become known as the Colfax Massacre, killing an estimated 150 freedmen in a campaign of intimidation designed to regain political control of the state and to end Reconstruction. The federal government sought to use the Fourteenth Amendment to end voter intimidation, but the *Cruikshank* ruling further eviscerated the power of the Fourteenth Amendment to protect black rights, by suggesting again that the amendment applied only to state action, not the actions of individuals, and so could not be used to control white-supremacist militias. The Court also drew upon its prior ruling in *Minor v. Happersett,* which rejected Victoria Woodhull's argument that the Fourteenth Amendment conferred suffrage, to renounce any federal interest in addressing access to voting. The net effect of the decision was to give the go-ahead to Southern Democrats to use private violence and informal militias to keep African Americans from the polls. Since the *Cruikshank* case completely drained the Fourteenth Amendment of its original purpose to protect black civil rights, its remaining purpose was so indeterminate that Field could in time make property protection the amendment's primary focus.[17]

In 1886, the year Gladden's book was published and eleven years after the Court's decision in *Cruikshank,* the U.S. Supreme Court took a decisive step toward using the Fourteenth Amendment to align the cause of corporations with the goals of Christian government. In *Santa Clara County v. Southern Pacific Railroad,* the Court ruled that a corporation counted as a person before the law and so received protection under the Fourteenth Amendment. Making a corporation a legal person with due process rights meant in principle that workingmen's organizations, which were not given a similar designation, could be seen in the eyes of the law as interfering with the right of two individuals—a worker and a corporation—to freely contract. In other words, by giving corporations legal protection from the Fourteenth Amendment, the Court rejected collective bargaining and blocked workers from using state legislatures to set limits on the workday or to require minimum levels of compensation.[18]

3.

Meanwhile, the new dissenters in the university continued to develop their rival system of authority. Although discoveries in biology and biblical studies had originally undermined the Christian foundation of the university system, they were not the most important disciplines in challenging the moral establishment. That honor fell to the new social sciences. The moral establishment claimed to provide authoritative guidance (and coercion) premised on Christianity as a foundation for the social and moral progress of the nation. But it relied on a social philosophy and a set of social theories that were, in principle, subject to empirical verification. Social science sought to arrive at solutions to society's problems through scientific study, which could test the ideas of the moral establishment and might even support them, depending on how the investigation proceeded. Moral establishmentarians even remained optimistic that if social science could be connected to the classical ideals of the university, in which science was but man's attempt to understand God and his creation, then social science might simply offer a more sophisticated means of social control.

This lack of clarity about the role of Christianity in social science stretched at least to the creation of the American Social Science Association (ASSA) in 1865. Less an academic organization than a ragtag collection of reformers, amateurs, and a handful of scholars, the ASSA sought to create new knowledge about the world for social and moral betterment. As the association developed, its amateurism and advocacy ran up against the developing ethos of scientific professionalism in the university. By 1878, when Benjamin Peirce, a devout Christian, Harvard mathematician, and father of the pragmatist Charles Sanders Peirce, became its president, the association already bordered on irrelevance. To resuscitate it, Peirce proposed merging the association with the then newly created Johns Hopkins University. But in rejecting the offer, Daniel Coit Gilman, the university president, cited the difference between "investigation & agitation" that distinguished the function of the social science association from that of a university. Gilman's rejection of the ASSA marked the emergence of social science from adolescence and required it to move away from the armchair activism that had characterized it up to that point.[19]

This rejection of advocacy promised (or threatened) to free social science from the control of Christianity, which caused further consternation among moral establishmentarians. Washington Gladden, in particular, saw this danger. Gladden wanted to harness social science to religious ends. He had happily embraced the new social disciplines at first as a rejection of what he considered the "greatly exaggerated individualism" that dissenters like Garrison, Stanton, and Ingersoll had supported in the past. Unlike that individualism, which exalted "[t]he sacredness of the personality" over the whole of society, social science, he claimed, remained attentive to "the relations and mutual obligations of persons" rather than to their absolute autonomy. Yet when social scientists moved away from activism, Gladden grew concerned that they might become hostile to Christianity's role in public life. Dismissing the inevitability of tension between a dogmatic religious system and an open-ended discipline of inquiry, Gladden insisted, "The relation of Social Science to Christianity is, in fact, the relation of an offspring to its parent. Social Science is the child of Christianity." Because Christianity, through the moral establishment, had sought to create an ideal social order that paid attention to social obligation, it had laid the foundation for what social science now sought to do. But instead of the natural alliance between social science and Christianity, there had arisen a "schism between Christians and Sociologists," Gladden acknowledged. Gladden wanted to reverse this development, harnessing social science to the purposes of Christianity so that the moral establishment might be consistently and permanently assured.[20]

Others joined Gladden in attempting to create a Christian social science to move the moral establishment in a more liberal direction. In 1885, the year before Gladden published his book, *Applied Christianity,* a group of scholar–activists led by the progressive Christian Richard T. Ely formed the American Economic Association. Joining Ely and Gladden at the association's inception were Lyman Abbott and Carroll D. Wright, the U.S. commissioner of labor whose office oversaw the gathering of statistics on marriage and divorce. Ely led his colleagues in transposing the imperatives of the moral establishment, which governed individual moral choices, into the new discipline of economics. He wanted to tame the economic choices of individuals and the economic behavior of corporations, which conservative moral establishmentarians had placed under an ethical shelter. The conveners of the association laid out a platform explaining that they viewed government "as an educational and ethical agency" that was necessary to all social progress. Because the economic laissez-faire that the moral establishment supported was "unsafe in politics and unsound in morals," the association proposed a new union of effort by "Church, state and science" to create a more comprehensive moral regime that reflected the realities of the industrial age. This effort would continue the connection between church and state that existed under the moral establishment, but the addition of science promised to regularize and perfect that union.[21]

The question facing the American Economic Association was just how far a connection between Christianity and social science could be pressed. The advocacy inherent in their stance seemed to run against the scholarly detachment required of an academic organization appealing to the authority of science. The resulting tensions undermined Ely's original vision just two years later, when the association rejected his statement of principles. As one of his strongest opponents complained, in Ely's conception the association seemed to masquerade as "a sort of church, requiring for admission to its full communion a renunciation of ancient errors, and an adhesion to the supposed new creed." That dogmatic limitation on economic research proved untenable in the long term, and the divergence between the two parties increased so much that in 1892 Ely resigned his position as secretary of the association in protest.[22]

The split between liberal Christian reformers and the social sciences became even more apparent a few years later with the establishment of the *American Journal of Sociology* in 1895. The journal was founded by Albion W. Small, who led the pioneering University of Chicago School of Sociology, identified himself as a Christian, and yet still rejected the affiliation of social science with Christianity. Small formed the organ in order to preempt a more reform-oriented journal of "Christian sociology," and in the journal's first issue he laid out the purpose of the new journal—and the purpose of sociology itself—in a way that distanced the discipline from the reform impulses of Gladden and Ely. As Small explained in his introductory essay, "The Era of Sociology," the discipline had arisen as a result of the Industrial Revolution, which had placed human beings in a state of mutual dependence that was little understood. The popular consciousness and dominant social philosophy regarding this interdependence Small considered undisciplined and rudimentary. By the late nineteenth century this popular social philosophy—the moral establishment—had reached intellectual bankruptcy. Professional sociology, Small insisted, would provide a better method for redirecting and controlling society. A return to the reforming social science that Gladden and Ely supported would compromise disciplinary rigor and make social science but a tool in the perpetuation of a defunct social system. "To many possible readers the most important question about the conduct of the JOURNAL will be with reference to its attitude toward 'Christian Sociology,'" he admitted. "[T]oward Christian sociology" in the abstract, he promised somewhat enigmatically that the journal would be "sincerely deferential." But "toward alleged 'Christian sociologists'" Small promised an attitude "severely suspicious."[23]

The issue was authority. Small rejected the kinds of authority proposed by the moral establishment, in which the mere declaration of a Christian foundation for morality provided enough credibility for its enforcement. The breakdown of society into industrial conflict and general malaise necessitated a new path forward, he claimed, not the same tired half-truths. "It is stupid and costly to let our thoughts about society be vague or wrong or partial," Small later insisted. "To live well we need to understand the circumstances that surround our attempts to live." That effort in turn required addressing another, more fundamental, set of questions, each of which also potentially challenged the moral establishment. In order to make sense of social life, Small suggested that sociologists needed a deeper understanding: "What are we human beings actually living for? What are we trying to bring about, on the whole, as the outcome of living? Are we making the best use of our resources to reach these ends that we have in view?" These questions implicitly rejected the answers that religion provided. Small even moved morals from under the thumb of religion and into the sociological fold. "Whatever may have been the prevalent form of moral philosophy," he insisted, "effective moral standards have always been the algebraic sum of concrete judgments about the things convenient for the persons judging." The task of the sociologist was to suggest paths forward based on actual behavior rather than religious ideals.[24]

Although Small cast the discipline in opposition to the moral establish-ment, he was savvier in his opposition than another dominant figure in soci-ology, Lester Frank Ward. Ward seemed to channel Ingersollian iconoclasm but, unlike Ingersoll, Ward thought the power of organized Christianity required more than the reorganization of society around the sanctity of the individual. Like Small, he saw the industrial age as a "revolt against that kind of *authority* which would force upon the people the primitive civilizations of by-gone centuries," but he worried that a pure revolt that rejected social authority without a replacement would create only chaos. "Co-operative organization is the order of the day," Ward declared, a task that required "the friends of liberalism" to unite against "the great and popular institution known as the Orthodox Church," whose teachings were in fact "the modified superstitions of barbarous ages."[25]

Some writers have seen Small as more open to the influence of Christian-ity than Ward was, two men on different ends of a spectrum within social science. In actuality, they fundamentally agreed that social science was a sec-ular affair. Small remained open to Christianity's utility so long as it did not impinge upon disciplinary rigor. He viewed Christianity in functional terms, as a means of promoting social harmony, but only when tamed by the scien-tific work of experts. In other words, he favored a subtle approach in subju-gating religion. As he explained in a letter to Ward, Small could not sympathize with Ward's views "especially on religious relations" and urged him not to broadcast his opinions "so freely upon religious subjects," lest he risk estranging people who might otherwise be attracted to their work. Small's comments suggested a disagreement more in public posture and tactics than in their understanding of the purpose of sociology. He explained to Ward, "There are thousands of men who hold to the substance of the traditional evangelical doctrines, who are yet theoretically willing to be convinced that any one of them is untenable." Studying the mechanisms of social control and industrial interdependence, Small believed, would help experts direct society into new directions with no foundation in Christianity, but only if they approached the subject from the right posture so as not to alienate people. By properly concealing their purposes, they might have a more powerful reach.[26]

Setting up the purpose of sociology in this way, while simultaneously disclaiming any intention of advocacy, Small subtly moved the moral establishment into the realm of science and stripped it of its connection to religion. As Daniel Seeley Gregory had claimed, "social control" was a Christian duty for property owners who sought "to increase the power of the moral and religious restraints" over their workers. Sociologists appropriated this language of social control to fashion their new role as experts in directing society. But as the theorist E. A. Ross emphasized, the sociologist should be careful not to declare his intentions. "The secret of order is not to be bawled from every housetop," Ross counseled. "The wise sociologist will show religion a consideration it has rarely met with from the naturalist. He will venerate a moral system too much to uncover its nakedness." In doing so, the sociologist would be able to align himself with those who wielded authority while observing a studious reticence in not telling the average man "how he is managed." Like most of the major social scientists of the late nineteenth century, Ross took the falseness of Christianity for granted. But, given the number of people who continued to look to religion as the basis of society, and given the increasing number of people willing to join churches in the last thirty years of the nineteenth century, he recommended circumspection. Social control, performed by sociologists, could act as an antidote to religious belief. Sociologists would function as the expert managers of this "secret," a group of secular clerics to lead the new secular society into the future.[27]

By the end of the nineteenth century, many social scientists had agreed upon the future role of experts in guiding society in directions more rational, scientific, and secular. By claiming that Christianity had exhausted itself as a source of authority and that America needed a new body of knowledge to carry it into the future, sociologists built their discipline on a theory of secularization that they would effect. At the same time, by reorienting research away from the transmission of timeless knowledge and toward open-ended inquiry, reformers promised to break the deadlock between the moral establishment and its dissenters. As Emil G. Hirsch, a reform rabbi in Chicago writing in the *American Journal of Sociology*, pointed out, "The dogmatism of the conservative produces the dogmatism of the radical. Ingersollism is the inevitable reaction against the bitterness of unscientific bibliolatry." Hirsch's rejection of Ingersollian iconoclasm, or rather his identification of it as the mirror image of unthinking Bible worship, suggested the power of the new knowledge forms emerging at the end of the nineteenth century. By assuming aspects of social control and investigation formerly held by the moral establishment, the social sciences made actual human beings the new standard of scholarly work and offered a new series of questions to be addressed in society. In rejecting the authority of a remote God who gave his command from up on high, they promised nothing less than the redefinition of humanity's intellectual and social world—centered not on God but on humans alone.[28]

4.

The purging of Christian control from social science finally gave opponents of the moral establishment a rival source of authority. The ongoing labor conflicts provided the battleground to advance their claims. If the Great Railroad Strike catalyzed concern over the moral establishment's relationship to industrial capitalism, the Pullman Strike of 1894 was the proximate cause for the coming deterioration of Protestant Christian control. After nearly two and a half decades of unbroken labor disputes, the Pullman Strike resembled the strike of 1877 but was more disruptive and lasted three times as long. The strike's leader, Eugene V. Debs, a labor organizer and future Socialist candidate for president, had a long history of dissent. As a young man in Terre Haute, Indiana, Debs had organized events for the Occidental Literary Club and in 1878 invited Robert Ingersoll to give an address entitled "The Religion of Past, Present, Future." So delighted was Debs that he invited Ingersoll back two years later, when Ingersoll gave his "Liberty of Man, Woman, and Child" speech linking his anti-Christian crusade to women's rights. Because Debs had already become involved in the labor movement, he joined Ingersoll's anti-Christian militancy with his own emerging labor radicalism. Ingersoll's iconoclasm and his willingness, as Debs put it in an 1893 article, to lead "from the jungles of superstition and despair to those highlands of vision and thought where great and good men and women live[d] above the polluted air of the bogs and fens of ignorance and intolerance" provided what Debs regarded as a model of progressive thought necessary for social progress. Yet, according to Debs, thought was not enough. Intellectual provocation needed to march hand-in-hand with labor organization to provide a counterweight to the power of industrial corporations. This led him to found the American Railway Union (ARU) in 1893 as an agent of social transformation. The ARU organized workers by industry rather than by job within the industry, as most unions had done to that point, and so formed a powerful challenge to the control of corporations by virtue of its ability to prompt concerted action by all the workers of particular company.[29]

The organization was tested less than a year after its formation when striking workers for the Pullman Company precipitated a showdown that paralyzed commercial distribution for the better part of two months. After President Grover Cleveland sent in federal troops, the strike spread out of the Midwest and into the East and the far West. Newspapers called for the end to lawlessness and painted Debs as an agent of chaos, licentiousness, and criminality. Finally, Peter S. Grosscup, a federal judge deeply hostile to the unions—which he considered a threat to "religion, government and civil liberty"—issued an injunction that the police could use to imprison striking workers, finally bringing the strike to an end. But he went a step further by summoning a grand jury to hear conspiracy charges against the leaders of the strike. Holding Debs in contempt for violating his injunction to stop striking, Grosscup consulted the U.S. attorney general, who charged Debs with violating the recently passed Sherman Antitrust Act. The original intent of the act had been to restrain corporations from unfairly fixing prices, but it was now used to prosecute union leaders for engaging in an alleged conspiracy to interfere with interstate commerce.[30]

After Debs was convicted, he appealed to the U.S. Supreme Court, which unanimously upheld the lower court's ruling, although on different grounds. The opinion was written by David Brewer, who extended his uncle Stephen Field's reasoning into further reaches of law. Brewer justified the validity both of the injunction and of Debs's subsequent contempt conviction in moral-establishment terms, claiming that the strike interfered with the prerogatives and rights of "the public at large." But the specifics of the ruling mattered less than the effect, which was to place the injunction, an antidemocratic judicial move that allowed a single judge to stop a strike and to set the penalty for failure to obey, at the heart of the moral establishment's crusade against unionism. Debs served six months in prison for his alleged conspiracy, but he saw his time in prison as a penalty for going against the moral code of the religious establishment, who used their connection to law to get what they wanted.[31]

Debs was right about the reason for his incarceration. Because proponents of the moral establishment viewed order itself as a moral category, the inherent disorder of strikes and the challenge to authority that establishmentarians saw as the inevitable wellspring of industrial discord led to a profound suspicion of Debs personally and the cause of unionism more broadly. Brewer was clear on this point in his subsequent extralegal writings, which sought to connect the logic of his decision in the *Debs* case to the jurisprudence of his uncle Stephen Field and the wider vision of Christian nationhood that Brewer thought the Court ought to uphold. As he observed in his 1902 book *American Citizenship*, a collection of lectures originally delivered at Yale, true religion served as the soil of any society and required moral growth in order for a society to flower and flourish. This morality received the protection of law to ensure consistent and vigorous moral growth. Brewer saw labor disputes as a new manifestation of the old desire to throw off "the restraints of law," now in the more threatening form of mob violence rather than individual protest. This new form of protest ran against the reality that the United States was a Christian nation, which, he claimed, required first and foremost that all of its citizens maintain "a high, clean, moral character." "The long lines of burning cars seen in Chicago at the time of the Pullman strike," Brewer insisted, were a failure of personal character and therefore a betrayal of the primary obligation of citizenship. The strike also flouted the authority by which the nation was held together, because personal character consisted in obeying authority. Brewer went so far as to claim that obedience served as a secondary requirement of citizenship, because "obedience insures peace and order." Strikes, to Brewer, stood as "a form of disobedience to constituted authority" that undermined "active virtue," destabilized the forms of Christian authority necessary for society, and ultimately threatened to destroy the Christian nation.[32]

Because Brewer occupied the center of the Court's majority alliance, his jurisprudence set the general trend of the Court during his tenure, and his explanation of the larger moral issues carried considerable weight both within and outside legal circles. His opinion in *Debs* garnered unanimous support from the rest of the Court, and it was this general sympathy for corporations as coordinating institutions, first suggested by Field and carried through by Brewer, that finally triumphed in the now infamous case of *Lochner v. New York* in 1905, which rejected the New York legislature's restriction of the working day to ten hours a day and sixty hours a week for people employed as bakers. The opinion, written by Brewer's ally, Rufus Peckham, claimed that the right to purchase or sell labor came under the protection of liberty guaranteed by the Fourteenth Amendment. To protect the rights of corporations and any man who needed freedom "to support himself and his family," the Court carved out limits to police power by aligning the government with the corporations and against unions. The façade of formalism allowed the Court first to make the corporation a person and then to make that person equal with a worker in the eyes of the law, therefore defining labor unions as illegal conspiracies designed to interfere with trade while legitimizing corporate control.[33]

Though the *Lochner* opinion represented the triumph of the gospel of wealth in law, it also displayed the beginning of the cracks in the support of the moral establishment. Far from unanimous, the Court was split 5–4. John Marshall Harlan led his colleagues Edward Douglas White and William R. Day in a formalistic dissent, but Oliver Wendell Holmes Jr. penned his own dissent, which went much further. Holmes had grown up within the New England literary circles of his father, a poet with connections to the Boston Transcendentalists, whose deep religious skepticism he internalized. After joining the Court in 1902 at the nomination of Theodore Roosevelt, his skepticism caused him to maintain a distance from organized Christianity and to regard much of his contemporaries' thought with a wry disdain that extended to what he saw as the facile reasoning of moral establishmentarians on the Court. In *Lochner*, Holmes cried foul because the Court's inconsistency was so blatant. In case after case, he pointed out, the Court had upheld the use of the police power to impinge on freedom of contract, including prohibiting stock sales on margin in California and supporting maximum-hour statutes for miners in Utah. Directly calling attention to the moral establishment, he called laissez-faire liberty a sham, since the Court had upheld Sunday laws and prohibitions of lotteries as part of police power, even though both also infringed on freedom of contract. All of this pointed to what Holmes clearly believed was the intellectual dishonesty of his opponents, who decided cases according to their own preferences or philosophical beliefs and then invented principles afterward.[34]

Holmes's dissent grew out of a jurisprudential orientation that would increase in influence in the coming years and would work to supplant the moral establishment. His genius (or danger, as his opponents saw it) came from his rejection of the dominant modes of legal thinking as sentimental and obfuscating. As he explained in "The Path of the Law," his groundbreaking *Harvard Law Review* article published a few years before *Lochner*, "When we study law we are not studying a mystery but a well known profession." Holmes wanted to peel back the mystery by rejecting the notion that law was a logical system rooted in the divine will. He wanted to do so because he understood the effects of the coercive power of law. Law was a human creation by which "the command of public force" was given to the courts. In cases before the court, he added, "the whole power of the state will be put forth, if necessary, to carry out their judgments and decrees." Because Holmes placed coercive power at the center of his legal theory, and because he admitted no higher principle by which the law operated, he endorsed pragmatism in the study of law as its first principle.[35]

This idea of pragmatism had particular relevance for his relationship to the moral establishment. By rejecting the notion that law had any architectonic structure or any overriding justification, Holmes presented law simply as a tool that society used to accomplish various ends. It had no independent essence rooted in logic, or nature, or religion. Stripping law of its divine cloak promised to reveal law as a series of rules that deployed coercive power to get specific results. Among the most powerful sources of confusion in the study of law, Holmes explained, was "the confusion between legal and moral ideas." The terminology of law invited this confusion by drawing upon phraseology that originated in moral theory. But law, according to Holmes, should regulate neither human intentions nor the conscience, which he took to be the guiding agent of morality, but rather should maintain codes of behavior that society as a whole considered desirable or advantageous. This utilitarian conception of law further dismissed any role for natural law or divine will in the norms enforced by the state.[36]

To accomplish a clear-minded reorientation of the law, Holmes recommended not the study of the past, though history necessarily played a role in law, or the study of logic, though opinions used logical inference, but the study of social science. "[T]he man of the future is the man of statistics and the master of economics," Holmes explained, because statistics and economics, the ability to consider probability and averages, paved the way for the accurate use of law as a tool to accomplish social ends. Holmes's jurisprudential theory fully embodied what has become known alternatively as legal "antiformalism" or "legal realism," both of which rejected the idea that a system, even a legal one, could be understood strictly in terms of its own internal dynamics. Only through social science, he claimed, could the operations of law be understood and wedded to larger social processes.[37]

This growing conflict between social science and the moral establishment finally entered case law in a particularly complicated opinion, the 1908 case of *Muller v. Oregon*, written by David Brewer for a unanimous court that included Holmes. The unanimity of the opinion belied the contradictions coursing through the case. The substance was fairly straightforward. In 1903, in order to protect the health of female workers, the State of Oregon passed restrictions on the number of hours that businesses could require women to work. Subsequently, Oregon convicted Curt Muller, the owner of a laundry, of requiring his female employees to work more than ten hours in a single day, which violated the Oregon labor law. Muller appealed the case to the U.S. Supreme Court and had every reason to expect the Court would side with him. After all, the Court had just ruled three years earlier in *Lochner* that the right to contract was protected by the Fourteenth Amendment, so employees and employers should be allowed to come to a private agreement about how much an employee should work. But in a surprise turn, the Court ruled that the state had a legitimate interest in protecting the health of female employees.[38]

The Court's ruling in *Muller* grew out of the logic of the moral establishment. Brewer claimed in his ruling that the difference in female physical structure and her responsibility for children and the home justified the Court's differing stances toward labor legislation for men and for women. Since "healthy mothers are essential to vigorous offspring," Brewer wrote, "the physical well-being of woman becomes an object of public interest and care in order to preserve the strength and vigor of the race." Brewer was careful to preserve the *Lochner* opinion by making clear that the ruling in *Muller* had no bearing on that case because of the different constitutions of men and women. The dependence of a woman upon a man and the subsequent "control" that he exerted over her, Brewer claimed, justified the Oregon legislation, regardless of any Fourteenth Amendment rights that *Lochner* might have established. On the whole, it was a classic piece of moral-establishment argumentation. Brewer grounded the opinion in women's difference from men, a difference not necessarily rooted in religion but in nature and in history, which presumed religion.[39]

Yet the more remarkable aspect of the case came not in the opinion or in its unanimity, but in a brief submitted by the counsel for the State of Oregon, Louis Brandeis. Prior to his appearance before the Court in *Muller*, Brandeis had already made a name for himself in legal circles, largely through an 1890 article in the *Harvard Law Review*, cowritten with his law partner Samuel Warren, entitled, "The Right to Privacy." The article's significance lay in its declaration of a new branch of law that had grown with the development of civilization and industry. "Political, social, and economic changes entail the recognition of new rights," Brandeis explained, a claim that rejected the moral establishment and instead pictured law as a living entity that adapted to new social situations. In this new industrial world, Brandeis claimed, "[t]he intensity and complexity of life" that resulted from "advancing civilization" necessitated the ability to "retreat from the world." Reasoning from established law that protected personal writing and all other personal productions from unauthorized publication, Brandeis insisted that these laws grew not from the protection of private property or intellectual property but from the principle of "an inviolate personality" and constituted nothing less than a right to privacy.[40]

In claiming that the right to privacy grew out of changed social circumstances, Brandeis gestured toward an emergent sociological jurisprudence that Holmes also supported in which law grew with the wider society. He completed this gesture in the brief he submitted for the *Muller* case, known as the "Brandeis brief." It marked a transformation in the presentation of evidence in law, drawing upon hundreds of sociological studies to show that long working hours threatened female health. For the first time in a brief submitted to the Supreme Court, Brandeis offered nonlegal, scientific data in order to prove his case. Brewer's opinion took note of Brandeis's brief and even praised it, but ultimately he buried much of his discussion of the brief in a footnote and tried not to use it in his reasoning. Brewer might have perceived that Brandeis's brief acted as Trojan horse that threatened the structures of authority that girded the moral establishment. By drawing upon social science, the brief undermined the moral establishment's reasoning even as it accepted its conclusions: that women were fundamentally different from men, and that women were guardians of the home and the young. In his acknowledgment of the brief, Brewer noted that the sociological studies it quoted were not, "technically speaking, authorities," because they contained "little or no discussion of the constitutional question" that the Court had to decide. He permitted himself only a curt recognition that the Court took "judicial cognizance of all matters of general knowledge" presented by the Brandeis brief before moving on to the constitutional question of balancing police power with due process in order to maintain the moral establishment.[41]

Yet in an important sense the Brandeis brief marked the first emergence of the powerful challenge to the moral establishment that came from social science. With its orientation toward empirical investigation and expert opinion outside of law, the brief moved fully away from the notion that Protestant Christianity offered an explicit foundation for morals. It assumed that morals were open to empirical study and that jurists could not simply imbue Protestant Christian morality with state power. Ultimately, the Brandeis brief showcased the intellectual precariousness of the moral establishment, a precariousness that would grow more problematic in the future.

LIBERAL AND CONSERVATIVE
MORAL VISIONS

1.

The Brandeis brief signaled more than just an intellectual challenge. As progressive liberals began to separate from both libertarian radicals and conservative moral establishmentarians, they came together as a new coalition of post-Christian dissenters and secularized Jews such as Louis Brandeis. Although Jews had been in the United States since the founding, they began to arrive in large numbers (along with Catholics) in the last three decades of the nineteenth century. By the second or third generation, many of these Jews had rejected the faith of their fathers and emerged as an important new secularizing force in American life. Secular Jews used their unique angle of vision into American culture to join post-Christian dissenters in critiquing the connection between Christianity and the state. This coalition shared much in common with proponents of the new social science, politicizing the structures of secular authority that social scientists offered and clarifying their emergent moral vision.[1]

The movement toward a coherent and politically viable liberal moral vision became particularly apparent in 1914 with the beginning of a new political magazine, the *New Republic*, which showcased exactly the kind of post-Christian gentile and Jewish alliance that was emerging. The magazine took its initial inspiration from the political theorist Herbert Croly. Born of post-Christian parents with a reformist streak, Croly became a synthesizer and popularizer of the growing reorientation of liberal political thought. A sometime attender of Harvard University who never managed to finish a degree, he held an editorial position at the *Architectural Record*, displaying no particular inclination to politics until the publication of his first book, *The Promise of American Life*, in 1909. The book appeared just as Theodore Roosevelt was leaving office, marking the emergence of a new perspective that would further the liberal progressive vision. The power of Croly's work came from his assumption that the American promise, which he defined as the achievement of "the democratic ideal," had not yet been realized in the new industrial age. The industrial transformation of the United States had created massive amounts of wealth, Croly noted, but wealth had been unfairly distributed, creating an inequality that violated the promise of democracy. In order to effect what he called "a morally and socially desirable distribution of wealth," Croly looked to the American state as the only entity large enough to counter-act the power of big business to bring about a true democracy.[2]

In looking to the national government to create economic justice, Croly reworked the function of governance in liberal political theory, exorcising the remaining ambiguities of the Brandeis brief and fully separating the liberal moral vision from its conservative counterpart. Croly insisted that the matu-ration of industrial capitalism had created both a new constellation of social obligations, thereby undermining the establishment's individualism in eco-nomic affairs, and "a promise of individual moral and intellectual emancipa-tion" from stultifying religious authority, undermining the establishment's desire to maintain morals and good order. On balance, Croly remained a lib-eral. He claimed that the radical diversity of American life—created through immigration and the centrifugal forces of market expansion—invalidated "the earlier instinctive homogeneity" that moral establishmentarians had sought to promote. "That homogeneity has disappeared never to return," Croly insisted—a good development, in his view. And echoing earlier liberal dissenters, Croly noted that the moral establishment's expectation of confor-mity "was dependent upon too many sacrifices of individual purpose and achievement" to the supposed good of the whole. But unlike the nineteenth-century anarchic dissenters, Croly acknowledged that "the social problem," by which he meant the labor problem, required a new social and political philos-ophy to replace the moral establishment. The new political philosophy had to be capable of promoting "solidarity" in American life without eliminating the "desirable individual and class distinctions" that were integral to a society that was liberal and free.[3]

Here Croly acknowledged a fundamental dilemma in liberal political theory that would puzzle thinkers for years to come. He agreed that diversity and individual autonomy rendered untenable the moral establishment's belief that the state ought to enforce a Christian moral code. A majority would never accept it. But he also saw that society required some principle of solidarity that would legitimize cultural and political authority. In other words, Croly saw that the central problem of liberal theory would be to come up with some basis for a legitimate cultural and political authority that could be accepted by everyone without presuming the conformity and homogeneity of the moral establishment.

Fortunately, Croly thought that a new spirit of progressivism—embodied by Theodore Roosevelt—had begun to move through the American people. Roosevelt had ascended to the presidency after William McKinley's assassination by an anarchist in 1901, and he had presided over the birth of the regulatory state. In Croly's opinion, Roosevelt gave expression to an emerging American nationalism that was the answer to the vexing question at the heart of liberalism. Croly called this new political orientation "constructive individualism." Given the realities of interdependence that the Industrial Revolution had created, he claimed that only a correct balance between individual rights and social structure, which made individualism constructive rather than destructive to the social whole, could sustain U.S. democracy. Achieving this balance required the use of the national government to establish a stable economic structure, guided by an administrative elite, within which the individual could flourish.[4]

Croly's intellectual achievement was considerable. He thought in grand architectonic terms that allowed him to recast the foundation of modern political and constitutional theory along liberal lines. He provided a persuasive reorientation of liberal political theory and liberal constitutionalism that allowed for the expansion of the American state into economic regulation while preserving individual rights. He would become one of the central fathers of modern liberal constitutional theory. But he also possessed a shrewd ability to publicize his thought. Once *The Promise of American Life* was published, Croly worked with his good friend Judge Learned Hand, who at the time served on the U.S. District Court for the Southern District of New York, to get the book to President Theodore Roosevelt, who had gone on safari immediately after leaving office. After reading it, Roosevelt wrote Croly to say how much he enjoyed the book, and within a month he announced a program of what he called the "New Nationalism," which would serve as a slogan for his unsuccessful run for the presidency in 1912. Though traces of the new nationalism could be found in Roosevelt's thought even prior to his reading Croly's book, many observers believed that Croly provided Roosevelt with his campaign slogan and, by implication, with his underlying philosophy.[5]

Unfortunately for Croly, Roosevelt was running as a third-party candidate who split the Republican ticket and lost to Woodrow Wilson, which revealed the somewhat limited popularity of liberal progressivism. While puzzling out a way forward in the aftermath of Roosevelt's defeat, a new voice appeared on the scene that grabbed Croly's attention. In 1913 Walter Lippmann—a sometime bohemian with radical connections, German Jewish parents, and socialist tendencies—published *A Preface to Politics*. During the entire election season, Lippmann had been in Maine pounding out his new manuscript, though he followed the election from afar and had developed sympathies for Roosevelt. Like Croly, Lippmann thought that politics needed to be remade to address twentieth-century realities. This required a shift away from the formalistic, axiomatic, and platitudinous thought of conservatives toward a politics that accounted for the actual life of human beings. Modern politics, Lippmann claimed, required the recognition that there was a human center to the universe, which the revolution "in education, morals, [and] religion" had created. Rejecting the hold of God over American culture, Lippmann claimed that modern politics must "become experimental towards life" rather than relying upon dead religious axioms. This attitude of free inquiry, so central to the scientific ideal of the university, would lead to the destruction of past idols, Lippmann predicted, especially as they related to "moral judgment." He acknowledged that his outlook relied upon a "dynamic conception of society" that many people found alarming. It detached society from any absolute foundation and recognized the contingency of modern life. It rejected that any creed was an expression of absolute truth and instead asked what purpose each individual creed served. "Suppose we recognize that creeds are instruments of the will," Lippmann proposed. "[H]ow would it alter the character of our thinking?" The question was largely rhetorical. He knew that it would revolutionize modern politics by rejecting the moral establishment and reorienting the state toward the emergent social-scientific research model of free inquiry and secular argumentation.[6]

The publication of Lippmann's book won him an international reputation that caught Croly's eye. But at this point in Lippmann's career, he had not totally given himself to the form of liberal progressive politics that Croly espoused. Lippmann moved among Greenwich Village radicals, frequented the salon of the sexually liberated and openly bisexual Mable Dodge, and marched with the socialist Big Bill Haywood and the anarchist Emma Goldman on behalf of striking textile workers. Although he advocated the creation of a practical body of knowledge through inquiry and experimentation, Lippmann nurtured a continued attraction to a radically democratic vision rather than rule by an administrative elite. What Lippmann and Croly shared was the belief that their central task was the rejection of religion from public life to pave the way for a new moral ideal of democracy.[7]

Despite their differences, Lippmann listened sympathetically as Croly pitched an idea for a new magazine that he claimed could become a vehicle to reorient U.S. political life. Such a magazine might offer a platform for rational exchange to influence policymakers and to clarify the lingering dilemmas of liberal–progressive theory that had prevented it from cohering into a singular movement. Since Lippmann had begun drifting away from the bohemians by 1913, while questioning socialism as an unrealistic ideal, Croly's overture came at the perfect moment to draw Lippmann fully out of the Village circle, even as both had actually begun to appropriate some of the bohemians' democratic orientation. By 1914 Lippmann and Croly had converged in their political views and, together with Walter Weyl, another secularized Jew who had earned a doctorate in economics at the University of Pennsylvania's Wharton School, started the *New Republic*, which became the powerful voice in liberal progressive thought that Croly had predicted.[8]

The attractiveness of their vision to liberals was immediately apparent in the popularity of the magazine. Though the *New Republic* was not the only new literary and journalistic venture that emerged out of early twentieth-century progressive politics, it was among the most important. It would come to embody the vision of an increasingly well-organized liberal intelligentsia who sought to turn both Washington policymakers and legal theorists against the moral establishment. The editors introduced the magazine as "an experiment" to provide "sufficient enlightenment to the problems of the nation and sufficient sympathy to its complexities." From the beginning, it attracted a wide variety of interested contributors. The wry and superior Harvard philosopher George Santayana penned regular columns. John Dewey, widely known as a philosophical pragmatist, a post-Christian religious theorist, and an educational reformer who had connections to Albion Small through the University of Chicago, also became a regular contributor. Randolph Bourne, a radical democratic theorist on the edge of the Village bohemian circle and one of Dewey's students, wrote for the magazine prior to World War I, after which the editors' support for the war caused the pacifist Bourne to end his connection. The editors also included contributions from W. E. B. Du Bois, whom Dewey knew through their mutual affiliation with the National Association for the Advancement of Colored People (NAACP), an organization that the magazine supported. Even Felix Frankfurter, the Jewish future Supreme Court justice who had worked in the Taft administration before decamping to Harvard Law School, was an informal member of the early *New Republic* working group.[9]

This wide variety of contributors allowed for a far-ranging articulation of the specific policy proposals floating among liberal–progressives in the second decade of the twentieth century. The editors criticized President Wilson for his obvious lack of interest in promoting black rights and his reliance upon Southern segregationists in his cabinet even after promising African Americans "absolute fair dealing . . . in advancing the interest of their race." They published a selection from Du Bois's first autobiography, *Darkwater*, on the slights, indignities, and dangers of being black in America. They criticized the absurdities of American family policy. For example, when the New York City Board of Education sought to induce married women to quit their teaching jobs and refused to hire any more married women as teachers, the magazine dismissed the school board as made up of "oldish and reactionary men" whose main concern was a lame attempt to uphold religion and morality. These writers translated the liberal progressive theory of Croly and Lippmann into specific policies. Civil rights, in the liberal–progressive moral vision, were embedded in economic social obligation. Only by recognizing the transformative power of the Industrial Revolution could politicians, political theorists, and public policymakers move beyond the platitudes of the moral establishment into what Croly called "industrial democracy."[10]

2.

While Croly and Lippmann hoped to mobilize the liberal intelligentsia, religious liberals also moved to consolidate their position, though at a trailing distance from their secular counterparts. Washington Gladden in particular continued to promote the vision of moral and religious progress that he had originally outlined in *Applied Christianity*, but as he did so his mission became increasingly secularized. Even after formulating the Social Gospel, he had wholeheartedly embraced the Southern civilizing mission, which showed the limits of his thought. Yet, noting the dramatic rise of lynching and Southern racism at the beginnings of Jim Crow, he concluded that the mission was inadequate to ensure black success, if not misguided entirely. After he was elected to head the American Missionary Association in 1901, Gladden began talking to black leaders other than Booker T. Washington, who had remained steadfast in support for the Southern moral establishment. In 1903 Gladden paid a visit to Atlanta University, where he met Du Bois, who gave Gladden a copy of his newly published book, *The Souls of Black Folk*. Gladden was so moved that he devoted most of his next Sunday's sermon to the book, asking his audience to consider the effect of "living in a civilization whose overwhelming sentiment puts you into a lower nature of being and means to keep you there." He acknowledged that Washington's emphasis on "economic efficiency," or the internalization of moral norms as a prerequisite to black economic success, was "a great need." But he observed, "Mr. Washington emphasizes the argument that if the Negro will but succeed in a material way all doors will be open to him. But that is not quite certain. The history of the Jews is evidence that industry and thrift do not disarm race prejudice." Gladden also claimed that Du Bois's book refuted Washington by explaining how "political degradation" rather than character defects or moral failings explained black poverty.[11]

Gladden's encounter with Du Bois transformed him. As he continued to develop his thinking, he internalized the emergent liberal–progressive notion that social context and social structure accounted for a lot of individual behavior. This in turn led him, beginning in 1904, to drop his earlier support for the Southern civilizing mission and to align the AMA with the emerging Du Bois faction of black leadership. Gladden's move represented a sharp break from the past and an important moment in the growth of religious liberalism. Although the AMA had already suffered a decline in influence in the South in the latter part of the nineteenth century, his assumption of the AMA presidency and his determination to steer it toward the Social Gospel marked the beginning of the institutionalization of liberal Christianity and its social ethic.[12]

The institutionalization began to gain steam in tandem with that of secular progressivism. By 1907, shortly after the publication of another important book on the Social Gospel by the liberal minister Walter Rauschenbusch, entitled *Christianity and the Social Crisis*, the Methodist General Conference settled upon a social creed that called for a living wage, the abolition of child labor, a limitation on the number of hours a person could work in a day, labor arbitration in cases of dispute, and other practical provisions supported by the labor movement. The Methodist creed in turn became the basis for an expanded social statement advanced by the newly formed Federal Council of Churches (FCC) in 1908, which came into being as a way to facilitate Protestant action in the Social Gospel vein. Unlike the Evangelical Alliance, the federal council welcomed black denominations and encouraged the incorporation of women's missionary societies into their respective denominational structures as an expression of gender equality.[13]

Yet the FCC did not easily overcome the conservative resistance to the Social Gospel. Those conservatives who became part of the FCC rejected the focus on structural amelioration over individual transformation. By 1912 the federal council had limped along for four years without having accomplished much, when around four hundred delegates met in Chicago for its second quadrennial session. Several delegates expressed concern with the council's focus on social justice and wanted a body that focused on evangelism and individual transformation to counterbalance the already formed Commission on the Church and Social Service. As a concession, the executive committee formed what it called a Committee on Evangelism. William H. Roberts, who was appointed the head of the committee, explained in his report to the convention just why conservatives disagreed with the broader council. When seeking to transform society, he claimed, "[t]he fundamental error to be overcome is sin, and external need can best be relieved by beginning with internal necessity." Enough delegates agreed with Roberts that the FCC created a permanent Commission on Evangelism, which furthered the usual moral establishment ideal within the larger organization. This tension between liberal Christianity's structural focus and conservatives' continued desire to promote a Christian nation through individual moral instruction produced instability both within the FCC and within the wider American Protestant universe. That instability would grow more pronounced as time went on.[14]

As Protestant leaders fought among themselves, the secular liberals at the *New Republic* also ran into problems. Although they had been remarkably successful at first in pushing their agenda onto the national policy stage, they encountered trouble in the messy realities of politics. After the first year of publication, the editors had managed to estrange themselves from Roosevelt, who objected to their mild criticism of him in one of their editorial columns. Adrift from power, with Roosevelt now antagonistic and Wilson ostensibly unsympathetic to their vision, the magazine's politics began to change when the Wilson administration—much to their surprise—began to move toward their nationalist ideal as war spread in Europe. This attraction grew stronger when, in 1916, Wilson nominated the liberal Brandeis to the U.S. Supreme Court. The *New Republic* editors increasingly saw in Wilson a leader who might come to embody liberal progressive thought, and they endorsed him in the 1916 presidential contest. They even dropped the label of "progressives" in favor of the old moniker, "liberals," having now successfully remade the term to include a social ethic that looked to the federal government for its enforcement.[15]

The union between Wilson and the *New Republic* remained happy for a time. When the United States entered the war, Wilson began elaborating a moral idealism that came close to the *New Republic*'s vision for the nation but projected it outward onto the world. American democratic ideals, in Wilson's vision, should be universally applied to other nations. In his rhetoric the war became a means to apply those ideas to the postwar international order. To that end Wilson laid out what became known as the Fourteen Points, which Lippmann helped draft. They articulated a framework for the reconstruction of the postwar world along national democratic lines. Once it became clear that the Fourteen Points were to form the basis for the armistice, Lippmann even helped write explanatory glosses to clarify their meaning. The *New Republic*'s vision of political democracy managed by a cadre of experts became official U.S. international policy.[16]

Yet, confronted with wartime nationalism, the *New Republic* editors were tripped up by the inherent tensions within their position. Although circulation soared during the war as the magazine became a major player in public policy, the editors misunderstood the degree to which the nationalism that they advocated could override individual rights rather than guarantee them. In the grip of war fever, Congress passed the Espionage Act of 1917, which prohibited speech that promoted insubordination among the U.S. armed forces or that sought to curtail enlistment into the military. It followed a year later with the Sedition Act of 1918, which prohibited any criticism of the U.S. government during war. Various people, almost all of them socialists or people otherwise on the political left, suffered arrest and trial for urging resistance to the draft or for speaking against the government's commitment to war. The movement to suppress speech brought into question how much Wilson supported the liberal vision of individual civil liberties within the strong national government, a point on which even the *New Republic* editors had never quite been clear. They seemed to assume that experts could craft the perfect progressive state in which the individual could be fit seamlessly into the social whole. Yet when faced with a robust nationalism, liberals realized that national imperatives might be at fundamental odds with individual rights.[17]

This dilemma emerged at about the same time in two other contexts. Wartime nationalism also yielded two constitutional amendments that furthered uncertainty over liberalism's understanding of the balance between social obligation and individual rights. In late 1917 Congress passed and the states subsequently ratified the Eighteenth Amendment, which prohibited the manufacture, sale, and transportation of alcohol in the United States. Although Wilson had no formal role in the amendment (no president does), and he had a long record of opposition to Prohibition, his administration had begun to cave to pressure from the anti-alcohol movement, which used the tools of nationalism that Wilson himself had exploited in wartime. In 1916 Wilson signed a bill outlawing alcohol in the District of Columbia, which would serve as a prelude to the passage of the Eighteenth Amendment. His weakness emboldened the Christian lobby that supported Prohibition, especially once they were able to link the elimination of drink with wartime rationing. Prohibition became a patriotic duty, a means of using grain in the service of the war effort. Once Congress had passed the Eighteenth Amendment, it followed with the Volstead Act of 1919, which set the parameters of enforcement for Prohibition. Wilson vetoed the act, but Congress quickly overrode his veto.[18]

Prohibition was the crowning triumph of the moral establishment. But it also recalled its recurrent demons: hypocrisy and failure, at least in the sense that Prohibition tended to intensify rather than suppress vice. Prohibition led to the culture of the speakeasy in the 1920s, which served as a nexus for the underground bohemia of loosened social and sexual mores of the Jazz Age. It also turned over the formerly legitimate business of alcohol production to criminal syndicates, who used the now fantastically profitable criminal enterprise to expand their operations into several competing organized-crime empires that later incorporated illegal drugs, gambling, prostitution, and the like.[19]

About the same time, Congress also moved in the other direction. In 1919 Congress passed the Nineteenth Amendment, which at long last gave women the vote. The Prohibition and women's suffrage movements had maintained an on-again, off-again connection through much of their history, so the two amendments' temporal proximity might seem unsurprising. But the case is not that clear. Although many early suffragettes had at one time been associated with the temperance movement, the majority had moved away from temperance by the Seneca Falls Convention in 1848. In the late nineteenth century the ascendancy of Frances Willard, the head of the Woman's Christian Temperance Union (WCTU), within the National-American Woman Suffrage Association, strengthened the connection of the two issues among conservative suffragettes but not necessarily among liberal ones. With Willard's death in 1898, the WCTU began to back away from its commitment to suffrage, and the movements began moving in distinct organizational directions. Since Stanton had died estranged from NAWSA in 1902 and Anthony had died in 1906, NAWSA had drifted, torn between conservatives who wanted suffrage to advance the moral establishment, pragmatists who supported the conservative vision as a means to their common end, and radicals who continued to reject anything but the re-envisioning of U.S. society. NAWSA did continue to add members, growing from 13,150 in 1893 to 75,000 in 1910, but its increased membership still paled in comparison to the population. It had relatively few successes as a result.[20]

The suffrage push got a jolt of energy in 1912, when Alice Paul and Lucy Burns, two radicals who worked in the British suffrage campaign and who rejected the dour conservatism within NAWSA, renewed the attempt to gain passage of a federal women's suffrage amendment, using arguments that accorded with liberal progressive politics. Rather than claiming the extension of women's maternal responsibility through suffrage, Paul and Burns simply argued that voting was a civil right. The day before Wilson's inauguration in 1913 they organized a march in Washington, D.C., to publicize their cause. By taking advantage of the hundreds of reporters and large crowds in town for the inauguration, they hoped to energize the movement. It was a publicity success, to say the least. A hostile crowd half a million strong gathered along the parade route on the day of the march, which resulted in a riot. The suffragists ultimately required a U.S. Cavalry unit to subdue the mob so that the parade could continue.[21]

The crowd's response demonstrated the still-widespread rejection of female suffrage, particularly when connected to civil rights. But Paul and Burns continued with their liberal–progressive agenda during the Wilson presidency, abandoning NAWSA's push for the vote as a means of moral regeneration for the nation and forming instead a counter-organization, the Congressional Union. By 1916 the Congressional Union had reconstituted itself again, as the National Woman's Party (NWP), which sought to advance the civil rights argument for women's suffrage in the political sphere. The NWP began an aggressive campaign of petitioning the government, mounting opposition movements against congressmen who voted against suffrage, and picketing the White House. Their demonstrations in front of the White House resulted in beatings, arrests, prison sentences, solitary confinement, and diets of bread and water. When the suffragists protested their treatment through hunger strikes, the authorities force-fed them. Paul protested so vociferously that she was moved to a psychiatric institution. The publicity was powerful and damaging to the establishment, and finally resulted in the Nineteenth Amendment, granting women the right to vote.[22]

The liberal–progressive responsibility for women's suffrage can be seen another way. Although some members of NAWSA supported both the Eighteenth and the Nineteenth Amendments, from a legislative standpoint Prohibition and women's suffrage represented two different policy orientations. Political scientists have shown that many of the congressmen who voted for Prohibition consistently voted down women's suffrage, and vice versa. These voting patterns demonstrate that the two issues anchored divergent political and moral visions. The first, exemplified by Prohibition, relied upon social control by harnessing nationalism to the prohibition of immoral behavior, the restriction of immigration, and the perpetuation of white supremacy. This was the moral establishment. The second, exemplified by women's suffrage, promoted a civil liberties agenda supported by the emergent liberal–progressive phalanx that resisted the efforts of moral-establishment supporters. These liberal and conservative moral visions remained in struggle through the 1920s.[23]

3.

The struggle intensified with the Red Scare of 1919–20. It was no accident that the Alien and Sedition Acts had been used mostly to prosecute people on the political left. Socialism lay at the left edge of the liberal–progressive phalanx, which made it a serious threat to the moral establishment and therefore more likely to be prosecuted under the wartime acts. Socialists offered the most consistent opposition to the establishment, calling for the nationalization of industry for the benefit of the workers. This challenge increased immediately following the end of World War I when, after a period of labor quiescence during the war, large and concentrated strikes paralyzed several industries. Industrial violence spiked to new levels of intensity. Race riots broke out in several cities. Someone mailed bombs to business and political leaders. Society seemed to be coming apart. U.S. Attorney General A. Mitchell Palmer blamed socialists and other radicals for the bombings, though these groups denied that they had been responsible. In June 1919 there were more bombings, and this time Palmer was a target. He somehow managed to survive the blast, though the bomb was so intense that it blew the bomber himself to pieces and body parts rained down on Franklin Delano Roosevelt's house across the street. For four months after the bombing, Palmer waited. Finally, on November 7, 1919, under the supervision of J. Edgar Hoover, federal authorities conducted a raid on the meetinghouses of the Union of Russian Workers in several cities and arrested hundreds of aliens and scheduled them for deportation.[24]

The Palmer Raids, as they came to be known, sought to quell the unrest and finally revealed to liberals just how awry their embrace of Wilson's nationalism had gone. Liberals had held out hope that there could still be a seamless integration of nationalism and individual rights that rejected any role for religion in law. But the Palmer Raids proved the potential malevolence of nationalism even during peacetime and made clear the naïveté of the liberal moral vision. Their optimistic hope in progress shaken, liberals became sober libertarians in their insistence on individual civil rights. Oliver Wendell Holmes emerged as one of the fiercest defenders of civil liberties. His nationalism had earlier allowed him to uphold the Alien and Sedition Acts for a unanimous Court in the case of *Schenck v. United States*, handed down on March 3, 1919. But the increasingly repressive U.S. government helped him quickly to a change of mind. Just eight months later, on November 10, 1919, nine days before the Palmer Raids began, the U.S. Supreme Court handed down another opinion, in *Abrams v. United States*, that again upheld the acts, but this time the Court broke 7–2, with Holmes and Brandeis dissenting.[25]

With the liberal political vision of the *New Republic* in disarray, the dissent of Holmes and Brandeis suggested the beginning of a recalibration of the moral vision that would guide liberal-progressivism for the next several decades. Although the Court cited Holmes's earlier opinion in *Schenck* to sustain the conviction in *Abrams,* Holmes now modified his position without acknowledging the change. "Persecution for the expression of opinions seems to me perfectly logical," Holmes explained in his *Abrams* dissent. "If you have no doubt of your premises or your power and want a certain result with all your heart[,] you naturally express your wishes in law and sweep away all opposition." By contrast, allowing people to speak freely required a certain amount of faith in the reasonableness of people, rather than a belief in their inherent depravity, such as the moral establishmentarians posited. Trusting people "is an experiment," Holmes admitted, "as all life is an experiment." Humans live their lives with limited perspectives that require us "to wager our salvation . . . based upon imperfect knowledge." But coercing silence from critics did not produce certainty, only repression. For the experiment to succeed given the tendency of zealots toward governmental coercion, Holmes asserted, Americans must "be eternally vigilant against attempts to check the expression of opinions that we loathe and believe to be fraught with death." The only exception to this freedom of expression was when that expression clearly and immediately threatened a lawlessness that would bring the experiment to an end. His "clear and present danger" test, as it came to be called, required a heightened level of stringency that would in time invalidate blasphemy laws and the like, though in the short term his eloquence could not hold back the wave of repression that the first Red Scare had begun.[26]

The dissents of Holmes and Brandeis began a trend among American liberals to see the Court as the chief agent in the protection of civil liberties for individuals and minorities. Their future dissents would elaborate on their reconsideration of the obligations of the citizen to the state and of the right of the government to shape its citizenship into a particular mold. As the Court continued to work through these issues in a series of First Amendment cases throughout the 1920s, Brandeis and Holmes often used their dissenting opinions to map out the changing tectonics of liberal jurisprudence, which threatened (or promised) to dismantle the moral establishment's presumption of a common morality anchoring national life. As Brandeis explained in a famous concurring opinion in *Whitney v. California*, which involved a California law forbidding the advocacy of violent political change, the perpetuation of democracy presumed a diversity of opinion rather than a consensus. "Those who won our independence by revolution were not cowards," he reasoned. "They did not fear political change. They did not exalt order at the cost of liberty." By seeking to perpetuate order over liberty, wartime nationalists and the moral establishmentarians before them had erred, exhibiting a preference for "authority" over "freedom," a hierarchy that Brandeis argued was unconstitutional and dangerous.[27]

The power of their jurisprudence built slowly, but they began to see its fruits by the end of the 1920s. In 1928 the Court heard the case of *Olmstead v. United States*, which furthered the question of how far the government could go in the policing of its citizens in an attempt to maintain morality. Given the emergence of organized crime under Prohibition, the government wanted to be able to wiretap in order to catch those engaged in a conspiracy to make and sell alcohol. The majority, in a 5–4 decision, upheld the use of wiretapping by invoking a common law rule that all evidence could be used even if it was illegally obtained. In essence, the Court held that even if the police violated the Fourth Amendment's prohibition of illegal search and seizure, the evidence could still be used without violating the Fifth Amendment's (and, by extension, the Fourteenth Amendment's) promise of due process. But the four dissenters to the majority had made something of a civil liberties turn, producing four different dissents. Holmes simply noted that the government should not be permitted to break the law while trying to enforce it. Justice Pierce Butler, who had not to that point displayed much concern for civil liberties (and would not in the future), wanted to narrow the issues under consideration but still agreed that the wiretapping was illegal and thought the plaintiffs ought to have a new trial with the evidence omitted. Brandeis's opinion was the most prescient. Drawing upon his earlier *Harvard Law Review* article, he claimed that the amendments to the Constitution protected a general right of privacy— "the right to be let alone"—in which the individual was protected from governmental intrusion. Applying the Constitution meant recognizing the general principles promoted by the framers and then seeking to adapt those principles to a changing world. Given the right to privacy, which was the vital principle of the Bill of Rights as a whole, government wiretapping violated the Fourth Amendment, and the use of that evidence in court violated the Fifth. Justice Harlan Fiske Stone, who had joined the Court in 1925 and would become one of its most reliable civil libertarians, concurred with elements of all three dissents.[28]

By the time of Brandeis's dissent in *Olmstead*, the essential outlines of the emerging liberal jurisprudence were becoming clearer, although it remained a minority position on the Court. Brandeis and Stone seemed ready to follow Holmes in remaining deferential to Congress in its regulation of business, while they stepped up their scrutiny of laws that violated civil rights. They sought to do so out of a belief that the liberties of national citizenship protected by the Fourteenth Amendment were those found in the Bill of Rights, which meant in principle that the Bill of Rights applied to both state and federal governments and that the federal judiciary had veto power over state and local laws that violated civil rights. Although the Court had shifted enough to agree in principle that the First Amendment had been incorporated into the Fourteenth, meaning that the rights of the First Amendment were relevant at all levels of government, the practical effect of that incorporation, and its role in defending civil rights, still remained in dispute.[29]

A 1931 case showed the limits of this shift. In *United States v. MacIntosh*, the federal government sought to uphold its decision to deny citizenship to a man originally from Canada. Congress had required citizens to swear an oath to defend the Constitution of the United States through military service, if necessary. MacIntosh wanted to modify the oath to say that he would do so within the limits of his conscience. He was not a pacifist in general but believed that some military actions were immoral, and he wanted to be able to decide for himself. The five-person majority ruled that he could not become a citizen because of his equivocal commitment to the United States. In the process it articulated the ideals of the moral establishment and set up the state as the interpreter of God's will. Although MacIntosh acknowledged "the right of the government to restrain the freedom of the individual for the good of the whole," the Court explained, he did so in a way that made "his own interpretation of the will of God the decisive test." Citing David Josiah Brewer's 1892 opinion, the Court noted, "We are a Christian people." This meant, according to the Court, that all had the equal right of religious freedom and all had the duty to obey God. It also meant that the government proceeded on the assumption "that unqualified allegiance to the Nation and submission and obedience to the laws of the land" were "not inconsistent with the will of God." In making this argument, the Court seemed to declare that it knew the will of God and that the nation's laws upheld it. At the same time, by claiming that the United States was composed of Christian people, the Court presumed that God was in favor of the government's actions, since the American government presumably embodied the Christian spirit of its people. This drained Christianity of any possibility of dissent from governmental action, aligning Christian purposes with those of the government.[30]

Holmes, Brandeis, Stone, and Chief Justice Charles Evans Hughes dissented. Hughes had just rejoined the Court in 1930. He had been an associate justice from 1910 to 1916 but resigned to run for president against Wilson. He often voted with the liberals, though he did not quite support economic regulation to the extent that they did. In his *MacIntosh* dissent, Hughes noted that the majority invoked Christianity but then made allegiance to God subordinate to obedience to civil authority. This aligning of Christianity with the state was actually dangerous to religion. "The essence of religion is belief in a relation to God involving duties superior to those arising from any human relation," Hughes maintained. One person or group's understanding of divinely obligated duties was bound to conflict with another's. By aligning Christianity and the state, as the majority sought to do, the moral establishment actually presented a danger to minority religions, which had long been a problem for Catholics, Mormons, Jews, and others. With the dissent in *MacIntosh*, the minority on the Court began broadening their civil liberties stance to include religious liberty in addition to free speech.[31]

4.

Meanwhile, the political landscape also began to change. Throughout the 1920s progressive liberals struggled in a political context that had turned increasingly conservative. After Wilson's presidency, Republicans had returned to the White House and remained through the 1920, 1924, and 1928 elections. Unlike progressive Republicans such as Theodore Roosevelt, who thought the industrial transformation required a new regulatory structure to tame big business, the Republicans of the 1920s transformed themselves into the party of big business and of the moral establishment. But with the beginning of the Great Depression in 1929, the old political alliances became scrambled as Hoover ran up against the bankruptcy of his governing ideology while trying to fight the Depression.[32]

In 1932, with the Republican Party reeling, Franklin Delano Roosevelt began to create a political movement within the Democratic Party that would bring the liberal vision into power for the next four decades. He initially returned to the progressive ideal of bringing all groups, including business interests, into his administration, seeking to create a new equilibrium that could perpetuate an industrial democracy, as Croly had wanted. But the business community began pulling out of the coalition midway through Roosevelt's first term, so in 1935 he threw his support to organized labor by signing the Wagner Act, which legitimized collective bargaining and forbade employers from interfering with union activity.[33]

Having been abandoned by business, in the election of 1936 Roosevelt shifted strategies to relying upon the masses in large Northern cities to carry him to victory, assembling an unlikely coalition of secular liberals, Protestant liberals, and Roman Catholics. The most important members of this new coalition were the Catholics, who had been divided since the late nineteenth century over the problem of labor but began to come together around the Catholic notion of social justice. Pope Leo XIII had begun the process in his famous 1891 encyclical, *Rerum Novarum*. The encyclical had something for everyone within the Roman Catholic Church. It endorsed the rights of labor, argued that the laboring classes were too often subject to "misery and wretchedness," and rejected the unlimited aggregation of wealth as a mark of character by suggesting that owners had obligations to their workers that limited their ability to cut wages, break strikes, and participate in violence. At the same time, the pope rejected socialism, endorsed private property, and claimed that only the Church could serve as an agent of justice between feuding parties. But in his 1899 letter *Testem Benevolentiae*, Leo also moved in what might have seemed to liberals to be a puzzling direction, rejecting what he called "Americanism," by which he meant individualism and free association. By the 1920s those twin impulses had solidified. In embracing social justice, the Catholic hierarchy pushed for the good of the community in all spheres of life, but rejected individualism and continued their support of the moral regulation of individuals. The hierarchy's embrace of social justice made Catholic adherents amenable to at least half of the liberal political vision—the part that included governmental regulation of business—which made them potential partners in a new coalition.[34]

In the face of Roosevelt's triumph in the 1936 election, the dissenters on the Court finally gained the upper hand. In 1937 the Court reversed its tendency to strike down laws that promoted economic regulation when, in a 5–4 opinion written by Chief Justice Hughes, it ruled that the Wagner Act was constitutional. Joining Hughes were Brandeis; Stone; Benjamin Cardozo, another secularized Jew who had replaced Holmes on the Court in 1932 and specifically advocated a sociological jurisprudence; and Owen Roberts, who had until that point voted against many New Deal measures. The shift proved decisive, as the liberal dissenters would thenceforth become a majority on the Court and able to elevate the liberal vision into law. A year later, in *United States v. Carolene Products Co.*, the Court fully moved away from the jurisprudence of Stephen Field and laid out its new liberal constitutional vision.

Although the case dealt with the ability of the government to regulate inter-state commerce, it was just as important for the Court's future role in the protection of civil liberties. In his opinion, Hughes promised that in the future the Court would presume the constitutionality of laws that furthered economic regulation, which allowed for the continued expansion of New Deal policies so long as those laws were not irrational or arbitrary. But in tandem with this new deference to Congress in its economic initiatives, the Court announced a new vigilance over civil liberties. "[T]he presumption of constitutionality" would be narrower for legislation that seemed specifically prohibited by the Constitution, especially those provisions "of the first ten amendments" that the Court thought had been "embraced within the Fourteenth." The Court left open how this supervision might work, but claimed oversight over the right to vote, the dissemination of information, the ability to organize politically, and the right to assemble peacefully. It also left open the possibility that the Court might need to direct a "more searching judicial inquiry" into the regulation of political processes directed at religious, national, and racial minorities, in an attempt to eliminate "prejudice" that violated minority rights.[35]

Through their series of minority opinions beginning in the 1920s, dissenters on the Court had crafted a legal philosophy that incorporated the liberal orientation of Lippmann and Croly into a jurisprudence that established the Court as a central protector of civil liberties. The *Carolene* opinion decisively established the Court's role in accordance with the liberal vision. But as the Court assumed the role of protector of civil liberties, it needed to clarify an issue that it had not addressed. How exactly did individual rights function in a democracy, and why were they so important to uphold? In 1939 the opportunity to clarify the issue came in *Schneider v. New Jersey*, the first case in which the Court applied the *Carolene* principle to religious freedom. A town in New Jersey had sought to use its police power to prohibit Jehovah's Witnesses from proselytizing. The Court struck down the law, explaining that the First Amendment right of free speech and freedom of the press were "vital to the maintenance of democratic institutions." Without freedom of speech the necessary deliberation about the common good so necessary to a democracy could not go forward, the Court claimed. The next year, in *Cantwell v. Connecticut*, the Court formally—and for the first time—incorporated the religion clauses of the First Amendment into the Fourteenth, which made them applicable to the states. This case also involved Jehovah's Witnesses. The State of Connecticut had given the secretary of the county public welfare council the ability to grant a license to solicit. The secretary denied the Witnesses a license and thus prohibited them from proselytizing. The Court struck down the law, declaring that it violated the Witnesses' free-exercise rights promised by the First Amendment.[36]

In striking down the law, the Court began to dismantle the moral establishment in several ways at once, while further fleshing out its liberal vision. First, it weakened the distinction between belief and action, which establishmentarians had earlier used to reject Mormon polygamy in *Reynolds v. United States*. The First Amendment's guarantee of free religious exercise entailed both the freedom to believe and the freedom to act, the Court now claimed. The first was absolute. The second was not. But the freedom to act could not be infringed without a compelling reason, which the state had not been able to demonstrate. Second, in *Cantwell* the Court began backing away from the idea that the state could define religion. Rather, the Court presumed that religious pluralism was the norm. The Connecticut system gave the state the final determination as to what constituted a religious cause, in effect giving the state the ability to define religion and so violating the promise of free exercise. In striking down the statute, the Court implicitly rejected the moral establishment argument in *Reynolds*, which dismissed polygamy as barbarism. The clear implication of *Reynolds* was that Mormon polygamy, if not Mormonism itself, was irreligious and so not protected by the First Amendment. In the Court's new formulation, such an easy definition of religion and irreligion became problematic, and the Court began backing away from any tendency to decide what constituted religion in a pluralized society. Third, the Court began to limit the police power of the state as established by common law. The judgment of what constituted a breach of the peace or the general welfare, which guided police power, rested upon powers "of the most general and undefined nature," the Court claimed. Rejecting a key intellectual maneuver of the moral establishment, the Court asserted that only when there was a "clear and present danger" to public safety could a state limit the rights of religion, which included the right of proselytizing if a believer thought it was his duty to do so. Simply noting what some considered a religion's bad tendency was not sufficient to limit religious rights. The reason for this limitation of governmental power went back to the maintenance of a democracy. Only by letting diversity flower could the United States avoid conflict and coercion, the Court claimed. By promoting religious liberty, the new majority explained, "many types of life, character, opinion and belief" could "develop unmolested and unobstructed." This diversity of character and opinion ultimately promised the most successful kind of democracy.[37]

But the Court had not entirely worked out what such a radical protection of diversity meant or why exactly it was necessary. Although the majority had rejected the moral establishment's presumption of moral consensus predicated upon a shared religious heritage, it had not yet addressed the felt need for some substitute for religion in order to provide social cohesion. Given this uncertainty, just one month later, in *Minersville School District v. Gobitis,* the Court delivered what appeared on first blush a contradictory opinion again involving the Jehovah's Witnesses. The Witnesses believed that God forbade saluting the American flag, which they thought made the state a kind of God. Unfortunately for the Witnesses, saluting the flag had become a legal requirement in many schools by 1940. In protesting the law, they claimed that they were being deprived of their rights of free exercise. The eight-person majority rejected their claim. Writing for the Court, Felix Frankfurter, who had been involved in the early planning of the *New Republic* and was appointed to the Court by Roosevelt in 1939, explained the dilemma. The case presented "conflicting claims of liberty and authority." Liberty of conscience would require the Witnesses to abstain from the ceremony. But authority required the state's ability "to safeguard the nation's fellowship." Social cohesion required some common commitments. The question the case raised was, where did the Court, given its embrace of diversity in a democracy, locate the unity that held the nation together? The *Gobitis* opinion presumed the diversity argument of *Cantwell,* even though it rejected the Witnesses' claims. The flag represented common aspirations, Frankfurter reasoned, so the saluting of the flag was necessary to perpetuate "the binding tie of cohesive sentiment." He elaborated, "Such a sentiment is fostered by all the agencies of mind and spirit which may serve to gather up the traditions of a people, transmit them from generation to generation, and thereby create that continuity of a treasured common life, which constitutes a civilization."[38]

The sole dissenter, Harlan Stone, agreed that the state had an interest in preserving social cohesion but claimed it could not do so at the expense of fundamental rights. "History teaches us that there have been but few infringements of personal liberty by the state which have not been justified, as they are here, in the name of righteousness and the public good, and few which have not been directed, as they are now, at politically helpless minorities," he wrote. Democracy required not merely the attempt to find cohesive sentiment, as Frankfurter claimed, but also the protection of rights "without which no free government can exist." Although Stone did not say so directly, his opinion seemed to imply what would become a new consensus: unity could be found only by a shared commitment to protecting the individual freedoms and rights that acknowledged American diversity.[39]

Stone elaborated on his point two years later when the majority of the Court again seemed to back away from the radicalism of its *Cantwell* ruling, claiming that the city of Opelika, Alabama, could require Jehovah's Witnesses to obtain a license to preach because they also sold books and pamphlets. The majority cited its previous decision in *Gobitis.* This time Stone was joined in his dissent by three Roosevelt appointees: Frank Murphy, who had replaced Pierce Butler in 1940; William O. Douglas, who had replaced Brandeis in 1939; and Hugo Black, who had replaced Willis Van Devanter in 1937. They joined Stone's dissent in full but also united in a separate opinion written by Murphy to clarify that they now regarded the *Gobitis* opinion, which all three had joined, as having been wrongly decided. Each had become convinced that America's "democratic form of government, functioning under the historic Bill of Rights, has a high responsibility to accommodate itself to the religious views of minorities, however unpopular and unorthodox those views may be." They added, "The First Amendment does not put the right freely to exercise religion in a subordinate position. We fear, however, that the opinions in these and in the *Gobitis* case do exactly that." The dissenters now claimed that the preservation of minority religious expression could be a form of social cohesion and constituted an important component in maintaining the social order. Their new formulation, which Stone had pioneered, rejected both the moral establishment's desire to preserve a general consensus based on a shared religious heritage and Frankfurter's desire to promote nationalism over individual rights.[40]

A year later, in *West Virginia Board of Education v. Barnette*, Stone's liberal vision became law as the Court rejected the *Gobitis* precedent in a 6–3 decision and declared that the Witnesses could not be made to salute the flag, a remarkable ruling given that it came in the middle of World War II. The Court thus brought to completion the line of thought that it had begun in *Cantwell v. Connecticut*, acknowledging that the maintenance of unity amid diversity was a key challenge in American democracy but rejecting the notion that exempting students who had religious objections to the salute would risk social dissolution. Writing for the Court was Robert H. Jackson, who replaced Stone as an associate justice in 1941 when Stone became Chief Justice upon the retirement of Hughes. "To sustain the compulsory flag salute," Jackson wrote, "we are required to say that a Bill of Rights which guards the individual's right to speak his own mind, left it open to public authorities to compel him to utter what is not in his mind." In rejecting Frankfurter's nationalist imperatives, the Court also rejected the logic of the moral establishment. Unlike Frankfurter, moral establishmentarians looked not to a flag salute but to the recitation of the Ten Commandments and Bible-reading as bases of moral cohesion. The judge in the nineteenth-century Thomas Whall case claimed explicitly that it did not matter whether the students believed the commandments or the Bible so long as they verbally acknowledged both as a means of inculcating a shared moral framework.[41]

The shift of reasoning from the nineteenth-century Whall case, to *Gobitis*, and finally to *Barnette* shows just how radical the Court's decision in 1940 was. With the *Cantwell* opinion, the Court entered an entirely different intellectual world. The nationalism that Frankfurter advanced had tapped into an old desire for a homogeneous consensus that the Court now claimed was inappropriate in American democracy. By acting as a guarantor of rights, the Court explained that it sought to provide "[a]ssurance that rights are secure," which in turn fulfilled Frankfurter's goal of prompting a greater support for government. Only by vigilant protection of civil rights could the national government expand its power to regulate business without endangering liberty. Frankfurter's desire to create social cohesion by coercing a uniform sentiment always came up short, the Court asserted. As moderate attempts at uniformity failed, more-severe techniques would become the norm. In turn, as pressure toward unity increased, so did division, as people slid out from under the pressure of conformity, which in turn ratcheted up the severity of the repression. Eventually, the Court claimed that the desire of the secular Frankfurter and his moral establishment forebears ended in the same place: "Compulsory unification of opinion achieves only the unanimity of the graveyard."[42]

Democracy needed a different principle. "[W]e apply the limitations of the Constitution with no fear that freedom to be intellectually and spiritually diverse or even contrary will disintegrate the social organization," the Court explained. Of course, "intellectual individualism and the rich cultural diversities" of the United States would inevitably result in "occasional eccentricity and abnormal attitudes." But ultimately, in the Court's reasoning, these did not threaten American cohesion. Quite the opposite. "It is in that freedom and the example of persuasion, not in force and compulsion, that the real unity of America lies," the Court concluded. If, in the conception of moral establishmentarians, a shared moral order had made democracy possible, the Court now came to the opposite conclusion. Only the defense of individual rights made democracy possible, and the only unity required was a shared agreement to protect the rights of all.[43]

11

THE LIBERAL MOMENT

1.

The direction of the Court from the 1920s to World War II seemed to herald the intellectual death of the moral establishment. But as its liberal jurisprudence developed, the Court prompted a pushback from both religious liberals and conservatives that intensified with the advent of the cold war.

Important changes in the religious landscape aided this resistance. These changes had been building for a long time. By the 1920s, as liberals on the Court began to advance their jurisprudence, the nascent split between religious liberals and conservatives had grown pronounced, and religious conservatives had become known as *fundamentalists* for their proclamation of what they considered the fundamentals of Christianity. Throughout the 1920s and 1930s, fundamentalists fought a determined battle with religious liberals for control of their denominations, but the liberals (or modernists, as they were sometimes called) emerged victorious. Consolidating their control in the major denominations and the Federal Council of Churches (FCC), religious liberals sought to use these and other organizations to direct U.S. law and politics. By the 1940s liberal Protestants had begun to partially embrace the liberal moral vision that was emerging on the Court, though they rejected or missed its frank secularity and connected it with their vision of Christianity. Casting aside any acknowledgment of their fundamentalist brethren and their Catholic counterparts, they presumed instead that liberal ecumenism allowed them to speak for all of Christianity under a new liberal regime.[1]

Meanwhile, conservative Protestants seemed temporarily to disappear. Unwilling to remain in denominations with people they considered heretics, fundamentalists retreated into their circles of small-denomination churches, fundamentalist colleges, and parachurch organizations to nurse their wounds.

Their intellectual position was an odd one. Like religious liberals, fundamentalists considered themselves trustees of American culture and guardians of American institutional life, both of which they claimed had been built upon Christianity. But with the advance of political and religious liberalism, fundamentalists grew increasingly alienated from society. Liberalism's blasé trust in the individual and its reluctance to use law in order to suppress licentiousness would, fundamentalists claimed, endanger the moral core of the United States, undermine the genius of the U.S. political arrangement, and halt the progress of the American project. Fundamentalists particularly objected to religious liberals in the FCC, whom they regarded as morally and spiritually bankrupt. In the face of liberal decadence, fundamentalists initially decided that their role was to play an American Cassandra as the United States suffered inevitable decline and extinction.[2]

But this was hardly a satisfying means of discharging their responsibility for America. Beginning in the 1940s, fundamentalists reemerged into public life, having grown unhappy with the futile effort of doing God's work by issuing wintry prophecies of the nation's impending doom. Trying to recapture their role as self-appointed societal trustees, after twenty years of small-scale institution-building, fundamentalists moved to shore up the decaying foundations of the moral establishment that had been allowed to crumble under what they saw as the careless gaze of the FCC. The first sign of this reemergence came in 1941, when Carl McIntire, a prickly minister in New Jersey who managed to estrange even other fundamentalists in his zeal for doctrinal purity, founded the American Council of Christian Churches (ACCC). The ACCC was designed to bring together fundamentalists to counter the liberalism of the FCC.[3]

Not all fundamentalists were satisfied. McIntire struck a schizophrenic, if not contradictory, pose: he declared the necessity of countering the public influence of the FCC, but at the same time affirmed the importance of remaining aloof from the world and avoiding doctrinal compromise. That stance could only cause fundamentalism to splinter into ever-smaller shards, as each group sought to maintain what it considered maximal doctrinal orthodoxy. His stance also did nothing to bring fundamentalism into conversation with the wider culture. Given these contradictions, other fundamentalists concluded that they needed a deeper engagement with American culture and life than McIntire had proposed—to be in the world but not of the world, as they would have explained it. Seeking to distinguish themselves from both the religious liberals in the FCC and the fundamentalists in the ACCC, the more moderate fundamentalists assumed the old label of *evangelicals*, a word that had dropped out of the vernacular because it lacked any real meaning, since both liberals and conservatives could claim the appellation during the height of the fundamentalist–modernist controversies.[4]

These latter-day evangelicals, or neo-evangelicals, believed that social transformation in the United States could come only through concerted evangelical action. Their goal was to reclaim the major institutions of American life that they had lost, redeeming and sanctifying the various structures of public authority and renewing the nation's legal and political commitment to the moral establishment. To that end, they formed the National Association of Evangelicals (NAE) in 1943. As Harold J. Ockenga, the association's first president, explained to the 1943 convention, God had preordained the United States as a haven for the persecuted religious minorities of Europe that arose out of the Protestant Reformation. His superintending objective gave the nation a mission to the world. "God must have had a purpose in forging one, great, united nation out of all these strains of population and thought," Ockenga reasoned. "God must have had a purpose in giving primarily to evangelical Protestantism the historic leadership of this great nation. That purpose unquestionably was the intention to diffuse the knowledge of God and truth through the Gospel unto the world." The NAE would return the nation to this divine purpose, he claimed.[5]

Although all three groups—evangelicals, fundamentalists, and religious liberals—claimed responsibility for American culture and society and supported some form of a moral establishment, each had differing conceptions of their responsibility, growing out of different theological stances and strategic considerations. Evangelicals sought what they considered a nice balance between fundamentalism and liberalism. Their disagreement with fundamentalists was primarily over strategy, not doctrine. As a promotional pamphlet for the NAE explained, the parties split over fundamentalism's "policy of indiscriminate destructive criticism." By settling into a completely antagonistic stance toward American culture, fundamentalism ultimately led "to the defeat of its own purposes." Put simply, fundamentalism was too oppositional, when it should be transformational. Evangelicals' problem with liberalism and the FCC was exactly the reverse. According to the NAE, the FCC lacked any coherent statement of faith or any consistent doctrinal principles, in spite of its claim to uphold national Christian purposes. As a result, the FCC, along with liberal Christianity more generally, lacked any constructive method of cultural engagement. It had gone too far in accommodating the world rather than challenging it and transforming it. In addition, the willingness of liberal Christians to cooperate with a whole host of non-Christian organizations represented to evangelicals the repudiation of Christian responsibility to maintain the godly foundations of American society.[6]

Evangelicals used the 1940s to build a series of institutions from which to launch their movement to reverse the liberalizing trend toward secularism. Though their perspective was essentially in line with the moral-establishment proponents of the nineteenth century, they lacked an institutional base after losing the battle for the major denominations in the 1920s and 1930s. This left them ill-equipped to respond when the Supreme Court began to dismantle the moral establishment. Bitter that liberal Protestants had failed in defense of Christian moral prerogatives—at least as evangelicals defined them—they were determined to set up a counter-network of power. In addition to the NAE, they founded an explicitly evangelical institution for training ministers, called Fuller Theological Seminary, in 1947, which promised to churn out more ministers that might align their churches with the evangelicals. They also began to develop their leadership at the top. Ockenga served as a behind-the-scenes organizational player in laying the framework for the emerging evangelical movement, but he ultimately lacked the personal charisma and dynamism to lead the new cadre of evangelicals that the NAE hoped to produce. For that, they needed a more compelling leader.[7]

They found him in the person of Billy Graham. Graham had emerged through an organization called Youth for Christ, a revivalistic pan-denominational group that had sought to convert young people. Graham came to the attention of those higher up in the evangelical movement through his 1949 Los Angeles revival campaign, a remarkable event that made him into a national figure when the newspaper mogul William Randolph Hearst decided to give his crusade major press coverage. Hearst's decision demonstrated the emerging power of evangelicalism and the kind of leadership that Graham could bring. As a nominal member of the enormous First Baptist Church of Dallas, headed by the arch-segregationist W. A. Criswell, Graham maintained a wide set of connections with conservative and racist fundamentalists throughout the South. But Graham hewed to a milder, if ambivalent, stance on racial issues that made him more of a national figure rather than merely a regional one. Graham also shared the evangelicals' commitment to cultural engagement, which furthered his appeal to potential converts and promised to broaden the evangelical base through conversion.[8]

Graham had real media savvy. He recognized the necessity of staying on message and controlling the medium. Rather than waiting for more favors from Hearst, in the mid-1940s Graham began laying the groundwork to create an evangelical media organization that would ensure he always had friendly coverage. His efforts finally came to fruition in 1956 with the creation of *Christianity Today*, which sought to provide a counterbalance to the more liberal *Christian Century*. Graham explained that the magazine sought to "plant the evangelical flag in the middle of the road, taking the conservative theological position but a definite liberal approach to social problems." He continued, "It would combine the best in liberalism and the best in fundamentalism without compromising theologically." For the editorship of the magazine, Graham tapped Carl F. H. Henry, whose 1947 manifesto *The Uneasy Conscience of Modern Fundamentalism* strengthened the intellectual basis for neo-evangelicalism's engagement with culture.[9]

Though Graham claimed that evangelicalism supported the liberal approach to social problems, he did not mean that he supported the liberal focus on social structure or the liberal belief in individual rights. He condemned what he called "the sin of tolerance" in an early *Christianity Today* article, claiming that "over-tolerance in moral issues" had threatened to unravel the American experiment. This over-tolerance had led to the crumbling of the moral establishment, which evangelicals now sought to reverse. Graham's relative friendliness toward liberalism stemmed from his support of cultural engagement in a way that liberals had continued but that fundamentalists had abandoned. For Graham, evangelical cultural engagement required the condemnation of moral pluralism rooted in unbelief and, closely connected for Graham, a strong embrace of anticommunism, which he saw as essential to preserving the Christian moral foundation of the United States. As the cold war heated up through the late 1940s and turned hot in the Korean conflict in 1950, Graham stood at the forefront of evangelical leaders who attributed the genius of the United States to its supposed foundation in Christianity, as opposed to the constructivist humanism of communist thought. Congress's addition of "under God" to the pledge of allegiance in 1954 and the declaration of "In God We Trust" as the national motto in 1956 grew out of the belief that theism or, more narrowly, Christianity provided a unique asset to the United States in the battle with godless communism. There were even renewed attempts at a Christian amendment to the Constitution, culminating in the Flanders Amendment of 1954, which asserted: "This Nation devoutly recognizes the authority and law of Jesus Christ, Saviour and Ruler of nations, through whom are bestowed the blessings of Almighty God." Although the amendment never made it out of Congress, it showed that evangelicals were worried that they might need an explicitly Christian constitutional foundation to rebuild the moral establishment.[10]

As evangelicals began to mobilize against communism, they seemed to be moving with the cultural currents. Many liberal Christians agreed that a broad embrace of theism aided the battle against communism, which suggested the possibility for cooperation. But the breadth of liberal alliances dwarfed that of evangelicals. Faced with what they considered a truly dangerous atheism, liberals softened their attitude toward Catholicism and Judaism to form a united monotheistic front, a religiously liberal notion of the moral establishment that would defend the American moral order against communism. By 1955, when the sociologist Will Herberg wrote *Protestant-Catholic-Jew*, which would become the definitive statement on the American religious enterprise at midcentury, American religious liberals had embraced a vanilla monotheism, as captured by Herberg's title. These three identities were really subsets, according to Herberg, of a larger American identity that rested upon a great "American religion." For Herberg, this mushy American religion stood for the "spiritual values" at the heart of U.S. democracy, "the fatherhood of God and brotherhood of man, the dignity of the human being, etc." So broad was the general religious agreement that Herberg equated this common religion with "the American Way of Life," which stood in antithesis to godless communism: "The American Way of Life is, at bottom, a spiritual structure, a structure of ideas and ideals, of aspirations and values, of beliefs and standards; it synthesizes all that commends itself to the American as the right, the good, and the true in actual life."[11]

Herberg was hardly alone in his analysis. In a Christmastime address in 1952, General Dwight D. Eisenhower, soon to be president, also articulated the frankly religious component of anticommunism. Eisenhower explained that the battle against communism was "a struggle for the hearts and souls of men—not merely for property or even merely for power." He added, "It is a contest for the beliefs, the convictions, the very innermost soul of the human being. Consequently, if we are to be strong we must be strong first in our spiritual convictions." In recounting a conversation that Eisenhower had with Soviet Marshal Georgi Zhukov about the differences between the Soviet and U.S. systems, the general explained that he was at a loss to know where to find common ground with Zhukov because of the fundamental irreconcilability of "the Bolshevik religion" and the American one. After quoting from the Declaration of Independence, Eisenhower claimed, "[O]ur form of Government has no sense unless it is founded in a deeply felt religious faith, and I don't care what it is. With us of course it is the Judo-Christian [sic] concept." Winning the fight against communism required getting back to those fundamentals, Eisenhower explained, which meant an acknowledgment that even those who were "so silly as to doubt the existence of an Almighty" needed to recognize that they were "still members of a religious civilization, because the Founding Fathers said it was a religious concept that they were trying to translate into the political world."[12]

Given this consensus, evangelicals would seem to have been well placed within the liberal anticommunist order, if they could only follow religious liberals in embracing Catholics. Evangelicals certainly supported Eisenhower in believing that the fight against communism represented not so much dueling empires in a battle for world domination as an epic moral struggle between good and evil, religion and irreligion. As Graham claimed, "Only as millions of Americans turn to Jesus Christ at this hour and accept him as Savior, can this nation possibly be spared the onslaught of a demon-possessed communism." Catholics agreed and seemed happy to be enfolded into the American religious order through anticommunism, especially since they had a long history of opposition to leftist causes. Phyllis Schlafly, the Catholic political activist who would become famous for her movement against the equal rights amendment, got her start in the anticommunist struggle and brought Catholic anticommunism to the grassroots. "We are engaged in a life-and-death struggle with the criminal underground whose leaders confidently expect to destroy our Church, our country, our freedom, the institution of the family, and everything else we hold dear," she claimed. William F. Buckley Jr., the Catholic intellectual who would go on to start the *National Review,* a conservative organ that provided an intellectual center to the still-nascent conservative movement, began in anticommunism as well. In his first book, *God and Man at Yale,* published in 1951, Buckley complained of what he considered "one of the most extraordinary incongruities" of the period: the university, which received "its moral and financial support from Christian individualism," had become a haven for anti-religious activity, which sought to convince "the sons of these supporters to be atheistic socialists."[13]

Evangelicals and conservative Catholics also shared a concern about domestic subversives, believing that communism provided as much of an internal threat as an external one. In 1953, as Joseph McCarthy began his inquisition into the political views of actors, entertainers, professors, and political figures, Graham praised those "who, in the face of public denouncement and ridicule, go loyally on in their work of exposing the pinks and the reds who have sought refuge beneath the wings of the American eagle." Claiming that Jesus himself provided the "classic example of loyalty to a divine purpose," Graham aligned Christian purposes with the United States and represented McCarthy as a follower of Jesus. That same year, the National

Association of Evangelicals passed a resolution supporting the prosecution by the McCarthy tribunal of liberal religious leaders, whom they saw as ideologically suspect. Similarly, in 1954, Buckley published a book entitled *McCarthy and His Enemies,* a vigorous defense of the soon-to-be disgraced senator, which supported McCarthy's belief that anticommunism required vigilance both at home and abroad and endorsed his witch-hunts. What Graham, the NAE, and Buckley shared was an abiding belief in order and a conviction that all who fell outside the narrow scope of the American moral order, as they defined it, worked for communist and subversive purposes. This convergence around anticommunism and a suspicion of nonconformism seemed to unite conservative Protestants and Catholics, laying the basis for future cooperation in renewal of the moral establishment.[14]

Yet evangelicals remained unable or unwilling to go as far as religious liberals in building interfaith alliances by reducing all belief to its lowest common denominator. As Will Herberg, who was Jewish, noted, by equating religion with the American way of life, many religious liberals exhibited the "secularism of a religious people, this religiousness in a secularist framework." The Judeo-Christian framework left little room for the transformation that evangelicals wanted or for a rehabilitation of the crumbling moral establishment, since it seemed to buttress the status quo. It also did not specifically recognize their claim that evangelical Christianity, not Judaism or Catholicism, had provided the historical foundation for public morals. Although Graham had presided over Eisenhower's Christian conversion, Eisenhower admitted the necessity of religious belief only in general. His flippant phrase— "and I don't care what it is"—could only strike evangelicals as lacking in true religious fervor. Eisenhower even went so far as to disclaim any intention of being "evangelical in . . . approach" while recommending that the nation hold to a religious foundation. His squishiness on doctrinal specifics only confirmed for evangelicals just how facile the American religious foundation, shorn of any specific evangelical content, might become if the FCC continued to allow the Supreme Court to deconstruct the moral establishment.[15]

In addition to objecting to any liberal doctrinal compromises, evangelicals remained wary of any alliance with Catholics, in particular, even though they agreed on much. The NAE had claimed as early as 1943, in a veiled reference to Catholicism, that the NAE sought "[t]o maintain and defend the American doctrine of the separation of church and state" from the attempts of Catholics to connect it in the Catholic hierarchy. That rejection of Catholicism proved unbending. In 1958 Phyllis Schlafly and her husband, Fred, proposed a joint Catholic–Protestant anticommunist organization to Dr. Fred

Schwarz, a Protestant who had founded the Christian Anti-Communism Crusade. Schwarz rejected their overture without much consideration because, he explained, many of his members were evangelical Protestants and would not stand for such a union. In 1959, with the Catholic John F. Kennedy campaigning for president, L. Nelson Bell, an executive editor of *Christianity Today* and Billy Graham's father-in-law, told the annual convention of the NAE, "Any country the Roman Catholic church dominates suppresses the rights of Evangelicals. . . . For that reason, thinking Americans view with alarm the possible election of a Roman Catholic as President of the United States." Bell's criticism equated "thinking Americans" with evangelicals. The implication, of course, was that someone else did the thinking for Roman Catholics, or that they were perhaps not American at all. These were not sentiments conducive to a new coalition, however virulent their anticommunism. Evangelicals wanted nothing less than a return to the moral establishment, working to maintain the conservative Protestant control that they had held in the past. Their ambivalence limited the extent to which the conservative countermovement could mobilize. But even with evangelical reluctance, by the late 1950s the foundation of a new movement was in place, anchored in anticommunism, a traditionalist conception of the place of morality in the American order, and a rejection of liberalism in religion and politics.[16]

2.

The anticommunist alliance between a growing evangelicalism and conservative Catholicism posed a challenge to the liberal Supreme Court, even though the alliance had not fully formed. At the same time, the cold war permeated the Court and everything else. This pressure from both within and without made the emergent liberal jurisprudence of the 1930s and early 1940s difficult to sustain, especially when it came to religion. Although that jurisprudence was never completely consistent, it had a generally secular thrust. But the fight against godless communism suggested that the frank secularism of prewar years, which promised (or threatened) to reject religion from public life, might not be tenable or even desirable.

The change registered almost immediately with the beginning of the cold war. In the past, moral establishmentarians had claimed that they supported the separation of church and state. In doing so, they drew upon a long tradition in which Protestants had advocated separation in order to exclude Catholics from public life while maintaining control. But in 1947, in *Everson v. Board of Education,* the Court stepped into the debate in a way that scrambled

Protestant claims and made it less likely that evangelicals could make use of the concept of church–state separation again. In *Everson,* the Court considered the constitutionality of a New Jersey law that paid for students' transportation to and from school, even if those schools were private and parochial. New Jersey's arrangement was part of a broader trend in which Protestants around the nation lost their grip on public school systems. Faced with large Catholic populations, many cities and states, particularly in the Northeast and the Midwest, began to explore ways to funnel money to parochial schools. In *Everson,* a 5–4 majority decided that New Jersey's arrangement could stand. Their argument threatened to undo many of the connections between religion and state that had existed throughout the nineteenth century. But just how the Court's opinion related to those prior debates remained unclear. The Court declared that the First Amendment's prohibition against laws respecting a religious establishment meant that the government could not aid religion at all, even if it did so on a non-preferential basis. And the government especially could not use any tax to support religious activity or religious institutions. Quoting Jefferson, the Court declared that the First Amendment had erected "a wall of separation between church and State," which required that the government observe scrupulous neutrality toward religion, neither supporting it nor persecuting it. This suggested that the Court had adopted a strict political secularism. But the majority actually upheld New Jersey's busing arrangement, which meant that the state was, at least in some sense, financially supporting parochial schools. The majority's argument consisted largely of a ringing endorsement of church–state separation as a way to prove its concern for the concept while at the same time affirming a connection between religion and the state.[17]

To the dissenters, the Court's opinion made no sense. They agreed with and even celebrated the majority's understanding of the First Amendment as creating a wall between church and state, but the dissenters all thought that that should have invalidated the New Jersey practice. To set the trajectory for cases in the future, the minority entered two opinions. The first was written by Justice Jackson, who simply noted, "[T]he undertones of the [majority] opinion, advocating complete and uncompromising separation of Church from State, seem utterly discordant with its conclusion yielding support to their commingling in educational matters." Jackson also joined the second dissent, written by Wiley Rutledge, a fierce liberal appointed by FDR in 1943. Rutledge's dissent was the longer of the two, and indicated a somewhat surprising transformation in liberal argumentation that threatened to muddy the constitutional waters. Rutledge, like everyone on the Court, accepted the separation of church and state. He admitted that *Everson* required that the Court determine for the first time what constituted an establishment of religion that was prohibited by the First Amendment. But instead of recognizing that the doctrine of the separation of church and state had long been used by Protestants to ensure religious control, and rather than demonstrating that the doctrine actually required a more thoroughgoing application to U.S. society in order to secularize U.S. public life, Rutledge claimed that the secularist understanding of Madison and Jefferson had always been understood by the Court and the American people. That concept, he claimed, constituted the genius of the American arrangement. Citing Madison's Memorial and Remonstrance against Virginia's 1785 plan to pay teachers of the Christian religion, Rutledge conflated Madison's desires with actual conditions and claimed that everyone had always recognized that the First Amendment sought "to create a complete and permanent separation of the spheres of religious activity and civil authority by comprehensively forbidding every form of public aid or support for religion." His presumption of a historic separation of church and state allowed him to look to Madison to provide the normative meaning of religious liberty. Instead of attempting to marshal evidence to support his rather startling claim, he gestured vaguely to "the Amendment's wording," to the arrangements of "history," and to "this Court's consistent utterances" as all somehow proving his point. The Court's approval of the New Jersey scheme threatened, according to Rutledge, "our great tradition of religious liberty," which had played a central part in American history. With Rutledge's dissent, the myth of American religious freedom entered into law.[18]

Everson proved pivotal in a number of ways and signaled the confusion and bitterness that was to come. All nine members of the Court accepted that the First Amendment required the complete separation of church and state. In one sense this represented the triumph of Madison's original vision of religious liberty, as Rutledge had claimed. With the passage of the Fourteenth Amendment and the subsequent incorporation of the establishment clause, thereby applying it to the states, the Court had duplicated Madison's long-ago scheme to modify the federal Constitution so that states would be prohibited from violating fundamental rights. This concern for rights and equality comported with the movement of the Court beginning in the 1940s. Yet the triumph of Madison's vision in theory came in an opinion discordant with the practice of complete church–state separation as Madison might have understood it, allowing the state to funnel money in support of transporting students to parochial schools. This dissonance between theory and practice betrayed a confusion that had entered the opinions of the Court in the postwar years. At the same time, *Everson* marked the beginning of a historical amnesia. Whatever Madison's or Jefferson's intent, strict separation had never existed in U.S. public life, law, and government. The assumption that strict separation had been the norm in the past threatened to place the legal transformation on a false historical foundation that undermined its intellectual rationale. Unlike Croly, or Lippmann, or Brandeis, who all saw the place of religion in public life as detrimental, the opinions in *Everson,* majority and dissenting alike, all pretended it had never existed. The Court assumed the myth of American religious freedom, taking on the mantle of what Rutledge called "our great tradition of religious liberty" in order to uphold their particular position. In this way, the Court placed a powerful, radically new jurisprudence upon the myth of historical continuity rather than forthrightly acknowledging why such a progressive jurisprudence was necessary in a modern democratic society.[19]

The historical amnesia deepened the following year in another case involving religion in the schools. In 1948, in *McCollum v. Board of Education,* the Court ruled, 8–1, that an Illinois program that allowed for voluntary religious instruction during school hours and on school property violated the separation of church and state. The board of education and its allies made two arguments. First, they claimed that the First Amendment's establishment clause restricted only Congress, and not the states. Failing that, they argued that, contrary to *Everson,* the First Amendment forbade only the preferential governmental support of one religion over others but not governmental aid to all religions. Both arguments would become compelling to religious conservatives in the 1970s. Hugo Black, who wrote the majority opinions in both *Everson* and *McCollum,* rejected the Board's arguments completely, noting that the majority and minority in *Everson* had held substantially the same position, regardless of their minor disagreement over the particulars of the case. Unwilling to reconsider what he considered the settled position of the Court, he did not engage in much further legal reflection. Others in the majority were not so reticent. Felix Frankfurter, who had a long and settled conception of church–state relations, offered a concurring opinion, joined by Jackson, Rutledge, and Harold Burton, a former Republican senator nominated by Truman in an effort to reach across party lines. Noting that a mere phrase—the separation of church and state—could not solve all disputes, Frankfurter wanted to elaborate on the underlying principle of separation that he saw the Court developing. To that end he recounted the history of common schooling in the United States, emphasizing that public schools had long been secular and nonsectarian. In his understanding, the power of the U.S. arrangement required secularity in public schools in order to train the citizen in his civic rather than religious duties. Yet his account, like that of Rutledge, ignored the long history of Protestant–Catholic conflict over the public schools and the reality of Protestant control. In doing so, he furthered a selective historical understanding, appealing again to what he saw as the great American principle of church–state separation that he claimed had only recently come under attack.[20]

Frankfurter's argument, like Rutledge's before him, was puzzling. He had been part of the early planning circle for the *New Republic* and so would have been aware that many of the editors and their allies had complained about the multiple connections between religion and the state and that they viewed the rejection of religion from public life as the fundamental liberal goal. He shared their view at that time. But with the rise of anticommunism, the liberals on the Court seemed to have shifted their thinking. The Court's invocation of the myth of American religious freedom instead positioned it as the conservative keeper of a unique American tradition that countered that of godless communism. In this way, the Court forestalled criticism that it engaged in social innovation that might lead to a secularized public sphere, since it acted only as a defender to incursions on American freedom that, it claimed, had been well established.[21]

This introduced intellectual instability in addition to historical falsehood into the evolving liberal jurisprudence, both of which showed the limits of mid-century cold war liberal thought. Postwar jurisprudence, while continuing to dismantle the moral establishment, lacked any apparent intellectual framework. It enunciated a principle of separation but then did not consistently follow it in practice. Without a clear sense of what it was doing and why, the Court's opinions became contradictory, yielding a confusing body of religious-liberty jurisprudence that never quite acknowledged the moral establishment that the Court had begun to dismantle. This tendency became apparent a few years later in the 1952 case of *Zorach v. Clauson*, when the Court again affirmed church–state separation while at the same time draining the formulation of much of its radical new vitality and repeating the old idea that religion formed the foundation of the American experiment. The case involved yet another educational-release program, in which students were let out of school to engage in religious exercises. The Court held in a 6–3 opinion that a New York City program to let students out during school time for voluntary sectarian religious instruction did not violate the separation of church and state. The majority opinion, written by Justice Douglas, who would in time become one of the strictest of church–state separatists on the Court, displayed odd rhetorical flights that clashed with his belief in separation. "We are a religious people whose institutions presuppose a Supreme Being," he claimed. State encouragement of religious instruction, according to Douglas, followed "the best of our traditions." Noting that he considered the New York arrangement an accommodation to the religion that provided a foundation for U.S. society, Douglas yoked the cold war argument of a religious foundation for American society to the perpetuation of religious instruction during school hours, even though it did not occur on school grounds. He even went so far as to suggest, in what would become a frequent allegation, that those who would strike down the New York scheme displayed "a callous indifference to religious groups" and betrayed a jurisprudential orientation "preferring those who believe in no religion over those who do believe."[22]

Black, Frankfurter, and Jackson each filed their own dissents. Confessing his mystification with the opinion of the Court, Black saw no difference between this arrangement and the Illinois plan that the Court had rejected just four years earlier in *McCollum,* except that New York had moved the religious instruction off-campus. Jackson and Frankfurter emphasized the religious coercion inherent in the arrangement. Because the religious instruction still used "the State's power of coercion" to advance religious ends, Jackson could not see how the arrangement could be made to square with the principle of church–state separation. He even felt compelled to point out that he sent his own children to private, religiously supported schools, in order to reject the majority's suggestion that opposition to New York's arrangement grew out of an anti-religious or atheistic orientation. "My evangelistic brethren," Jackson complained, "confuse an objection to compulsion with an objection to religion."[23]

3.

After *Zorach,* the Court did not hear another establishment-clause case for the remainder of the decade. Yet the Court did not settle into a conservative posture. Instead, it moved in other, clearer directions that had just as much import for the moral establishment. In 1953 Eisenhower appointed Earl Warren as the chief justice, inaugurating a period of determined liberalism. The radicalism of the Court's commitment to individual rights became apparent in the year after Warren's appointment, with one of the most important cases of the twentieth century, *Brown v. Board of Education.* In its unanimous decision written by Warren, the Court began dismantling segregation, a foundational part of the Southern moral order. Overturning *Plessy v.*

Ferguson, *Brown* was the culmination of the revolution of sociological juris-prudence that had begun with the Brandeis brief. It cited psychological and historical studies that showed black children had internalized a feeling of infe-riority as a result of their experience of segregation. This feeling of inferiority provided a basis on which to dismiss the Court's earlier endorsement of sepa-rate but equal educational arrangements, noting that such arrangements were illegitimate under the equal protection clause of the Fourteenth Amendment. "[P]sychological knowledge" and "modern authority" showed that separate but equal was inherently unequal, the Court explained. In making its claim, the Court returned to the argument about diversity and democracy that it began developing in the early 1940s. Compulsory education demonstrated how important it was to American "democratic society" that U.S. citizens underwent formal schooling. Education awakened children "to cultural values," diversity and equality chief among them, that were necessary for the maintenance of democracy.[24]

In many ways, the Court's decision in *Brown* began the cultural upheaval of the 1960s, even though it came in 1954. Although the religion decisions of the late 1940s had been alarming to conservatives, they did not inspire the mas-sive resistance that came after the Court's decision in *Brown*. *Brown* indicated the extent to which the Court's thinking on democracy, diversity, and equality could reshape and even reject the moral establishment. Throughout the South, white communities mobilized to resist the Court's anti-segregationist ruling by blockading schoolhouses, forming white citizen councils to defend white supremacy, and petitioning state legislators and politicians to maintain their commitment to states' rights to segregate. Religious leaders were often at the forefront of these protests. Meanwhile, the participants in the civil rights movement, which accelerated with the Montgomery bus boycott the year after *Brown*, responded by stepping up their demand for the full inclusion of black Americans into American democracy. Led by the charismatic minister Martin Luther King Jr., the bus boycott began a movement that combined liberal reli-gious rhetoric with nonviolent actions that forced a confrontation with authorities. The civil disobedience of the civil rights movement and its tactics of nonviolent engagement served as an exemplar for the many activists that joined in the civil rights protests in the early 1960s and then moved in even broader directions with the women's rights movement, the gay rights move-ment, and other groups calling for radical democracy and equality. As the battle for civil rights heated up, the nation descended into what many regarded as a kind of civil war that scrambled old political alliances and eroded the governing consensus.[25]

These radical movements of the 1960s, more than anything else, contributed to the ultimate destruction of the moral establishment. Since they often had a completely secular foundation and, in the case of second-wave feminists, antiwar protesters, and white allies of the black civil rights movement, were often led by Jews rather than Protestants or Catholics, the new movements created powerful vehicles that rejected Protestant moral authority and its enshrinement in law. This challenge grew as the civil rights movement moved into high gear. King's March on Washington in 1963, the Freedom Summer in Mississippi in 1964, and the campaign in Alabama in 1965 produced several legislative achievements. The 1964 Civil Rights Act eliminated discrimination in schools, employment, and public places. The 1965 Voting Rights Act outlawed discrimination in access to the polling booth. The 1965 Immigration and Nationality Act abolished national quotas and threw open the nation's doors to Eastern Europeans, Latin Americans, Asians, and Africans. All promised to remake American life. Together the Civil Rights Act and the Voting Rights Act eliminated the most egregious cases of the governmentally endorsed violations of individual rights, while the Immigration Act promised to accelerate the demographic transformation of the United States, making diversity the lodestone of the liberal political tradition.[26]

Faced with these large-scale movements and startling political achievements, the leaders of liberal Christianity, rather astonishingly, dropped their proprietary claim to the nation and ceased to presume that they spoke for all of Christianity. Their disinterest in promoting the Christian-nation ideal that had been used to uphold the moral establishment indicated the degree to which secular liberal thinking had undermined liberal Protestantism. It also suggested the powerful extent to which the liberalizing trend terminated in public secularism. Embracing this new focus on secular rights, liberal Protestants fully joined the liberal consensus and in some cases even turned to the radicalism of the movements of the 1960s. As they did so, mainline Protestant denominations, which had served as a redoubt of religious liberalism, suffered demographic collapse. No longer an institutional vehicle for a distinctly Christian voice, liberal Protestantism saw many parishioners drift instead into other forums of activism and social activity, move their membership to conservative churches, or drop out altogether.[27]

When liberal Protestants lost interest in promoting the Christian nation and turned toward the promotion of individual rights, evangelicals remained at the ready to advance the moral establishment's cause. As events moved ahead of them, evangelicals were initially uncertain how to respond, torn between an allegiance to the old moral order and a new appreciation, advanced by Billy Graham, that their theology might require racial equality. But even Graham, with his comparative racial moderation, which made him uncharacteristic in a sea of Southern fundamentalist and evangelical racism, projected an ambivalent posture toward the civil rights movement. Although he held desegregated revival campaigns and used his evangelical belief in the equality of each individual before God to provide what some saw as tacit support for civil rights, he never really warmed to the movement and often resisted it. This resistance grew out of his Southern background and his evangelical concern for deference to established authority, which convinced him that massive white resistance to desegregation was unhelpful but also made him reject the nonviolent civil disobedience of the civil rights movement. After every major milestone in the movement, Graham welcomed the change and then called for an end to civil rights demonstrations, effectively pleading for everyone to accept the status quo. In 1963, after four teenage girls died in the Sixteenth Street Baptist Church bombing in Birmingham, Graham toed the standard Southern and white supremacist line in his radio program when he referenced "a growing suspicion that the bombings may be from professionals outside Alabama who want to keep the racial problem at fever pitch in the South," which put blame for the bombing on black subversives rather than white racists. Once Graham came under the influence of J. Edgar Hoover, who convinced him that many civil rights activists were communists, Graham began to fret in public about "subversive groups penetrating the civil rights movement," casting the movement as a threat to American values. In 1965 Graham reiterated his philosophical resistance to protest in a television and radio broadcast. "If the law says that I cannot march or I cannot demonstrate, I ought not to march and I ought not to demonstrate," he explained. Then, he added, "And if the law tells me that I should send my children to a school where there are both races, I should obey that law also." Graham's ambivalence toward civil rights was characteristic of white evangelicalism as a whole. From *Christianity Today*'s founding in 1956 through the March on Washington in 1963, the magazine maintained a consistently distant posture toward the civil rights movement, asserting that law could only go so far: people needed not a change of laws but a change of heart through conversion. The practical effect of this posture was a lukewarm support for civil rights in the abstract but little actual enthusiasm for the movement.[28]

The debate over black civil rights demonstrated just how confused the religious arguments over the moral establishment had become. Leaders of the radical and reformist movements of the 1960s rejected religion and doctrinally based moral authority in favor of a pluralist political order, one that recognized the social problems of racial injustice and economic polarization. But to conservative evangelicals, pluralism threatened the place of their moral authority in law, which they understood as historically vital to the sustenance of the United States.

Catholics too remained ambivalent. The hierarchy that determined Catholic doctrine came down firmly in support of equality and integration, considering it a moral imperative facing the international and multiethnic church in the post-Hitler era. Working sometimes even in advance of the civil rights movement, the church threatened the excommunication of parishes that resisted integration. The clerical hierarchy right up through Pope Pius XII sought to purge racial barriers and prejudice within the Church. This commitment to liberal causes and diversity continued to grow throughout the 1960s and became a cornerstone of Catholic belief in the immediate aftermath of the Second Vatican Council.[29]

But whatever the Church's official position, at the grassroots level many Catholics remained hostile. Led by William Buckley, many conservative Catholics believed civil rights were yoked to the historical utopianism of communism. Buckley's opposition was not surprising. As he explained in a 1957 editorial entitled "Why the South Must Prevail," the unrest of the civil rights movement showed that the white South was "entitled to take such measures as . . . necessary to prevail, politically and culturally." The white South was entitled to do so even when it lacked the requisite numbers to work through democratic channels because, "for the time being," it was "the advanced race." Rather than listening to the "ever-so-busy egalitarians and anthropologists," with their claim of universal suffrage, Buckley explained that the more important issue, even more important than democracy, was "the claims of civilization." Drawing a connection between British imperialism in Kenya, which chose civilization over barbarism in imposing white rule, Buckley summed up his point. "If the majority wills what is socially atavistic," he claimed, "then to thwart the majority may be, though undemocratic, enlightened. It is more important for any community, anywhere in the world, to affirm and live by civilized standards, than to bow to the demands of the numerical majority." Christian civilization required holding back the licentiousness of the masses and asserting a standard of decency, by which he meant, of course, state-sponsored segregation. Should it be impossible to hold back the civil rights movement, Buckley grimly explained, the white South, as the agent of Christian civilization, had to decide whether or not "the prevalence of its will" merited "the terrible price of violence." Given that the acceptance of barbarism was the only alternative to violence, Buckley's editorial seemed to suggest that there really would be no choice at all.[30]

Faced with such moral-establishmentarian rhetoric, Martin Luther King responded as a man of faith who rejected the simplistic understanding of order that both Buckley and the more moderate Graham upheld. In his famous 1963 letter from the Birmingham city jail—it was addressed to white clergyman of the city, but it could easily have been addressed to national leaders as well—King wrote, "Injustice anywhere is a threat to justice everywhere. We are caught in an inescapable network of mutuality, tied in a single garment of destiny. Whatever affects one directly affects all indirectly." In one sense, this sounded like a concern for the community as a moral unit, but, unlike moral establishmentarians, King recognized that this mutual interconnectedness required a strong commitment to individual rights. Moral establishmentarians, such as Graham and Buckley, thought that order, structure, and authority stood as the uppermost concern in society because individuals needed to be tamed by the community in order to be fit for society. Graham, in particular, believed that such a taming could come only through evangelical conversion, which began the process of Christian sanctification through a church. But King rejected such an understanding, claiming that order had to be paired with inclusion in the political process and individual self-determination for it to be legitimate. Moral establishmentarians failed to understand, King explained, that "groups are more immoral than individuals," which undermined the basic argument for the moral establishment. King did believe in a moral law, a morality on which human law should be based. But unlike moral establishmentarians, King claimed that the moral law tended toward individual rights. "Any law that uplifts human personality is just," he claimed. "Any law that degrades human personality is unjust." Those moral establishmentarians who were "more devoted to 'order' than to justice" misunderstood the basic requirements of the moral law.[31]

4.

Ultimately, this pluralist political orientation undid more than just segregation. As the 1960s progressed, and as the civil rights movement spawned numerous offshoots that sought to push a rights agenda in other aspects of society, the Court's jurisprudence moved toward a complete dismantling of the moral establishment. Under Warren, the Court took a number of liberal stands, first on the issue of race in the 1950s and then expanding in a wide variety of directions with the cultural developments of the 1960s. But as it did so, philosophical clarity and historical accuracy continued to elude the Court, placing the liberal revolution on uncertain intellectual footing.

The Court began in 1961 with *Torcaso v. Watkins*, which declared that freedom of religion included the freedom not to believe in anything. The case involved a Maryland law—representative of a wide variety of laws dating from the nineteenth century—that required all notary publics to declare their belief in the existence of God. Since the early nineteenth century, the belief in God or a future state of rewards and punishments had been a requirement for witnesses to appear before a court, for officeholders to assume office, and for the performance of a wide variety of other civic functions in several states, though those laws were less frequently enforced by the twentieth century. Ignoring the ubiquity of these laws and citing a past history of religious liberty, the Court explained in a unanimous opinion written by Justice Black that the Maryland law, and by implication others like it, violated the U.S. history of religious freedom, which had always been capacious in its embrace of religious traditions. Because Buddhism, Taoism, and even secular humanism were religious traditions that did not require a belief in God, the Court ruled that requiring a belief in the existence of God violated the Constitution and trespassed on the diversity of American religion.[32]

Torcaso followed the earlier pattern of intellectually evasive and historically misinformed reasoning. Determined to move in a liberal direction but suffering from historical amnesia in the belief that expansive religious freedom was part of the national character, the Court continued to draw upon a false history to support its opinions. Oddly, the Court's invocation of an exceptional history of freedom masked its actual expansion of rights and left unexplained why, given this history of freedom, the Court's actions were needed in the first place. This lack of intellectual clarity went hand-in-hand with a failure to recognize the logical terminus of many of its own opinions, which often pushed the Court in more-radical directions than it had been initially prepared to go. Because religion and the state had so many connections, the Court's declaration of the separation of church and state threatened to upend many aspects of U.S. governance in ways that it consistently was unable to anticipate. Given their belief in the myth of religious freedom, the jurists on the Court seemed unaware of those implications until a case came before it, at which point the Court sometimes pressed its jurisprudence to its logical conclusion and sometimes drew back, which created even more legal murk.

The same year that the Court decided *Torcaso*, two other cases showcased this tendency. In *McGowan v. Maryland*, the Court again seemed to recognize its dilemma when it upheld Sunday laws as a valid exercise of police power. In doing so, the Court rejected the claim of appellants who asserted that Sunday laws constituted an establishment of the Christian religion. The Court did acknowledge that Sunday laws originally had a religious purpose, but claimed that by the eighteenth century, when the First Amendment was proposed and ratified, a secular justification for the laws had begun to emerge. Citing Stephen Field, the Court noted that those secular justifications had now become ubiquitous. Combined with this secular justification, the long history of Sunday laws and their extensive adoption across the nation determined their constitutionality, the Court ruled. "Laws setting aside Sunday as a day of rest are upheld," the Court claimed, "not from any right of the government to legislate for the promotion of religious observances, but from its right to protect all persons from the physical and moral debasement which comes from uninterrupted labor." Because the Court assumed the myth of religious freedom, it could not properly acknowledge the role of the Sunday laws in maintaining Christian power.[33]

The sole dissent, by William O. Douglas, also started a soon-to-be familiar pattern. Douglas was among the most historically conscious members of the Warren Court and so saw that the Court's liberal jurisprudence would require the overturning of many precedents. Cutting through what he considered the Court's evasive opinion, Douglas put his finger on the issue. "The question is not whether one day out of seven can be imposed by a State as a day of rest," he retorted. "The question is whether a State can impose criminal sanctions on those who, unlike the Christian majority that makes up our society, worship on a different day or do not share the religious scruples of the majority." Noting that the acts prohibited by Sunday legislation—shopping, working, some forms of recreation—were "innocent acts," aside from the religious scruples concerning the day, he refused to support what he implied was the majority's insincere claim that Sunday observance sought only to protect persons from moral and physical debasement. Freedom of religion required also the freedom from religion, Douglas maintained, while Sunday laws mandated religious observance—the cessation of labor—that had been required by the Fourth Commandment. "No matter how much is written, no matter what is said," Douglas complained, the Court could not evacuate the religious origin of the Sunday laws nor eviscerate the religious reason behind their continued enforcement. Only the power of the Christian majority had clouded the Court's ability to see that enforcing the Christian Sabbath was essentially the same as enforcing Ramadan fasting, which the Court would never dream of upholding. "Today we retreat from that jealous regard for religious freedom which struck down a statute because," quoting his own concurring opinion in *Board of Education v. Barnette*, "it was a 'handy implement for disguised religious persecution.'"[34]

That same year, the Court also declined to take its liberal embrace of the rights of the individual to the logical conclusion. According to many liberals, the individual stood in some sense abstracted from the myriad social forms in which he or she was embedded, which is why liberals could so consistently argue for individual rights. The individual stood naked before the state, denuded of race or sex or religion and regarded only as a citizen. That had been Elizabeth Cady Stanton's argument when she dissolved the women's suffrage organization to form the American Equal Rights Association, promising "to bury the woman in the citizen." By contrast, in the moral establishment's understanding, the individual stood embedded in the many mediating institutions that directed individual behavior. The state could compel individuals when they bucked those institutions' influence. This was especially true for women, whom the moral establishment had relegated to the home. The placing of women in the home did not take the form of bald coercion, as in the case of African Americans and segregation. Instead, women were placed on a pedestal and idolized as pure and virtuous, and as the interpreters of divine morality for the child. The courts had consistently referenced this special place of the woman in the family when upholding her so-called privileges, which exempted women from the duties of citizenship such as jury duty or military service. To many women these supposed privileges felt more like a cage than a pedestal. These privileges also had the effect of using some women's exemption from duty to deny other women their rights, such as the ability to come to trial before a jury of peers that included other women. In *Hoyt v. Florida*, the Court unanimously displayed the limits of its liberalism when it rejected the argument of Gwendolyn Hoyt, a woman from Florida who argued that her conviction by an all-male jury for killing her husband had violated her rights. "Despite the enlightened emancipation of women from the restrictions and protections of bygone years," the Court explained, "woman is still regarded as the center of home and family life." These "special responsibilities" meant that women could not be compelled to serve on a jury, even if it placed other women at a disadvantage. Sex equality did not come under the protection of the Fourteenth Amendment.[35]

Given its lack of philosophical and historical clarity, the Court continued to address the moral establishment with a confused and contradictory logic. Just the next year the Court resumed its liberal march in one of the most famous (or infamous) religious liberty cases, *Engel v. Vitale*, which rejected the use of prayer in schools. At issue before the Court was New York State's

Regents' prayer, which invoked the blessing of the Almighty as part of what the state considered the moral and spiritual training of students. In its 7–1 opinion, the Court again appealed to history to strike down school prayer, asserting that many of the immigrants had come to the United States to escape religious persecution. "By the time of the adoption of the Constitution," Black wrote for the Court, "our history shows that there was a widespread awareness among many Americans of the dangers of a union of Church and State." But invoking the mythical history of religious freedom only gave the impression that the Court did not recognize how far-reaching its opinion actually was. Only Douglas, in a concurring opinion, saw what the *Everson* opinion actually meant if followed consistently. Noting that the case raised the question of whether the government could, according to the Constitution, pay for religious exercises, Douglas explained that the U.S. government at both the federal and state levels was at the time "honeycombed with such financing." Rather than implying that school prayer constituted an aberration from the larger history of freedom, Douglas saw that there had always been myriad connections between religion and the state and that these would be severed if the Court followed *Everson* to its logical conclusion.[36]

In 1963 the Court extended its ruling to exclude Bible-reading from the public schools and to reject the argument that Bible-reading was a nonsectarian exercise designed primarily to advance morals. Its historically inaccurate reasoning also continued. Rather than acknowledge that it was overturning a practice dating back to the beginning of public schooling in the United States, the Court again acted as though the Pennsylvania practice under consideration had been aberrant. Relatively speaking, the arrangement under consideration was somewhat tolerant. School officials read from multiple versions of the Bible, including the King James version, which was supported by conservative Protestants; the Douay version, which was supported by Catholics; the Revised Standard version, which was supported by liberals; and what the Court referred to as "the Jewish Holy Scriptures." All readings occurred without prefatory statements, which again emphasized the Protestant belief in the self-interpretation of scripture but insulated the district from the charge of sectarianism. Anyone wanting to opt out of the exercise could do so. But the father of the children who had filed the suit claimed that all those excused from the Bible-reading would be considered atheists or even atheistic communists. The family was Unitarian. Yet the suit was also joined by Madalyn Murray (soon to be Madalyn Murray O'Hair), an avowed atheist whose presence broadened the import of the case by allowing the Court to reemphasize that the freedom of religion included the freedom of irreligion.[37]

The Court's 8–1 opinion again invoked its now-standard historical myths. It recounted U.S. history as a history of religious freedom before summarizing the Court's recent adjudication on religious liberty, which implicitly lined up the Court's opinions with the wider history of American freedom and made the Court the enforcer of the long tradition of freedom. Yet its final result also squared with the Court's new emphasis on individual rights and equality, even for the nonreligious. Writing for the Court, Justice Tom Clark, who had been appointed by Truman in 1949, rejected the school district's argument. The district claimed Bible-reading as an aid, in its words, to "the promotion of moral values, the contradiction of the materialistic trends of our times, the perpetuation of our [American] institutions and the teaching of literature." But in providing exemptions and using various translations, the Court noted that the school board implicitly acknowledged the religious nature of the ceremony. Rather than ensuring the wide acceptance of the practice, these exemptions laid bare a fundamentally religious rationale for Bible-reading in public schools that could not be hidden by a claim of "nonreligious moral inspiration." After noting that even small trickles in the betrayal of principle could soon become a raging river, the Court concluded with the words of Madison, "[I]t is proper to take alarm at the first experiment on our liberties," which again construed the Court as the long-standing guardian of historic American freedoms.[38]

As the confused opinions kept coming, the Court's reasoning left many questions unanswered and riddled its jurisprudence with unanticipated tensions. By underselling the liberalizing rationale for their decisions—which, aside from Douglas, the justices apparently did not fully see—the Court created a damaging uncertainty as to its purpose in taking on these cases. In not acknowledging past religious power and not explaining that that power had led to an unfair exclusion or coercion of individuals, the Court left obscure the reason that it felt compelled to act in the first place, which in turn allowed conservatives to press their claims without acknowledging their desire for a return to coercion. After the Court's rejection of Bible-reading in schools, and the same day King gave his "I Have a Dream" speech in front of the Lincoln Memorial, Billy Graham used a crusade in Los Angeles to comment on the liberal movement. Noting that people of the world had been crying out for freedom through marches and demonstrations, Graham predicted, "If our Supreme Court continues this trend toward throwing God and the Bible out of our national life, there may some day be a march on Washington that will dwarf the one held today for civil rights." Graham's comment implied that the Court's jurisprudence sought to strip Americans of civil rights rather than expand them. While suggesting that the liberal movement had resulted in licentiousness, with "the greatest crime wave in history and broken homes, and suicides, and racial tension," Graham called the nation back to the Bible as its moral center and foundation of freedom, a foundation that was belied by his implicit reliance on a coercion that the Court never sought to explicitly challenge.[39]

Yet the Court's liberal march did continue. By 1965 the Court had finally expanded religious freedom to include political, sociological, and philosophical reasoning. The case involved conscientious objectors to the Vietnam War. Congress had made provision for objectors who held that a Supreme Being required their refraining from war. Rather than strike down the law, the Court issued a unanimous opinion that interpreted it in such as way as to broaden the exemption to almost anyone who presented a principled objection. In explaining its reasoning, the Court drew upon the assumption that all departures from the norm of Christian belief had to be explained in terms of a functional equivalency. When a person's objection was "sincere and meaningful" and when the belief assumed an importance "in the life of its possessor parallel to that filled by the orthodox belief in God," then the Court declared that that person qualified for an exemption to the draft. En route to its decision, the Court overturned its prior opinion in *MacIntosh,* which had rhetorically aligned the will of God with the actions of the United States government. The Court did so because it now recognized that the diversity of the United States required an acknowledgment of the many moral traditions by which a person might conscientiously object to war. Douglas, ever more radical, issued a concurring opinion noting that although none of the petitioners before the Court was an avowed atheist, he wanted to make clear that the Court's ruling ought to be applied equally to an explicitly irreligious person.[40]

That same year, Douglas wrote for the Court in a 7–2 opinion in *Griswold v. Connecticut* when it overturned a Connecticut law that forbade the use of contraceptives. Citing the constitutional revolution in which the Bill of Rights had been incorporated in the Fourteenth Amendment and employing a genuinely historical mode of argumentation, Douglas summarized the past movement of the Court. Their past decisions implied that the guarantees of the Bill of Rights had "penumbras, formed by emanations from those guarantees that help give them life and substance." The First Amendment, in particular, had "a penumbra where privacy is protected from governmental intrusion." The "[v]arious guarantees" promised in the Bill of Rights combined with the historical development of American jurisprudence to "create zones of privacy" that the government must honor. In this way, Douglas brought the right-to-privacy concept first put forward by Brandeis into the mainstream of constitutional law. By declaring the right to privacy as an emanation from various protections of the Bill of Rights, the Court moved to shield the individual from moral sanction and governmental coercion, allowing the individual to make choices within a zone of protection.[41]

Given these trends toward more-intensive rights claims, conservative resistance to the liberalizing development of modern society grew harsher. Conservatives foresaw the dissolution and disorder that moral establishmentarians had long warned would come with the absence of restraint. In the summer of 1965, after the eruption of the Watts Riots in Los Angeles, which lasted six days and caused dozens of deaths and thousands of injuries, Billy Graham again channeled evangelical anger at what many saw as the inevitable breakdown of society once Christian moral authority was removed from U.S. law and politics. Visiting Watts after order had been restored, Graham spoke darkly of the "great racial revolution" that the riots signified. Watts constituted the revolution's "dress rehearsal," according to Graham, with "sinister forces" that sought to overthrow the American order. As in the past, Graham called on King, who had nothing to do with the rioting, to halt further civil rights demonstrations and called for a congressional response that might restore a permanent sense of order. Graham's disgust at the direction of the liberalizing movement would soon prompt him to engage in more-overt political action.[42]

Two years later the Court moved to dismantle a final vestige of formal segregation, striking down in a unanimous opinion a Virginia anti-miscegenation law prohibiting interracial marriage. After Mildred Jeter and Richard Loving were married in Washington, D.C., the couple moved to Virginia. Once they settled they were arrested for violating Virginia's anti-miscegenation statute. After they pled guilty, the circuit court judge sentenced them to one year in jail and then suspended the sentence for twenty-five years, provided they moved from Virginia and did not return. The judge explained that his decision and the law were guided by religious considerations: "Almighty God created the races white, black, yellow, malay and red, and he placed them on separate continents. And but for the interference with his arrangement there would be no cause for such marriages. The fact that he separated the races shows that he did not intend for the races to mix." The U.S. Supreme Court struck down the ruling and reversed its prior opinion in Pace v. Alabama, which had upheld anti-miscegenation laws. Because the clear purpose of the Fourteenth Amendment had been to prevent invidious discrimination on the basis of race, the Court explained, anti-miscegenation laws could not stand. But the Court went even further—with important ramifications for the gay rights movement—when it declared, "The freedom to marry has long been recognized as one of the vital personal rights essential to the orderly pursuit of happiness by free men."[43]

The Court rounded out the decade in 1969, when it drew upon its ruling in *Griswold* to strike down a Georgia law that made it illegal to view obscene material in the home. Writing for the unanimous Court was Thurgood Marshall, the first black Supreme Court justice, who had worked on the *Brown* case for the plaintiffs and joined the Court in 1967 at the nomination of President Lyndon Baines Johnson, just two years after the United States began to ensure that African Americans had the right to vote and the same year that the Court outlawed anti-miscegenation statutes. Writing in *Stanley v. Georgia*, Marshall held that an individual's ability to view material that others found obscene constituted one of the fundamental rights of a free society, "the right to be let alone—the most comprehensive of rights and the right most valued by civilized man." "If the First Amendment means anything," he continued, "it means that a State has no business telling a man, sitting alone in his own house, what books he may read or what films he may watch." Georgia's claim that anti-obscenity laws fell within the police power of the state could be understood, Marshall explained, only as "the assertion that the State has the right to control the moral content of a person's thoughts." Marshall remained skeptical of the ability of the state to exert moral control over the individual at all. "Whatever the power of the state to control public dissemination of ideas inimical to the public morality," a power that he left in some doubt, the state could not do so by invading the right to privacy.[44]

Marshall's opinion represented the capstone of the Court's effort to dismantle the moral establishment. Although its rulings were often historically confused, the Court's general thrust was clear and motivated by a new commitment to equality and individual rights that had emerged in the 1940s and intensified during the civil rights movement. The Court declared that freedom of religion included the freedom to believe in nothing at all; rejected prayer and Bible-reading in schools as part of moral training; broadened the definition of religion to include ethical, sociological, and philosophical views that informed a person's moral convictions; overturned several Comstock laws by declaring a right to privacy emanating from the Bill of Rights; rejected the state's police power to enforce anti-miscegenation laws; and ruled that the right of privacy included the right to view obscene material in one's home. Its actions were not entirely consistent, though. They could not have been. Resting its doctrine of separation on a mythical historical foundation while confronting the density of connections between religion and the state, the

Court took on too much without knowing what it was doing and soon realized the limits of its jurisprudence. In particular, the Court upheld Sunday laws as part of the secular protection of health and morals and declared that women had primary responsibility for the home, two key components of the moral establishment that retreated from complete equality. But even with these tensions, the Court effected significant movement toward the acceptance of a pluralist America, divorcing law from Christian moral norms in a way that severely undercut Christian power and emphasized the equal and individual rights of all.

Many were unhappy with these developments, which made the decisions precarious. Graham's comments after the Watts Riots—flailing against a society that seemed to be falling apart—gave expression to a countermovement that had been building for some time and would migrate into the Republican Party after the Democrats accepted the mantle of civil rights. It was not an unexpected development. After signing the 1964 Civil Rights Act, Lyndon Johnson had despondently confided to his aide, Bill Moyers, "I think we just delivered the South to the Republican Party for a long time to come." Though Johnson had won election in 1964 with a large majority, the domestic unrest, conservative resistance to the radicalism of the Court, and fragmentation of political progressives in the face of the Vietnam War had left him bereft of support by 1968, so much so that he withdrew from his reelection attempt early in the primary season. After Martin Luther King was assassinated in April 1968, the two major leaders responsible for the civil rights successes had been destroyed. Although Hubert Humphrey, the eventual 1968 Democratic nominee, was the sitting vice president, Richard Nixon won an easy majority in the Electoral College, even after splitting the South with the racist governor from Alabama, George Wallace. Nixon then provided the new Republican strategy that challenged liberal jurisprudence and sought to rehabilitate the moral establishment.[45]

12

A MORAL MAJORITY?

1.

Nixon's election was the beginning of the conservative realignment that would, in less than twelve years, reorient U.S. political life and inaugurate the culture wars that consumed most of the last two decades of the twentieth century. He ran as the candidate who would restore law and order after the social upheavals of the late 1960s, and Billy Graham, who had a long history of support for Nixon, moved to align evangelicals with this emerging political majority. During the tumultuous summer of 1967, Graham praised the people who had turned away from the "rioting and rebellion" and were instead turning to Jesus, "a 'quiet revolution'" that fed into Nixon's calls for law and order. Nixon's campaign promises tapped into this weariness with social upheaval and assured voters, in a devastating part of his acceptance speech during the Republican nominating convention, that he would represent "the forgotten Americans, the non-shouters, the non-demonstrators" whom Nixon later gathered under the rubric of the "silent majority."[1]

Graham and Nixon came to collaborate throughout much of Nixon's 1968 campaign and subsequent presidency. Graham had wide-ranging connections to religious bankers and businessmen who had hosted many of his crusades and constituted an important bloc of the Republican Party. He also had multiple connections to racist Southern fundamentalists and evangelicals whom Nixon drew upon as he sought to rework the U.S. political map. This new coalition took a little while to build. Though Nixon split the Southern vote with George Wallace in 1968, the results were promising, suggesting a way for Republican electoral dominance. In 1969 Kevin Phillips, a Nixon campaign strategist and later Republican Party operative, wrote a book entitled *The Emerging Republican Majority* that codified the plan, which he further summarized in a 1970 interview with the *New York Times.* Arguing that Johnson had been right when he saw that Democratic alignment with civil rights would cost his party, Phillips explained, "The more Negroes who register as Democrats in the South, the sooner the Negrophobe whites will quit the Democrats and become Republicans. That's where the votes are." Once Southern whites had realigned with the Republican Party, Phillips predicted that they would deliver the Southern electoral votes, which would create a winning Republican coalition for at least a generation.[2]

This became known as Nixon's Southern Strategy, but it went hand-in-hand with a larger strategy in the Republican Party that joined religion and race. Since the civil rights movement had spawned other movements for expanding rights, race continued to be the signifier for a whole host of other issues. As Nixon's close advisor (and, later, convicted Watergate conspirator) John Ehrlichman explained, by reframing public housing, law and order, or public school busing in such a way that the voter "could avoid admitting to himself that he was attracted by a racist appeal," Nixon was able to make implicit racist gestures to gain votes from those who did not consider themselves racist. It worked because the strategy drew upon the overarching idea that individuals each had their place in an ordered society. "That subliminal appeal to the antiblack voter," in Ehrlichman's words, was especially effective for evangelicals who followed Graham and read *Christianity Today.* Their theoretical commitment to black rights could be trumped by a tacitly racist appeal that promoted an ordered society. This allowed them to vote for policies that circumscribed black rights while maintaining psychological equilibrium by not confronting their implicit racism.[3]

Such craven political posturing did have dangers that even Kevin Phillips recognized, admitting, "The popular conservative majority now taking shape . . . *is* vulnerable to aberration." Since the new Republican coalition drew upon "apprehensive bourgeois and law-and-order-seeking individuals," he acknowledged "a proclivity to authoritarianism and over-reaction to the liberal-engendered permissiveness and anarchy of the sixties." Yet others saw the movement as a solution to the problem of political demagoguery, as Lee Atwater, the Republican political operative who joined Reagan's White House, ran the elder Bush's 1988 campaign, and then became the chairman of the Republican National Committee, later explained. "You start out in 1954 by saying, 'Nigger, nigger, nigger,'" he said of conservatives' tactics after *Brown.* But that strategy could not last, given the success of the civil rights movement. "By 1968," he went on, "you can't say 'nigger'—that hurts you. Backfires. So you say stuff like forced busing, states' rights and all that stuff. You're getting so abstract now [that] you're talking about cutting taxes, and all these things you're talking about are totally economic things and a byproduct of them is [that] blacks get hurt worse than whites. And subconsciously maybe that is part of it. I'm not saying that. But I'm saying that if it is getting that abstract, and that coded, that we are doing away with the racial problem one way or the other. You follow me—because obviously sitting around saying, 'We want to cut this,' is much more abstract than even the busing thing, *and* a hell of a lot more abstract than 'Nigger, nigger.'" This coding of race, as Atwater put it, helped solve what he understood as America's "racial problem," which he seemed to see less as a problem of structural discrimination than as a problem of getting Republicans elected.[4]

In any case, this authoritarianism that Phillips predicted, which had been inherent in the moral establishment, set in immediately. As Graham told a crowd at one of his crusades, at which Nixon spoke, "I'm for change, but the Bible teaches us to obey authority," a statement that buttressed Nixon's leadership as the result of God's appointment and implicitly rejected the radical subversion of Christian authority that characterized the late 1960s. Graham actually provided one of the most useful tools in Nixon's strategy. He used his evangelical prestige to burnish Nixon's conservative credentials and to provide cover for the new politics of race. Because Graham had sought to remain aloof from social struggle around the civil rights movement, his endorsement disguised the implicitly racial appeals that Nixon was making while sacralizing Nixon's vision of law and order. As Kenneth Chafin, the director of evangelism for the Southern Baptist Convention and a frequent Graham consultant, explained, "I've never heard Billy make real strong statements on race. The purpose for which he sets up a crusade is basically not designed to address itself to race."[5]

By avoiding the specific issue of race, Graham paved the way for the Nixon strategy and the platform for the emerging conservative coalition. Partly, this stemmed from Graham's theology, which rendered him skeptical of any attempt to effect social transformation other than through Christian conversion and the traditional restraints imposed by communities. In contrast to King, who dreamed that "one day, right there in Alabama, little black boys and black girls will be able to join hands with little white boys and white girls as sisters and brothers," Graham thought that "[o]nly when Christ comes again will the lion lie down with the lamb and the little white children of Alabama walk hand in hand with the little black children." Graham's millennialism presumed that interracial hostility would last until Christ's return.[6]

Yet Graham claimed his emerging alliance with Nixon not as a movement into partisan politics or as a participation in coded race-baiting, but as a logical extension of the battle against Satan that he had been waging since his first anticommunist pronouncements of the 1950s. When Graham went so far as to allow Nixon to address one of his revival meetings, the first time a president had done so, he disclaimed any intention of engaging in a political act. "I wouldn't think that you'd call the President political," he protested. To Graham, at least publicly, Nixon was his office, a national leader embodying the American order that Graham sought to buttress and restore. But this posture pulled him deeper into partisan politics than he wanted to admit. In a conversation with Nixon that the president secretly taped in 1972, Graham gave Nixon campaign advice, urging him to orient his reelection effort on a platform of "integrity" that focused on the restoration of law and order that Nixon supposedly had effected. He needed to be proactive in setting up this image, Graham explained, because the media could not be counted upon to represent their cause fairly, a phenomenon that Nixon angrily attributed to the Jews he believed controlled the media. Graham agreed, lamenting what Jews were "doing to this country," perhaps a recognition of the role secular Jews had played in the radical movements of the 1960s and the general liberalization of U.S. society.[7]

Liberals were not fooled by this hypocritical posture of political neutrality but had difficulty fighting it because it operated on such a subtle level. The "Nixon–Graham doctrine of the relation of religion to public morality and policy," as the liberal theologian Reinhold Niebuhr labeled the emerging countermovement, shrouded law and order in what Niebuhr saw as "an aura of sanctity on contemporary public policy." It coded evangelical desires and masked racism behind a less obvious rhetoric, rejecting the liberalizing movement and seeking a rehabilitation of the moral establishment.[8]

2.

While Nixon and Graham worked together on the political front, other conservatives were busy in the courts. One of the most important consequences of the polarization of the 1960s was conservatives' increased interest in law, which they saw as a means of turning back the tide of liberalism in U.S. society that the Court both promoted and legitimized. As a first attempt to rein in the liberal tendencies of the Court, Nixon nominated Warren Burger to usher in a more conservative era of jurisprudence when Earl Warren retired as chief justice in 1969. But the addition of Burger did not measurably change the liberal trend of the Court, though it did slow and further confuse its jurisprudence.

Just one year after he was appointed, Burger got the chance to begin putting his stamp on religious-liberty law in a case involving tax exemptions for churches, one of the most important means of state support for religion. The plaintiffs in the case claimed that tax exemptions violated the establishment clause of the First Amendment. Writing for the 8–1 majority, Burger claimed that tax exemption did not violate the establishment clause and, in the process, moved away from the Warren Court's confident pronouncements on the First Amendment's meaning. "The Establishment and Free Exercise Clauses of the First Amendment are not the most precisely drawn portions of the Constitution," Burger explained. He also acknowledged "considerable internal inconsistency in the opinions of the Court" that had arisen in part from the Court's "too sweeping utterances." By distancing himself from the absolute church–state separation of the Warren Court, Burger made room for the multitudinous connections between religion and the state that had been the historical norm and that conservatives wanted to maintain. In the case before the Court, Burger claimed that the long history of tax exemptions for churches, which they received in exchange for public service, was sufficient evidence of their constitutionality. But his belief in a history of freedom made him blind to a passive or proxy establishment that had operated through much of U.S. history and that sustained tax exemption.[9]

Douglas, in what would become an increasingly frequent occurrence, stood in dissent. "I would suppose that in common understanding one of the best ways to 'establish' one or more religions is to subsidize them," he reasoned, "which is what a tax exemption does." In contrast to Burger and the rest of the Court, Douglas recognized not just past coercion but also the revolutionary transformation of jurisprudence since the Civil War. Douglas sounded like a teacher lecturing a group of not very bright students. The constitutional revolution of the Fourteenth Amendment "involved the imposition of new and far-reaching constitutional restraints on the States," he explained. "Nationalization of many civil liberties has been the consequence of the Fourteenth Amendment, reversing the historic position that the foundations of those liberties rested largely in state law." When the First Amendment was incorporated into the Fourteenth, many long-standing practices had to be declared unconstitutional, Douglas noted, citing prayer and Bible-reading in schools as two prominent examples. In this way, he clarified the point on which Burger had slipped up. If the First Amendment did not apply to the states, then Douglas agreed that states could grant tax exemptions to churches just as they could grant tax exemptions to any other kind of organization. But once the First Amendment did apply to the states, then churches ought to lose tax exemption because the vast majority of churches did not constitute "social welfare programs within the reach of police power." Even if they did offer social services, Douglas reasoned that churches still could not qualify for tax exemption, because then the government would favor believers over nonbelievers, which ran against the purpose of the First Amendment "to promote a viable, pluralistic society."[10]

As the cases kept coming, this split between Burger and Douglas became the animating division on the Court. Both agreed that the past jurisprudence had been unacceptably inconsistent, but Burger concluded that it had been the fault of the original principle of church–state separation, while Douglas believed that the principle just needed to be consistently applied. In *Lemon v. Kurtzman*, Burger had another chance to rework the jurisprudence. At issue was, once again, the problem of states (Pennsylvania and Rhode Island) funneling money to private, parochial schools, this time by paying for private school teachers' salaries and books when they were not explicitly sectarian. Burger, writing for the Court, invalidated the practice. "The language of the Religion Clauses of the First Amendment is at best opaque," Burger asserted. Claiming that the prior holdings of the Court that called for total church–state separation were not really possible to enforce, he proposed a three-part test that has since become known as the *Lemon* test. To pass constitutional muster, Burger explained, a program must have (1) a secular purpose that (2) neither advances nor inhibits religion nor (3) promotes excessive entanglement of the government with religion. In the case in question, Burger ruled that the program both had a secular purpose and did not advance or inhibit religion, at least in theory. But to ensure that the teachers paid by the program did not use the money for sectarian ends, the state would have to set up an extended program of surveillance that would foster an entanglement with religious schools and so was impermissible.[11]

Douglas agreed that religious-liberty law needed rationalization but thought that Burger's reasoning was wrong-headed. Any consideration of paying schools must acknowledge, Douglas claimed, the "obvious fact that the *raison d'être* of parochial schools is the propagation of a religious faith." Exhibiting a real sense of history, Douglas noted that although they taught secular subjects, parochial schools had come into existence largely because Protestant groups had seized the public school system to propagate their own religious faith. In attempting to funnel money to a teacher who ostensibly taught secular subjects, the legislature conceived of a history or literature class as a separate institute rather than "part of the organic whole" that fostered religious education. Burger's tacit acceptance of the legislation's secular purpose remained oblivious to the function and history of parochial schools as religious bodies that emerged in a context of religious conflict. His test, in turn, took the Court further away from the more urgent issue of completely secularizing the public school system that it had begun with *Engel v. Vitale*.[12]

For all their differences, Douglas and Burger agreed on the outcome of *Lemon,* which struck down public aid to parochial schools. This disagreement in reasoning but agreement on outcome continued in other cases. As much as Burger sought to halt the liberal march, he had imbibed the prior liberal opinions whose logic, even when strained by myriad philosophical and historical tensions, still compelled surprising decisions. None was more surprising or momentous than the opinion in *Roe v. Wade* (1973), which would galvanize the emerging conservative coalition. *Roe* touched on all the issues that animated the moral establishment, with a specific focus on the place of women. The Court had begun its reconsideration of the rights of women two years earlier in *Reed v. Reed,* when it ruled for the first time that discrimination on the basis of sex, not just race, was forbidden by the equal protection clause of the Fourteenth Amendment. Moving away from the kind of reasoning it had employed just ten years earlier in *Hoyt v. Florida,* the Court dropped all talk of the family as woman's sphere. By putting the Fourteenth Amendment to work protecting women from discrimination based on sex, the Court required the law to regard a woman primarily as an individual, not as a matron or mother. This further abstracted the woman from the family, which had been a central mediating institution in the moral establishment, and rendered her as simply a citizen before the state. In *Roe* the Court took this idea further by employing the privacy doctrine originally devised by Brandeis and brought into law by Douglas in *Griswold v. Connecticut. Roe* declared that a woman's decision to have an abortion was a private moral choice in which the state had no business involving itself.[13]

The 7–2 majority opinion—written by Harry Blackmun, whom Nixon had appointed in 1971 upon the recommendation of Chief Justice Burger—was a model of historically informed legal scholarship. Blackmun began by noting that common law had distinguished between abortions that occurred prior to quickening—the first felt movements of the fetus—and abortions performed afterward. Common law offered minimal scrutiny of abortions done prior to quickening. This distinction disappeared over the course of the nineteenth century as more-stringent statutory codes were passed in tandem with (though Blackmun did not note it in the opinion) the expansion of religious power. Blackmun observed, "[A]t the time of the adoption of our Constitution, and throughout the major portion of the 19th century, abortion was viewed with less disfavor than under most American statutes currently in effect [in 1973]." Given the relative freedom of the past, Blackmun reasoned that no historical precedent could support the antiabortion laws because they were of relatively recent vintage. Then, drawing upon Brandeis's notion of a right to privacy, Blackmun suggested that abortion was covered under that right, which allowed individuals to make moral choices within a wider political context of disagreement. The woman's right to privacy meant that the state had no business making a moral decision for her. Yet Blackmun did acknowledge that the state had an interest in protecting human life, which meant that the right to privacy was not absolute. Once the fetus became viable, which Blackmun decided was the third trimester of pregnancy, but not before then, the state could provide regulations or even proscribe abortion. What was remarkable about the decision was its detachment. Absent was any language of morality, even though Blackmun was treading on hotly disputed moral ground. Instead he used a consistent vocabulary of personal choice, individual consultation, and professional medical judgment, all within the context of a right to privacy in making a difficult moral decision.[14]

More than anything else, *Roe* solidified the modern conservative coalition by bringing conservative Catholics, evangelicals, and fundamentalists together under the flag of the Republican Party. Prior to *Roe*, abortion had been largely a Catholic issue, growing out of the Catholic theological commitment to support life in all its forms. But *Roe* demonstrated to conservatives across the religious divide the powerful political implications of abortion and the deep instability wrought by the pluralization of ethical norms during the 1960s. By rooting a woman's right to an abortion in the fundamental right of privacy, the Court conceived of the citizen as a point of pure moral self-determination. Apart from communal standards, religious pressure, or mediating institutions previously responsible for aiding and softening the coercive power of law, the individual alone became responsible for moral choice. *Roe* served as a culmination of the many cases that reconsidered the relations and obligations of the citizen to the state and called into question the extent to which the state had the right to legislate public morality. The Court had increasingly undermined the traditional role of the state in defining an official morality and instead presumed and even nurtured a diversity of religious and moral opinion.

According to conservatives, the outcome of such jurisprudence could be only moral anarchy, societal dissolution, and the breakdown of anything approaching civilized existence. The fact that the Court had so carefully translated a moral issue involving the preservation of life into the language of privacy, personal choice, and medical judgment suggested to conservatives the absolute loss of a moral compass directing state policy. *Roe* represented to conservatives the larger trend toward the breakdown of mediating institutions and the abdication of Christian authority in government. It was the triumph of liberalism and the death knell for the moral establishment.

Other concurrent developments seemed to reinforce the danger of an absolute collapse of Christian moral authority. Even more worrisome than *Roe,* to some conservatives, was the newly passed equal rights amendment (ERA), which Congress had authorized in 1972. Alice Paul, the radical suffragette who pushed Congress during the Wilson administration to embrace women's suffrage, had originally proposed the ERA. By the time the amendment finally passed Congress it stated quite simply, "Equality of rights under the law shall not be denied or abridged by the United States or by any state on account of sex." That simple statement operated as a Trojan horse through which the moral outrage of *Roe* would be multiplied many times over, claimed Phyllis Schlafly, a central figure in the emerging Catholic–Protestant conservative coalition. Equal rights, in Schlafly's estimation, meant the further devaluing of the family by considering a woman primarily as a citizen rather than a wife or a mother. To mobilize against this, she formed a new grassroots coalition with the goal of capturing the Republican Party for traditionalists who sought to buttress the remains of the moral establishment and bring it back wherever possible. Unlike Billy Graham, Schlafly had always been an explicit, rather than implicit, partisan. She had also long distrusted Nixon. When he self-destructed in the Watergate controversy and finally resigned the presidency in 1974, Schlafly used it as an opportunity to reorient the Republican Party.[15]

Schlafly's campaign against the ERA proved powerful in part because she used it to clarify what she saw as the fundamental differences between liberal and conservative political philosophy. As she explained in an early article against the ERA in her monthly newsletter, the *Phyllis Schlafly Report*, the American woman had the most privileges of any person in world history because the family functioned as a basic social unit as a result of America's "Judeo-Christian civilization." Men and women had different responsibilities both within and without this basic social unit. Because women had babies, they raised the children, while men became responsible in law and custom primarily for material support, which in turn resulted "in all women, in effect, being put on a pedestal." The ERA, with its focus on individual rights and its conception of women as citizens rather than merely mothers or wives, ran counter to this conservative vision and introduced the threat of disaster. Hinting at the issue of race, Schlafly noted, "In other civilizations, such as the

African and the American Indian, the men strut around wearing feathers and beads and hunting and fishing . . . while the women do all the hard, tiresome drudgery including the tilling of the soil (if any is done)." The final barb, "if any is done," conjured the old belief in laziness and lack of character that had served as a justification for both slavery and segregation and implicitly painted what she considered "the American way" as a white, bourgeois phenomenon. By advocating a consistent set of liberal individual rights, the "'equal rights' fanatics" sought to knock the woman from her pedestal and remove the protection that the law had given her, which could result only in the cultural degeneracy characterizing other, non-white civilizations.[16]

To resist this assault, Schlafly founded STOP ERA, which showcased the grassroots power of the new coalition and its rejection of the liberal view of U.S. society and culture. As a broad coalition of devotees of the traditional family, STOP ERA had the power of numbers, inundating politicians with literature and campaigning against those who supported equal rights. Schlafly's efforts had immediate effect. A year after Congress had passed the ERA, thirty states had ratified the amendment, and its ultimate approval seemed merely a matter of time. But as Schlafly's campaign developed, the pace slowed dramatically. In 1974 three states ratified it. In 1975 one did. Finally, in 1977, another followed, which meant three states were still needed for the amendment's final ratification. It stalled there.[17]

Meanwhile, evangelicals were coming into alignment with conservative Catholics such as Schlafly. Billy Graham did not participate in this movement, busy as he was trying to rehabilitate his nonpartisan image after Nixon's expulsion had sullied it. But others responded quite fiercely. One of the most important was Francis Schaeffer, a former trainee of the fundamentalist Carl McIntire. In the 1940s after Schaeffer moved out of McIntire's shadow and into more-mainstream evangelical circles, he developed a reputation as something of an intellectual. His basic thesis, repeated again and again in a large number of books that sold millions of copies, was that U.S. culture and Western civilization had both been founded upon Christianity. That foundation had been steadily eroded by secular humanists and other liberal elites, he claimed, which placed freedom on an indeterminate foundation and seemed to portend a coming barbarism. Schaeffer had remained initially cool to the antiabortion movement, considering it a Catholic issue that was too overtly political. He preferred instead to focus on less obviously political concerns. But his son, Frank Schaeffer, who was responsible for the fundraising arm of the ministry and had become part of the ever-larger evangelical machine, thought otherwise, though he was not at first able to convince his father. In

1955 after building a following as a Christian intellectual, Francis decamped to a Swiss chateau that he opened as a study house, where he remained to write books and to cultivate an oracular persona. But he stayed in touch with the U.S. evangelical movement through his son, who traveled among the wealthy evangelical elite. As a result of his travels, Frank Schaeffer recognized that abortion could mobilize the evangelical electorate, since the *Roe* decision cut across so many beliefs that evangelicals had held dear. While shooting a film series based on one of Francis's books, *How Should We Then Live?*, Frank finally convinced his father to take a stand on the abortion debate, devoting the final two episodes to the issue.[18]

Their decision had profound implications for the evangelical movement and for the rise of the Christian Right, given Schaeffer's stature among evangelicals. *How Should We Then Live?* remains standard viewing in evangelical high schools and colleges, so much so that it still brings Frank Schaeffer several thousand dollars per year in royalties, decades after the documentary was made. The series made the elder Schaeffer into an international evangelical celebrity and helped mobilize a generation of evangelicals against abortion, drawing them into the Republican Party and into cooperation with conservative Catholics. Schaeffer had already laid the intellectual basis for such cooperation with non-evangelicals and even non-Christians in a 1970 book, *The Church at the End of the Twentieth Century*. Attuned as he was to the many cultural currents swirling in the United States, Schaeffer realized that many groups who might not agree with evangelical theology could still support evangelical ends. Rather than allies, these people were what he called "cobelligerents," persons uniting on a specific issue but disagreeing on the ultimate basis for their cause—and often unaware of the implicitly Christian foundation of their belief. With the rise of social issues such as abortion, women's rights, obscenity, and so on, Schaeffer gave evangelicals a conceptual basis by which to become partners with Catholics within the Republican Party.[19]

Schaeffer's concept of co-belligerence also helped cement the final piece of the puzzle that would allow for a complete coalescence of conservative Protestants and Catholics in a movement to catapult Ronald Reagan to victory and revive the Republican Party. That final piece was the 1979 rise of the Moral Majority. The group was led by the formerly separation-minded Southern fundamentalist Jerry Falwell, who, according to Mel White, a one-time ghostwriter for several members of the Religious Right, including Falwell, admired Schaeffer and adopted his strategy of co-belligerency. In White's words, Falwell used the notion of co-belligerency to explain his search for "an army of 'nonbelievers'" that could enact what Falwell thought of as "God's will for the nation." Falwell shared the political theology that conservative Catholics and evangelicals had adopted in seeking to restore the moral establishment, but he needed the concept of co-belligerency to overcome his sectarian animosity. Once he did so, his organization became a powerful force. As Falwell explained in his 1980 book *Listen, America!*, he believed that God had favored the United States because the Founders had "established America's laws and precepts on the principles recorded in the laws of God, including the Ten Commandments." These religious principles expressed themselves in a moral code that had held society together, but that code had come under attack since the 1960s. "We are quickly moving toward an amoral society where nothing is either absolutely right or absolutely wrong," Falwell fretted. With the disappearance of absolute moral clarity, U.S. society was "crumbling," marked by an erosion of stability that left the United States "morally sick." Citing all the moral flash points that had arisen since the 1960s—abortion, prayer and Bible-reading in schools, pornography, homosexuality, and the dignity of the family—Falwell proposed that the Moral Majority could be a union of all the various interests that wanted to preserve the genius of America in order to renew the moral establishment.[20]

Schlafly, Schaeffer, and Falwell represented three powerful grassroots groups that had an interest in rehabilitating the moral establishment. All three groups—conservative Catholics, evangelicals, and fundamentalists—agreed that the cultural authority of conservative Christianity provided the foundation for the United States. They all thought that a dedicated group of liberal radicals was seeking "the abolition of truth and morality," in Schaeffer's words. Their union against this common enemy finally allowed them to overcome sectarian divisions. If Schaefer's concept permitted Protestants to cooperate with Catholics, it was Schlafly's grassroots political strategy, replicated in countless organizations, that became the cornerstone of this conservative countermovement. Her strategy was, like that of Lyman Beecher, a response to a liberal democratizing movement in politics, without entirely embracing democracy. While not overtly racist herself, she claimed that cultural authority in a diverse society was best held by the (implicitly) white trustees of Judeo-Christian civilization. She saw U.S. culture as inherently hierarchical, built upon families with men as the head of the household and women in charge of the home. This hierarchy presumed a wider context of proper authority upon which the U.S. order had once been based and upon which activists hoped it might one day again be based. By the time the ERA ratification period expired in 1982, the conservative restoration of the moral establishment, now centered on the notion of family values rather than overtly on race, appeared imminent.[21]

3.

As the grassroots conservative movement built momentum, conservative legal activists moved to find a coherent alternative to liberal jurisprudence. While searching for a solution, they adopted two tactics. The first was characterized by a cognizance of the emerging Republican majority and the grassroots political power that conservatives possessed. Claiming that many of the questions addressed by the Court over the last two decades had been more properly political than legal, conservatives suggested that the Court ought to defer to the legislative branch, particularly when it addressed social questions. This tack essentially rejected the Court's earlier *Carolene* decision to defer to the legislature in economic matters while subjecting issues of fundamental rights to a "more searching judicial inquiry" in order to protect the rights of minorities. Conservatives claimed that the *Carolene* principle had created a pattern of judicial activism that short-circuited the political process in an overly zealous attempt to eradicate prejudice and defend the rights of minorities. But conservatives were not consistent, as a subsequent development in conservative legal theory showed. "Originalism," as the new doctrine came to be called, suggested that the meaning of the Constitution had been fixed at its ratification, and any departure from that meaning was invalid. This enabled conservatives to discount large portions of the last century of constitutional development that they did not like, while claiming to be upholding the Constitution's original meaning as they, not the judicial tradition, understood it.[22]

The single most important person in the emerging conservative jurisprudence was not Chief Justice Burger but William Rehnquist, whom Nixon had appointed to the Court in 1972 and whom Reagan made Chief Justice in 1986. Rehnquist had clerked under Jackson during *Brown v. Board of Education* and wrote a memo defending the separate-but-equal doctrine of *Plessy v. Ferguson.* Although he disowned the memo in his confirmation hearings, it showcased the emerging conservative judicial philosophy to which he subscribed while on the bench. As he saw it, the Court primarily served as a neutral arbiter between the branches of government, remaining deferential to the legislature and not needing to protect minority and individual rights. "The Constitution, of course, deals with individual rights, particularly in the first Ten and the Fourteenth Amendments," he admitted, but in attempting to defend those rights the Court had too often been in "hot water." Since the Court was being asked to defend the individual rights of black children in *Brown,* Rehnquist applied this doctrine specifically to race in a way that he would do only rarely in the future. Noting that the appellants held a view "palpably at variance with precedent and probably with legislative history," Rehnquist claimed that it was quite clear that segregation did not constitute "one of those extreme cases which commands [judicial] intervention." "To the argument . . . that a majority may not deprive a minority of its constitutional right," he continued, "the answer must be made that while this is sound in theory, in the long run it is the majority who will determine what the constitutional rights of the minority are," a claim that rejected Madison's constitutional reasoning while claiming original intent. Rather than the Court "read[ing] its own sociological views into the Constitution," Rehnquist concluded, "I think *Plessy v. Ferguson* was right and should be re-affirmed."[23]

As the politics of race was folded into the Nixon strategy of law and order, this explicitly racial thinking faded into conservatives' view of judicial deference to the legislature and the careful perpetuation of states' rights. The new conservative philosophy became immediately useful in trying to rebuild the moral establishment. In 1977, in *Maher v. Roe*, the Court held in a 6–3 decision that states were not compelled to fund non-therapeutic abortions for women on welfare and could, in fact, advance a state preference for the continuation of the pregnancy. Connecticut, like many other states, had seen antiabortion activists mobilizing against *Roe* by limiting access to abortion. The majority, in effect, gave the go-ahead to these efforts by stepping back from its *Carolene* promise of oversight for individual rights, a shift that Rehnquist had suggested in his memo. Only three justices dissented, which indicated the growing conservative shift. William J. Brennan, appointed by Truman in 1956, wrote for Marshall and Blackmun, outlining the minority's consternation. Brennan noted that the Court had repeatedly held, after *Carolene*, that states could not infringe upon fundamental rights, which meant not just denying rights outright but inhibiting the exercise of rights through legislative impediments. Because *Roe* had declared abortion part of the fundamental right to privacy, the minority reasoned that states could not declare an official preference toward the preservation of a pregnancy by refusing to fund all non-therapeutic abortions for the poor. Instead, women on welfare, like women on private insurance, had the "fundamental right to make that choice free from state interference."[24]

Three years later the Court moved to apply the same thinking to the national level in a 5–4 decision in *Harris v. McCrae*. After antiabortion activists had such success on the state level, Henry Hyde of Illinois, a Catholic Republican, introduced an amendment to an unrelated bill that prohibited all federally funded abortions, even if one was necessary for the health of the mother. The district court originally struck down the Hyde Amendment, claiming that it violated the First Amendment's prohibition of a religious establishment. The majority on the Court rejected the district court's ruling, repeating its reasoning in *Maher*. In rejecting the district court's claim, the Court noted that antiabortion was not solely a religious issue but had instead arisen from "'traditionalist' values toward abortion," a statement that discounted the historical evidence marshaled by Blackmun in *Roe*, which showed that women had a much freer access to abortion before the religious expansion that had occurred over the course of the nineteenth century.[25]

In this decision and in the future, the assertion of history by conservative jurists often became a vehicle for false nostalgia. William Brennan, joined by Blackmun and Marshall, wrote a fiery dissent (Stevens penned his own), arguing that the Hyde Amendment could only be considered "a transparent attempt by the Legislative Branch to impose the political majority's judgment of the morally acceptable and socially desirable preference on a sensitive and intimate decision that the Constitution entrusts to the individual." But the Hyde Amendment went a step further by attempting to "foist that majoritarian viewpoint" only upon the small segment of society who were poor and required state aid, which discriminated against the segment that, "because of its position of political powerlessness, is least able to defend its privacy rights from the encroachments of state-mandated morality." The discrimination against the poor made the amendment doubly noxious, trouncing fundamental rights by interfering with a private decision and doing so on a discriminatory basis.[26]

As the Court trended conservative, its decisions became more fractured, and the high level of agreement characterizing the 1950s and 1960s became rare. Yet conservatives were able only to chip away at liberal decisions, never to completely rid jurisprudence of liberalism. Conservatives continued to use history to buttress their claims to originalism, but its use was often an empty gesture to mask an ideological agenda. As conservatives increasingly turned to history, liberal jurists began to move away from the false history that had accompanied earlier decisions and instead began to analyze the historical claims that conservatives were making. In the process, the debate over law became as much a debate over history. In 1983, for example, the Court declined to continue its liberal jurisprudence, when it ruled that religious acts in state-sponsored contexts other than schools—such as opening legislative sessions with a prayer—were perfectly valid. Writing for the six-person majority, Burger drew upon the past to prove his point. Noting that such religious ritual was "deeply embedded in the history and tradition" of the United States, in which legislative and other official prayers had "coexisted with the principles of disestablishment and religious freedom," Burger acknowledged past religious practice but only in the context of his asserted myth of religious freedom. "In light of the unambiguous and unbroken history of more than 200 years," he claimed, "there can be no doubt that the practice of opening legislative sessions with prayer has become part of the fabric of our society." He continued, "To invoke Divine guidance on a public body entrusted with making the laws is not, in these circumstances, an 'establishment' of religion or a step toward establishment."[27]

Since Douglas had retired in 1975, the task of rebuttal fell to William Brennan, joined by Thurgood Marshall; again, Stevens penned a separate dissent. Brennan was scathing in his critique of the majority's reasoning, claiming that their invocation of history missed all the essential points. He noted that the majority had assumed that the Constitution was "a static document" that remained "fixed for all time by the life experience of the Framers," rather than a document of flexible principles whose application changed as society transformed. Given this originalist impulse, Brennan observed that the majority opinion did not even attempt to square its reasoning with the past reasoning of the Court, ignoring the Court's multiple opinions that incorporated fundamental rights into the Fourteenth Amendment and neglecting the body of jurisprudence that would mandate the prohibition of legislative prayer, regardless of its long historical standing. Brennan was particularly contemptuous of the idea that past practice and original meaning had any relevance when it came to the subject of religion. He quoted Justice Joseph Story, who had claimed that the First Amendment was designed to advance nonsectarian Christian belief rather than "Mahometanism [sic], or Judaism, or infidelity, by prostrating Christianity." Brennan rejected Story's assumption of the Christian prerogatives in law, which had been part of the legal architecture of the past and seemed to offer a basis for conservatives in the present. Those assumptions were simply untenable in any constitutional regime concerned with equal protection and democratic inclusion, he claimed. The majority's "focus here on a narrow piece of history" actually bastardized any real historical consciousness, including a consciousness of the Court's own past decisions, and ultimately invoked history only to cloak their "betrayal of the lessons of history."[28]

Brennan concluded his stinging dissent with an observation that was also a prediction. "If the Court had struck down legislative prayer today, it would likely have stimulated a furious reaction," he conceded. "But it would also, I am convinced, have invigorated both the 'spirit of religion' and the 'spirit of freedom.'" In making such a prediction, Brennan drew upon the long-held liberal belief that the separation of church from state provided for the vitality of both and protected each from the other. That had been Madison's belief and it had been expressed many times by liberals on the Court. But the opposite was also true, he implied. If church and state were not separate, particularly in a government with a large and widening bureaucratic apparatus, then religious partisans who sought to inject religion into government ran the risk that religion could be subjected to governmental regulation. The trend toward state regulation began the same year in a highly controversial case, *Bob Jones University v. United States*, brought by a fundamentalist college that believed that the races ought not to mix because God had intended to keep them separate. For years, the college had been an important stop for Republican presidential candidates during the primary season, and an important part of the Southern Strategy. After the civil rights movement, the Internal Revenue Service (IRS) began clamping down on schools that discriminated on the basis of race, as Bob Jones did first by admitting only white students and then, under pressure from the IRS, by admitting nonwhite students but segregating them or instituting special rules that limited their equal participation once they had been admitted. After a nearly ten-year battle with the recalcitrant university, the IRS revoked the school's tax-exempt status. When Bob Jones sued, the National Association of Evangelicals, the Republican senator (and future Senate majority leader) Trent Lott, and the Church of Latter-Day Saints all filed amicus briefs in support of Bob Jones by claiming a violation of religious freedom. The Court, in an 8–1 opinion written by Burger, upheld the IRS's decision with the explanation that because racial discrimination was against long-standing public policy, the university had lost its right to tax exemption, since it no longer conferred the public benefit that the tax exemption required. Brennan had rightly predicted that if the state supported religion then religion inevitably became the subject of state control.[29]

The following year the Court decided another case that again showed the danger for religious groups who sought to use the government to further their ends, though conservatives continued to push for the connection of religion and the state by claiming that it was an essential aspect of a democratic society whose majority was Christian. The Court was asked to consider the legality of a nativity scene, or crèche, erected by the City of Pawtucket, Rhode Island. The mayor of Pawtucket had explained that those who wanted to dismantle the nativity scene sought to establish another religion, the religion of secularism. He supported the crèche for the purpose of keeping "Christ in Christmas." Writing for the majority in the 5–4 decision, Chief Justice Burger explained that the display did not violate the establishment clause because the city had a secular purpose for the display—the celebration of a secular holiday, notwith-standing its religious origins or the comments of the mayor. Burger again turned to the past, citing "an unbroken history of official acknowledgment by all three branches of government of the role of religion in American life from at least 1789." This allowed him to root the crèche in historical precedent, again ignoring the constitutional revolution of the Fourteenth Amendment and its application to religious liberty in the 1940s and 1950s.[30]

In the main dissent, joined by Marshall, Blackmun, and Stevens, Brennan once again returned to what he considered the first principles that the conser-vative members of the Court seemed unable to comprehend. Noting the mayor's explanation for the crèche as an attempt to keep Christ in Christmas, Brennan wondered how the Court could arrive at such a willfully blind ruling. "I refuse to accept the notion implicit in today's decision that non-Christians would find that the religious content of the crèche is eliminated by the fact that it appears as part of the city's otherwise secular celebration of the Christ-mas holiday," he complained. Displaying a far greater religious sympathy than the majority who remained intent on maintaining religion in public life, Brennan further explained the difference between the crèche and the other displays. The scene of Mary, Jesus, and Joseph in a manger "is the chief sym-bol of the characteristically Christian belief that a divine Savior was brought into the world and that the purpose of this miraculous birth was to illuminate a path toward salvation and redemption." He continued, "For Christians, that path is exclusive, precious, and holy. But for those who do not share these beliefs, the symbolic reenactment of the birth of a divine being who has been miraculously incarnated as a man stands as a dramatic reminder of their dif-ferences with Christian faith." Contrary to the majority's claim that the crèche simply re-created a historical event as part of a holiday tableau, Brennan claimed that it was rather "best understood as a mystical re-creation of an event that lies at the heart of the Christian faith." Since the Court's decision drained the crèche of inherent religious content, he explained, it ought to be "offensive" to those Christians "[for] whom the crèche has profound significance."[31]

But he did not stop there. To the majority's assertion that such displays were part of the nation's religious heritage, Brennan acidly observed: "[T]he Court's approach suggests a fundamental misapprehension of the proper uses of history in constitutional interpretation." Historical precedent was never enough to justify a practice, especially given the constitutional revolution of the Fourteenth Amendment. But in this case Brennan also chastised the Court for bad history. As he noted, the widespread celebration of Christmas and the display of the crèche did not occur until well into the nineteenth century, after the decline of Puritan hostility to Christmas that, though he did not say so, went hand-in-hand with evangelical expansion. But instead of analyzing that history in any persuasive way, Brennan explained, "[T]he Court takes a long step backwards to the days when Justice Brewer could arrogantly declare for the Court that 'this is a Christian nation.' Those days, I had thought, were forever put behind us by the Court's decision in *Engel v. Vitale*, in which we rejected a similar argument advanced by the State of New York that its Regents' Prayer was simply an acceptable part of our 'spiritual heritage.'" Rather than an innocuous demonstration of holiday spirit, the display, Brennan thought, "should be recognized for what it is: a coercive, though perhaps small, step toward establishing the sectarian preferences of the majority at the expense of the minority."[32]

In minimizing precedent, appealing to a false history, and trivializing the profound religious significance of the crèche in order to renew majoritarian control over individual religious rights, the conservative members of the Court had adopted the same duplicity as the moral establishment, claiming religious freedom and religious heritage while trivializing religious belief and doctrine by secularizing it to support government action. As the conservative thrust became clearer, the divisions on the Court became more bitter, with conservatives continuing to display little historical consciousness, and liberals, somewhat belatedly, seeking to rebuild liberal jurisprudence on a clearer historical foundation. The result was something approaching gridlock, as individual decisions sometimes turned conservative and sometimes liberal but without any coherent rationale.

In 1985, in yet another 5–4 decision, the conservative Court upheld a Georgia sodomy law, which again displayed its moral-establishmentarian aspirations using spurious historical reasoning. Rejecting the argument that the right of privacy had any relevance in consensual sexual relations between adults, the majority held that the proscriptions against sodomy had ancient historical roots. Since the law had no rational basis other than the belief that same-sex intimacy was immoral and unacceptable, the issue came down to whether such a determination could be maintained in law. Writing for the Court was White, who along with Rehnquist had dissented in *Roe*. He claimed that because law was "constantly based on notions of morality," merely asserting that law had a moral basis, any moral basis, offered a reasonable constitutional ground for the Court to uphold it, the right of privacy notwithstanding. Blackmun wrote in a dissent joined by Brennan, Marshall, and Stevens, putting a fine point on what he saw as the conservatives' goal. Although the Court had claimed that the case was merely about the legitimacy of sodomy, Blackmun thought that the case was really about a more fundamental issue: the right all citizens had "in controlling the nature of their intimate associations with others," an entitlement that ought to be protected by the right of privacy as individuals worked out their lives according to their own moral light. Responding to several amicus briefs that cited the Judeo-Christian heritage of the nation and the proscriptions against homosexuality in the Bible as a reason for upholding sodomy law, Blackmun reminded the Court that "[t]he legitimacy of secular legislation" depended on whether the government was able to "advance some justification for its law beyond its conformity to religious doctrine." The majority had not shown any such justification. Instead, the Court's ruling promoted religious intolerance. In their attempt to "enforce private morality" through the law, the Court had forgotten that the government cannot gratify religious intolerance by punishing private behavior any more than it could "punish such behavior because of racial animus."[33]

The increasingly conservative drift of the Court and its recurrent breakdown into 5–4 decisions brought intense attention and anticipation of the next judicial appointee. Because liberals feared and conservatives hoped that the appointment would move the Court decisively toward the rejection of liberal jurisprudence, when Justice Lewis F. Powell Jr. announced retirement in 1987, both sides mobilized. Seeking to advance a new moral establishment, Reagan nominated Robert Bork, a former solicitor general in the Nixon and Ford administrations who had since become a U.S. Appeals Court justice for the District of Columbia circuit. Bork also possessed scholarly credentials, having been a professor of law at Yale.[34]

Bork's opinions as a judge and his extensive extralegal writings made clear his fierce dedication to the ideals of the moral establishment. As Bork explained his position in a 1984 pamphlet entitled *Tradition and Morality in Constitutional Law* and published by the American Enterprise Institute, he saw "moral harm" inflicted by a licentious individual on the community as a primary concern of law. Because liberals tended to discount such harm, Bork saw their deference to "the autonomy of the individual" as a continual push toward "the privatization of morality" that relied upon a state-sponsored "moral relativism." To support his jurisprudence and to criticize liberalism he drew upon history, which he claimed undermined the abstract theory of rights that liberals promoted. "Our constitutional liberties arose out of historical experience and out of political, moral, and religious sentiment," Bork explained. "They do not rest upon a general theory." The liberal attempt to break the connection of religion, morality, and law worked to subvert both "democratic control" and "the history" that brought "life, rootedness, and meaning" to Americans' rights. Ultimately, according to Bork, liberal jurisprudence could only end badly, which, he asserted, any student of history would know. He claimed that liberals ignored the basic difference "between the American and the French revolutions" and the legal systems they had created, one of which had proven remarkably stable and the other one of which had not. The American Revolution had been conservative and had focused on the virtue of a community rooted in religious and moral concerns, while the French Revolution had focused on individual rights in a new secular regime. For those who missed his implication that liberalism had resulted in anarchy and then despotism, Bork concluded that, of the two revolutions, "the outcome for liberty was much less happy under the regime of 'the rights of man.'"[35]

Reagan's nomination of Bork, given his extensive paper trail and public utterances, was a frontal attack on liberal jurisprudence and an attempt to pull off a decisive move to the right that might seal a conservative legal revolution. But, ultimately, the clarity of Bork's establishmentarian ambitions sank his candidacy. Given that he would have replaced Powell, a moderate who had bucked the most-conservative jurists on the Court, Bork's nomination proved too controversial. As then Senator Joseph Biden, the chairman of the Senate Judiciary Committee, explained, were Bork to be replacing one of the other conservative justices, it "would be a whole different ball game." But a Democratic Senate was not about to endorse the decisive move to the right that Bork's nomination heralded.[36]

Condemnations of Bork began to emerge from several directions. The Biden Report, a report prepared at the behest of Biden to assess Bork's nomination, argued that Bork's rejection of the right of privacy discarded the "text, history and tradition of the Constitution." Ted Kennedy went further, in a sustained attack on Bork on the floor of the Senate. "Robert Bork's America is a land in which women would be forced into back-alley abortions, blacks would sit at segregated lunch counters, rogue police would break down citizens' doors, schoolchildren could not be taught about evolution, writers and artists would be censored at the whim of government, and the doors of the Federal courts would be shut on the fingers of millions of citizens for whom the judiciary is often the only protector of individual rights that are at the heart of our democracy," Kennedy claimed. It sounded a lot like America under the moral establishment.[37]

There was also a parallel public campaign to block Bork's confirmation. Black civil rights groups were alarmed that Bork had criticized the liberal reasoning in several civil rights cases, including *Brown*, though he claimed to uphold the Court's mandate of desegregation. Television ads by liberal groups began to warn that Bork's confirmation would have disastrous consequences for civil liberties, and many law professors wrote op-eds denouncing his nomination.[38]

The campaign was too much. In October 1987 the judiciary committee voted 9–5 against Bork's nomination, and the Senate as a whole voted it down 58–42 later that month. The major legacy of the Bork confirmation hearings was the introduction of a new level of public antagonism into the judicial nomination process, with long-standing consequences for future appointees. But the eventual nomination and confirmation of Anthony Kennedy to Powell's seat placed another conservative moderate on the bench without ushering in a conservative revolution.

4.

The failure of Bork's nomination and the animosities it stirred demonstrated the extent to which legal reasoning had become hostage to wider political division. The moral gulf between liberals and conservatives that had been opened in the 1960s produced a spate of 5–4 opinions and showcased deep division not just over the individual cases but over proper jurisprudence in the abstract. Conservatives sought to maintain majority religious prerogatives, often channeled through the legislative process, by disclaiming any interest in providing judicial scrutiny of fundamental religious rights and by invoking a religious past to which they sought to return. Those religious prerogatives included the maintenance of majoritarian moral norms, as in the case of sodomy and abortion laws, and the public honoring of God in political and legal forums. Liberals, meanwhile, supported continued judicial scrutiny in order to uphold fundamental rights, rather than deference to legislative authority. This meant upholding the right to privacy, in which all individuals were free to make their own moral decisions, at least within certain limits. The liberal flank wanted to separate church and state and to privatize controversial moral choices, in effect reducing the power of the mediating institutions upon which the moral establishment relied and making the individual the locus of moral decision-making.

Liberals did occasionally win a case in spite of the general conservative drift. In 1989 the Court was asked to rule on the constitutionality of a nativity scene inside a courthouse and of a menorah and Christmas tree in front of a government building, both in Pennsylvania. The opinion was complicated, with some justices voting to remove one or the other of the displays, some voting to remove them both, and some voting to keep them both, but ultimately the nativity scene had to be removed while the menorah and Christmas tree were allowed to stay. Blackmun announced the opinion of the Court, returning again to first principles. He acknowledged that when the First Amendment was written it had perhaps been "understood to protect only the diversity within Christianity," but constitutional law had evolved so that now the Court protected everyone. In attempting to bring real history back into constitutional jurisprudence, Blackmun even went so far as to consider the meaning of the religious heritage of the nation, which the conservatives had been so fond of using to justify their opinions and which Bork had used to support the reincorporating of religion and morality into law. "The history of this Nation, it is perhaps sad to say, contains numerous examples of official acts that endorsed Christianity specifically," Blackmun admitted, "but this heritage of official discrimination against non-Christians has no place in the jurisprudence of the Establishment Clause." Instead, he explained, the premise of the establishment clause, as it had evolved through the opinions of the Court, required "a respect for religious pluralism" rather than the covert—or, in the case of Bork, overt—establishmentarian ideals of the conservatives.[39]

It soon became apparent, if it had not been obvious all along, that conservatives were not interested in equally maximizing religious liberty for all—just those of Judeo-Christian heritage. This was a broader foundation than the original moral establishment, which perhaps showed the durable nature of liberalism's accomplishment, but it still struggled to account for the religious diversity of American life. In 1990 the Court was asked to decide whether the Native American Church in Oregon, whose members ingested a controlled substance as part of religious ritual, could be exempt from drug laws on religious grounds. Writing for the three other conservative justices, and, somewhat oddly, for the liberal justice Stevens, Antonin Scalia, who had been appointed in 1986 by Reagan, revealed that conservative justices were not motivated by the protection of religion in general but of the Christian majority's religion in particular. The Court had previously ruled that the government needed a compelling reason to infringe on religious practice, since religious freedom was a fundamental right. Scalia rejected that standard and the underlying *Carolene* principle that supported it, explaining that if the government needed a compelling reason to infringe upon fundamental rights, then it would not be able to do many things that it wished to do. "Any society adopting such a system would be courting anarchy," and, he held, the danger of anarchy grew "in proportion to society's diversity of religious beliefs, and its determination to coerce or suppress none of them." In other words, a society must coerce some people's actions through the use of law, and it must do so even when those actions arise out of religious beliefs. Should a society decide not to suppress some religious exercises using the coercion of law, Scalia wrote, it would devolve into a mess with no one in control. Waiving the Court's obligation to scrutinize religious-liberty claims to see if the government had a compelling reason for its actions, Scalia explained that society did not have "the luxury" of protecting all religious belief and action except in cases in which they threatened the highest orders of society, which had been the standard in the past. Instead, deferring to the legislative and executive branches, the Court explained that government could, but need not, provide an exemption for religious belief, subject to the political will of the majority. "It may fairly be said that leaving accommodation to the political process will place at a relative disadvantage those religious practices that are not widely engaged in," Scalia admitted. But majoritarianism was, against the claims of Madison and many of the Constitution's framers, an "unavoidable consequence of democratic government." Scalia presumed the freedom of traditional Christian forms of religion, which had the support of the majority, but left the door wide open for the regulation of other nontraditional forms, as in the past, through criminal law.[40]

Sandra Day O'Connor, who had been appointed by Reagan in 1981, wrote a separate concurring opinion because she considered Scalia's reasoning a dangerous departure from established precedent. Accepting the Court's settled position that the government had to show some compelling reason for outlawing religious behavior, O'Connor ruled that the state had a compelling interest in limiting a controlled substance. As for Scalia's belief that penalizing non-majority religions was an unavoidable outcome of democracy, O'Connor responded, "[T]he First Amendment was enacted precisely to protect the rights of those whose religious practices are not shared by the majority and may be viewed with hostility." The past decisions of the Court showed ample justification for the role of the Court in mitigating what O'Connor called "the harsh impact of majoritarian rule." But, to Scalia's credit, he did not engage in the usual kabuki theater of invoking a history of religious liberty while trying to limit religious liberty in the present. Instead, he noted more forthrightly than other conservatives that a well-ordered society placed limits on liberty, and showed that conservatives sought a return to the moral establishment of yesteryear.[41]

Shortly after the *Smith* opinion, the Court went through an upheaval, as four of its members were replaced in five years. Following the Bork debacle, judicial nominations became ever more scripted, as presidents sought to avoid bitter nomination fights. George H. W. Bush had a shot at reshaping the Court when two liberal stalwarts, Brennan and Marshall, retired in 1990 and 1991, respectively. But Bush's nominations of David Souter and Clarence Thomas failed to achieve the desired effect, because only Thomas emerged as a conservative. Shortly after Bill Clinton took office, he made up for the loss of Marshall's liberal seat when Byron White, who had dissented in *Roe,* retired and was replaced by Ruth Bader Ginsburg, an active litigant for feminist causes. The following year, Blackmun retired and was replaced by Stephen Breyer.

The new additions changed the players without changing the fundamental dynamic on the Court. Liberals continued to have occasional success in forming alliances with the swing justices, particularly when either Kennedy or O'Connor was allowed to write the majority opinion. But, often, merely preserving a past liberal decision was considered a victory. In 1992 prior to the addition of Ginsburg and Breyer, the 5–4 Court had upheld *Roe v. Wade* in *Planned Parenthood v. Casey.* Kennedy, O'Connor, and Souter delivered the jointly written majority opinion, which Stevens and Blackmun joined in part. The liberal–moderate coalition formed again in 2003 in *Lawrence v. Texas,* when Anthony Kennedy wrote for the Court to strike down sodomy laws. The 6–3 opinion completed the movement toward privatization that had begun with *Griswold.* Kennedy summarized the general trend of the Court toward recognizing a right to privacy by which the individual is shielded from state intrusion into moral issues. The Court's prior opinion in *Bowers,* which had upheld sodomy laws, departed from this general trend, according to Kennedy. He acknowledged that for many people homosexuality violated religious beliefs and ran afoul of moral ideals. But in a nod to liberal conceptions of pluralism and the place of diverse moral sentiment in U.S. society, Kennedy explained that criminalizing homosexual conduct actually involved a broader issue: whether a majority can use the coercive apparatus of the state to impose its moral views through criminal law. Just thirteen years earlier, in *Employment Division v. Smith,* Scalia had held that it could do just that, and moral-establishment proponents had made that argument whenever it had been convenient. Kennedy was not persuaded. The Court struck down all sodomy laws in the United States and, by implication, affirmed that the majority could not use the power of the state to impose its moral views through criminal law. Scalia wrote for Rehnquist and Thomas in a bitter dissent. He claimed that the Court's opinion opened the door to full-scale licentiousness because "laws against bigamy, same-sex marriage, adult incest, prostitution, masturbation, adultery, fornication, bestiality, and obscenity" were also permissible only if states could enact "laws based on moral choices." Scalia cited the "impossibility of distinguishing homosexuality from other traditional 'morals' offenses" to decry how far-reaching the opinion was. If the Court rejected all such laws, Scalia predicted a busy and activist Court in the future.[42]

But conservatives remained the actual activists in attempting to strike down liberal precedent, though the presence of O'Connor held back their most radical efforts. Perhaps the most important victory came in a 2002 case that approved a voucher plan by which parents could use tax money to send their children to private, parochial schools. The Court's opinion, written by Rehnquist, held that the plan did not fall afoul of the First Amendment because it had a secular purpose—the education of children—and provided for true choice, in which parents could take their children to a parochial school or a non-parochial private school, or leave them in public school. Either way, he held, religion had not been advanced. Yet a concurring opinion by Clarence Thomas wondered whether the First Amendment really ought to apply to the states. Thomas's opinion showed just how far the conservative bloc might attempt to roll back the constitutional developments of the preceding half century. Thomas, in effect, questioned the incorporation of the First Amendment into the Fourteenth and seemed to want a return to the days of the moral establishment when states could do as they pleased.[43]

The fragmentation of the Court and the disarray in its jurisprudence became fully apparent in 2005, when the Court showed how impotent law had become in adjudicating religious and political disputes. Ruling in two separate cases on the public display of the Ten Commandments, it allowed one display to remain and ordered two others removed. In the first case, *McCreary v. ACLU*, the Court struck down two displays found in county courthouses in Kentucky. Both displays were erected by religious conservatives in an attempt to prove the religious heritage of the United States and the foundational role of Christianity in U.S. law and government. The Court ruled in a 5–4 opinion written by Souter that the displays had no secular intent and violated the establishment clause of the First Amendment. Scalia wrote for Rehnquist, Thomas, and Kennedy in dissent, again laying out the conservative principles. Moving against the *Lemon* test, Scalia rejected the notion that the government must be neutral with regard to religion. He claimed that the neutrality principles had been brought into disrepute because the Court had "not had the courage (or the foolhardiness) to apply the neutrality principles consistently." The problem, as Scalia saw it, was that "[i]f religion in the public forum had to be entirely nondenominational, there could be no religion in the public forum at all." Citing the nation's "historical practices," Scalia recommended a return to the nineteenth-century ideal of public and governmental affirmation of monotheistic religion in general. "Publicly honoring the Ten Commandments is thus indistinguishable, insofar as discriminating against other religions is concerned, from publicly honoring God," he explained. Because publicly honoring God had a long tradition that, though he did not say so, had increased with evangelical expansion, it did not conflict with the establishment clause, which meant that the establishment clause did not require neutrality in governmental treatment of religion.[44]

Yet the same day, the Court also upheld another display of the Ten Commandments, this time a marble monument erected in 1961 on the Texas Capitol's grounds. The display was given to the state just as the Court approached the height of its liberal decisions on the separation of church and state. Unlike in the Kentucky case, the Court produced no majority opinion. It instead yielded a messy plurality of Rehnquist, Kennedy, Scalia, and Thomas, who voted to keep the display; three concurrences by Scalia, Thomas, and Breyer (in judgment but not in reasoning); and three dissents by Stevens, O'Connor, and Souter, with Ginsburg joining both Stevens and Souter and Stevens also joining Souter. The swing vote in the two cases was Breyer, who thought that the forty-year history of the display somehow provided it with a legitimate secular purpose. That secular purpose was further buttressed, he claimed, by the stated intention of the donating group, who had asserted that the Ten Commandments formed the basis for American "civic morality."[45]

That same year marked the beginning of a major breakthrough for conservatives when O'Connor retired. President George W. Bush nominated John G. Roberts Jr., a longtime trial attorney who had clerked under Rehnquist and been appointed to the U.S. Appeals Court for the District of Columbia by Bush in 2003. Unlike Bork, Roberts had only a minimal paper trail to suggest his jurisprudence, so he looked like a brilliant strategic choice to replace the moderate O'Connor. The stakes were raised even higher when Rehnquist died in September and Bush nominated Roberts as chief justice.

The nomination hearings offered a curious but telling view of the changed political momentum. Rather than pushing a liberal jurisprudence, liberals clung to the liberal judgments of the past, pressing Roberts on his beliefs about abortion and civil rights and on the role of precedent in future decisions. Roberts complied by emphasizing his judicial restraint and his belief that the Court should narrowly tailor its opinions to address the minimal question at hand with the largest possible majority on the Court. But not all were convinced. Representative John Lewis, an icon of the civil rights movement, feared that the Court under Roberts might "no longer hear the people's cries for justice," and a familiar coalition of liberal Democrats, civil rights workers, and feminists lined up against the nomination. Democrats were divided and worried about appearing overly obstructionist. Their unwillingness to filibuster gave the united Republicans a go-ahead to confirm Roberts, 78–22. At the end of October, Bush nominated Samuel Alito Jr. to fill O'Connor's seat, a more controversial choice because of Alito's clearer judicial conservatism. During the hearings, he got into some trouble because of a statement he made while working for the Reagan administration in which he called Bork "one of the most outstanding nominees" of the twentieth century. But Alito danced his way out of danger, emphasizing that he had many (unspecified) disagreements with Bork and was only speaking as a member of the political administration at the time. He was confirmed by a much more divided Senate by a vote of 58–42.[46]

The additions of Alito and Roberts turned out to be fateful as the Court has veered sharply to the right. In its first full term, the Roberts Court upheld a federal law limiting abortions, curbed the free-speech rights of students at public schools, denied a woman the right to sue for sex discrimination (on narrow procedural grounds), and, most controversially, curtailed the ability of schools to use racially conscious criteria to preserve or promote racial integration, all in 5–4 decisions. At the end of the term, a frustrated Stephen Breyer took the extraordinary step of reading his dissenting opinion to the Court, which included a shot at the supposed judicial restraint of Roberts. "It is not often in the law that so few have so quickly changed so much," Breyer observed bitterly. Subsequent terms have generated a clearer rightward shift, never more apparent than in the 2010 decision that corporations can spend unlimited money in U.S. elections, a decision that drew upon the nineteenth-century decision in *Santa Clara County v. Southern Pacific Railroad* that corporations were persons before the law. Though it has yet to make any momentous decision specifically on religion, it seems but a matter of time. When the Court does so, it is likely that the decision will continue to aid political conservatives and religious activists in rehabilitating the moral establishment.[47]

CONCLUSION: MORAL MAXIMALISM
AND RELIGIOUS CONTROL

The debate over the public role of religion in American life has now entered its sixth decade of intense conflict. Religious conservatives believe that the United States exists as a free society because of its divinely ordained moral foundation. The institutions of civil society, especially the church, the family, and the many voluntary organizations with religious origins, buttress the state's efforts to enforce the moral norms that have made the United States great. When these mediating institutions fail, in the conservative view, the coercion of law must step in to tame rogue individuals. By contrast, liberals claim that individuals ought to be trusted to make moral choices. In a world of divergent moral ideals, only by allowing individuals to make those choices can the United States avoid coercive authoritarianism. These two largely irreconcilable visions of American political life have produced an acrid debate that continues today.

Yet the remarkable thing about this fifty-year-long conflict is not its singularity, but its historical regularity. This debate has, in fact, been ongoing since the founding, a fact that is also disputed in the competing visions of national life. Conservatives claim that the United States has always honored Christianity above other religions, recognizing the role of religion as the foundation of morals to be enforced in law. Historical honesty requires an acknowledgment that this moral establishment did exist for a long time, as conservatives claim. It also requires an acknowledgment that the establishment was contested in the past, just as its attempted rehabilitation is contested in the present. It was contested because the establishment used coercion to further religious ends that many found objectionable. The frequent invocation of religious freedom has obscured that in actual practice Christian moral and religious ideas pervaded American law and society and formed critical boundaries circumscribing that freedom. Religious partisans assumed control of law and governance and used those tools to coerce dissenters based on their religiously derived moral convictions.

Stripping away the myth of American religious freedom and conceding the coercive role of religion in enforcing moral norms through law requires an alteration of several key terms and assumptions in the current debate. Common ways of talking about religion's role in U.S. law and politics fail in various ways. Most evince what the intellectual historian David Hollinger has called "patterns of engagement and evasion." Unwilling to look squarely at past forms of religious coercion, participants in the contemporary debate too often selectively deploy the myth of religious freedom for partisan political ends. In order to move beyond the shibboleths that govern discussion of religion in American life, we must reject the bad history that informs the debate.[1]

The first step is to reject several theoretical conceptions, or at least to modify them significantly. I am most concerned to refute the claim that the moral establishment was a *civil religion*, in the celebrated parlance of the sociologist Robert Bellah. Bellah first proposed the idea of an American civil religion in a 1967 essay in which he asserted that American society was coming apart. His was a call to reaffirm common American values. He claimed to be echoing John Dewey's ideal of a common faith, Walter Lippmann's notion of a shared public philosophy, and Arthur M. Schlesinger Jr.'s concept of a vital center. But Bellah's concept, unlike Dewey's or Lippmann's (though like Schlesinger's), presumed a kind of uniformity that never existed. Subsequent commentators took the concept in wildly contradictory directions, much to Bellah's dismay. Today it has essentially been appropriated by the Religious Right. Richard John Neuhaus, for example, the late editor of the conservative Catholic monthly *First Things*, construed civil religion as the equivalent of "political religion" or "public religion," in which religious ideals form, or ought to form, a sacred canopy over the public square. Neuhaus claimed that he, like Bellah, was "politically devoted to what used to be, and may be again, the 'vital center' of liberal democracy," a center that Neuhaus saw as essentially religious.[2]

These conceptions of civil religion both revel in the same fantasy. That is, they share a belief in the consensual nature of American civil religion—a society gathered around a common religious center whose uniform and voluntary support makes possible a harmonious and socially integrated whole. As Bellah claimed, "[T]he relation between religion and politics in America has been singularly smooth. . . . [T]he civil religion was able to build up without any bitter struggle." This society without conflict is a daydream, a chimera. Though proponents of the moral establishment have historically used the language of consensus, they relied upon coercion. And they never over-came the objections of dissenters, nor were they able to stamp them out.[3]

The moral establishment was also not, as some have claimed, just *religious politics*, the penchant toward organization and political mobilization or the right of association that forms a healthy part of any functioning civil society. Civil society in modern democracies consists of a set of nongovernmental institutions that remain apart from government in order to counterbalance the power of the state. They are the voluntary expressions of like-minded peoples' association and can, but need not, form the basis of political organization and lobbying. Churches, political groups such as MoveOn.org and the Christian Coalition, and women's groups such as the National Organization for Women or STOP ERA, to name just a few, are all examples of the kinds of groups that thrive in a functioning civil society. But a healthy civil society in a modern liberal democracy also requires the right of disassociation, so that individuals who do not share the interests or ideas of others are free to congregate alternatively (or not at all) without repercussion. At bottom, civil society protects individuals from governmental intrusion and nongovernmental oppression. It preserves a disorderly space that provides a buffer between the power of the state and the freedom of individuals and serves as a breeding ground for the contentious politics that are a healthy part of modern democracies. These ideas about civil society are exactly those that emerged out of liberal political thought, beginning with that of Holmes and Brandeis in the 1920s.[4]

Given how long it took before political theorists understood that liberal democracy should embrace civil society in this way, and given the fact that it is still contested in some quarters, it is anachronistic to understand the moral establishment as an expression of religious politics growing out of voluntary association in civil society. Quite the opposite. It was resistance to the moral establishment that provided the historical context for the emergence of liberal democratic theory. True, in the early nineteenth century, moral establishmentarians conceded to institutional disestablishment, which had the effect of admitting that governments should not provide formal support for specific religious sects, thereby relegating religion to what we today would call civil society. But the concession was only skin deep. Proponents of the moral establishment yoked religion to morals and enshrined them in law. And the religion they meant was Christianity, and, often more narrowly, Protestant Christianity, even when they failed to say so. This moved religion from the realm of civil society directly into the realm of the state, with Protestant Christianity quite clearly receiving preferential support from the government, which in turn enforced its moral norms. It also shielded religion from the realm of politics, at least in its most forthright form. After all, politics entails a struggle for power that operates within established political rules. The legal provisions of the moral establishment, by contrast, created the rules of politics by defining the limits of dissent through the regulation of the moral behavior on which the polity was supposed to be dependent.

Because the moral establishment was not just an expression of religious politics and not exclusively confined to civil society, it cannot be reduced to *moral suasion*, or the appeal of private citizens to their fellows to do what is right, which is how many writers have claimed that religious reform worked in the United States. The determination of religious partisans to use law to enforce morality shows the extraordinary degree to which they were not committed solely to moral suasion. As the sociologist Pierre Bourdieu has argued, the law is almost uniquely a text that produces its own effects. When a jurist declared that the United States was a Christian nation—a frequent occurrence in the nineteenth century—his proclamation made it so. Though the meaning of that utterance might be in dispute, and other judges in other jurisdictions might disagree, where that utterance was binding it was backed by the full force of the state. This was hardly moral suasion.[5]

Similarly, the moral establishment cannot be considered an *informal religious establishment*, another common characterization among writers trying to make sense of the public role of Protestantism in American history. Informal, in the normal meaning, suggests an arrangement without connection to law that relies on tacit political agreements or covert social mechanisms for its enforcement. Such an arrangement usually draws upon majoritarian or consensual bases. The late nineteenth-century U.S. Supreme Court's embrace of morals in law that were detached from any explicit religious belief might suggest an informal religious establishment, since it granted Protestants de facto rather than explicit primacy. But such a reading obscures the fact that the moral establishment had a connection to law that was sometimes more forthright in connecting morality and religion and sometimes less so. The upshot was a religious coercion by the state that used law to accomplish its ends. Given this connection to law, while the moral establishment was not a self-described religious establishment, it cannot plausibly be characterized as informal.[6]

I do not mean to suggest that the informal establishment was unreal. The multiple and ad hoc networks of religious organizations in the nineteenth century created informal pressures on dissenters and provided the cultural conditions that helped perpetuate the moral establishment. But the moral establishment featured formal, legal coercion in the enforcement of moral ideals. Those ideals, as Kent, Story, and more lately Scalia have noted, came from Christianity, even when jurists failed to say so. The claims of the moral establishment may have been unstable and never free of their own contradictions, but they were sufficiently compelling for much of American history to allow significant religious control of the law. As the informal establishment crumbled with the influx of Catholics, Jews, and secularists in the last part of the nineteenth century, there was a concerted campaign against the moral establishment that eventually dismantled this coercive connection between religion and the state. In order to make this narrative clear and to focus on the connections between the state and religion, I have suggested that, far from informal, the moral establishment was a religious establishment by proxy. *Proxy religious establishment* avoids historical anachronism while capturing the contradictions, fissures, and ambiguity of what was going on and still putting a fine point on the preferential place of Christianity in the legal system.

Acknowledging the preference given to Christianity in the past undermines the frequent invocation of the myth of religious freedom in the present, particularly in law. The courts have too often indulged in self-congratulation when exulting religious liberty, thus obfuscating the nation's historically coercive regime. Ultimately, the protestations of liberal dissenters make this regime visible. Dissenters showed that the symbolic universe that sustained and legitimated the moral establishment was not consensual. They challenged the validity of the moral establishment in courts, before legislatures, at state constitutional conventions, in critical organs such as journals and newspapers, or through organizations engaged in grassroots political mobilization. These dissenters were liberal in the sense that they stood for the self-determination of the individual. In characterizing dissenters as liberals, I am not invoking a contemporary understanding of the word but using the language of historical actors in order to trace the development of liberal thought through time. Pope Leo XIII claimed that proponents of "liberalism" were following the dictates of "naturalists or rationalists" in seeking to overthrow the connection between religion and morality. Anthony Comstock claimed that free-love proponents, "[l]iberals," and "infidels" were all seeking to overthrow the restraints of morality. Freethought proponents claimed that the sponsors of the Blaine Amendment sought to catch both "the Evangelical and the Liberal votes at the same time" by staying vague on the amendment's purpose so as to appeal to both groups' radically opposed interests. Following the Civil War, Elizabeth Cady Stanton's speeches received the support of the National Liberal League, which also offered an alliance to Susan B. Anthony, who demurred because such an association put off "the religionists." If dissenters were liberal, then the moral establishment was illiberal, which further undercuts the typical narrative of religious freedom.[7]

Of course, not all political liberals were religiously liberal. There are those, such as Rabbi Abraham Joshua Heschel, whose conservative religious beliefs prompted liberal political activism in the civil rights movement and opposition to the Vietnam War. In many cases truly conservative religious ideals can sustain liberal and even revolutionary political beliefs because the originators of religious traditions—Jesus of Nazareth and John Calvin, for example— were often more supple and iconoclastic thinkers than were their later followers. But though conservative religious beliefs can support liberal political positions, they have not often done so. In general, there has been a strong enough overlap between liberal politics and liberal religious belief and, conversely, between conservative politics and conservative religious belief that the language of liberalism captures something important. That was why so many historical actors from all sides of the dispute drew upon it. As the liberal critic Lionel Trilling claimed, liberalism has "[as] its first essential imagination" a belief in "variousness and possibility, which implies the awareness of complexity and difficulty." This belief in complexity suggested that people require a measure of freedom to work out their own ideas in the face of the world's baffling inscrutability. At bottom, liberalism's affirmation of pluralism, reason, and freedom situated its proponents in conflict with the fundamental affirmation of the moral establishment: that God's decree set standards so that moral truths were equally applicable to all people across time and space and formed the proper and singular basis of U.S. law and society. The moral establishment featured a narrow appeal to transcendent religious ideals, which often led to the illiberal legal and political policies that characterized much of the American past.[8]

Coming to terms with this past requires a fundamental shift in the current debate. Too often liberals have followed the pattern of the postwar Supreme Court in invoking the religious freedom of the past as a reason for their resistance to conservative arguments in the present. Such an argument obscures the necessity of liberal jurisprudence and divorces that jurisprudence from the burdens of the history out of which it arose. By buying into the myth, liberals must contort their arguments in a way that only weakens them. Conservatives, too, have often misrepresented the past in political arguments and legal opinions. When conservatives claim that historical practices and the American religious heritage require the continued preferential place of Christianity—or sometimes, more generically, monotheism—in American public life, they obscure the fundamentally coercive nature of those past practices. Conservatives have been especially egregious in invoking history while ignoring its fullest ramifications. They appeal to religious heritage as sufficient to explain the meaning of the First Amendment but neglect to acknowledge that the Bill of Rights did not apply to the states until incorporated into the Fourteenth Amendment, thereby ignoring the Court's rupture with state precedents in determining constitutional meaning. In the process, they elide the issue of coercion by presuming a consensual and happy past of freedom.

When pressed, some conservatives, such as Scalia, admit the coercive nature of these moral norms but seek refuge in the argument that law of all kinds relies upon coercion in order to maintain certain kinds of behavior. The act of making something illegal draws upon the coercive capacities of the state to enforce the law. Because all law is coercive, to extrapolate from Scalia's opinions, there is no contradiction in saying both that the moral establishment was coercive and that the history of the United States was a history of freedom. After all, tax law coerces, but most of us have no problem saying that tax law makes possible the enforcement of the rights and liberties afforded citizens of the United States. At the same time, the moral establishment's connection of religion and morals correctly acknowledged that both religion and law deal in norms. Although the creation and maintenance of those norms is not the only function of either religion or law, that function certainly lies at the center of their respective arenas. And the legality of an act implies its correspondence with some kind of agreed-upon standard of behavior, which often comes from religion. All of this would seem to support conservative claims that seek to bury illiberalism in the concept of legality. But in making their case, conservative arguments ultimately misunderstand or misrepresent the operations of the moral establishment.

There is a better way. As the legal scholar Robert Cover has argued, we each live in a universe of meaning in which law plays an important but not all-encompassing role. That universe of meaning emerges most fully from various social and collective forces—religion chief among them—that produce multiple and often contradictory standards of ethical behavior. In the American liberal tradition, the law works to allow the coexistence of many ethical standards. If left alone in anarchic relation, these various moral beliefs would destroy one another. Law mediates the nation's varied norms, which arise from its many religious beliefs (or nonreligious beliefs). In other words, law maintains what the moral philosopher Michael Walzer has called "moral minimalism" rather than the moral maximalism rooted in a religious tradition.[9]

Cover and Walzer are heirs to modern, pluralistic moral thought. They begin with the recognition of plural moral standards that arise from multiple religious, ethnic, and cultural norms, in order to elaborate a political and legal philosophy broad enough to allow many groups, with many different moral claims, to live under the same law. If religious and, to a degree, moral pluralism are hallmarks of a modern liberal society, then morality that is enforced by law must be tied to reason and subject to argumentation about how moral standards advance good in a way that is agreeable to many different groups. But proponents of a renewed moral establishment seem to recognize no distinction between the strong, fully elaborated moralities of religious communities and the weak forces of law that are necessary to regulate the multiple moral worlds that exist in the United States. They claim instead that clear and unambiguous religious principles formed the foundation for the U.S. political and social order. Latter-day proponents of the moral establishment seek an integrated society in which there is no separation between the fully elaborated morality of a religious community and the weaker but more shared morality of a pluralistic political community. All of this is in keeping with the moral establishment that they seek to rehabilitate.

An honest account of the past does not support such a rehabilitation. The dominant narratives of U.S. history—the myth of American religious freedom—simply cannot explain the moral establishment's reliance upon legal coercion to propagate religiously derived moral norms. Those dominant narratives have no means of accounting for coercion arising from a narrow religious sensibility that was not consensually shared by the population, not merely a function of religious politics, not simply propagated through moral suasion, not solely maintained by social pressure, and not an inevitable function of legality and legal norms. Instead, the moral establishment of the past was an active program that maintained religious control over U.S. society through law. To put the issue this way provides the key to understanding religious and political conflict in the present. The narrative of religious freedom that too often frames the debate acts only to obscure the limits of freedom, the coercion born of religious ideals, the lack of religious liberty, and the struggle for power and control that are hidden from view in many contemporary histories and legal opinions.

To move forward we must first confront and assume the burdens of history. The liberal Supreme Court decisions of the 1940s began to remove the preferential standing of Christianity in order to acknowledge the competence of the individual and the plural moral universe that had existed, but remained suppressed, for a long time. But because both liberals and conservatives assumed a past of unbroken religious freedom, their historical assumptions obscured the deep moral divisions and the true stakes of these debates. Conservatives, in particular, have been hiding behind the myth of religious freedom. Were they not allowed to do that, their position would be rejected by a majority of Americans, as Bork's nomination showed. Conversely, liberals have been reluctant to acknowledge past religious power for fear that it would strengthen conservative jurisprudence. In doing so, they have given up the most compelling argument for their own jurisprudence, which was originally to liberate the individual from religious oppression that used the apparatus of the state. Were liberals to more forthrightly acknowledge that history, it would strengthen their position and result in better law.

What we need now is a philosophy of judicial minimalism that relies on an adequate conception of our past. By clearing the ground of historical myths and erroneous concepts, we can reenter political and legal conversation on a new foundation. Rather than positing the exceptional nature of our freedom, we should recognize that the past has been characterized by fundamental tensions that have existed since the American Revolution and have become particularly heated in the last fifty years. The central issue in these disputes is how to adjudicate between diverse constituencies with competing ethical claims within a moral framework that might be acceptable in law. In the past, as now, there were deep cleavages in American cultural life—highly contested moral ideas and disagreements about mutual obligations—that the debates failed to solve. Instead of attempting to balance competing moral ideals, religious partisans drew upon law to coerce cultural conformity, and seek to do so again. Rejecting the myth of American religious freedom helps clarify the coercion inherent in the conservative legal agenda. It also makes clear that rather than being a narrow quarrel over church and state, the debate involves a pair of more profound questions that remain unanswered: what minimal moral standards do we expect of one another, and how do we maintain them with fairness to all?

ACKNOWLEDGMENTS

This book was made possible by a 2009 Research Initiation Grant from University Research Services and Administration at Georgia State University (GSU), a 2009 Summer Research Grant from the history department at GSU, a 2007–8 postdoctoral fellowship from the Visiting Scholars Program of the American Academy of Arts and Sciences, a 2008 summer seminar fellowship with the Institute for Constitutional Studies at the George Washington University Law School, a 2005–7 Liebmann Fellowship from the Dolores Zohrab Liebmann Foundation, 2005 and 2006 summer research fellowships from the University of North Carolina at Chapel Hill (UNC) history department, a 2005 Summer Stipend from the UNC Center for the Study of the American South, and a 2005 George Mowry Dissertation Research Grant from the UNC history department. Portions of this work have appeared previously under the title "The Civilizing Mission of Booker T. Washington," *Journal of Southern History* 73 (May 2007): 323–62, and are reprinted by permission of the *Journal of Southern History*.

I am indebted to my dissertation advisor, John Kasson, for his help when this project was a dissertation. His books and classes showed me what good history is and how it works. He also showed me how useful it can be to write out of ambivalence rather than passion. Fitz Brundage, Peter Filene, Michael Lienesch, and Grant Wacker, who made up my dissertation committee, all read the manuscript at that intermediate point. Their suggestions for research direction and improvement, their willingness to write countless recommendation letters, and their continued belief both in the project and in me were a great boon. They also taught me a lot. My master's degree advisor, Thomas Haskell, presided over a transitional period in my intellectual life. His stamp is evident throughout this book, even though he did not read it in advance. Others read various portions at various times. For their criticism and intellectual exchange I would like to thank David Davis, D. G. Hart, Vincent Lloyd, Kathryn Lofton, Laurie Maffly-Kipp, Pauline Maier, Genna Rae McNeill, Phil Sinitiere, Pat Spacks, and Ann Ziker. Jayna Hoffacker and Michael Arndt, my master's advisees and research assistants, read the manuscript and helped me fact-check it.

The people at Oxford University Press did a superb job. Production editor Christine Dahlin moved it through the final process with calm professionalism. Jackie Doyle, my copyeditor, put the manuscript in order and helped, as no one else ever has, to incorporate the quotations into my prose. I am especially grateful to my editor, Theo Calderara, who saw from the beginning what I was trying to accomplish. He proved to be all that I could have hoped for in an editor, reading and critiquing the manuscript to help me express what I wanted to say and to make the book more accessible.

Several people deserve special thanks. David Hollinger gave me great criticism and encouragement when he read the book proposal and subsequent manuscript. Ed Blum helped me both shorten the manuscript and make its point clearer. Jenna Gray-Hildenbrand made me consider that a liberal moral establishment also sought to use the state. John Kaag gave me the single most important sentence in the preface. Ben Wise distracted me from writing in the best of ways, with meals, conversations over beer, our shared enthusiasm for photography, and random middle-of-the-day phone calls. He helped with the manuscript, of course, but more importantly he was a great friend while I wrote. Alston Wise made many dinners for me while I was in Cambridge and let me join in the nightly ritual of ice cream, bad TV, and affectionate argument. Rob Baker welcomed me to the GSU history department and then closely read the entire manuscript, lending his legal expertise and writerly skill to save me from many errors. Joy Rohde did more than anyone else to shape the book. Her unrelenting intellectual engagement challenged me to rethink, to rewrite, and to rearrange again and again. She also introduced me to Somerville restaurants, Greyhounds, and roller derby. Sandra Sehat, my mom, has always supported me in my various intellectual wanderings over the last fifteen years, even when they made no sense to anyone other than me. Finally, Connie Moon Sehat, my wife, has been my intellectual partner and my partner in life, letting me explore the world with her, showing me love, and trying to remind me what is important.

I am dedicating this book to the two people who originally prompted me to think about the proper relationship between norms, religious values, and culture. Davey Naugle will probably not agree with my conceptualization or my argument. Consequently, he bears no responsibility for the book other than providing the impetus for its production. My college encounter with his thought has offered a consistent touchstone in my intellectual life—even as I have critiqued many aspects of my prior religious belief. This book reflects my intellectual debt to him. Brian Sartor might be more likely to agree with me, but I cannot be sure, and his agreement is beside the point. Since encountering Naugle's ideas with me, Brian has been my most consistent interlocutor. We have discussed the relationship of Christianity and culture for more than fifteen years, with the exchange changing as we did. I offer this book to both as a continuation of the conversation.

NOTES

Preface

1. Alexis de Tocqueville, *Democracy in America*, trans. Harvey C. Mansfield and Delba Winthrop (Chicago: University of Chicago Press, 2000), 280–281.
2. In making this claim, I am indebted here and throughout to Jon Butler, "Historiographical Heresy: Catholicism as a Model for American Religious History," in *Belief in History: Innovative Approaches to European and American Religion*, ed. Thomas Kselman (Notre Dame: University of Notre Dame Press, 1991), 286–309.

Introduction

1. *New York Times*, May 21, 1887 (both quotations). For the extended story, see Orvin Larson, *American Infidel: Robert G. Ingersoll, A Biography* (New York: Citadel, 1962), 214–217.
2. *Philadelphia Press*, May 24, 1884, reprinted in Robert G. Ingersoll, *The Works of Robert G. Ingersoll*, ed. C. P. Ferrell (New York: Ingersoll, 1900), 8:202.
3. Robert Wuthnow and John H. Evans, eds., *The Quiet Hand of God: Faith Based Activism and the Public Role of Mainline Protestantism* (Berkeley and Los Angeles: University of California Press, 2002), ix (first quotation); John Witte Jr., *Religion and the American Constitutional Experiment*, 2nd ed. (Boulder: Westview, 2005), xiii (second quotation).
4. "Romney's 'Faith in America' Address," *New York Times*, December 6, 2007, http://www.nytimes.com/2007/12/06/us/politics/06text-romney.html. For representative statements of other religious conservatives, see Robert H. Bork, *Slouching towards Gomorrah: Modern Liberalism and American Decline* (New York: Regan Books, 1996); William J. Bennett, *The Broken Hearth: Reversing the Moral Collapse of the American Family* (New York: Doubleday, 2001); Gertrude Himmelfarb, *The De-Moralization of Society: From Victorian Virtues to Modern Values* (New York:

Knopf, 1995); Richard John Neuhaus, *The Naked Public Square: Religion and Democracy in America* (Grand Rapids, Mich.: Eerdmans, 1984); Ellis Sandoz, *Republicanism, Religion, and the Soul of America* (Columbia: University of Missouri Press, 2006).

5. "Romney's 'Faith in America' Address," *New York Times*, December 6, 2007, http://www.nytimes.com/2007/12/06/us/politics/06text-romney.html (first quotation); Isaac Kramnick and R. Laurence Moore, *The Godless Constitution: A Moral Defense of the Secular State* (New York: Norton, 2005), 14 (second quotation); Randall Balmer, *Thy Kingdom Come: How the Religious Right Distorts the Faith and Threatens America* (New York: Basic Books, 2006), ix (third and fourth quotations).

6. *Barron v. Baltimore*, 32 U.S. 243 (1833), at 247 (quotation); *Permoli v. New Orleans*, 44 U.S. 589 (1845). On Marshall's evangelical tendencies, see Clifford S. Griffin, *Their Brothers' Keepers: Moral Stewardship in the United States, 1800–1865* (New Brunswick, N.J.: Rutgers University Press, 1960), 276; Henry Otis Dwight, *The Centennial History of the American Bible Society* (New York: Macmillan, 1916), 544.

7. *An Inquiry into the Moral and Religious Character of the American Government* (New York: Wiley & Putnam, 1838), 198 (first and second quotations), 185 (third and fourth quotations), italics in original.

8. For the church membership statistics and data showing the evangelical lead in the expansion, see Roger Finke and Rodney Stark, *The Churching of America, 1776–2005: Winners and Losers in Our Religious Economy*, 2nd ed. (New Brunswick, N.J.: Rutgers University Press, 2005), 23, 56.

9. For two archetypal examples of the frequent connection of U.S. religious freedom and the unfolding of U.S. liberties, see Alan Heimert, *Religion and the American Mind: From the Great Awakening to the Revolution* (Cambridge, Mass.: Harvard University Press, 1966); Nathan O. Hatch, *The Democratization of American Christianity* (New Haven, Conn.: Yale University Press, 1989).

10. John Stuart Mill, "De Tocqueville on Democracy in America [I]," *London Review* 1 (October 1835), 85–129, reprinted in John Stuart Mill, *The Collected Works of John Stuart Mill*, ed. J. M. Robson (Toronto: University of Toronto Press, 1963–1991), 18:178 (first three quotations); Alexis de Tocqueville, *Democracy in America*, trans. Harvey C. Mansfield and Delba Winthrop (Chicago: University of Chicago Press, 2000), 236 (fourth quotation), 241 (fifth quotation), 278 (sixth quotation).

11. On Tocqueville's limitations, see Rogers M. Smith, *Civic Ideals: Conflicting Visions of Citizenship in U.S. History* (New Haven, Conn.: Yale University Press, 1997), 14–30.

12. On civic myths, see ibid., 30–39.

13. New Hampshire Constitution of 1784, part 1, art. 6 (both quotations). All citations to constitutions are taken either from William F. Swindler, ed., *Sources and Documents of United States Constitutions*, 11 vols. (Dobbs Ferry, N.Y.: Oceana, 1973–1979),

or *Constitutions of the United States, National and State*, 2nd ed., 6 vols. (Dobbs Ferry, N.Y.: Oceana, 1974–).

14. Richard Hofstadter, *Anti-Intellectualism in American Life* (New York: Knopf, 1963), 20.

Chapter 1

1. Ezra Stiles to Benjamin Franklin, January 28, 1790, in *The Olive Branch* (New York: New-York Universalist Book Society, 1828), 1:211 (all quotations).

2. Benjamin Franklin to Ezra Stiles, March 9, 1790, in Benjamin Franklin, *The Writings of Benjamin Franklin*, ed. Albert Henry Smyth (New York: Macmillan, 1907), 10:84 (all quotations).

3. Ibid., 10:84 (first three quotations), 85 (fourth through sixth quotations).

4. Franklin, "Speech in the Convention at the Conclusion of Its Deliberations," in Franklin, *Writings*, 9:607 (first quotation), 608 (second quotation). On John Adams's marginal relevance in U.S. political thought, see Gordon S. Wood, *The Creation of the American Republic, 1776–1787* (Chapel Hill: University of North Carolina Press, 1969), 567–592.

5. On the multiple intellectual currents at the time of the American Revolution and their resolution in a pattern of constitutionalism, see Wood, *Creation of the American Republic*; Bernard Bailyn, *Ideological Origins of the American Revolution* (Cambridge, Mass.: Belknap Press, 1967).

6. On the vanguard radicalism of Pennsylvania, see Wood, *Creation of the American Republic*, 83–90. On the Whig belief in the people as the rightful repository of power and rights, see Jack N. Rakove, *Original Meanings: Politics and Ideas in the Making of the Constitution* (New York: Knopf, 1996), 310–316. On the trouble with democracy, see Gordon S. Wood, *The Radicalism of the American Revolution* (New York: Knopf, 1992), 145–168.

7. Merle Curti, *The Growth of American Thought*, 3rd ed. (New York: Harper & Row, 1964), 104–108 (Franklin quotation on p. 107).

8. Pennsylvania Constitution of 1776, Declaration of Rights, arts. 2 (first and third quotations) and 5 (second quotation); Plan of Government, sec. 10 (fourth quotation).

9. Benjamin Rush, *Observations upon the Present Government of Pennsylvania: In Four Letters to the People of Pennsylvania* (Philadelphia: Styner & Cist, 1777), 4 (first quotation); Benjamin Franklin to Joseph Priestley, August 21, 1784, in Franklin, *Writings*, 9:266 (second quotation), italics in original. Note that Franklin only loosely paraphrased the actual provision, which can be found in the Pennsylvania Constitution of 1776, Plan of Government, sec. 10.

10. Henry Muhlenberg, "Abstract of a Letter of Rev. Henry Melchior Muhlenberg," *Pennsylvania Magazine of History and Biography* 22, no. 1 (1898): 129.

11. Ibid., 130.

12. For Muhlenberg's account of events, see ibid., 129–131.

13. Pennsylvania Constitution of 1776, sec. 45 (all quotations).

14. Muhlenberg, "Abstract of a Letter," 130 (both quotations).

15. For other examples of old-line Protestant discontent with the constitution, see J. Paul Selsam, *The Pennsylvania Constitution: A Study in Revolutionary Democracy* (Philadelphia: University of Pennsylvania Press, 1936), 218–221 (first and second quotations on p. 218); Muhlenberg, "Abstract of a Letter," 131 (third through fifth quotations); Anne H. Wharton, "Thomas Wharton, Jr., First Governor of Pennsylvania under the Constitution of '76," *Pennsylvania Magazine of History and Biography* 5, no. 4 (1881): 432–433.

16. "Demophilus" in the *Pennsylvania Gazette*, March 19, 1777, quoted by Selsam, *Pennsylvania Constitution*, 220 (both quotations). On the debate over the constitution, its rocky passage, and the subsequent instability of the state, see Selsam, *Pennsylvania Constitution*, 205–254.

17. See the chart of state constitutional provisions in David Sehat, "The American Moral Establishment: Religion and Liberalism in the Nineteenth Century" (PhD diss., University of North Carolina at Chapel Hill, 2007), 266–286.

18. North Carolina Constitution of 1776, arts. 34 (first quotation), 32 (second quotation); New Jersey Constitution of 1776, arts. 18 (third quotation), 19 (fourth quotation). For similar provisions promising religious liberty but protecting Christianity or, more narrowly, Protestant Christianity, see Delaware Declaration of Rights and Fundamental Rules of 1776, arts. 2, 3; Delaware Constitution of 1776, art. 22; Maryland Declaration of Rights of 1776, arts. 33, 35; Maryland Constitution of 1776, art. 55; Vermont Constitution of 1777, ch. 2, sec. 9; Georgia Constitution of 1777, art. 6; South Carolina Constitution of 1778, arts. 3, 12, 13, 38; New Hampshire Constitution of 1784, part 1, arts. 4, 5, 6; part 2, "Senate," "House of Representatives," and "President." On the discrimination against Jews in Connecticut and Rhode Island, see Morton Borden, *Jews, Turks, and Infidels* (Chapel Hill: University of North Carolina Press, 1984), 13.

19. On civic republicanism, see Bailyn, *Ideological Origins of the American Revolution*; Wood, *Creation of the American Republic*; J. G. A. Pocock, *The Machiavellian Moment: Florentine Political Thought and the Atlantic Republican Tradition*, 2nd ed. (Princeton, N.J.: Princeton University Press, 2003).

20. On Christian republicanism, see Mark A. Noll, *America's God: From Jonathan Edwards to Abraham Lincoln* (New York: Oxford University Press, 2002), 53–92.

21. On the Enlightenment trust in reason to determine morals, see John G. West Jr., *The Politics of Revelation and Reason: Religion and Civic Life in the New Nation* (Lawrence: University Press of Kansas, 1996), 74–78, 117–134.

22. On John Jay, see Walter Stahr, *John Jay: Founding Father* (New York: Hambledon & London, 2005).

23. New York Constitution of 1777, art. 38 (all quotations).

24. *Journals of the Provincial Congress, Provincial Convention, Committee of Safety and Council of Safety of the State of New York, 1775–1777* (Albany: Thurlow Weed, 1842), 1:844 (both quotations).

25. John Jay to John Murray Jr., October 12, 1816, in John Jay, *The Correspondence and Public Papers of John Jay*, ed. Henry P. Johnston (New York: G. P. Putnam's, 1890–1893), 4:391 (first four quotations), 393 (fifth quotation), italics in original.

26. New York Constitution of 1777, art. 38 (first and third quotations); *Journals of the Provincial Congress*, 1:845 (second quotation).

27. Virginia Constitution of 1776, Declaration of Rights, sec. 16 (all quotations).

28. Thomas Jefferson, "A Bill for Establishing Religious Freedom," in Thomas Jefferson, *The Papers of Thomas Jefferson*, ed. Julian P. Boyd (Princeton, N.J.: Princeton University Press, 1950–), 2:545–546 (first quotation), 546 (second quotation). On Jefferson's attempt to pass his bill, see Thomas E. Buckley, *Church and State in Revolutionary Virginia, 1776–1787* (Charlottesville: University Press of Virginia, 1977), 38–62.

29. Massachusetts Constitution of 1780, part 1, arts. 2 (first quotation) and 3 (second quotation); part 2, ch. 4, art. 1 (third quotation).

30. John Adams, *The Defence of the Constitutions of Government of the United States of America,* in John Adams, *The Works of John Adams*, ed. Charles Francis Adams (Boston: Little, Brown, 1851–1865), 4:293 (first, third through fifth quotations), 292 (second quotation).

31. Isaac Backus, "A Door Opened for Christian Liberty" (1783), in Isaac Backus, *Isaac Backus on Church, State, and Calvinism: Pamphlets, 1754–1789*, ed. William G. McLoughlin (Cambridge, Mass.: Belknap Press, 1968), 436 (first two quotations); John Leland, "The Yankee Spy" (1794), in John Leland, *The Writings of Elder John Leland*, ed. L. F. Greene (1845; repr., New York: Arno, 1969), 220 (third through fifth quotations), 224 (sixth through eighth quotations).

32. The distinction between the symbolism of politics and the distribution of power and institutional formation comes from Richard Hofstadter, *The Paranoid Style in American Politics and Other Essays* (New York: Knopf, 1965), viii–ix.

33. Massachusetts Constitution of 1780, part 1, art. 3 (both quotations).

34. Maryland Declaration of Rights of 1776, art. 33 (quotation); Delaware Declaration of Rights of 1776, rule 3; North Carolina Constitution of 1776, art. 32; Georgia Constitution of 1777, art. 56; New Hampshire Constitution of 1784, art. 5; New York Constitution of 1777, art. 38.

35. See the chart of state constitutional provisions in Sehat, "American Moral Establishment," 266–286. Vermont and South Carolina each ratified two constitutions between 1776 and 1787, and Connecticut lived under its colonial charter without passing a constitution until 1818. On the various civil incapacities levied on Jews, Unitarians, and agnostics, see Leonard W. Levy, *The Establishment Clause: Religion and the First Amendment*, 2nd ed. (Chapel Hill: University of North Carolina Press, 1994), 77–78.

Chapter 2

1. On evangelicalism in the South, see Christine Leigh Heyrman, *Southern Cross: The Beginnings of the Bible Belt* (New York: Knopf, 1997); Rhys Isaac, *The Transformation of Virginia, 1740–1790* (Chapel Hill: University of North Carolina Press, 1982). On evangelicalism in general, see Mark A. Noll, *America's God: From Jonathan Edwards to Abraham Lincoln* (New York: Oxford University Press, 2002), 9–18. On the rapid progress of evangelical expansion, see Roger Finke and Rodney Stark, *The Churching of America, 1776–2005: Winners and Losers in Our Religious Economy*, 2nd ed. (New Brunswick, N.J.: Rutgers University Press, 2005), 55–116.

2. On the evangelical population of Virginia and their contribution to the debate, see Thomas E. Buckley, *Church and State in Revolutionary Virginia, 1776–1787* (Charlottesville: University Press of Virginia, 1977), 173–182.

3. Thomas Jefferson, "A Bill for Establishing Religious Freedom," in Thomas Jefferson, *The Papers of Thomas Jefferson*, ed. Julian P. Boyd (Princeton, N.J.: Princeton University Press, 1950–), 2:545–553 (both quotations on p. 546).

4. Isaac Backus, *An Appeal to the Public for Religious Liberty* (1773), in Isaac Backus, *Isaac Backus on Church, State, and Calvinism: Pamphlets, 1754–1789*, ed. William G. McLoughlin (Cambridge, Mass.: Belknap Press, 1968), 309 (all quotations), italics in original.

5. On the evangelical argument for the connection of church and state, see Philip Hamburger, *Separation of Church and State* (Cambridge, Mass.: Harvard University Press, 2002), 65–78.

6. Petition quoted in Buckley, *Church and State*, 74 (both quotations).

7. "A Bill 'Establishing a Provision for Teachers of the Christian Religion,'" in Buckley, *Church and State*, 188–189 (first and second quotations on p. 188); George Washington to James Madison, November 17, 1788, in James Madison, *The Papers of James Madison*, ed. William T. Hutchinson and William M. E. Rachal (Chicago: University of Chicago Press, 1962–1991), 11:351 (third quotation). For Madison's reading of the bill, see James Madison to Thomas Jefferson, January 9, 1785, in Madison, *Papers*, 8:228–229.

8. Jack N. Rakove, *James Madison and the Creation of the American Republic*, 3rd ed. (New York: Pearson/Longman, 2007); Ralph Louis Ketcham, *James Madison: A Biography* (New York: Macmillan, 1971).

9. James Madison, *Memorial and Remonstrance against Religious Assessments*, in Madison, *Papers*, 8:295–306 (first quotation on p. 299, second and third quotations on p. 301, fourth through sixth quotations on p. 302). On Madison's parliamentary moves to get to the recess, see Buckley, *Church and State*, 108–112.

10. On the eighteenth-century conception of rights, see John Phillip Reid, *The Constitutional History of the American Revolution* (Madison: University of Wisconsin Press, 1986–1993), 1:3–113; Bernard Bailyn, *Ideological Origins of the American Revolution* (Cambridge, Mass.: Belknap Press, 1967), 184–198. On the idea of the sovereignty of the people as a central component in protecting rights, see Gordon S.

Wood, *The Creation of the American Republic, 1776–1787* (Chapel Hill: University of North Carolina Press, 1969), 344–389. On Madison's view of rights and the difference between procedural rights and the inalienable rights of the individual, see Jack N. Rakove, *Original Meanings: Politics and Ideas in the Making of the Constitution* (New York: Knopf, 1996), 310–316; Jack N. Rakove, *Declaring Rights: A Brief History with Documents* (Boston: Bedford, 1998), 17–31, 99–107. On rights talk and its present-day significance for both detractors and proponents, see Mary Ann Glendon, *Rights Talk: The Impoverishment of Political Discourse* (New York: Free Press, 1991); Ronald Dworkin, *Taking Rights Seriously* (Cambridge, Mass.: Harvard University Press, 1977).

11. For a nice overview of the other petitions, see Buckley, *Church and State*, 136–153 (all quotations on p. 140).

12. The threefold categories of the institutional, ceremonial, and moral establishment come from John Witte Jr., but he applies them only to the Massachusetts Constitution of 1780. I use his terminology, but I have developed the threefold conception beyond Witte's original use. Given his suggestion that the Massachusetts arrangement could provide a model for today, which runs against my focus on the coercion inherent in the various forms of establishment, Witte would likely not be in agreement with my argument. See John Witte Jr., "'A Most Mild and Equitable Establishment of Religion': John Adams and the Massachusetts Experiment," in *Religion and the New Republic: Faith in the Founding of America*, ed. James H. Hutson (Lanham, Md.: Rowman & Littlefield, 2000), 18–22.

13. For the text of the original bill and subsequent emendations, see Jefferson, *Papers*, 2:545–553 (first quotation on p. 545, third and fifth quotations on p. 546, fourth quotation on pp. 545–546); Virginia Constitution of 1776 Declaration of Rights, sec. 16 (second quotation). For an account of the legislative back-and-forth, see Buckley, *Church and State*, 155–164.

14. Washington to Madison, November 5, 1786, in Madison, *Papers*, 9:162 (both quotations).

15. Madison to Edmund Randolph, April 15, 1787, in Madison, *Papers*, 9:379 (first quotation); Madison, "Vices of the Political System of the United States," in Madison, *Papers*, 9:345–358 (second quotation on p. 345, third through fifth quotations on p. 356).

16. Madison, "Vices of the Political System of the United States," in Madison, *Papers*, 9:357 (first quotation); Madison to Jefferson, October 24, 1787, in Madison, *Papers*, 10:214 (second and third quotations).

17. For a summary of Madison's goals going into the convention, see the editorial explanation in Madison, *Papers*, 10:3.

18. "The Virginia Plan," in Madison, *Papers*, 10:12–18. On the function of institutional checks and balances, see Wood, *Creation of the American Republic*, 471–518.

19. Madison to Jefferson, September 6, 1787, in Madison, *Papers*, 10:163–164 (first quotation), italics in original where the letter was encoded; Jefferson to Madison, June 20, 1787, in Madison, *Papers*, 10:64 (second quotation).

20. U.S. Constitution, art. 7 (first quotation); Madison to Jefferson, October 24, 1787, in Madison, *Papers*, 10:212 (second through fifth quotations); Jefferson to Madison, December 20, 1787, in Madison, *Papers*, 10:335–339.

21. On the concerns over the godless constitution, see Isaac Kramnick and R. Laurence Moore, *The Godless Constitution: A Moral Defense of the Secular State* (New York: Norton, 2005), 26–45.

22. Merrill Jensen, John P. Kaminski, and Gaspare J. Saladino, eds., *The Documentary History of the Ratification of the Constitution* (Madison: State Historical Society of Wisconsin, 1976–), 9:xix–xx. On the importance of Virginia in influencing the remaining states, see Tench Coxe to Madison, May 19, 1788, in Madison, *Papers*, 11:51–52.

23. Daniel Carroll to Madison, May 28, 1788, in Madison, *Papers*, 11:65.

24. Jensen, Kaminski, and Saladino, *Documentary History*, 9:951 (first quotation), 10:1213 (second and third quotations), 9:1052 (fourth and fifth quotations).

25. Ibid., 10:1223 (both quotations). For the final vote count, see the editors' note in ibid., 10:1512–1515.

26. For the exchange of intelligence about Henry's activities and Madison's uncertainty about what to do, see Edmund Randolph to Madison, November 10, 1788; Madison to Randolph, November 23, 1788; Madison to Washington, December 2, 1788; George Lee Tuberville to Madison, December 14, 1788; George Nicholas to Madison, January 2, 1789; Benjamin Johnson to Madison, January 19, 1789, in Madison, *Papers*, 11:338–339, 362–364, 376–378, 396–397, 406–409, 423–425.

27. Jefferson to Madison, July 31, 1788, in Madison, *Papers*, 11:212 (first two quotations); Madison to Jefferson, October 17, 1788, in Madison, *Papers*, 11:297 (third through sixth quotations); Jefferson to Madison, November 18, 1788, in Madison, *Papers*, 11:353–354 (seventh quotation).

28. Madison to Thomas Mann Randolph, January 13, 1789, in Madison, *Papers*, 11:416 (first quotation); Madison to George Eve, January 2, 1789, in Madison, *Papers*, 11:405 (second and third quotations). Also see Madison to a Resident of Spotsylvania County, [January 27, 1789], in Madison, *Papers*, 11:428–429.

29. Madison to Jefferson, October 17, 1788, in Madison, *Papers*, 11:297 (quotation). For the breakdown of the vote by county, see Madison, *Papers*, 11:438–439, note 1.

30. Joseph Gales, ed., *Debates and Proceedings in the Congress of the United States* (Washington, D.C.: Gales & Seaton, 1834–1856), 1:451 (first quotation), 452 (second quotation). This source is commonly called the *Annals of Congress* and is hereafter cited as *Annals of Congress*.

31. Madison to Jefferson, October 17, 1788, in Madison, *Papers*, 11:297 (first and second quotations); Gales, *Annals of Congress*, 1:757 (third quotation).

32. Gales, *Annals of Congress*, 1:757 (first and second quotations), 758 (third through sixth quotations).

33. Ibid., 1:796.

34. Ibid., 1:452 (first quotation), 783 (second and third quotations), 784 (fourth through sixth quotations). The debate may not have been recorded in its entirety, which would help explain the relatively small amount of controversy.

35. Madison to Richard Peters, August 19, 1789, in Madison, *Papers*, 12:346–347 (first quotation), 347 (second quotation); Gales, *Annals of Congress*, 1:734 (third and fourth quotations), 735 (fifth through eighth quotations), 737 (ninth quotation), 738 (tenth and eleventh quotations); Madison to Alexander White, August 24, 1789, in Madison, *Papers*, 12:352 (twelfth and thirteenth quotations).

36. For the Senate version of the amendment, see *Journal of the First Session of the Senate of the United States* (Washington: Gales & Seaton, 1820), 77. On the Senate's lack of a record of debate, see Rakove, *Declaring Rights*, 186.

37. Madison to Edmund Pendleton, September 14, 1789, in Madison, *Papers*, 12:402 (first, third, and fourth quotations); Gales, *Annals of Congress*, 1:451 (second quotation). On the maneuvering following the Senate's revisions, see the letters in Helen E. Veit, Kenneth R. Bowling, and Charlene Bangs Bickford, eds., *Creating the Bill of Rights: The Documentary Record from the First Federal Congress* (Baltimore: Johns Hopkins University Press, 1991), 291–300.

38. Gales, *Annals of Congress*, 1:948 (first quotation), 451 (second quotation).

39. Jefferson to Madison, August 28, 1789, in Madison, *Papers*, 12:363; Ronald Dworkin, *Is Democracy Possible Here? Principles for a New Political Debate* (Princeton, N.J.: Princeton University Press, 2006), 55–57. The utter ambiguity of the First Amendment is evident in the overwhelming number of articles trying to make sense of it. Between 2000 and 2005 scholars published nearly 2,000 articles on religious-liberty law. See John Witte Jr., *Religion and the American Constitutional Experiment*, 2nd ed. (Boulder: Westview, 2005), xvi. The Court has had a difficult time with the indeterminacy of the amendment. The resulting jurisprudence on the First Amendment has been a fly in the teeth of legal scholars, who complain of the inconsistency, the opacity, and the general unpredictability of the Court's opinions. One scholar, Jesse H. Choper, has even gone so far as to argue that the First Amendment's two religion clauses are self-referentially incoherent. According to Choper, the Court must define what religion means in order to protect free religious exercise (the second clause), but to define religion is necessarily to choose among alternative conceptions of religion, which could then be said to establish that one conception over others, thereby violating the establishment clause. See Jesse H. Choper, "Defining 'Religion' in the First Amendment," *University of Illinois Law Review* 1982, no. 3: 579–613; Jesse H. Choper, "The Religion Clauses of the First Amendment: Reconciling the Conflict," *University of Pittsburgh Law Review* 41 (Summer 1980): 673–701.

Chapter 3

1. For the church statistics, see Roger Finke and Rodney Stark, *The Churching of America, 1776–2005: Winners and Losers in Our Religious Economy*, 2nd ed. (New Brunswick,

N.J.: Rutgers University Press, 2005), 22–24. There is near-universal agreement among historians and sociologists of religion about the very low percentage of church membership in 1776 and its expansion during the nineteenth century. For concurring assessments, see R. Laurence Moore, "Charting the Circuitous Route toward Religious Liberty," *Modern Intellectual History* 2 (April 2005): 114. On the distinction between church membership and church adherence, which might account for these low numbers, see Patricia U. Bonomi and Peter R. Eisenstadt, "Church Adherence in the Eighteenth-Century British American Colonies," *William and Mary Quarterly*, 3rd series, vol. 39 (April 1982): 245–286; Finke and Stark, *Churching of America*, 27–35; Richard J. Carwardine, *Evangelicals and Politics in Antebellum America* (New Haven, Conn.: Yale University Press, 1993), 43–48. But even if church adherence was twice as large as church membership in the eighteenth century, the percentages remain lower in 1776 and higher in 1900 than what we might expect in a decline model. For the denominational breakdown, see Finke and Stark, *Churching of America*, 56.

2. On the expansion of evangelical Protestantism (including the church-expansion statistics), see Finke and Stark, *Churching of America*, 23, 55–116 (Methodist statistic on p. 57); Jon Butler, *Awash in a Sea of Faith: Christianizing the American People* (Cambridge, Mass.: Harvard University Press, 1990), 257–288 (church statistics on pp. 282–284); Mark A. Noll, *America's God: From Jonathan Edwards to Abraham Lincoln* (New York: Oxford University Press, 2002), 161–186 (statistic on ministers on p. 166). On the growth of the population as a whole, see Herbert S. Klein, *A Population History of the United States* (New York: Cambridge University Press, 2004), 244.

3. On the presence of hearers, see Carwardine, *Evangelicals and Politics*, 43.

4. On the evangelical synthesis, see Noll, *America's God*, 161–208. On the essentially ordered, rather than disordered, process of the revivals and the Awakening, see Donald G. Mathews, "The Second Great Awakening as an Organizing Process, 1780–1830: An Hypothesis," *American Quarterly* 21 (Spring 1969): 23–43. On the shared general characteristics of the emergent Protestant denominations, see Robert T. Handy, *Undermined Establishment: Church–State Relations in America, 1880–1920* (Princeton, N.J.: Princeton University Press, 1991), 8–12.

5. On the emergent power of evangelicals in American cultural and political life, see Noll, *America's God*, 187–208.

6. On disputes over the nature of this commercial transformation (or evolution), see the special issue "Capitalism in the Early Republic," *Journal of the Early Republic* 16 (Summer 1996): 159–308; and Naomi R. Lamoreaux, "Rethinking the Transition to Capitalism in the Early American Northeast," *Journal of American History* 90 (September 2003): 437–461.

7. Alexis de Tocqueville, *Democracy in America*, trans. Harvey C. Mansfield and Delba Winthrop (Chicago: University of Chicago Press, 2000), 482–492, 500–506.

8. Ibid., 483.

9. Ibid., 501 (first quotation), 504 (second and third quotations). There is an element of reductionism in Tocqueville's analysis that dissolves religious experience into

the nonreligious terms of social control. Tocqueville himself was aware of the objection. He acknowledged that religious believers had, through their own experiences, come to their belief in terms and by explanations that had their own integrity apart from any exterior, nonreligious explanation. But his acknowledgment did not change his conviction of a nonreligious explanation for religious belief. He explained, "[I]nterest is the principal means [that] religions themselves make use of to guide men, and I do not doubt that it is only from this side that they take hold of the crowd and become popular" (ibid., 505).

10. Ibid., 501 (quotation). Here I am both acknowledging Rogers Smith's warning against using Tocqueville as a key to U.S. civic identity, and aligning my analysis with Smith's multiple-traditions approach. Tocqueville's focus on egalitarianism and democratization ignored the illiberal exclusions that characterized the American past. I take Tocqueville's account as a starting point to understand why evangelicals would remain so ambivalent about democracy, thereby using Tocqueville to undermine an approach to U.S. law and politics that rests on a unitary tradition. See Rogers M. Smith, *Civic Ideals: Conflicting Visions of Citizenship in U.S. History* (New Haven, Conn.: Yale University Press, 1997), 14–20.

11. South Carolina Constitution of 1790, art. 8, sec. 1; Pennsylvania Constitution of 1790, art. 9, sec. 4; Delaware Constitution of 1792, art. 1, sec. 1.

12. Vermont Constitution of 1793, ch. 2, sec. 39; Maryland Constitution of 1776 as amended in 1810, art. 13; Connecticut Constitution of 1818, art. 1, sec. 4 (first quotation), art. 7, sec. 1 (second and third quotations); New Hampshire Constitution of 1784, part 1, art. 6 (fourth quotation); Massachusetts Constitution of 1780, art. 3 (fifth and sixth quotations); North Carolina Constitution of 1776 as amended in 1835, art. 4, sec. 2. For a close account of the process of institutional disestablishment, which he somewhat confusingly calls "political disestablishment," see Steven K. Green, *The Second Disestablishment: Church and State in Nineteenth-Century America* (New York: Oxford University Press, 2010), 3–145. I regret that Green's book appeared too late for me to make full use of it in preparing this manuscript.

13. Thomas E. Buckley, *Church and State in Revolutionary Virginia, 1776–1787* (Charlottesville: University Press of Virginia, 1977), 140 (both quotations). This emphasis on the limits of democratic thought among even those who rejected the institutional establishment runs in tension with the claims of Nathan O. Hatch, *The Democratization of American Christianity* (New Haven, Conn.: Yale University Press, 1989). Hatch himself has to admit that even many evangelicals who used the rhetoric of democracy did so in the promotion of "authoritarian" control that sometimes included "religious dictatorship," which he characterizes a "curious paradox" (p. 11). My own view is that Hatch overstates both the degree to which the constitutional framers were committed to democracy and the degree to which evangelicals used the language of democracy or sought to embody it. Several recent works on Virginian Baptists, who were supposed to be at the forefront of democratic thought in their ecclesiology and in their embrace of church–state separation,

demonstrate just how much they reinforced the dominant moral ideals and the hierarchical structure of Virginian society, rejecting or modifying democracy in important ways. These books directly take on the Hatch thesis in a more monographic vein and work in concert with my broader claims. See Jewel L. Spangler, *Virginians Reborn: Anglican Monopoly, Evangelical Dissent, and the Rise of the Baptists in the Late Eighteenth Century* (Charlottesville: University of Virginia Press, 2008), 119–166; Charles F. Irons, *The Origins of Proslavery Christianity: White and Black Evangelicals in Colonial and Antebellum Virginia* (Chapel Hill: University of North Carolina Press, 2008); Janet Moore Lindman, *Bodies of Belief: Baptist Community in Early America* (Philadelphia: University of Pennsylvania Press, 2008).

14. For the classic argument that the dispute over religion in politics was a partisan affair, see Arthur M. Schlesinger Jr., *The Age of Jackson* (Boston: Little, Brown, 1945), 350–360.

15. Lyman Beecher, "Autobiographical Statement on the 1818 Disestablishment of the 'Standing Order' in Connecticut, 1864," in *Making the Nonprofit Sector in the United States: A Reader*, ed. David C. Hammack (Bloomington: Indiana University Press, 1998), 119 (both quotations).

16. Ibid., 122 (all quotations). On the religious rapprochement between evangelicals and old-line religious groups, see Sidney E. Mead, *The Lively Experiment: The Shaping of Christianity in America* (New York: Harper & Row, 1963), 52–54.

17. Lyman Beecher, *Lectures on Scepticism*, 3rd ed. (Cincinnati: Corey & Webster, 1835), 58 (first quotation), 57 (second quotation); Lyman Beecher, "A Reformation of Morals Practicable and Indispensable," in *Sermons* (Boston: John P. Jewett, 1852), 92 (third quotation).

18. Beecher, "A Reformation of Morals," 92 (first quotation); Beecher, *Lectures on Scepticism*, 79 (second quotation).

19. Beecher, "A Reformation of Morals," 93 (first quotation), 92–93 (second quotation).

20. For an incomplete list of the many reform organizations, see Charles I. Foster, *An Errand of Mercy: The Evangelical United Front, 1790–1837* (Chapel Hill: University of North Carolina Press, 1960), 275–279. On the expansion of voluntary organizations to reform U.S. society, see Ronald G. Walters, *American Reformers, 1815–1860*, rev. ed. (New York: Hill & Wang, 1997); Paul S. Boyer, *Urban Masses and Moral Order in America, 1820–1920* (Cambridge, Mass.: Harvard University Press, 1978), 22–53; Carroll Smith-Rosenberg, *Religion and the Rise of the American City: The New York City Mission Movement, 1812–1870* (Ithaca, N.Y.: Cornell University Press, 1971); Clifford S. Griffin, *Their Brothers' Keepers: Moral Stewardship in the United States, 1800–1865* (New Brunswick, N.J.: Rutgers University Press, 1960). On the interlocking connection of Protestant social thought with the institutional structures of the Protestant establishment, see William R. Hutchison, *Religious Pluralism in America: The Contentious History of a Founding Ideal* (New Haven, Conn.: Yale University Press, 2003), 65–83.

21. Beecher, "A Reformation of Morals," 95 (all quotations).

22. Richard R. John, "Taking Sabbatarianism Seriously: The Postal System, the Sabbath, and the Transformation of American Political Culture," *Journal of the Early Republic* 10 (Winter 1990): 517–567 (quotation on p. 558).

23. For one example of scholars claiming that the evangelical failure to prevent Sunday mail delivery demonstrates the speciousness of the Christian-nation ideal, see Isaac Kramnick and R. Laurence Moore, *The Godless Constitution: A Moral Defense of the Secular State* (New York: Norton, 2005), 131–149. On the end of Sunday mail service, see Gaines M. Foster, *Moral Reconstruction: Christian Lobbyists and the Federal Legislation of Morality, 1865–1920* (Chapel Hill: University of North Carolina Press, 2002), 134.

24. On James Kent and the role of the state court judges in nineteenth-century jurisprudence, see G. Edward White, *The American Judicial Tradition: Profiles of Leading American Judges* (New York: Oxford University Press, 1976), 35–63.

25. *People v. Ruggles*, 8 Johns. 290 (1811), at 290.

26. On the party affiliation of the judges, see Leonard W. Levy, *Blasphemy: Verbal Offense against the Sacred, from Moses to Salman Rushdie* (New York: Knopf, 1993), 402.

27. *People v. Ruggles*, 8 Johns. at 294 (first, second, fourth, and fifth quotations), 295 (third and seventh quotations), 296 (sixth quotation). For an excellent overview of the Christian-nation maxim, see Steven K. Green, "The Rhetoric and Reality of the Christian Nation Maxim in American Law, 1810–1920" (PhD diss., University of North Carolina at Chapel Hill, 1997).

28. *Commonwealth v. Sharpless*, 2 Serg. & Rawle 91 (1815), at 102 (first quotation), 103 (second and third quotations).

29. *Commonwealth v. Wolf*, 3 Serg. & Rawle 48 (1817), at 49 (first through fourth quotations), 51 (fifth and sixth quotations).

30. *Updegraph v. Commonwealth*, 11 Serg. & Rawle 394 (1824), at 398 (first quotation), 399 (second through fourth quotations).

31. On the bad tendency test, see David M. Rabban, *Free Speech in Its Forgotten Years* (New York: Cambridge University Press, 1997).

32. Nathaniel H. Carter and William L. Stone, *Reports of the Proceedings and Debates of the Convention of 1821, Assembled for the Purpose of Amending the Constitution of the State of New York* (Albany: E. & E. Hosford, 1821), 463 (first and third quotations), 462 (second quotation).

33. Ibid., 464 (first quotation), 465 (second and third quotations).

34. Ibid., 575 (first quotation), 576 (second through fourth quotations).

35. Thomas Jefferson to John Cartwright, June 5, 1824, in Thomas Jefferson, *The Writings of Thomas Jefferson*, ed. Albert Ellery Bergh (Washington, D.C.: Thomas Jefferson Memorial Association, 1904), 16:48 (first through third quotations), 51 (fourth quotation).

36. Joseph Story to Edward Everett, September 15, 1824, and Joseph Story, "Christianity a Part of the Common Law," in Joseph Story, *The Life and Letters of Joseph*

Story, ed. William W. Story (Boston: Little, Brown, 1851), 1:430 (first quotation), 433 (second quotation).

37. *State v. Chandler*, 2 Del. 553 (1837), at 553 (first quotation), 555 (second quotation), 564 (third quotation), 567 (fourth through sixth quotations), italics original.

38. *Commonwealth v. Kneeland*, 37 Mass. 206 (1838), at 217 (first quotation), 218 (second and third quotations), 221 (fourth quotation), 219–220 (fifth quotation), 220 (sixth quotation). For the party affiliation of the dissenting justice, see Levy, *Blasphemy*, 422.

39. Jefferson to Cartwright, June 5, 1824, in Jefferson, *Writings*, 16:48 (first quotation); *State v. Chandler*, 2 Del. at 555 (second quotation). On blasphemy law's place in the wider system of religious jurisprudence, see Sarah Barringer Gordon, "Blasphemy and the Law of Religious Liberty in Nineteenth-Century America," *American Quarterly* 52 (December 2000): 682–719.

40. *Vidal et al. v. Philadelphia*, 43 U.S. 127 (1844), at 198 (both quotations).

41. Ibid., at 198 (first quotation), 200 (second quotation). For Story's fuller interpretation of the First Amendment and its implications for religious liberty more generally, see Joseph Story, *A Familiar Exposition of the Constitution of the United States* (Boston: Marsh, Capen, Lyon, & Webb, 1840), 259–261.

42. *Permoli v. New Orleans*, 44 U.S. 589 (1845). In *Permoli*, the Court reiterated, in a more specific application, its earlier decision handed down for a unanimous court by John Marshall in *Barron v. Baltimore*, 32 U.S. 243 (1833), that the Bill of Rights was never intended to apply to the states. On the requirement to swear belief in the existence of God and an afterlife, see Chester James Antieau, Phillip Mark Carroll, and Thomas Carroll Burke, *Religion under the State Constitutions* (Brooklyn: Central Book, 1965), 107–111. See also *State v. Chandler*, 2 Del. at 567; *An Inquiry into the Moral and Religious Character of the American Government* (New York: Wiley & Putnam, 1838), 131–133; Carter and Stone, *Reports of the Proceedings and Debates*, 463–466.

43. Carter and Stone, *Reports of the Proceedings and Debates*, 574 (first quotation), 575 (second and third quotations).

Chapter 4

1. Nathaniel H. Carter and William L. Stone, *Reports of the Proceedings and Debates of the Convention of 1821, Assembled for the Purpose of Amending the Constitution of the State of New York* (Albany: E. & E. Hosford, 1821), 576 (both quotations).

2. *Gelly v. Cleve*, cited in 1 Ld. Raym. 147 (1694), in Helen Tunnicliff Catterall, ed., *Judicial Cases Concerning American Slavery and the Negro* (Washington, D.C.: Carnegie Institution of Washington, 1926–1937), 1:10 (first quotation). The Virginia blue law and John Rolfe are quoted in the editorial notes by Catterall, *Judicial Cases Concerning American Slavery*, 1:54 (second quotation), 55 (third quotation).

3. John Woolman quoted by Thomas L. Haskell, *Objectivity Is Not Neutrality: Explanatory Schemes in History* (Baltimore: Johns Hopkins University Press, 1998), 279 (both quotations). On the Quaker role in early antislavery efforts, see Arthur Zilversmit, *The First Emancipation: The Abolition of Slavery in the North* (Chicago: University of Chicago Press, 1967), 55–58.

4. Thomas Hamm, *The Quakers in America* (New York: Columbia University Press, 2003), 13–36.

5. Zilversmit, *First Emancipation*, 82–83, 109–138, 169–200.

6. *Journals of the General Conference of the Methodist Episcopal Church* (New York: Carlton & Phillips, 1855), 1:22 (first quotation), 23 (second and third quotations).

7. Ibid., 37, 40, 41 (quotation), 44, 60–65. For the changes in the *Discipline* and its deference to Southern sensibilities, see *The Doctrines and Discipline of the Methodist Church*, 12th ed. (New York: T. Kirk, 1804), 215–216; *The Doctrines and Discipline of the Methodist Episcopal Church*, 16th ed. (New York: Hitt & Ware, 1813), 209–210. Quakers themselves struggled with how to move forward in the nineteenth century. See Ryan P. Jordan, *Slavery and the Meetinghouse: The Quakers and the Abolitionist Dilemma, 1820–1865* (Bloomington: Indiana University Press, 2007).

8. "American Colonization Society: A Memorial to the United States Congress," in Albert P. Blaustein and Robert L. Zangrando, eds., *Civil Rights and African Americans: A Documentary History* (Evanston, Ill.: Northwestern University Press, 1991), 70 (all quotations). On Lyman Beecher's support for colonization, see Bertram Wyatt-Brown, *Lewis Tappan and the Evangelical War against Slavery* (Cleveland: Press of Case Western Reserve University, 1969), 85.

9. On Beecher's inconsistency, see Wyatt-Brown, *Lewis Tappan*, 85.

10. See Christine Leigh Heyrman, *Southern Cross: The Beginnings of the Bible Belt* (New York: Knopf, 1997); Cynthia Lynn Lyerly, *Methodism and the Southern Mind, 1770–1810* (New York: Oxford University Press, 1998); Sylvia R. Frey, *Come Shouting to Zion: African American Protestantism in the American South and British Caribbean to 1830* (Chapel Hill: University of North Carolina Press, 1998); Donald Mathews, *Religion in the Old South* (Chicago: University of Chicago Press, 1977).

11. Charles C. Jones, *Religious Instruction of the Negroes in the United States* (Savannah, Ga.: Thomas Purse, 1842), 125 (first and second quotations), 125–126 (third quotation), 143 (fourth quotation).

12. Charles Cotesworth Pinckney, *An Address Delivered in Charleston, before the Agricultural Society of South-Carolina*, reprinted in Jeffrey Robert Young, ed., *Proslavery and Sectional Thought in the Early South, 1740–1829: An Anthology* (Columbia: University of South Carolina Press, 2006), 246 (first three quotations); Jones, *Religious Instruction of the Negroes*, 126 (fourth and eighth quotations), 130 (fifth through seventh quotations); [Frederick Dalcho], *Practical Considerations Founded on the Scriptures, Relative to the Slave Population of South-Carolina* (Charleston: A. E. Miller, 1823), 6 (ninth and tenth quotations). Jones has a useful litany of excerpts

from other Southern Christian writers that agree with his assessment. See Jones, *Religious Instruction of the Negroes*, 140–153.

13. Elizabeth Fox-Genovese, *Within the Plantation Household: Black and White Women in the Old South* (Chapel Hill: University of North Carolina Press, 1988), 64 (quotation). Also see Jeffrey Robert Young, *Domesticating Slavery: The Master Class in Georgia and South Carolina, 1670–1837* (Chapel Hill: University of North Carolina Press, 1999), 123–160; Eugene D. Genovese, *Roll, Jordan, Roll: The World the Slaves Made* (New York: Vintage, 1976), 3–7.

14. For examples of the claim that Southern religion was individualistic and apolitical, see John B. Boles, *The Great Revival, 1789–1805: The Origins of the Southern Evangelical Mind* (Lexington: University of Kentucky Press, 1972), 125–142; Rufus B. Spain, *At Ease in Zion: Social History of Southern Baptists, 1865–1900* (Nashville, Tenn.: Vanderbilt University Press, 1967), 149–173. For a look at how deeply implicated evangelicals were in slavery's justification, see Elizabeth Fox-Genovese and Eugene D. Genovese, *The Mind of the Master Class: History and Faith in the Southern Slaveholder's Worldview* (New York: Cambridge University Press, 2005).

15. Robert L. Dabney, *A Defence of Virginia [and through Her, of the South] in Recent and Pending Contests against the Sectional Party* (New York: E. J. Hale & Son, 1867), 229 (all quotations). On the univocal claim of Southern clerics that the system of slavery was sanctioned by God, see Eugene D. Genovese, *A Consuming Fire: The Fall of the Confederacy in the Mind of the White Christian South* (Athens: University of Georgia Press, 1998), 1–33; Mitchell Snay, *Gospel of Disunion: Religion and Separatism in the Antebellum South* (New York: Cambridge University Press, 1993).

16. Dabney, *A Defence of Virginia*, 259 (first through fourth quotations), 260 (fifth quotation).

17. *Commonwealth v. Turner*, 26 Va. 678 (1827), at 680 (first two quotations), 681 (third and fourth quotations), 686 (fifth and sixth quotations). On the curse of Ham, see Genovese, *Consuming Fire*, 4. For other examples of the courts' declaration of the inapplicability of common law and subsequent reluctance to intervene in the affairs of the household, see *State v. Hale*, 9 N.C. 582 (1823); *George (a slave) v. State*, 37 Miss. 316 (1859).

18. *State v. Mann*, 13 N.C. 263 (1829), at 266 (first through sixth quotations), 267 (seventh quotation) (1829). For a particularly sensitive treatment of this case and an explanation of its wider relationship to Southern slave law, see Thomas D. Morris, *Southern Slavery and the Law, 1619–1860* (Chapel Hill: University of North Carolina Press, 1996), 190–193.

19. *Neal v. Farmer*, 9 Ga. 555 (1851), at 582 (all quotations), italics in original.

20. *State v. Cantey*, 2 Hill 614 (1835), in Catterall, *Judicial Cases Concerning American Slavery*, 2:359 (first quotation); *Cooper and Worsham v. Mayor and Aldermen*, 4 Ga. 68 (1848), at 72 (second quotation); *State v. Jowers*, 33 N.C. 555 (1850), at 556 (third and fourth quotations), 556–557 (fifth quotation). For examples of convicted free

African Americans being sold back into slavery, see *Mabry v. Commonwealth*, 4 Va. 396 (1824); *Aldridge v. Commonwealth*, 4 Va. 447 (1824).

21. *Dred Scott v. Sandford*, 60 U.S. 393 (1857), at 407 (first and second quotations), 409 (third through sixth quotations).

22. On the Hicksite change in theology and praxis, see H. Larry Ingle, *Quakers in Conflict: The Hicksite Reformation* (Knoxville: University of Tennessee Press, 1986).

23. Hamm, *Quakers in America*, 39–46, especially p. 44.

24. On Garrison's relationship to Beecher, see Wendell Phillips Garrison and Francis Jackson Garrison, *William Lloyd Garrison: The Story of His Life* (New York: Century, 1885–1889), 1:78, 212–215.

25. Wyatt-Brown, *Lewis Tappan*, 78–79 (quotation on p. 78).

26. On the early subscribers to the *Liberator*, see Aileen S. Kraditor, *Means and Ends in American Abolitionism: Garrison and His Critics on Strategy and Tactics, 1834–1850* (New York: Pantheon, 1969), 4.

27. *Liberator*, December 14, 1833 (all quotations). On Garrison's role in drafting the Declaration, see Lewis Tappan to the Editor of the *Liberator*, March 19, 1852.

28. On evangelical activism, see Ronald G. Walters, *American Reformers, 1815–1860*, rev. ed. (New York: Hill & Wang, 1997); Clifford S. Griffin, *Their Brothers' Keepers: Moral Stewardship in the United States, 1800–1865* (New Brunswick, N.J.: Rutgers University Press, 1960); Charles I. Foster, *An Errand of Mercy: The Evangelical United Front, 1790–1837* (Chapel Hill: University of North Carolina Press, 1960).

29. Kraditor, *Means and Ends*, 78–81.

30. *Liberator*, December 12, 1835.

31. On the abolition controversy at Lane, see Robert Samuel Fletcher, *A History of Oberlin College* (Oberlin, Ohio: Oberlin College, 1943), 1:150–178.

32. *Liberator*, July 23, 1836 (first two quotations); Garrison to the *New England Spectator*, July 30, 1836, in William Lloyd Garrison, *The Letters of William Lloyd Garrison*, ed. Walter M. Merrill and Louis Ruchames (Cambridge, Mass.: Belknap Press, 1971–1981), 2:148 (third and fourth quotations).

33. *Liberator*, August 6, 1836 (all quotations).

34. For the history of the Grimké sisters, see Gerda Lerner, *The Grimké Sisters from South Carolina: Pioneers for Women's Rights and Abolition*, rev. ed. (Chapel Hill: University of North Carolina Press, 2004), 3–99.

35. "Pastoral Letter of the Massachusetts Congregationalist Clergy (1837)," in Aileen S. Kraditor, ed., *Up from the Pedestal: Selected Writings in the History of American Feminism* (Chicago: Quadrangle, 1968), 51 (both quotations). For Paul's enjoinment of women's silence, see 1 Corinthians 14:34–35.

36. Garrison to George W. Benson, April 7, 1838, in Garrison, *Letters*, 2:345 (first and second quotations); June 6, 1839, Journals, Lewis Tappan Papers, Prints and Manuscript Division, Library of Congress (third quotation).

37. Tappan's letter to Phelps is paraphrased by Garrison in a letter to George Benson, August 26, 1837, Garrison, *Letters*, 2:290–291.

38. Garrison and Garrison, *William Lloyd Garrison*, 2:177 (first quotation), italics in original; *Liberator*, September 28, 1838 (all subsequent quotations).

39. Lewis Tappan, quoted by Wyatt-Brown, *Lewis Tappan*, 193.

40. James G. Birney, "View of the Constitution of the American A. S. Society as connected with the 'No-Government' Question," reprinted in the *Liberator*, June 28, 1839 (all quotations), italics in original.

41. June 6, 1839, Journals, Lewis Tappan Papers, Prints and Manuscript Division, Library of Congress (first quotation); Garrison to Oliver Johnson, August 5, 1839, in Garrison, *Letters*, 2:526 (second and third quotations).

42. November 14, 1839, Journals, Lewis Tappan Papers, Prints and Manuscript Division, Library of Congress.

43. On the organizational limitations of the society, see Wyatt-Brown, *Lewis Tappan*, 198.

44. For Tappan's involvement with the case, see ibid., 205–212. For the opinion, see *United States v. Libellants and Claimants of the Schooner Amistad,* 40 U.S. 518 (1841).

45. Lewis Tappan quoted by Wyatt-Brown, *Lewis Tappan*, 292.

46. Lewis Tappan, *History of the American Missionary Association: Its Constitution and Principles, Etc.* (New York: n.p., 1855), 21 (first quotation), 23 (second quotation).

47. On Lewis Tappan's role in the AMA, see Wyatt-Brown, *Lewis Tappan*, 292–322. On the AMA's success in uniting the various evangelical players that were unable to come together in the AFASS, see the organizing members of the association in Tappan, *History of the American Missionary Association*, 20.

Chapter 5

1. Elizabeth Cady Stanton, Susan B. Anthony, and Matilda Joslyn Gage, *The History of Woman Suffrage* (Rochester: Susan B. Anthony, 1881–1887), 1:54–61 (quotations on p. 55).

2. Genesis 3:16 (RSV) (first quotation); William Blackstone, *Commentaries on the Laws of England*, 12th ed. (London: Strahan & Woodfall, 1793), 441 (second quotation). See also James Kent, *Commentaries on American Law*, 5th ed. (New York: James Kent, 1844), 2:74–94; Tapping Reeve, *The Law of Baron and Femme*, 2nd ed. (Burlington: Chauncey Goodrich, 1846); Edward D. Mansfield, *The Legal Rights, Liabilities, and Duties of Women* (Salem: John P. Jewett, 1845).

3. Linda K. Kerber, *No Constitutional Right to Be Ladies: Women and the Obligations of Citizenship* (New York: Hill & Wang, 1998), 8–33; Sandra F. VanBurkleo, *"Belonging to the World": Women's Rights and American Constitutional Culture* (New York: Oxford University Press, 2001), 1–57.

4. "Tenth National Woman's Rights Convention," in Elizabeth Cady Stanton and Susan B. Anthony, *The Selected Papers of Elizabeth Cady Stanton and Susan B. Anthony*, ed. Ann D. Gordon (New Brunswick, N.J.: Rutgers University Press,

1997–), 1:411 (quotation); Elisabeth Griffith, *In Her Own Right: The Life of Elizabeth Cady Stanton* (New York: Oxford University Press, 1984), 30–39.

5. "Woman's Rights Convention, Held at Seneca Falls," July 19–20, 1848, in Stanton and Anthony, *Selected Papers*, 1:80 (both quotations).

6. Robert H. Abzug, *Cosmos Crumbling: American Reform and the Religious Imagination* (New York: Oxford University Press, 1994), 183–193 (especially pp. 190–193).

7. Ibid., 190–193. On the political uses of the womanly ideal, see Barbara Leslie Epstein, *The Politics of Domesticity: Women, Evangelism, and Temperance in Nineteenth-Century America* (Middletown, Conn.: Wesleyan University Press, 1981).

8. "Woman's Rights Convention, Held at Seneca Falls," July 19–20, 1848, in Stanton and Anthony, *Selected Papers*, 1:77 (both quotations).

9. Stanton, Anthony, and Gage, *History of Woman Suffrage*, 1:535–536.

10. Ibid., 1:536 (first quotation), 540 (second and third quotations), 382 (fourth through seventh quotations), italics in original.

11. "Elizabeth Cady Stanton's Letter," September 6, 1852, in ibid., 1:850 (first three quotations), 851 (fourth quotation).

12. Lawrence M. Friedman, "Rights of Passage: Divorce Law in Historical Perspective," *Oregon Law Review* 63, no. 4 (1984): 651–657; Richard H. Chused, "Married Women's Property Law, 1800–1850," *Georgetown Law Journal* 71 (June 1983): 1359–1425.

13. "Address by ECS to the Legislature of New York," in Stanton and Anthony, *Selected Papers*, 1:240–260.

14. Ibid., 1:245 (first quotation); Kent, *Commentaries*, 2:74 (second through fourth quotations); Joseph Story, *Commentaries on the Conflict of Laws Foreign and Domestic*, 3rd ed. (Boston: Little, Brown, 1846), 193–234.

15. Mansfield, *Legal Rights, Liabilities, and Duties of Women*, 20 (first quotation), 235 (second and third quotations), 261–262 (fourth quotation), 262 (fifth through seventh quotations), italics in original. For other treatise writers who explicitly connected Christianity and marriage law, see Sarah Barringer Gordon, *The Mormon Question: Polygamy and Constitutional Conflict in Nineteenth-Century America* (Chapel Hill: University of North Carolina Press, 2002), 65–68, 138.

16. "Address by ECS to the Legislature of New York," in Stanton and Anthony, *Selected Papers*, 1:253 (first quotation), 245 (second quotation).

17. Kent, *Commentaries*, 2:106 (quotation). For a helpful assessment of the many contradictions of coverture, see Kerber, *No Constitutional Right to Be Ladies*, 3–46.

18. "From the Diary of SBA," in Stanton and Anthony, *Selected Papers*, 1:270.

19. Lucy Stone to Antoinette Blackwell Brown, August 1849, in Lucy Stone and Antoinette Blackwell Brown, *Friends and Sisters: Letters between Lucy Stone and Antoinette Blackwell Brown, 1846–1893*, ed. Carol Lasser and Marlene Deahl Merrill (Urbana: University of Illinois Press, 1987), 56 (both quotations), italics in original. Although Stone would eventually marry, it would be a tortuous negotiation and resulted in not legally binding marriage documents that defined rights and responsibilities. See

Lucy Stone and Henry B. Blackwell, *Loving Warriors: Selected Letters of Lucy Stone and Henry B. Blackwell, 1865 to 1893*, ed. Leslie Wheeler (New York: Dial, 1981), 108–114. On the active participation of several prominent suffrage proponents including Lucy Stone in the freethought movement, see Stow Persons, *Free Religion: An American Faith* (New Haven, Conn.: Yale University Press, 1947), 132–133.

20. Stanton to Anthony, January 24, 1856, and Stanton to Anthony, June 10, 1856, in Stanton and Anthony, *Selected Papers*, 1:316 (first quotation), 325 (second through fourth quotations).

21. Anthony to Lucy Stone, June 16, 1857, in Stanton and Anthony, *Selected Papers*, 1:345 (both quotations), emphasis in original.

22. "Address by ECS to the American Anti-Slavery Society," in Stanton and Anthony, *Selected Papers*, 1:409 (first and second quotations), 410 (third quotation).

23. "Tenth National Woman's Rights Convention," in Stanton and Anthony, *Selected Papers*, 1:420 (first quotation), 426 (second quotation).

24. *Proceedings of the Tenth National Woman's Rights Convention*, May 10 and 11, 1860 (Boston: Yerrington & Garrison, 1860), in Elizabeth Cady Stanton and Susan B. Anthony, *The Papers of Elizabeth Cady Stanton and Susan B. Anthony*, ed. Patricia G. Holland and Ann D. Gordon (Wilmington, Del.: Scholarly Resources, 1991), reel 9: frame 658 (first quotation); *New York Daily Tribune*, May 14, 1860 (second quotation); Stanton to Martha Wright Coffin, July 12, 1860, in Stanton and Anthony, *Selected Papers*, 1:436 (third quotation).

25. Anthony to Wendell Phillips, April 29, 1861, in Stanton and Anthony, *Selected Papers*, 1:464 (first quotation), 465 (second quotation).

26. Lyman Beecher, *Lectures on Scepticism*, 3rd ed. (Cincinnati: Corey & Webster, 1835), 62 (both quotations).

Chapter 6

1. Abraham Lincoln, "Second Inaugural Address," in Abraham Lincoln, *The Collected Works of Abraham Lincoln*, ed. Roy P. Basler (New Brunswick, N.J.: Rutgers University Press, 1953–1955), 8:333 (both quotations).

2. Philip Schaff, "Slavery and the Bible," *Mercersburg Review* 13 (April 1861): 316 (first quotation); *The Liberator*, January 10, 1845 (second quotation); Garrison to James Miller McKim, July 19, 1845, in William Lloyd Garrison, *The Letters of William Lloyd Garrison*, ed. Walter M. Merrill and Louis Ruchames (Cambridge, Mass.: Belknap Press, 1971–1981), 3:307 (third quotation).

3. Schaff, "Slavery and the Bible," 317 (all quotations).

4. On free labor, see Eric Foner, *Free Soil, Free Labor, Free Men: The Ideology of the Republican Party before the Civil War* (New York: Oxford University Press, 1995), 11–39.

5. Many writers have noted the bourgeois character of nineteenth-century civilizing missions. See Frederick Cooper and Ann Laura Stoler, eds., *Tensions of Empire:*

Colonial Cultures in a Bourgeois World (Berkeley and Los Angeles: University of California Press, 1997); Thomas C. Holt, "'An Empire over the Mind': Emancipation, Race, and Ideology in the British West Indies and the American South," in *Region, Race, and Reconstruction: Essays in Honor of C. Vann Woodward*, ed. J. Morgan Kousser and James M. McPherson (New York: Oxford University Press, 1982), 283–313.

6. Chase and Cragin both quoted by Mark Wahlgren Summers, "With a Sublime Faith in God and in Republican Liberty," in *Vale of Tears: New Essays on Religion and Reconstruction*, ed. Edward J. Blum and W. Scott Poole (Macon: Mercer University Press, 2005), 112 (first through fourth quotations), 124 (fifth and sixth quotations).

7. On white conditions set for black stays in churches and the quote from Alabama Baptist Convention *Minutes*, see Kenneth K. Bailey, "The Post–Civil War Racial Separations in Southern Protestantism: Another Look," *Church History* 46 (December 1977): 453–456 (first quotation on p. 455); Lucius H. Holsey, "The Colored Methodist Episcopal Church," in *Afro-American Religious History: A Documentary Witness*, ed. Milton C. Sernett (Durham, N.C.: Duke University Press, 1985), 235 (second quotation), 235–236 (third quotation).

8. Thomas R. R. Cobb, *An Inquiry into the Law of Negro Slavery in the United States of America* (Philadelphia: T. & J. W. Johnson, 1858), 1:49 (quotation). For the general fear of a lapse into barbarism, see I. A. Newby, *Jim Crow's Defense: Anti-Negro Thought in America, 1900–1930* (Baton Rouge: Louisiana State University Press, 1965), 54–79 (especially pp. 70–77).

9. *Laws of the State of Mississippi, 1865* (Jackson, Miss., 1866), in David E. Shi and Holly A. Mayer, eds., *For the Record: A Documentary History of America*, 2nd ed. (New York: Norton, 2004), 1:582 (all three quotations). On the black codes generally, see Eric Foner, *Reconstruction: America's Unfinished Revolution, 1861–1877* (New York: Perennial Classics, 2002), 198–216.

10. U.S. Constitution, Fourteenth Amendment, Section 1. On the role of the Civil Rights Act of 1866 and the Fourteenth Amendment in changing the logic of American citizenship laws, see Rogers M. Smith, *Civic Ideals: Conflicting Visions of Citizenship in U.S. History* (New Haven, Conn.: Yale University Press, 1997), 286–346; Foner, *Reconstruction*, 251–261.

11. On the operating budget of the AMA compared to other benevolent societies, see Ralph E. Luker, *Social Gospel in Black and White: American Racial Reform, 1885–1912* (Chapel Hill: University of North Carolina Press, 1991), 13. For a general history of the AMA and its predominance in teacher training, see Joe M. Richardson, *Christian Reconstruction: The American Missionary Association and Southern Blacks, 1861–1890* (Athens: University of Georgia Press, 1986), 109–119 (statistic on teacher training on p. 119). For a sympathetic reading of the mission, see Edward J. Blum, *Reforging the White Republic: Race, Religion, and American Nationalism, 1865–1898* (Baton Rouge: Louisiana State University Press, 2005), 51–86.

12. Michael E. Strieby, ed., *The Nation Still in Danger, or, Ten Years after the War: A Plan* (New York: American Missionary Association, 1875), 2 (first quotation), 6 (second and third quotations), 7 (fourth quotation).

13. Oliver Otis Howard, *The Autobiography of Oliver Otis Howard, Major General, United States Army* (New York: Baker & Taylor, 1907), 2:584 (first and second quotations), 585 (third and fourth quotations).

14. Richardson, *Christian Reconstruction*, 76 (first quotation); Howard, *Autobiography*, 2:213 (second quotation), 220 (third quotation) 220–221 (fourth quotation), 221 (fifth and sixth quotations); John W. Alvord, ed., "Ninth Semi-Annual Report," *Semi-Annual Reports on Schools for Freedmen, Numbers 1–10, January 1866–1870* (New York: AMS Press, 1980), 39 (seventh through ninth quotations). For Howard's account of his conversion to evangelicalism, see Howard, *Autobiography*, 1:82. I am indebted to David L. Davis for alerting me to the Alvord work in general and the quotation in particular.

15. For an extended account of Freedmen's Bureau and AMA cooperation, see Richardson, *Christian Reconstruction*, 75–84. On the practice of dual appointments, see E. Allen Richardson, "Architects of a Benevolent Empire: The Relationship between the American Missionary Association and the Freedmen's Bureau in Virginia, 1865–1872," in *The Freedmen's Bureau and Reconstruction: Reconsiderations*, ed. Paul A. Cimbala and Randall M. Miller (New York: Fordham University Press, 1999), 121.

16. On Armstrong's history in Hawaii, schooling under Hopkins, and early maneuvering to establish Hampton Institute, see Robert Francis Engs, *Educating the Disfranchised and Disinherited: Samuel Chapman Armstrong and Hampton Institute, 1839–1893* (Knoxville: University of Tennessee Press, 1999), 1–85. On the multiple personnel and ideological connections between the two organizations and Armstrong's maneuvering and subsequent AMA commission, see Richardson, "Architects of a Benevolent Empire," 119–139. On the Evangelical Alliance, see Philip D. Jordan, *The Evangelical Alliance for the United States of America, 1847–1900: Ecumenicism, Identity, and the Religion of the Republic* (New York: Edwin Mellen, 1982).

17. Samuel Chapman Armstrong, "Lessons from the Hawaiian Islands," *Journal of Christian Philosophy* 3 (January 1884): 213 (first through third quotations), 214 (fifth and sixth quotations); Samuel Chapman Armstrong, *Armstrong's Ideas on Education for Life*, ed. Francis Greenwood Peabody (Hampton, Va.: Hampton Institute, 1913), 41 (fourth quotation).

18. For Hampton's curriculum, cost, and teachers, see M. F. Armstrong and Helen W. Ludlow, *Hampton and Its Students* (New York: G. P. Putnam's, 1874), 165–170. For Armstrong's views on the cost and benefits of industrial education, see Armstrong, *Armstrong's Ideas on Education for Life*, 23 (first quotation), 18 (second and third quotations); Armstrong, "Lessons from the Hawaiian Islands," 216 (fourth quotation).

19. On black churches and schools as primary Klan targets, see Foner, *Reconstruction*, 428. On the social foundation of the Klan in white churches and the leadership by white ministers, see W. Scott Poole, "Confederate Apocalypse: Theology and Violence in the Reconstruction South," in Blum and Poole, *Vale of Tears*, 36–52 (quotation on p. 47).

20. *The Freedmen's Record*, December 1866, 205 (first two quotations); *New York Times*, March 29, 1868 (third through fifth quotations). On the general movement toward forgiveness of the South, see Blum, *Reforging the White Republic*, 87–119; Daniel W. Stowell, *Rebuilding Zion: The Religious Reconstruction of the South, 1863–1877* (New York: Oxford University Press, 1998), 162–186. I draw heavily upon Blum's work for the next several paragraphs.

21. *New York Times*, March 29, 1868 (first quotation); Harriet Beecher Stowe, *Men of Our Times; or, Leading Patriots of the Day* (Hartford, Conn.: Hartford Publishing, 1868), 567 (second and third quotations), italics in original.

22. On the Third Great Awakening, see William G. McLoughlin, *Revivals, Awakenings, and Reform: An Essay on Religion and Social Change in America, 1607–1977* (Chicago: University of Chicago Press, 1978), 141–178. For the church membership statistics, see Roger Finke and Rodney Stark, *The Churching of America, 1776–2005: Winners and Losers in Our Religious Economy*, 2nd ed. (New Brunswick, N.J.: Rutgers University Press, 2005), 23. On Moody's revivals and the sectional rapprochement that sustained evangelical expansion, see Blum, *Reforging the White Republic*, 120–145.

23. "Eleventh National Woman's Rights Convention," May 10, 1866, in Elizabeth Cady Stanton and Susan B. Anthony, *The Selected Papers of Elizabeth Cady Stanton and Susan B. Anthony*, ed. Ann D. Gordon (New Brunswick, N.J.: Rutgers University Press, 1997–), 1:586.

24. Ellen Carol DuBois, *Feminism and Suffrage: The Emergence of an Independent Women's Movement in America, 1848–1869* (Ithaca, N.Y.: Cornell University Press, 1978), 162–202.

25. Ibid., 53–104, 162–202.

26. *The Slaughterhouse Cases*, 83 U.S. 36 (1873), at 62 (first quotation), 74 (second quotation). On the Fourteenth Amendment and the Court's early interpretation, see Richard C. Cortner, *The Supreme Court and the Second Bill of Rights: The Fourteenth Amendment and the Nationalization of Civil Liberties* (Madison: University of Wisconsin Press, 1981), 3–11. On the use of police power to constrain democracy, see Christopher L. Tomlins, *Law, Labor, and Ideology in the Early American Republic* (New York: Cambridge University Press, 1993), 60–97, especially pp. 95–97. Of course, police power extended beyond the moral establishment to include public health regulations and other legitimate aspects of governance. On the *Slaughterhouse Cases*, which were prompted by health regulations, see Ronald M. Labbé and Jonathan Lurie, *The Slaughterhouse Cases: Regulation, Reconstruction, and the Fourteenth Amendment* (Lawrence: University Press of Kansas, 2003).

27. *Slaughterhouse Cases*, 83 U.S. at 62 (first quotation), 87 (second quotation).

28. Louis R. Harlan, *Booker T. Washington: The Making of a Black Leader, 1856–1901* (New York: Oxford University Press, 1972), 109–156.

29. "A Speech before the National Educational Association," July 16, 1884, in Booker T. Washington, *The Booker T. Washington Papers*, ed. Louis Harlan (Urbana: University of Illinois Press, 1972–1989), 2:261 (first through fourth quotations), Mark 5:9, 15; Luke 8:30 (fifth quotation).

30. "A Speech Delivered before the Women's New England Club," January 27, 1890, in Washington, *Papers*, 3:27.

31. Ibid. (all quotations).

32. Washington, "The Colored Ministry: Its Defects and Needs," in Washington, *Papers*, 3:72–73 (first quotation), 73 (second through fifth quotations).

33. Ibid., 3:74 (quotation), italics in original. For more on Washington's mode of operation, his attempt to balance shifting constituencies, and his engagement with various black denominational leaders, see David Sehat, "The Civilizing Mission of Booker T. Washington," *Journal of Southern History* 73 (May 2007): 323–362.

34. *Pace & Cox v. State*, 69 Ala. 231 (1881), at 232 (quotation). For the decision of the U.S. Supreme Court, see *Pace v. Alabama*, 106 U.S. 583 (1883).

35. *Civil Rights Cases*, 109 U.S. 3 (1883).

36. W. E. B. Du Bois, *The Souls of Black Folk*, ed. Henry Louis Gates Jr. and Terri Hume Oliver (1903; repr., New York: Norton, 1999), 35 (first quotation); Washington, "The Standard Printed Version of the Atlanta Exposition Address," September 18, 1895, in Washington, *Papers*, 3:584 (second through fifth quotations), 585 (sixth through ninth quotations).

37. *Plessy v. Ferguson*, 163 U.S. 537 (1896), at 544 (first and second quotations), 550 (third and fourth quotations), 551 (fifth quotation).

38. *Official Proceedings of the Constitutional Convention of the State of Alabama, May 21st, 1901 to September 3rd, 1901* (Wetumpka, Ala.: Wetumpka Printing, 1941), Day 2 (second through sixth quotations), Day 6 (first quotation), Day 7 (seventh through tenth quotations).

39. *New York Times*, April 15, 1903 (first through sixth, eleventh through fifteenth quotations); Washington, *Papers*, 7:119 note 1 (seventh through tenth quotations).

40. Schaff, "Slavery and the Bible," 316 (first quotation); *New York Times*, April 15, 1903 (second quotation).

Chapter 7

1. "Speech by ECS on Free Love," in Elizabeth Cady Stanton and Susan B. Anthony, *The Selected Papers of Elizabeth Cady Stanton and Susan B. Anthony*, ed. Ann D. Gordon (New Brunswick, N.J.: Rutgers University Press, 1997–), 2:396 (all quotations).

2. Barbara Goldsmith, *Other Powers: The Age of Suffrage, Spiritualism, and the Scandalous Victoria Woodhull* (New York: Knopf, 1998), 63–71, 104–109, 156–162, 246–257. For Woodhull's argument that the Fourteenth and Fifteenth amendments together granted suffrage to women, and her testimony before the U.S. House Judiciary Committee to that effect, see Elizabeth Cady Stanton, Susan B. Anthony, and Matilda Joslyn Gage, *The History of Woman Suffrage* (Rochester: Susan B. Anthony, 1881–1887), 2:443–448.

3. Stanton to Lucretia Coffin Mott, April 1, 1871, in Stanton and Anthony, *Selected Papers*, 2:427 (first quotation), 428 (second and third quotations).

4. Stanton, Anthony, and Gage, *History of Woman Suffrage*, 2:159 (first quotation), 157 (second quotation), 161 (third and fourth quotations).

5. For the complete history of the Beecher–Tilton affair, see Altina L. Waller, *Reverend Beecher and Mrs. Tilton: Sex and Class in Victorian America* (Amherst: University of Massachusetts Press, 1982).

6. On Woodhull's growing disrepute, see Waller, *Reverend Beecher and Mrs. Tilton*, 1–7.

7. On Woodhull's attempt to connect herself to Beecher, see "Victoria C. Woodhull's Complete and Detailed Version of the Beecher–Tilton Affair," facsimile reproduction in Victoria Woodhull, *The Victoria Woodhull Reader*, ed. Madeleine B. Stern (Weston, Mass.: M & S Press, 1974).

8. Victoria Woodhull, "The Principles of Social Freedom," facsimile reproduction in Woodhull, *Victoria Woodhull Reader*.

9. Ibid., 3 (first quotation), 42 (second through fifth quotations). Compare Woodhull's argument to the arguments of Andrews in Stephen Pearl Andrews, Horace Greeley, and Henry James, *Love, Marriage and Divorce and the Sovereignty of the Individual* (1853; repr., New York: Source Book Press, 1972).

10. Victoria Woodhull to Isabella Beecher Hooker, August 8, 1871, in Charles F. Marshall, ed., *The True History of the Brooklyn Scandal* (Philadelphia: National Publishing, 1874), 334 (first four quotations); Henry Ward Beecher to Isabella Beecher Hooker, April 25, 1872, in Marshall, *True History of the Brooklyn Scandal*, 334 (fifth through seventh quotations), italics in original; "From the Diary of SBA," Sunday, May 12, 1872, Stanton and Anthony, *Selected Papers*, 2:494 (eighth quotation).

11. Victoria Woodhull to Henry Ward Beecher, November 19, 1871, in Marshall, *True History of the Brooklyn Scandal*, 358 (first quotation); Victoria Woodhull to Henry Ward Beecher, June 3, 1872, in Marshall, *True History of the Brooklyn Scandal*, 363 (second quotation); "Victoria C. Woodhull's Complete and Detailed Version of the Beecher–Tilton Affair," facsimile reproduction in Woodhull, *Victoria Woodhull Reader*, 3 (third and fourth quotations).

12. "Victoria C. Woodhull's Complete and Detailed Version of the Beecher–Tilton Affair," facsimile reproduction in Woodhull, *Victoria Woodhull Reader*, 13 (first quotation), 19 (second through fourth quotations).

13. On Comstock's involvement in the affair, see Nicola Beisel, *Imperiled Innocents: Anthony Comstock and Family Reproduction in Victorian America* (Princeton, N.J.: Princeton University Press, 1997), 76–87.

14. Victoria Woodhull, "The Naked Truth; or, the Situation Reviewed!" facsimile reproduction in Woodhull, *Victoria Woodhull Reader*, 1 (both quotations). On the number of times the story appeared in the *New York Times*, see Paul A. Carter, *The Spiritual Crisis of the Gilded Age* (DeKalb: Northern Illinois University Press, 1971), 115.

15. Marshall, *True History of the Brooklyn Scandal*, 179 (first quotation), 184 (second quotation).

16. Ibid., 272 (first quotation), 393 (second quotation and block quotation).

17. Victoria Woodhull, "Tried as By Fire; or, The True and The False, Socially," facsimile reproduction in Woodhull, *Victoria Woodhull Reader*, 3 (first quotation), 5 (second quotation), 28 (third through sixth quotations).

18. On the Tiltons' post-trial fate, see Waller, *Reverend Beecher and Mrs. Tilton*, 11. For Woodhull's post-trial story, see Goldsmith, *Other Powers*, 429–431, 440–447.

19. E. L. Godkin, "Chromo-civilization," *Nation*, September 24, 1874, 201 (first quotation), 202 (second through fourth quotations).

20. James Schouler, *A Treatise on the Law of Domestic Relations*, 2nd ed. (Boston: Little, Brown, 1874), 3–22 (third through fifth quotations on p. 17). On the place of Schouler and Bishop in postbellum family law, see Hendrik Hartog, *Man and Wife in America: A History* (Cambridge, Mass.: Harvard University Press, 2000), 16.

21. Joel Prentiss Bishop, *Commentaries on the Law of Married Women* (Boston: Little, Brown, 1873–1875), 1:iv (first quotation), 2:viii (second quotation); Joel Prentiss Bishop, *Commentaries on the Law of Marriage and Divorce*, 6th ed. (Boston: Little, Brown, 1881), 1:2 (third quotation).

22. Bishop, *Commentaries on the Law of Marriage and Divorce*, 2:205 (first four quotations), 207 (fifth quotation). On Bishop's success, in particular, see Michael Grossberg, *Governing the Hearth: Law and the Family in Nineteenth-Century America* (Chapel Hill: University of North Carolina Press, 1985), 21–30. For examples of how the judiciary used Bishop and Schouler to limit the effectiveness of the women's rights property acts, see Norma Basch, *In the Eyes of the Law: Women, Marriage, and Property in Nineteenth-Century New York* (Ithaca, N.Y.: Cornell University Press, 1982), 200–223.

23. Carroll D. Wright, *A Report on Marriage and Divorce in the United States, 1867 to 1886* (Washington, D.C.: Government Printing Office, 1889), 25 (both quotations). On the number of divorces, see ibid., 139–140. On the formation of the New England Divorce Reform League, its reorganization as the National Divorce Reform League, and the petition to Congress, see Lynne Carol Halem, *Divorce Reform: Changing Legal and Social Perspectives* (New York: Free Press, 1980), 34–40.

24. U.S. Constitution, art. 4, sec. 1 (quotation). On the success of religious conservatives in tightening divorce law and its administration, see Halem, *Divorce Reform*,

34–40. On the rise of the migratory divorce, Nelson Manfred Blake, *The Road to Reno: A History of Divorce in the United States* (New York: Macmillan, 1962), 116–243. For an early example of criticism used against Indiana and later Maine, see Horace Greeley and Robert Dale Owen, *Divorce, being a Correspondence between Horace Greeley and Robert Dale Owen* (1860; repr., New York: Source Book Press, 1972).

25. "Victoria C. Woodhull's Complete and Detailed Version of the Beecher–Tilton Affair," facsimile reproduction in Woodhull, *Victoria Woodhull Reader*, 3 (first quotation); Friedman, "Rights of Passage," 662 (second and third quotations). On the National Divorce Reform League's attempt to muster a constitutional amendment, see Halem, *Divorce Reform*, 36–40.

26. *Bradwell v. Illinois*, 83 U.S. 130 (1873), at 141 (both quotations).

27. *Minor v. Happersett*, 88 U.S. 162 (1875).

28. Stanton to the Editor [Francis Abbot], *Index*, in Stanton and Anthony, *Selected Papers*, 3:265 (first quotation), 266 (second quotation); Stanton to Isabella Beecher Hooker, November 28, 1877, in Stanton and Anthony, *Selected Papers*, 3:342 (third quotation). On Francis Abbot and Free Religionists, see Stow Persons, *Free Religion: An American Faith* (New Haven, Conn.: Yale University Press, 1947). For Ingersoll's speech, see Ingersoll, "Liberty of Man, Woman and Child," in Robert G. Ingersoll, *The Works of Robert G. Ingersoll*, ed. C. P. Ferrell (New York: Ingersoll, 1900), 1:329–398. For Anthony's letter, see Susan B. Anthony to Robert G. Ingersoll, January 1, 1877, in Elizabeth Cady Stanton and Susan B. Anthony, *The Papers of Elizabeth Cady Stanton and Susan B. Anthony*, ed. Patricia G. Holland and Ann D. Gordon (Wilmington, Del.: Scholarly Resources, 1991), reel 19: frames 418–421.

29. "Third Decade Celebration at Rochester, New York," in Stanton and Anthony, *Selected Papers*, 3:386–399 (quotation on p. 393).

30. Anthony to Isabella Beecher Hooker, July 14, 1873, in Stanton and Anthony, *Selected Papers*, 2:618 (first quotation), 619 (second and third quotations), emphasis in original.

31. Stanton to the Editor, *Index*, July 22, 1878, in Stanton and Anthony, *Selected Papers*, 3:399 (first quotation). For Abbot's response, see the editorial comment by Ann D. Gordon in Stanton and Anthony, *Selected Papers*, 3:400 note 1. For Anthony's concern about deterring the "religionists," see Stanton and Anthony, *Selected Papers*, 3:400 note 2.

32. Stanton to Anthony, May 21, 1880, in Stanton and Anthony, *Selected Papers*, 3:537 (first and second quotations), italics in original; Stanton, Anthony, and Gage, *History of Woman Suffrage*, 1:16 (third quotation); Gage, "Women, Church, and State," in Stanton, Anthony, and Gage, *History of Woman Suffrage*, 1:753–799.

33. "The Race Problem: Miss Willard on the Political Puzzle of the South," *Voice*, October 23, 1890, p. 8 (all quotations). On the rejection of Stanton's amendments, see Susan B. Anthony and Ida Husted Harper, *The History of Woman Suffrage* (Rochester, N.Y.: Susan B. Anthony, 1902), 4:58–61, 75–77.

34. Elizabeth Cady Stanton, *The Woman's Bible* (1895/1898; repr., Boston: Northeastern University Press, 1993), part 1, p. 20 (both quotations). For the back history of the *Woman's Bible*, see Kathi Kern, *Mrs. Stanton's Bible* (Ithaca, N.Y.: Cornell University Press, 2001), 103–106, 135–171.

35. Stanton, *Woman's Bible*, part 1, p. 61 (both quotations).

36. On the general response to the *Woman's Bible*, see Kern, *Mrs. Stanton's Bible*, 172–222 (first quotation on p. 172); Stanton, *Woman's Bible*, part 2, p. 7 (second quotation), pp. 7–8 (third quotation).

37. Stanton, *Woman's Bible*, part 1, p. 11 (all quotations), italics in original.

38. Anthony and Harper, *History of Woman Suffrage*, 4:254 (first quotation), 263 (second quotation), 264 (third through sixth quotations).

39. Frances E. Willard, *Home Protection Manual: Containing an Argument for the Temperance Ballot for Women* (New York: "The Independent" Office, 1879). On the organizational fallout of the censure, see Kern, *Mrs. Stanton's Bible*, 198–206.

Chapter 8

1. John T. McGreevy, *Catholicism and American Freedom: A History* (New York: Norton, 2003), 7–11 (quotation on p. 8).

2. Howard K. Beale, *A History of Freedom of Teaching in American Schools* (New York: Scribner's, 1941), 207–218.

3. Horace Mann, *The Republic and the School: Horace Mann on the Education of Free Men*, ed. Lawrence A. Cremin (New York: Teachers College Press, 1957), 106 (both quotations).

4. See Mann's explanation of nonsectarianism in ibid., 98–112.

5. "In the Police Court of Boston, Massachusetts. April, 1859. Commonwealth, on Complaint of Wall vs. M'Laurin F. Cooke," *American Law Register* 7 (May 1859): 420 (first and second quotations), 421 (third quotation).

6. Ibid., 417–426.

7. Roger Finke and Rodney Stark, *The Churching of America, 1776–2005: Winners and Losers in Our Religious Economy*, 2nd ed. (New Brunswick, N.J.: Rutgers University Press, 2005), 121.

8. Claudia Carlen, ed., *The Papal Encyclicals* ([Wilmington, N.C.]: McGrath, 1981), 1:236 (first quotation), 238 (second and third quotations), 239 (fourth quotation).

9. For Decree 426 and its translation, see Bernard Julius Meiring, *Educational Aspects of the Legislation of the Councils of Baltimore, 1829–1884* (New York: Arno, 1978), 278 (all quotations).

10. My treatment of the Cincinnati Bible Wars in this paragraph and following is indebted to Tracy Fessenden, *Culture and Redemption: Religion, the Secular, and American Literature* (Princeton, N.J.: Princeton University Press, 2007), 73–83.

11. *The Bible in the Public Schools: Arguments before the Superior Court of Cincinnati in the Case of* Minor v. Board of Education of Cincinnati *(1870) with the Opinions of the Court and the Opinion on Appeal of the Supreme Court of Ohio* (New York: Da Capo, 1967), 6–7 (first quotation), 7 (second quotation); Fessenden, *Culture and Redemption*, 76–77.

12. Ohio Constitution of 1851, art. 1, sec. 7 (first three quotations), art. 6, sec. 2 (fourth and fifth quotations); *Bible in the Public Schools*, vii–xvii.

13. *Bible in the Public Schools*, 375 (first two quotations), 379 (third quotation), 381 (fourth and fifth quotations).

14. *Board of Education v. Minor*, 23 Ohio St. 211 (1872), at 244 (first quotation), 243 (second quotation).

15. Ibid., at 245 (first and second quotations), 248 (third quotation), 250 (fourth quotation), 250–251 (fifth quotation), 251 (sixth quotation).

16. "Something Significant," *Christian Advocate*, October 7, 1875, 316 (first quotation); "An Open Letter," *Index*, November 4, 1875, 522 (second quotation); *Congressional Record* (Washington, D.C.: Government Printing Office, 1873–), 4:5189 (third quotation). On Grant and Blaine, see Steven K. Green, "The Blaine Amendment Reconsidered," *American Journal of Legal History* 36 (January 1992): 42–57. For my discussion of the Blaine Amendment as a whole, I am indebted to Green.

17. Green, "Blaine Amendment Reconsidered," 56.

18. "The Republican Party and the School Question," *Index*, September 7, 1876, 426 (both quotations).

19. *Congressional Record*, 4:5190–5191 (quotation on p. 5190).

20. Ibid., 4:5453.

21. Ibid., 4:5562 (first three quotations), 5584 (fourth and fifth quotations).

22. Ibid., 4:5589 (all quotations), 5595 (final vote).

23. Green, "Blaine Amendment Reconsidered," 47.

24. Carlen, *Papal Encyclicals*, 2:8 (first quotation), 51 (second through fourth quotations), 110 (fifth quotation), 114 (sixth and seventh quotations).

25. Ibid., 2:172 (all quotations).

26. See chart of state constitutional provisions governing religion in David Sehat, "The American Moral Establishment: Religion and Liberalism in the Nineteenth Century" (PhD diss., University of North Carolina at Chapel Hill, 2007), 271–286.

27. See Decrees 194–213 in Meiring, *Educational Aspects*, 293–318. On the growth of the parochial school system by 1920, see Jay P. Dolan, *The American Catholic Experience: A History from Colonial Times to the Present* (New York: Doubleday, 1985), 293. See also the 1875 directive from Rome, "Instruction of the Congregation de Propaganda Fide Concerning Catholic Children Attending American Public Schools, November 24, 1875," reprinted in John Tracy Ellis, ed., *Documents of American Catholic History*, rev. ed. (Wilmington, Del.: Michael Glazier, 1987), 2:405–408.

28. Jan Shipps, *Sojourner in the Promised Land: Forty Years among the Mormons* (Urbana: University of Illinois Press, 2000), 229–243.

29. On Smith's turn to polygamy, see Richard Lyman Bushman, *Joseph Smith: Rough Stone Rolling* (New York: Knopf, 2005), 323. On the secrecy of the official doctrine even after it was put into writing, see Fawn M. Brodie, *No Man Knows My History: The Life of Joseph Smith, the Mormon Prophet*, 2nd ed. (New York: Knopf, 1971), 343–344. On Brigham Young's announcement of the doctrine, see Gordon, *Mormon Question*, 1.

30. Gordon, *Mormon Question*, 111–116.

31. *Reynolds v. United States*, 98 U.S. 145 (1879), at 164 (first through fifth, seventh, and eighth quotations), 165 (sixth quotation).

32. Robert Baird, *Religion in America, or, An Account of the Origin, Relation to the State, and Present Condition of the Evangelical Churches in the United States*, 2nd ed. (New York: Harper, 1856), 252.

33. *Ex parte Newman*, 9 Cal. 502 (1858), at 520 (first quotation); *Commonwealth v. Wolf*, 3 Serg. & Rawle 48 (1817), at 51 (second quotation).

34. *Davis v. Beason*, 133 U.S. 333 (1890), at 341 (first and third quotations), 342 (second quotation), 342–343 (fourth quotation), 343 (fifth and sixth quotations).

35. *Latter-Day Saints v. United States*, 136 U.S. 1 (1890), at 48 (first quotation), 49 (second quotation), 51 (third quotation), 67 (fourth quotation).

36. Sehat, "American Moral Establishment," 271–286.

37. For a good account of the backroom political movements that denied him the governorship, see Orvin Larson, *American Infidel: Robert G. Ingersoll, a Biography* (New York: Citadel, 1962), 76–80, 89–98.

38. Robert G. Ingersoll, *The Works of Robert G. Ingersoll*, ed. C. P. Ferrell (New York: Ingersoll, 1900), 1:7 (first quotation), 169 (second quotation), 75 (third quotation), 179 (fourth quotation).

39. On Comstock's concerns, vice efforts, and law, see Anthony Comstock, "The Suppression of Vice," *North American Review* 135 (November 1882): 484–489 (quotation on p. 488). For the Comstock Law of 1873, see Anthony Comstock, *Traps for the Young*, ed. Robert Bremner (1883; repr., Cambridge, Mass: Belknap Press, 1967), xii note 9.

40. *Ex parte Jackson*, 96 U.S. 727 (1878), at 736 (both quotations). Field's view was in keeping with many of the court rulings in the late nineteenth century. See Michael Les Benedict, "Victorian Moralism and Civil Liberty in the Nineteenth-Century United States," in *The Constitution, Law, and American Life: Critical Aspects of the Nineteenth-Century Experience*, ed. Donald G. Nieman (Athens: University of Georgia Press, 1992), 91–122; Mark Warren Bailey, *Guardians of the Moral Order: The Legal Philosophy of the Supreme Court, 1860–1910* (DeKalb: Northern Illinois University Press, 2004), 113–141. On Ingersoll's petition to Congress, see Gaines M. Foster, *Moral Reconstruction: Christian Lobbyists and the Federal Legislation of Morality, 1865–1920* (Chapel Hill: University of North Carolina Press, 2002), 53.

41. Comstock, *Traps for the Young*, 184 (first and second quotations), 197 (third quotation), 186 (fourth quotation), 237 (fifth quotation).

42. For several examples of legal intimidation used against Ingersoll, see the press accounts in Ingersoll, *Works*, 8:13–15, 72–80, 202–204 (first and third quotations on p. 202, second and fourth quotations on p. 203, fifth quotation on p. 204), 266–268. For an account of the Delaware Chief Justice and the Delaware grand jury, see Larson, *American Infidel*, 161–164.

43. David McAllister, T. H. Acheson, and William Parsons, *Christian Civil Government in America: The National Reform Movement, Its History and Principles*, 6th ed. (Pittsburgh: National Reform Association, 1927), 16 (first through third quotations), 17 (fourth through seventh quotations).

44. Ibid., 140–148 (first and second quotations on p. 143, third quotation on p. 144, fourth quotation on p. 145, fifth quotation on p. 148).

45. For some of Brewer's extensive extralegal writings, see David J. Brewer, *American Citizenship* (New York: Scribner's, 1902); David J. Brewer, *The Twentieth Century from Another Viewpoint* (New York: Fleming H. Revell, 1899); David J. Brewer, *The United States a Christian Nation* (Philadelphia: John C. Winston, 1905). For an excellent, concise overview of Brewer's life and work, consult Owen M. Fiss, "Brewer, David Josiah," in *The Oxford Companion to the Supreme Court of the United States*, ed. Kermit L. Hall (New York: Oxford University Press, 1992), 89–91.

46. Brewer, *United States a Christian Nation*, 49 (first quotation), 54 (second quotation), 55 (third quotation), 65 (fourth and fifth quotations); *Church of the Holy Trinity v. United States*, 143 U.S. 457 (1892), at 471 (sixth quotation).

47. *Congressional Record*, 4:5584.

48. Lyman Beecher, "A Reformation of Morals Practicable and Indispensable," in *Sermons* (Boston: John P. Jewett, 1852), 95.

Chapter 9

1. Alan Trachtenberg, *The Incorporation of America: Culture and Society in the Gilded Age* (New York: Hill & Wang, 2007); Martin J. Sklar, *The Corporate Reconstruction of American Capitalism, 1890–1916: The Market, the Law, and Politics* (New York: Cambridge University Press, 1988).

2. Melvyn Dubofsky and Foster Rhea Dulles, *Labor in America: A History*, 7th ed. (Wheeling, Ill.: Harlan Davidson, 2004), 108–111.

3. *New York Times*, July 30, 1877 (quotation). For more examples of the Protestant response to the Great Railroad Strike, see Henry F. May, *Protestant Churches and Industrial America* (New York: Harper, 1949), 91–111 (especially pp. 91–99).

4. The term "libertarian radicalism" comes from David M. Rabban, *Free Speech in Its Forgotten Years* (New York: Cambridge University Press, 1997), 23.

5. Noah Porter, *The American Colleges and the American Public*, new ed. (New York: Scribner's, 1878), 207 (quotation). On the distinction between science and religion and the desire for autonomous communities of inquiry, see David A. Hollinger, "Inquiry and Uplift: Late Nineteenth-Century American Academics and the Moral Efficacy of Scientific Practice," in *The Authority of Experts: Studies in History and Theory*, ed. Thomas L. Haskell (Bloomington: Indiana University Press, 1984), 142–156, especially pp. 147–150. On the moral impulse in the nineteenth-century college, see Laurence R. Veysey, *The Emergence of the American University* (Chicago: University of Chicago Press, 1965), 21–56; Julie A. Reuben, *The Making of the Modern University: Intellectual Transformation and the Marginalization of Morality* (Chicago: University of Chicago Press, 1996).

6. Grant Wacker, "The Demise of Biblical Civilization," in *The Bible in America: Essays in Cultural History*, ed. Nathan O. Hatch and Mark A. Noll (New York: Oxford University Press, 1982), 121–138.

7. John W. Burgess, *Reminiscences of an American Scholar: The Beginnings of Columbia University* (New York: Columbia University Press, 1934), 147 (first quotation), 147–148 (second quotation), 148 (third quotation).

8. On the organization of knowledge and the new disciplines, see John Higham, "The Matrix of Specialization," and Edward Shils, "The Order of Learning in the United States: The Ascendancy of the University," in Alexandra Oleson and John Voss, eds., *The Organization of Knowledge in Modern America, 1860–1920* (Baltimore: Johns Hopkins University Press, 1979), 3–18, 19–50; Peter Novick, *That Noble Dream: The "Objectivity Question" and the American Historical Profession* (New York: Cambridge University Press, 1988), 47–60. On the end of the moral philosophy capstone in the 1870s, see Reuben, *Making of the Modern University*, 90.

9. Mark Hopkins, *Lectures on Moral Science* (Boston: Gould & Lincoln, 1862), 102–105 (both quotations on p. 103).

10. See, for example, Jean Miller Schmidt, *Souls or the Social Order: The Two-Party System in American Protestantism* (Brooklyn: Carlson, 1991), xxxv–xxxvii.

11. Daniel Seeley Gregory, *Christian Ethics; or, The True Moral Manhood and Life of Duty: A Textbook for Schools and Colleges* (Philadelphia: Eldredge & Brother, 1875).

12. Ibid., 265 (first quotation), 223 (second quotation), 224 (third quotation), 294 (fourth and fifth quotations). Gregory's support of owners over workers was representative of much of the moral literature. See, for example, William Makepeace Thayer, *Tact, Push, Principle*, 29th ed. (Boston: J. H. Earle, 1880); Mark Hopkins, *The Law of Love and Love as a Law; or, Christian Ethics*, rev. ed. (New York: Scribner's, 1881), 155–181; James McCosh, *Our Moral Nature, Being a Brief System of Ethics* (New York: Scribner's, 1892), 24–25; William Lawrence, "The Relation of Wealth to Morals," *World's Work* 1 (January 1901): 286–292.

13. Samuel Lane Loomis, *Modern Cities and Their Religious Problems* (New York: Baker & Taylor, 1887), 74 (first quotation), 75 (second through fourth quotations).

14. Washington Gladden, *Applied Christianity: Moral Aspects of Social Questions* (Boston: Houghton Mifflin, 1886), 33.

15. For two examples of the historians that emphasize the ascendancy of the Social Gospel, see Gary Dorrien, *The Making of American Liberal Theology: Imagining Progressive Religion, 1805–1900* (Louisville: Westminster John Knox Press, 2001), 261–334; William R. Hutchison, *Religious Pluralism in America: The Contentious History of a Founding Ideal* (New Haven, Conn.: Yale University Press, 2003), 84–110.

16. U.S. Constitution, Fifth Amendment (second quotation), Fourteenth Amendment, sec. 1 (first quotation); *The Slaughterhouse Cases*, 83 U.S. 36 (1873). On Field's relationship with Hopkins, see Jack Beatty, *Age of Betrayal: The Triumph of Money in America, 1865–1900* (New York: Knopf, 2007), 148–149. On Field's jurisprudence, see Charles W. McCurdy, "Stephen J. Field and the American Judicial Tradition," in Philip J. Bergan, Owen M. Fiss, and Charles W. McCurdy, *The Fields and the Law: Essays* (San Francisco and New York: United States District Court for the Northern District of the California Historical Society and the Federal Bar Council, 1986), 5–19.

17. *United States v. Cruikshank,* 92 U.S. 542 (1875). On the Colfax Massacre, see LeeAnna Keith, *The Colfax Massacre: The Untold Story of Black Power, White Terror, and the Death of Reconstruction* (New York: Oxford University Press, 2008).

18. *Santa Clara County v. Southern Pacific Railroad,* 118 U.S. 394 (1886).

19. Thomas L. Haskell, *The Emergence of Professional Social Science: The American Social Science Association and the Nineteenth-Century Crisis of Authority* (Urbana: University of Illinois Press, 1977), 149–167 (quotation on p. 154). On the tension between professionalization and advocacy, see Mary O. Furner, *Advocacy and Objectivity: A Crisis in the Professionalization of American Social Science, 1864–1905* (Lexington: University Press of Kentucky, 1975).

20. Gladden, *Applied Christianity,* 194 (first through third quotations), 214 (fourth quotation), 215 (fifth quotation).

21. Richard T. Ely, "Report on the Organization of the American Economic Association," *Publications of the American Economic Association* 1 (March 1886): 6 (first quotation), 7 (second and third quotations). On the beginnings of the AEA, see Haskell, *Emergence of Professional Social Science,* 177–189.

22. A. W. Coats, "The First Two Decades of the American Economic Association," *American Economic Review* 50 (September 1960): 555–574 (quotation on p. 558). On the larger struggle over objectivity, see Robert C. Bannister, *Sociology and Scientism: The American Quest for Objectivity, 1880–1940* (Chapel Hill: University of North Carolina Press, 1987).

23. Albion W. Small, "The Era of Sociology," *American Journal of Sociology* 1 (July 1895): 1 (second quotation), 15 (third through seventh quotations). On Small's decision to found the journal in order to preempt a more reform-oriented one to protect disciplinary integrity, see Dorothy Ross, "The Development of the Social

Sciences," in Oleson and Voss, *Organization of Knowledge in Modern America*, 113–121 (first quotation on p. 117). Ross enlarges on this account in Dorothy Ross, *The Origins of American Social Science* (New York: Cambridge University Press, 1991), and Dorothy Ross, ed., *Modernist Impulses in the Human Sciences, 1870–1930* (Baltimore: Johns Hopkins University Press, 1994).

24. Albion W. Small, "The Sociologist's Point of View," *American Journal of Sociology* 3 (July 1897): 149 (first two quotations), 151 (third quotation), 169 (fourth and fifth quotations).

25. Lester Frank Ward, "The Situation," *Iconoclast* 1 (March 1870): 2 (first through third quotations), 1 (fourth and fifth quotations), italics in original.

26. Albion W. Small, Lester Frank Ward, and Bernhard J. Stern, "The Letters of Albion W. Small to Lester F. Ward," *Social Forces* 12 (December 1933): 163–173 (all quotations on p. 165).

27. Gregory, *Christian Ethics*, 265 (first two quotations); Edward Alsworth Ross, *Social Control: A Survey of the Foundations of Order* (New York: Macmillan, 1901), 441 (third through sixth quotations).

28. Emil G. Hirsch, "The American University," *American Journal of Sociology* 1 (September 1895): 130–131. See Small's claim that all early sociologists shared the same basic vision in spite of terminological difference in Albion W. Small, *General Sociology: An Exposition of the Main Development in Sociological Theory from Spencer to Ratzenhofer* (Chicago: University of Chicago Press, 1905), 397–403. Small's claim is supported by the extensive study of Christian Smith, "Secularizing American Higher Education: The Case of Early American Sociology," in *The Secular Revolution: Power, Interests, and Conflict in the Secularization of American Public Life*, ed. Christian Smith (Berkeley and Los Angeles: University of California Press, 2003), 97–159.

29. Eugene V. Debs, "Robert G. Ingersoll," *American Journal of Politics* 2 (February 1893): 202 (third quotation). On Debs's invitation to Ingersoll, and Ingersoll's speeches, see Ingersoll to Debs, December 29, 1879, and Debs to Ingersoll, [February?] 2, 1881, in Debs, *Letters of Eugene V. Debs*, ed. J. Robert Constantine (Urbana: University of Illinois Press, 1990), 1:12–13 (first two quotations on p. 12). On Debs's life, see Nick Salvatore, *Eugene V. Debs: Citizen and Socialist*, 2nd ed. (Urbana: University of Illinois Press, 2007).

30. Peter S. Grosscup, "Our Old American Freedom," *North American Review* 210 (December 1919): 753 (quotation); Dubofsky and Dulles, *Labor in America*, 158–166.

31. *In re Debs*, 158 U.S. 564 (1895), at 586.

32. David J. Brewer, *American Citizenship* (New York: Scribner's, 1902), 25 (first quotation), 35 (second quotation), 24 (third quotation), 94 (fourth quotation), 98 (fifth and sixth quotations).

33. *Lochner v. New York*, 198 U.S. 45 (1905), at 59 (quotation). On Brewer's position at the center of the Court's controlling coalition, see Owen M. Fiss, "David J. Brewer: The Judge as Missionary," in Bergan, Fiss, and McCurdy, *Fields and the Law*, 57.

34. On Holmes as critic of the Court, see Ken I. Kersch, *Constructing Civil Liberties: Discontinuities in the Development of American Constitutional Law* (New York: Cambridge University Press, 2004), 147–155, 287–292.

35. Oliver Wendell Holmes Jr., "The Path of the Law," *Harvard Law Review* 10 (March 1897): 457 (all quotations).

36. Ibid., 458.

37. Ibid., 469 (first quotation); Thomas L. Haskell, *Objectivity Is Not Neutrality: Explanatory Schemes in History* (Baltimore: Johns Hopkins University Press, 1998), 232 (second quotation); Morton J. Horwitz, *The Transformation of American Law, 1870–1960: The Crisis of Legal Orthodoxy* (New York: Oxford University Press, 1992), 5 (third quotation). On probability and statistics, see Ian Hacking, *The Taming of Chance* (New York: Cambridge University Press, 1990). On Holmes's view of the law as a tool and its connection to probability, see Louis Menand, *The Metaphysical Club* (New York: Farrar, Straus, & Giroux, 2001), ix–xii, 339–347.

38. *Muller v. Oregon*, 208 U.S. 412 (1908).

39. Ibid., at 421 (all quotations).

40. Samuel D. Warren and Louis D. Brandeis, "The Right to Privacy," *Harvard Law Review* 4 (December 1890): 193 (first two quotations), 196 (third through fifth quotations), 205 (sixth quotation).

41. *Muller v. Oregon*, 208 U.S. at 420 (second and third quotations), 421 (fourth quotation). For the Brandeis Brief, see Brief for Appellee, *Muller v. Oregon*, 208 U.S. 412 (No. 107).

Chapter 10

1. On the secular Jewish and post-Christian coalition, see David A. Hollinger, "Jewish Intellectuals and the De-Christianization of American Public Culture in the Twentieth Century," *Science, Jews, and Secular Culture: Studies in Mid-Twentieth-Century American Intellectual History* (Princeton, N.J.: Princeton University Press, 1996), 17–41; Ken I. Kersch, *Constructing Civil Liberties: Discontinuities in the Development of American Constitutional Law* (New York: Cambridge University Press, 2004), 290–292.

2. Herbert Croly, *The Promise of American Life* (New York: Macmillan, 1909), 17 (first quotation), 23 (second quotation). On Croly's upbringing and biography, see Charles Forcey, *The Crossroads of Liberalism: Croly, Weyl, Lippmann, and the Progressive Era, 1900–1925* (New York: Oxford University Press, 1961), 11–16.

3. Croly, *Promise of American Life*, 139 (all quotations).

4. Ibid., 441.

5. On Croly's courtship of Roosevelt and the similarity and dissimilarity of their political thought, see Forcey, *Crossroads of Liberalism*, 123–144 (quotation on p. 127).

6. Walter Lippmann, *A Preface to Politics* (New York: Mitchell Kennerley, 1913), 85 (first quotation), 107 (second quotation), 200 (third quotation), 221 (fourth quotation), 224 (fifth and sixth quotations). Lippmann here fully embraced what David Hollinger has called the "intellectual gospel." See David A. Hollinger, "Justification by Verification: The Scientific Challenge to the Moral Authority of Christianity in Modern America," in *Religion and Twentieth-Century American Intellectual Life*, ed. Michael J. Lacey (Washington, D.C., and Cambridge: Woodrow Wilson International Center for Scholars and Cambridge University Press, 1989), 116–135 (quotation on p. 123).

7. On Lippmann's involvement with the Village bohemians, see Nancy Cohen, *The Reconstruction of American Liberalism, 1865–1914* (Chapel Hill: University of North Carolina Press, 2002), 237–238. On the bohemians in general, see Christine Stansell, *American Moderns: Bohemian New York and the Creation of a New Century* (New York: Metropolitan Books, 2000).

8. Forcey, *Crossroads of Liberalism*, 52–87, 153–177.

9. *New Republic*, November 7, 1914, 3 (both quotations). On Dewey and Du Bois's association, see David Levering Lewis, *W. E. B. Du Bois: The Fight for Equality in the American Century, 1919–1963* (New York: Henry Holt, 2000), 252. On Frankfurter's connection to the *New Republic*, see Forcey, *Crossroads of Liberalism*, 181–182.

10. *New Republic*, November 21, 1914, 5 (first quotation); W. E. B. Du Bois, "On Being Black," *New Republic*, February 18, 1920, 338–341; "Restoring the Family," *New Republic*, November 28, 1914, 9 (second quotation); Herbert Croly, *Progressive Democracy* (New York: Macmillan, 1914), 378 (third quotation).

11. On Gladden's ascension to the AMA presidency and his pivot toward Du Bois, see Ronald C. White Jr., *Liberty and Justice for All: Racial Reform and the Social Gospel (1877–1925)* (New York: Harper & Row, 1990), 130–141 (all quotations on p. 138).

12. On Gladden's invitation to Du Bois, see ibid., 140. On the significance of institutionalization, see William R. Hutchison, *Religious Pluralism in America: The Contentious History of a Founding Ideal* (New Haven, Conn.: Yale University Press, 2003), 106–110.

13. Walter Rauschenbusch, *Christianity and the Social Crisis* (New York: Macmillan, 1907). For the founding statement of the FCC, see H. Shelton Smith, Robert T. Handy, and Lefferts A. Loetscher, eds., *American Christianity: An Historical Interpretation with Representative Documents* (New York: Scribner's, 1960–1963), 2:394–397. On the beginnings of the Federal Council of Churches, see Robert A. Schneider, "Voice of Many Waters: Church Federation in the Twentieth Century," in *Between the Times: The Travail of the Protestant Establishment in America, 1900–1960*, ed. William R. Hutchison (New York: Cambridge University Press, 1989), 95–121. For the Methodist social creed, see Charles Howard Hopkins, *The Rise of the Social Gospel in American Protestantism, 1865–1915* (New Haven, Conn.: Yale University Press, 1940), 291. On the inclusion of African Americans and women in the FCC, see Hutchison, *Religious Pluralism in America*, 137.

14. Charles S. MacFarland, ed., *Christian Unity at Work: The Federal Council of the Churches of Christ in America in Quadrennial Session at Chicago, Illinois, 1912*, 4th ed. (New York: The Federal Council of the Churches of Christ in America, 1913), 153 (quotation). On the initial jockeying to create the Committee on Evangelism, see Jean Miller Schmidt, *Souls or the Social Order: The Two-Party System in American Protestantism* (Brooklyn: Carlson, 1991), 131–136.

15. On the *New Republic*'s changing relationship to Roosevelt and Wilson, and its new use of the term "liberals" rather than "progressives," see Forcey, *Crossroads of Liberalism*, 253–263 (quotations on p. 255).

16. On progressives and World War I, see William E. Leuchtenburg, *The Perils of Prosperity, 1914–1932*, 2nd ed. (Chicago: University of Chicago Press, 1993), 30–48. On Lippmann's role in drafting and glossing the Fourteen Points, see Godfrey Hodgson, *Woodrow Wilson's Right Hand: The Life of Colonel Edward M. House* (New Haven, Conn.: Yale University Press, 2006), 188.

17. On the Espionage and Sedition Acts, see David M. Rabban, *Free Speech in Its Forgotten Years* (New York: Cambridge University Press, 1997), 248–298. On the magazine's spike in circulation and influence during the war, see Forcey, *Crossroads of Liberalism*, 278. On the wartime demise of the *New Republic*'s vision, see David W. Noble, "The *New Republic* and the Idea of Progress, 1914–1920," *Mississippi Valley Historical Review* 38 (December 1951): 387–402.

18. Gaines M. Foster, *Moral Reconstruction: Christian Lobbyists and the Federal Legislation of Morality, 1865–1920* (Chapel Hill: University of North Carolina Press, 2002), 203–219.

19. On Prohibition and organized crime, see Michael A. Lerner, *Dry Manhattan: Prohibition in New York City* (Cambridge, Mass.: Harvard University Press, 2007), 255–288.

20. On the WCTU's cooling on suffrage and the drift of NAWSA, see Ross Evans Paulson, *Liberty, Equality, and Justice: Civil Rights, Women's Rights, and the Regulation of Business, 1865–1932* (Durham, N.C.: Duke University Press, 1997), 118–128. For the membership numbers and relative lack of success in the suffrage campaign, see Stanley Coben, *Rebellion against Victorianism: The Impetus for Cultural Change in 1920s America* (New York: Oxford University Press, 1991), 94.

21. Coben, *Rebellion against Victorianism*, 94–96.

22. Ibid., 96–97.

23. On the different issue alignments around Prohibition and women's suffrage, see Eileen Lorenzi McDonagh, "The Significance of the Nineteenth Amendment: A New Look at Civil Rights, Social Welfare, and Woman Suffrage Alignments in the Progressive Era," *Women & Politics* 10, no. 2 (1990): 59–94; Eileen L. McDonagh, "Issues and Constituencies in the Progressive Era: House Roll Call Voting on the Nineteenth Amendment, 1913–1919," *Journal of Politics* 51 (February 1989): 119–136. For methodological assumptions in the political science study of issue alignments, see Paul Burstein, "Policy Domains: Organization, Culture, and Policy Outcomes," *Annual Review of Sociology* 17, no. 1 (1991): 327–350.

24. Donald Johnson, *The Challenge to American Freedoms: World War I and the Rise of the American Civil Liberties Union* (Lexington: University Press of Kentucky, 1963), 125–145.

25. *Schenck v. United States*, 249 U.S. 47 (1919); *Abrams v. United States*, 250 U.S. 616 (1919).

26. *Abrams v. United States*, 250 U.S. at 630 (first six quotations). On the origins of the clear and present danger test, see Rabban, *Free Speech in Its Forgotten Years*, 7–8 (seventh quotation on p. 8), 285–298, 342–344.

27. *Whitney v. California*, 274 U.S. 357 (1927), at 377 (all quotations).

28. *Olmstead v. United States*, 277 U.S. 438 (1928), at 478.

29. For more on this shift, see Richard C. Cortner, *The Supreme Court and the Second Bill of Rights: The Fourteenth Amendment and the Nationalization of Civil Liberties* (Madison: University of Wisconsin Press, 1981), 3–11, 38–62.

30. *United States v. MacIntosh*, 283 U.S. 605 (1931), at 619 (first quotation), 625 (second through fifth quotations). For related opinions, see also *United States v. Schwimmer*, 279 U.S. 644 (1929); *United States v. Bland*, 283 U.S. 636 (1931).

31. *United States v. MacIntosh*, 283 U.S. at 633–634.

32. Leuchtenburg, *Perils of Prosperity*, 84–103, 241–264.

33. William E. Leuchtenburg, *Franklin D. Roosevelt and the New Deal, 1932–1940* (New York: Harper & Row, 1963), 143–166.

34. Claudia Carlen, ed., *The Papal Encyclicals* ([Wilmington, N.C.]: McGrath, 1981), 2:241 (first quotation). On *Rerum Novarum*'s role in the Catholic divide over labor in the United States and the sometimes strained connection between Catholics and liberals, see John T. McGreevy, *Catholicism and American Freedom: A History* (New York: Norton, 2003), 131–138, 153–157. On the papal rejection of Americanism and modernism, see Jay P. Dolan, *In Search of an American Catholicism: A History of Religion and Culture in Tension* (Oxford: Oxford University Press, 2002), 99–117 (second quotation on p. 108). On the new political type that characterized the post-1936 liberal Democratic base, see Leuchtenburg, *Franklin D. Roosevelt and the New Deal*, 184–185.

35. *National Labor Relations Board v. Jones and Laughlin Steel Corporation*, 301 U.S. 1 (1937); *United States v. Carolene Products Co.*, 304 U.S. 144 (1938), at 152 note 4 (all quotations). On the foundational shift in jurisprudence that the *Carolene* principle marked, see James Hitchcock, *The Supreme Court and Religion in American Life* (Princeton, N.J.: Princeton University Press, 2004), 1:154–155.

36. *Schneider v. New Jersey*, 308 U.S. 147 (1939), at 161 (quotation); *Cantwell v. Connecticut*, 310 U.S. 296 (1940).

37. *Cantwell v. Connecticut*, 310 U.S. at 308 (first and second quotations), 310 (third and fourth quotations).

38. *Minersville School District v. Gobitis*, 310 U.S. 586 (1940), at 591 (first two quotations), 596 (third and fourth quotations).

39. Ibid., at 604 (first quotation), 606–607 (second quotation).

40. *Jones v. Opelika*, 316 U.S. 584 (1942), at 624 (both quotations).

41. *West Virginia State Board of Education v. Barnette*, 319 U.S. 624 (1943), at 634 (both quotations). For the judge's claim in the Thomas Whall case, see "In the Police Court of Boston, Massachusetts. April, 1859. Commonwealth, on Complaint of Wall vs. M'Laurin F. Cooke," *American Law Register* 7 (May 1859): 423.

42. *West Virginia State Board of Education v. Barnette*, 319 U.S. at 636 (first quotation), 641 (second quotation).

43. Ibid., at 641 (first quotation), 641–642 (second quotation), 642 (third quotation), 646 (fourth quotation). See also *Murdock v. Pennsylvania*, 319 U.S. 105 (1943), which overturned the Court's previous opinion in *Jones v. Opelika*. On the Court's shift in its conception of democracy, see David Sikkink, "From Christian Civilization to Individual Civil Liberties: Framing Religion in the Legal Field, 1880–1949," in *The Secular Revolution: Power, Interests, and Conflict in the Secularization of American Public Life*, ed. Christian Smith (Berkeley and Los Angeles: University of California Press, 2003), 344–346. On the legal movement of the Stone and Vinson Courts and the unstable body of jurisprudence that resulted from their adjudication, see William M. Wiecek, *The Birth of the Modern Constitution: The United States Supreme Court, 1941–1953* (New York: Cambridge University Press, 2006), 1–9.

Chapter 11

1. On the fundamentalist–modernist controversies, see George M. Marsden, *Fundamentalism and American Culture*, 2nd ed. (New York: Oxford University Press, 2006). On religious liberalism and its political transformation, see David A. Hollinger, "The Realist-Pacifist Summit Meeting of March 1942 and the Political Reorientation of Ecumenical Protestantism in the United States," *Church History* 79 (forthcoming, September 2010).

2. Grant Wacker, "Uneasy in Zion: Evangelicals in Postmodern Society," in *Evangelicalism and Modern America*, ed. George Marsden (Grand Rapids, Mich.: Eerdmans, 1984), 17–28.

3. Joel A. Carpenter, *Revive Us Again: The Reawakening of American Fundamentalism* (New York: Oxford University Press, 1997), 13–56, 144–147.

4. On neo-evangelicalism and its revival, see George M. Marsden, "Contemporary American Evangelicalism," in *Southern Baptists and American Evangelicals: The Conversation Continues*, ed. David S. Dockery (Nashville: Broadman & Holman, 1993), 31, 33–34.

5. *United . . . We Stand: A Report of the Constitutional Convention of the National Association of Evangelicals* (Boston: NAE, 1943), 10 (both quotations). On the beginning of the NAE, see Carpenter, *Revive Us Again*, 147–160.

6. *United . . . We Stand*, 39 (both quotations).

7. George M. Marsden, *Reforming Fundamentalism: Fuller Seminary and the New Evangelicalism* (Grand Rapids, Mich.: Eerdmans, 1987).

8. Carpenter, *Revive Us Again*, 211–226.

9. Marsden, *Reforming Fundamentalism*, 157–161 (both quotations on p. 158); Carl F. H. Henry, *The Uneasy Conscience of Modern Fundamentalism* (Grand Rapids, Mich.: Eerdmans, 1947).

10. Billy Graham, "The Sin of Tolerance," *Christianity Today*, February 2, 1959, 3–5 (first two quotations on p. 3); Stephen J. Whitfield, *The Culture of the Cold War*, 2nd ed. (Baltimore: Johns Hopkins University Press, 1996), 77–100 (third and fourth quotations on p. 89). On the Flanders Amendment, see "The Congress: Hunting Time," *Time*, May 24, 1954, 23 (fifth quotation).

11. Will Herberg, *Protestant-Catholic-Jew: An Essay in American Religious Sociology* (Garden City: Doubleday, 1955), 52 (first through third quotations), 88 (fourth and fifth quotations).

12. *New York Times*, December 23, 1952.

13. Graham quoted by Whitfield, *Culture of the Cold War*, 81 (first quotation). Phyllis Schlafly quoted by Donald T. Critchlow, *Phyllis Schlafly and Grassroots Conservatism: A Woman's Crusade* (Princeton, N.J.: Princeton University Press, 2005), 75 (second quotation); William F. Buckley Jr., *God and Man at Yale: The Superstitions of "Academic Freedom"* (Chicago: Regnery, 1951), xi (third and fourth quotations), xi–xii (fifth quotation).

14. Billy Graham, *Labor, Christ, and the Cross* (Minneapolis: Billy Graham Evangelistic Association, 1953), 6 (both quotations); William F. Buckley Jr., *McCarthy and His Enemies: The Record and Its Meaning* (Chicago: Regnery, 1954). On the relationship of Catholics and liberals, see John T. McGreevy, *Catholicism and American Freedom: A History* (New York: Norton, 2003), 211–212. On the NAE's resolution, see Mark Silk, "The Rise of the 'New Evangelicalism': Shock and Adjustment," in *Between the Times: The Travail of the Protestant Establishment in America, 1900–1960*, ed. William R. Hutchison (New York: Cambridge University Press, 1989), 281.

15. Herberg, *Protestant-Catholic-Jew*, 15 (first quotation); *New York Times*, December 23, 1952 (second and third quotations). On Graham's role in Eisenhower's conversion, see Whitfield, *Culture of the Cold War*, 87–88.

16. *United . . . We Stand*, 39 (first quotation); *New York Times*, April 11, 1959 (second and third quotations). On Schlafly's overture to and rejection by Schwarz, see Critchlow, *Phyllis Schlafly*, 80. On Bell as Graham's father-in-law, see "The Preaching and the Power," *Newsweek*, July 20, 1970, 51.

17. *Everson v. Board of Education*, 330 U.S. 1 (1947), at 16.

18. Ibid., at 19 (first quotation), 31–32 (second quotation), 32 (third through fifth quotations), 44 (sixth quotation).

19. Ibid., at 44. Wiecek argues that the difference between the Stone and Vinson Courts lies largely in the fact that the former took up free-exercise issues and the

latter took up establishment issues. But, as he notes, the two are necessarily related, and the reasoning of the Court during the Jehovah's Witnesses cases, even though those cases are classified under free-exercise jurisprudence, necessarily addressed the government's ability to decide whether a sect's activities could be considered religious and therefore could receive a license to proselytize. In turn, the act of adopting a definition of religion, as Jesse Choper has argued, could be said to establish that definition, which in turn violates the non-establishment clause. So these two kinds of cases cannot be so easily separated. See William M. Wiecek, *The Birth of the Modern Constitution: The United States Supreme Court, 1941–1953* (New York: Cambridge University Press, 2006), 203–205; Jesse H. Choper, "Defining 'Religion' in the First Amendment," *University of Illinois Law Review* 1982, no. 3: 579–613; Jesse H. Choper, "The Religion Clauses of the First Amendment: Reconciling the Conflict," *University of Pittsburgh Law Review* 41 (Summer 1980): 673–701.

20. *McCollum v. Board of Education*, 333 U.S. 203 (1948).

21. For the effects of the cold war on the Court, see Wiecek, *Birth of the Modern Constitution*, 535–618.

22. *Zorach v. Clauson*, 343 U.S. 306 (1952), at 313 (first quotation), 314 (second through fourth quotations).

23. Ibid., at 323 (first quotation), 324 (second and third quotations).

24. *Brown v. Board of Education*, 347 U.S. 483 (1954), at 494 (first and second quotations), 493 (third and fourth quotations). On the Court's break from establishment-clause jurisprudence, see James Hitchcock, *The Supreme Court and Religion in American Life* (Princeton, N.J.: Princeton University Press, 2004), 1:160.

25. See Michael J. Klarman, *From Jim Crow to Civil Rights: The Supreme Court and the Struggle for Racial Equality* (New York: Oxford University Press, 2004), 344–442; Maurice Isserman and Michael Kazin, *America Divided: The Civil War of the 1960s*, 3rd ed. (New York: Oxford University Press, 2008).

26. Harvard Sitkoff, *The Struggle for Black Equality, 1954–1992*, rev. ed. (New York: Hill & Wang, 1993). On the importance of Jews and other post-Protestants in creating reform vehicles, see Hollinger, "The Realist-Pacifist Summit Meeting of March 1942.

27. Wade Clark Roof and William McKinney, "Denominational America and the New Religious Pluralism," *Annals of the American Academy of Political and Social Science* 480 (July 1985): 24–38; Roger Finke and Rodney Stark, *The Churching of America, 1776–2005: Winners and Losers in Our Religious Economy*, 2nd ed. (New Brunswick, N.J.: Rutgers University Press, 2005), 246.

28. Graham quoted by Steven P. Miller, *Billy Graham and the Rise of the Republican South* (Philadelphia: University of Pennsylvania Press, 2009), 109 (first quotation), 94 (second quotation), 113–114 (third quotation), 114 (fourth quotation). On *Christianity Today*'s ambivalence toward the idea of civil rights, see Mark G. Toulouse,

"*Christianity Today* and American Public Life: A Case Study," *Journal of Church and State* 35 (Spring 1993): 255. For my treatment of Billy Graham here and what follows, I am deeply indebted to Miller's book. For a contemporary sociological examination of the problem of race in evangelical thought, see Michael O. Emerson and Christian Smith, *Divided by Faith: Evangelical Religion and the Problem of Race in America* (New York: Oxford University Press, 2000).

29. On the Catholic hierarchy's commitment to equality, see McGreevy, *Catholicism and American Freedom*, 208–211.

30. William F. Buckley Jr., "Why the South Must Prevail," *National Review*, August 24, 1957, 148 (first quotation), 149 (second through tenth quotations).

31. Martin Luther King Jr., "Letter from Birmingham City Jail," in Martin Luther King Jr., *A Testament of Hope: The Essential Writings and Speeches of Martin Luther King, Jr.*, ed. James Melvin Washington (San Francisco: Harper, 1991), 290 (first quotation), 292 (second quotation), 293 (third and fourth quotations), 295 (fifth quotation).

32. *Torcaso v. Watkins*, 367 U.S. 488 (1961).

33. *McGowan v. Maryland*, 366 U.S. 420 (1961), at 436 (both quotations).

34. Ibid., at 561 (first and second quotations), 562 (third quotation), 572 (fourth quotation), 572 footnote 6 (fifth and sixth quotations).

35. "Eleventh National Woman's Rights Convention," in Elizabeth Cady Stanton and Susan B. Anthony, *The Selected Papers of Elizabeth Cady Stanton and Susan B. Anthony*, ed. Ann D. Gordon (New Brunswick, N.J.: Rutgers University Press, 1997–), 1:586 (first quotation); *Hoyt v. Florida*, 368 U.S. 57 (1961), at 61–62 (second quotation), 62 (third and fourth quotations). On women's rights and their privileges that continued in law during this time, as well as a compelling argument for the illegitimacy of special privileges in the liberal tradition, see Linda K. Kerber, *No Constitutional Right to Be Ladies: Women and the Obligations of Citizenship* (New York: Hill & Wang, 1998), 124–220.

36. *Engel v. Vitale*, 370 U.S. 421 (1962), at 429 (first and second quotations), 437 (third quotation).

37. *School District of Abington Township v. Schempp*, 374 U.S. 203 (1963), at 207.

38. Ibid., at 223 (first quotation), 224 (second quotation), 225 (third quotation).

39. King, *A Testament of Hope*, 217 (first quotation); *Los Angeles Times*, August 29, 1963 (second and third quotations).

40. *United States v. Seeger*, 380 U.S. 163 (1965), at 166 (both quotations).

41. *Griswold v. Connecticut*, 381 U.S. 479 (1965), at 484 (first, third, and fourth quotations), 483 (second quotation).

42. Graham quoted by Miller, *Billy Graham*, 128 (all quotations).

43. *Loving v. Virginia*, 388 U.S. 1 (1967), at 3 (first quotation), 12 (second quotation).

44. *Stanley v. Georgia*, 394 U.S. 557 (1969), at 564 (first quotation), 565 (second through fourth quotations), 566 (fifth quotation).

45. Bill Moyers, "Second Thoughts: Reflections on the Great Society," *New Perspectives Quarterly* 4 (Winter 1987): 41 (quotation). On Johnson's popular margin of

victory in 1964 and Nixon's Electoral College results in 1968, see Isserman and Kazin, *America Divided*, 131, 250.

Chapter 12

1. Graham and Nixon quoted by Steven P. Miller, *Billy Graham and the Rise of the Republican South* (Philadelphia: University of Pennsylvania Press, 2009), 124 (first quotation), 125 (second through fourth quotations).
2. *New York Times*, May 17, 1970 (quotation); Kevin P. Phillips, *The Emerging Republican Majority* (New Rochelle, N.Y.: Arlington House, 1969).
3. John Ehrlichman, *Witness to Power: The Nixon Years* (New York: Simon & Schuster, 1982), 223 (first quotation), 222 (second quotation).
4. *New York Times*, May 17, 1970 (first through third quotations); Alexander P. Lamis, "The Two-Party South," in *Southern Politics in the 1990s*, ed. Alexander P. Lamis (Baton Rouge: Louisiana State University Press, 1999), 8 (fourth through seventh quotations).
5. "The Preaching and the Power," *Newsweek*, July 20, 1970, 50 (first quotation), 53 (second quotation).
6. King, "I Have a Dream," in Martin Luther King Jr., *A Testament of Hope: The Essential Writings and Speeches of Martin Luther King, Jr.*, ed. James Melvin Washington (San Francisco: Harper, 1991), 219 (first quotation); "The Preaching and the Power," 52 (second quotation).
7. "The Preaching and the Power," 55 (first quotation). On Graham's unacknowledged connection to partisan politics, see Miller, *Billy Graham*, 124–154 (second and third quotations on p. 145).
8. "The Preaching and the Power," 55 (both quotations).
9. *Walz v. Tax Commission*, 397 U.S. 664 (1970), at 668 (all quotations).
10. Ibid., at 701 (first through fourth quotations), 708–709 (fifth quotation), 716 (sixth quotation).
11. *Lemon v. Kurtzman*, 403 U.S. 602 (1971), at 612.
12. Ibid., at 628 (first quotation), 641 (second quotation).
13. *Reed v. Reed*, 404 U.S. 71 (1971). For the backstory to this case, see Linda K. Kerber, *No Constitutional Right to Be Ladies: Women and the Obligations of Citizenship* (New York: Hill & Wang, 1998), 199–206.
14. *Roe v. Wade*, 410 U.S. 113 (1973), at 140.
15. Donald T. Critchlow, *Phyllis Schlafly and Grassroots Conservatism: A Woman's Crusade* (Princeton, N.J.: Princeton University Press, 2005), 212–218 (quotation on p. 213).
16. Phyllis Schlafly, "What's Wrong with 'Equal Rights' for Women?" *Phyllis Schlafly Report*, February 1972 (all quotations).
17. Critchlow, *Phyllis Schlafly*, 218–227.

18. Frank Schaeffer, *Crazy for God: How I Grew Up as One of the Elect, Helped Found the Religious Right, and Lived to Take All (or Almost All) of It Back* (New York: Carroll & Graf, 2007), 260–274. On Graham's retreat from partisan politics, see Miller, *Billy Graham*, 182–199.

19. Francis A. Schaeffer, *Complete Works of Francis Schaeffer: A Christian Worldview*, 2nd ed. (Westchester, Ill.: Crossway, 1982), 4:30.

20. Mel White, *Stranger at the Gate: To Be Gay and Christian in America* (New York: Simon & Schuster, 1994), 145 (first and second quotations); Jerry Falwell, *Listen, America!* (Garden City: Doubleday, 1980), 29 (third quotation), 117 (fourth and fifth quotations), 120 (sixth quotation).

21. Schaeffer, *Complete Works*, 5:423 (quotation). On the end of the ERA, see Critchlow, *Phyllis Schlafly*, 281.

22. *United States v. Carolene Products Co.*, 304 U.S. 144 (1938), at 152 note 4 (first quotation). On originalism, see Jack N. Rakove, *Original Meanings: Politics and Ideas in the Making of the Constitution* (New York: Knopf, 1996), 3–22 (second quotation on p. 3).

23. *Congressional Record*, 117:45440 (first through fourth, seventh quotations), 45441 (fifth, sixth, and eighth quotations).

24. *Maher v. Roe*, 432 U.S. 464 (1977), at 488.

25. *Harris v. McRae*, 448 U.S. 297 (1980), at 319.

26. Ibid., at 332 (all quotations).

27. *Marsh v. Chambers*, 463 U.S. 783 (1983), at 786 (first two quotations), 792 (third through fifth quotations).

28. Ibid., at 816 (first and second quotations), 817 (third through fifth quotations).

29. Ibid., at 822 (both quotations); *Bob Jones University v. United States*, 461 U.S. 574 (1983).

30. *Lynch v. Donnelly*, 465 U.S. 668 (1984), at 701 (first quotation), 674 (second quotation).

31. Ibid., at 708 (first three quotations), 711 (fourth quotation), 712 (fifth and sixth quotations).

32. Ibid., at 718 (first quotation), 718–719 (second quotation), 725 (third quotation).

33. *Bowers v. Hardwick*, 478 U.S. 186 (1985), at 196 (first quotation), 206 (second quotation), 211 (third and fourth quotations), 212 (fifth quotation), 211–212 (sixth quotation).

34. John Ehrman, *The Eighties: America in the Age of Reagan* (New Haven, Conn.: Yale University Press, 2005), 144.

35. Robert H. Bork, *Tradition and Morality in Constitutional Law* (Washington, D.C.: American Enterprise Institute, 1984), 3 (first four quotations), 8 (fifth through eleventh quotations).

36. Neal Devins and Wendy L. Watson, eds., *Federal Abortion Politics: A Documentary History* (New York: Garland, 1995), 3:71–73 (quotation on p. 71).

37. Ibid., 3:72 (first quotation), 130 (second quotation).

38. Ehrman, *Eighties*, 143–147.

39. *County of Allegheny v. ACLU*, 492 U.S. 573 (1989), at 590 (first quotation), 604 (second quotation), 604–605 (third quotation), 610 (fourth quotation).

40. *Employment Division v. Smith*, 494 U.S. 872 (1990), at 888 (first three quotations), 890 (fourth and fifth quotations).

41. Ibid., at 902 (both quotations).

42. *Planned Parenthood v. Casey*, 505 U.S. 833 (1992); *Lawrence v. Texas*, 539 U.S. 558 (2003), at 590 (all quotations).

43. *Susan Tave Zelman v. Doris Simmons-Harris*, 536 U.S. 639 (1995).

44. *McCreary v. ACLU*, 545 U.S. 844 (2005), at 890 (first quotation), 893 (second and third quotations), 894 (fourth quotation).

45. *Van Orden v. Perry*, 545 U.S. 677 (2005), at 701.

46. *New York Times*, September 13, 2005; September 15, 2005 (first quotation); January 10, 2006; January 11, 2006 (second quotation).

47. *New York Times*, July 1, 2007 (quotation); January 21, 2010.

Conclusion

1. David A. Hollinger, "Patterns of Engagement and Evasion," in *Debating the Divine: Religion in 21st Century American Democracy*, ed. Sally Steenland (Washington, D.C.: Center for American Progress, 2008), 77. See http://www.americanprogress. org/issues/2008/06/debating_the_divine.html.

2. Richard John Neuhaus, *The Naked Public Square: Religion and Democracy in America* (Grand Rapids, Mich.: Eerdmans, 1984), vii (first quotation), 20 (second quotation), viii (third quotation). Bellah's original essay is Robert N. Bellah, "Civil Religion in America," in *Beyond Belief: Essays on Religion in a Post-Traditional World* (New York: Harper & Row, 1970), 168–189. For Bellah's subsequent attempt to rein in the definitional unclarity of the concept, see Robert N. Bellah and Phillip E. Hammond, *Varieties of Civil Religion* (San Francisco: Harper & Row, 1980). For his admission that civil religion was not a properly analytic concept—and was even sectarian in its major thrust—see Robert N. Bellah, *The Broken Covenant: American Civil Religion in Time of Trial*, 2nd ed. (Chicago: University of Chicago Press, 1992), vi–xiii.

3. Bellah, "Civil Religion in America," 180–181.

4. On civil society, see Ernest Gellner, *Conditions of Liberty: Civil Society and Rivals* (New York: Allen Lane/Penguin, 1994); Ralf Dahrendorf, *After 1989: Morals, Revolution and Civil Society* (New York: St. Martin's Press, 1997), 37–48.

5. For the classic claim that the U.S. political arrangement embraced persuasion over coercion, see Sidney E. Mead, *The Lively Experiment: The Shaping of Christianity in America* (New York: Harper & Row, 1963), 16–37. On Bourdieu's legal theory, see Richard Terdiman, "Translator's Introduction to Pierre Bourdieu, 'The Force of

Law: Toward a Sociology of the Juridical Field,'" *Hastings Law Journal* 38 (July 1987): 805–813.

6. On the informal establishment, see William R. Hutchison, *Religious Pluralism in America: The Contentious History of a Founding Ideal* (New Haven, Conn.: Yale University Press, 2003); Robert T. Handy, *Undermined Establishment: Church–State Relations in America, 1880–1920* (Princeton, N.J.: Princeton University Press, 1991); William R. Hutchison, ed., *Between the Times: The Travail of the Protestant Establishment in America, 1900–1960* (New York: Cambridge University Press, 1989).

7. Claudia Carlen, ed., *The Papal Encyclicals* ([Wilmington, N.C.]: McGrath, 1981), 2:173 (first two quotations); Anthony Comstock, *Traps for the Young*, ed. Robert Bremner (1883; repr., Cambridge, Mass.: Belknap Press, 1967), 184 (third and fourth quotations); "The Republican Party and the School Question," *Index*, September 7, 1876, 426 (fifth quotation); Elizabeth Cady Stanton and Susan B. Anthony, *The Selected Papers of Elizabeth Cady Stanton and Susan B. Anthony*, ed. Ann D. Gordon (New Brunswick, N.J.: Rutgers University Press, 1997–), 3:400 note 2 (sixth quotation).

8. Lionel Trilling, *The Liberal Imagination: Essays on Literature and Society* (New York: Viking, 1950), xv (both quotations). On Heschel, see Edward K. Kaplan and Samuel H. Dresner, *Abraham Joshua Heschel: Prophetic Witness* (New Haven, Conn.: Yale University Press, 2007).

9. Robert M. Cover, *Narrative, Violence, and the Law: The Essays of Robert Cover*, ed. Martha Minnow, Michael Ryan, and Austin Sarat (Ann Arbor: University of Michigan Press, 1992); Michael Walzer, *Thick and Thin: Moral Argument at Home and Abroad* (Notre Dame, Ind.: University of Notre Dame Press, 1994), 1 (quotation).

INDEX

moral establishment (*continued*)
  and Mormonism, 168–173
  new coalition after *Roe,* 262–266
  and Nineteenth Amendment, 214–216
  and Prohibition, 213–215
  and public schooling, 155–168
  and social science, 193–198, 202–204
  Southern, 77–84, 111–132, 151
  and women's rights, 97–108, 147–154
Moral Majority, 265–266
moral minimalism, 289
moral suasion, 286, 290
Mormons (or Mormonism),
  Mitt Romney as, 3
  and public school education, 157
  and religious freedom, 168–173, 179, 220,
    223, 271
Morris, Gouverneur, 24
Mott, Lucretia, 99–101, 135
Moulton, Francis, 136
Moyers, Bill, 254
Muhlenberg, Henry, 16, 18–22, 28
Muller v. Oregon, 202–204
Murphy, Edgar Gardner, 131
Murphy, Frank, 224–225
Muslims, 18, 20, 27, 44, 69, 247, 270
myth of American religious freedom,
  as a civic myth, 7, 290
  and contemporary debate, 284, 287–288, 291
  defined, 4–7
  in law, 237–240, 246–247, 249–250, 253, 270

National-American Woman Suffrage Associa-
    tion, 151–155, 214–215
National Association for the Advancement of
    Colored People, 209
National Association of Evangelicals, 229–230,
    233–235, 271
National Association of Spiritualists, 137, 139
National Divorce Reform League, 145–146, 180
National Education Association, 125
*National Labor Relations Board v. Jones and
    Laughlin Steel Corporation,* 221–222
National Reform Association, 176–179
National Review, 233
National Woman's Party, 215
National Woman Suffrage Association, 123, 133,
    135, 138, 141–142, 150–152
Neal v. Farmer, 82–83

Neuhaus, Richard John, 284
New Deal, 4, 220–222
New Departure, 135, 147
New England Divorce Reform League, 145
New England Freedmen's Aid Society, 121
New Hampshire Constitution of 1784, 8, 20,
    28, 55, 66
New Hampshire law, 75
New Jersey Constitution of 1776, 21–22
New Jersey law, 1, 75, 222, 236–237
New Republic,
  as catalyst of liberal progressivism, 205,
    209–210, 212–213
  and Felix Frankfurter, 224, 239
  and World War I, 217
New York Constitution of 1777, 22–24, 28,
    60–61
New York Constitution of 1821, 63–64
New York law,
  and abolition, 75
  and blasphemy, 60–61, 66
  and labor, 200–201
  and public schooling, 239–240, 248–249
  and women's rights, 103
Niebuhr, Reinhold, 258
Nineteenth Amendment, 214–216
Nixon, Richard,
  appointments to the U.S. Supreme Court,
    258, 261, 267
  and the conservative movement, 263–264,
    278
  and the Southern Strategy, 254–258, 268
noblesse oblige, 53, 188
nonresistance, 91–92
nonsectarianism,
  and Christianity, 270
  and law, 171, 179, 188, 249
  and morals, 62, 68, 157
  and public schooling, 158, 161–162, 164, 166,
    238, 249
North Carolina Constitution of 1776, 21–22,
    28, 55
North Carolina law, 81–84

O'Connor, Sandra Day, 278–282
O'Hair, Madalyn Murray, 249
obscenity law,
  and Anthony Comstock, 174–175
  and Religious Right, 265

invalidated by the U.S. Supreme Court, 253, 279

as supported by evangelicalism, 58

and Victoria Woodhull, 140, 142

Ockenga, Harold J., 229–230

Ohio Constitution of 1851, 160–161

Ohio law, 160–162

Olmstead v. United States, 218–219

Oregon law, 202–203

originalism, 267, 269–270

Pace v. Alabama, 128, 252

Palmer, A. Mitchell, 216

Palmer, John M., 173

Palmer Raids, 216–217

paternalism, 79–82, 95

Paul, Alice, 214–215, 263

Peckham, Rufus, 200

Peirce, Benjamin, 193

Peirce, Charles Sanders, 193

Pendleton, Edmund, 48

Penn, William, 19

Pennington, J.W.C., 95

Pennsylvania Constitution of 1776, 16–22, 24, 26, 35

Pennsylvania Constitution of 1790, 54

Pennsylvania law,

and blasphemy, 2, 62, 176

and Christianity, 75

and indecency, 61–62

and religious displays, 276

and Sabbath law, 62, 171

and the schools, 249, 260

People v. Ruggles, 60–66

Permoli v. New Orleans, 4, 68

Peters, Richard, 47

Phelps, Amos A., 91, 95

Phillips, Kevin, 255–257

Phillips, Wendell, 97, 108, 123

Pinckney, Charles Cotesworth, 78

Pius XII, 244

Planned Parenthood v. Casey, 279

Plessy v. Ferguson, 129, 240–241, 267–268

pluralism,

and democracy, 218, 223–225, 241–242

and equal protection, 277, 279

and evangelicalism, 231, 244

and liberal progressivism, 206, 288–290

Madison's vision of, 39

and morality, 158, 245–246, 251, 262

and religion, 277

and Roman Catholicism, 244

police power

and Sabbath law, 247

and the First Amendment, 222–223, 253, 260

and the Fourteenth Amendment, 124, 130, 201, 204

polygamy, 168–173, 223

Porter, Noah, 145, 185–186

Post, Amy, 149

Powell, Lewis F., Jr., 274–276

pragmatism, 202

Presbyterians (or Presbyterianism),

as abandoned by Robert Ingersoll, 173

as abandoned by Sarah and Angelina Grimké, 90

Benjamin Rush as, 18

as a branch of evangelicalism, 52

and the moral establishment, 18, 19, 78, 80, 88

as old-line establishmentarians, 16, 31, 52

Priestley, Joseph, 18

privacy, right to,

enters constitutional law, 251–253

and Louis Brandeis, 203–204, 218

and Robert Bork, 275

and *Roe v. Wade,* 261–262, 268–269

and sodomy law, 273–274, 279

and Victoria Woodhull, 139

Prohibition, 213–215, 218

Protestant Reformation, 26, 166, 229

Protestants (or Protestantism), see specific group or denomination

Pullman Strike, 198–200

Quakers (and Quakerism)

antislavery activism, 74–75, 85–86

Hicksite revolution, 85–86

in women's movement, 90, 99, 101, 135

Rauch, F.W., 160

Rauschenbusch, Walter, 211

Reagan, Ronald,

judicial nominations of, 267, 274–275, 277, 278

and Moral Majority, 265

political operatives of, 256, 282

Reconstruction, 111–124, 191–192